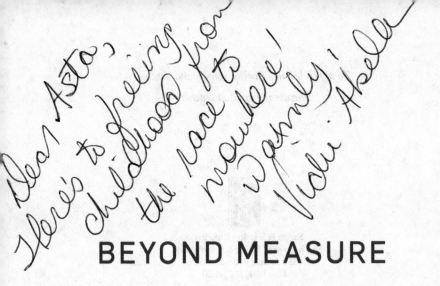

Dear Asta,
Here's to freeing
childhood from
the race to
nowhere!
Warmly,
Vicki Abeles

BEYOND MEASURE

Rescuing an Overscheduled, Overtested, Underestimated Generation

VICKI ABELES

WITH GRACE RUBENSTEIN

SIMON & SCHUSTER PAPERBACKS

New York London Toronto Sydney New Delhi

To my children—Shelby, Jamey, and Zak—

who are my greatest teachers

Simon & Schuster Paperbacks
An Imprint of Simon & Schuster, Inc.
1230 Avenue of the Americas
New York, NY 10020

First Simon & Schuster trade paperback edition October 2016

SIMON & SCHUSTER PAPERBACKS and colophon are
registered trademarks of Simon & Schuster, Inc.

For information about special discounts for bulk purchases,
please contact Simon & Schuster Special Sales at
1-866-506-1949 or business@simonandschuster.com.

The Simon & Schuster Speakers Bureau can bring
authors to your live event. For more information or to book
an event contact the Simon & Schuster Speakers Bureau at
1-866-248-3049 or visit our website at www.simonspeakers.com.

Manufactured in the United States of America

1 3 5 7 9 10 8 6 4 2

The Library of Congress has cataloged the hardcover edition as follows:

Abeles, Vicki.
Beyond measure : rescuing an overscheduled, overtested, underestimated
generation / by Vicki Abeles.
pages cm
1. Educational change—United States. 2. Overpressure
(Education) 3. Motivation in education—United States.
4. Academic achievement—United States. 5. Students—
Academic workload—United States. I. Title.
LA217.2.A24 2015
370.973—dc23 2015022235

ISBN 978-1-4516-9923-4
ISBN 978-1-4516-9924-1 (pbk)
ISBN 978-1-4516-9925-8 (ebook)

Contents

Foreword

Lynda Weinman, founder of Lynda.com

I AM A POSTER child for someone who was failed by standardized education but who found personal and professional success despite the experience.

I started out as a happy student who thrived in and loved school. But when my parents went through an acrimonious divorce, sending my siblings and me back and forth to and from unwanting guardians in whose homes I suffered neglect and abuse, my life took a terrible turn. No longer thrilled just to please teachers and parents, I struggled to find meaning in my lessons. School felt impersonal and irrelevant. No one really knew me there. I went from getting straight A's to becoming more and more depressed, disenfranchised, and disengaged. By middle school I was getting C's and D's. I dreamed of dropping out.

What saved me was a chance at a wholly different kind of learning. I found a high school that afforded students two rare gifts—choice and trust—allowing me to hew my studies to my own curiosity, with teachers' support. At this pivotal time in my life, when I could have easily given up and been drawn down a darker path, I instead learned to believe in myself beyond how school defined me. My new education connected me with my passions and motivated me to work for something more than a grade.

My story is not unique. Today, millions of young people are checking out, alienated by an educational culture that obsesses over products—transcripts, test scores, top-ranked college admissions—while missing the diverse potential and passions of individual people. At the same time, millions of others are swept up in the rush to rank and measure each student. These beleaguered young people spend their whole childhoods racing for perfection, or giving up altogether like I almost did, driving themselves to hollow exhaustion to meet an impossible ideal. This kind of high-stakes childhood is an experience that, as a parent, I know all too well.

My exposure to divergent forms of education was still with me when, in 1995, I cofounded an online learning company called Lynda.com, offering online video lessons in design, computer, and business skills to learners inside and outside the classroom. The company recently sold to LinkedIn for a record-breaking sum and now serves hundreds of millions of people around the world, a testament to the hunger for new ways of learning.

As a hiring manager for the past twenty years, I have seen firsthand how hard it is to find employees who are self-motivated, creative thinkers, and contributors versus followers. Job seekers emerging from a school system and a culture at large that place the most value on what can be measured possess fewer of the hard-to-measure interpersonal skills of leadership, problem solving, and creativity. Given that most factory jobs are destined to be filled by robots and computerized automation, and that some of the most intriguing vocations of today didn't even exist ten years ago, it is essential to rethink our education system and move away from the drills and rote learning of facts that can be better retrieved by computers than human beings. To really give our kids the best chance to flourish, we have to teach them how to think, lead, innovate, and contribute. Beyond the prospect of good jobs, we owe kids these better lessons so that they may forge good lives—equipped to be engaged, stimulated, complete human beings.

All of this was on my mind when I saw Vicki Abeles's film, *Race to Nowhere*, with hundreds of parents and teachers at a community screening in Santa Barbara, California, a few years ago. I witnessed the vibrant discussion afterward, as the audience shared their own similar stories, hopes, fears, and dreams for their students and children. Vicki's film stirred strong emotion in me too, as I have worn the shoes of a student, parent, teacher, and employer. In all of these roles, I've personally experienced the downside of high-stakes testing and standardized learning. My early school experiences were strikingly similar to many of those featured in *Race to Nowhere*. And the innovative high school that changed the trajectory of my life was strikingly similar to many of the inspiring schools that are written about in this book.

In both of her documentaries and now this book, Abeles has tuned in to one of the most important problems of our time. She is a brave champion for the widespread movement to change education from a one-size-fits-all factory model to a dynamic and personal approach that promotes our innate creativity and natural thirst for lifelong growth and learning.

I believe, along with Vicki and the other experts she cites in her book, that it is critical to place primary value on human creativity and wellness in order to create a viable economy for future generations and a balanced life for our children. Our current education system is not only outdated and ineffective, but it is dangerous to our children; the health effects of too much stress and pressure are resulting in physical and mental problems of epidemic proportions.

In our school system's zest to measure, grade, rank, promote, and punish, we have lost touch with what matters most—creating healthy, happy children who love to learn, want to contribute to the world, and can tackle the enormous problems of our times with innovative ideas and solutions. Because the truth is that success is not defined by grades, degrees, or money. It is reflected in the quality of life you lead and how you carry your values and purpose into making a positive impact.

Vicki's book tells the stories of students, parents, and teachers who are breaking free of the past and forging new systems of learning. She has devoted her life's work to telling the stories of the disenfranchised and disconnected, and presents solutions and research for how to change the system to foster thinking, creativity, wellness, and optimism.

Her words and research will shed new light on new information and actions that will reverse the tide of our broken education system. Change is not going to come from the top down, it is going to come from those affected by our broken systems. The time is now, and you can be part of this change. Join us, read and share this book, and be brave. It is time to stop perpetuating what isn't working and move toward a brighter and healthier future for all.

The stakes have never been higher for us to get it right.

"Numbered Identity"

Tira Okamoto, 17, Lowell High School, San Francisco

I am 2040, 31, and 3.67.
I am 500 words on the Common App.
I am the stacks of Scantron tests that lie on my bedroom floor.
I am the SAT, ACT, and AP test-prep books.
I am one of the millions of bubbles I will have filled out by the
    time I graduate from high school.
I am a student being taught by teach-to-the-test teachers.
I am instructional minutes and A-G graduation requirements.
I am the eight hours of high school.
I am the five hours of homework.
I am the less than five hours of sleep.
I am a test crammer who hardly remembers the information
    after the test.
I am the AP machine, the bubble robot.
I am the repeat.
I am a product of the system.
I am standardized.
What more do you want?
Why can't I be known as
A dancer with crazy curly hair
A bike rider who loves to read books.
An avid baseball fan whose passion is global communication
    and relations.
Why am I just a
Numbered Identity?

Introduction

IN HOMES AND classrooms across America, a silent epidemic is raging. It afflicts the eight-year-old lying awake, pulling his hair with worry over tomorrow's test. The seventeen-year-old straining to keep up in AP chemistry on top of the three other AP classes and two sports and four clubs that she thought she needed on her résumé. And the thirteen-year-old still studying past one a.m., wondering in the back of her bleary mind if *this*—this never-ending contest for credentials, this exhaustion, this feeling of meaninglessness—is all life is.

The scourge affects teachers, too, who feel pressured to push children through impossible piles of information instead of pursuing fewer, richer experiences that might teach them more. And it ravages families, who see their hard-studying teen little more than ten minutes a day and can't understand how such a curious, playful child became a spiritless workaholic.

This illness is the Race to Nowhere. Its source is an education culture gone crazy with competition, and a society so obsessed with one narrow vision of success that it's making our children sick. Once contained to ambitious adult professionals, the sickness now afflicts children, who absorb the message that sprinting for the "top" is the only way to succeed. Still fragile and impressionable, they feel they must outshine their peers with perfect performances in every realm: school, test scores, sports, arts, and activities. If they fall short, they believe they have failed.

As a result, some children have ended up in pediatricians' and psychologists' offices with stress-induced illnesses that could last a lifetime. Others will avoid medical trouble but will nonetheless miss the chance to enjoy their childhoods, explore genuine interests, and discover who they really are.

A grassroots movement is growing to cure this disease. In my travels across the country since the release of my first film, *Race to Nowhere*, and in researching my new film, *Beyond Measure*, I have found a veritable army of fellow change makers. There are hundreds of thousands of parents and students, teachers and school administrators, who all share the conviction that our kids deserve something better. We want to see our children for more than a hurried few minutes at dinner. We want schools to be a place where kids go to feel stimulated and supported, not ranked and sorted, and where the great poet, peacemaker, or political debater is valued as highly as the adept test taker. Like all caring adults, we want our children to grow into happy, healthy, financially independent citizens. But we see that the mad dash to outachieve one another is actually worsening their chances. The participants in this movement refuse to accept the false notion that the highest grades and the fattest childhood résumés represent the only path to a worthy life. Instead, we envision a world in which a child with a healthy body, a creative mind, and a contented heart—not simply an Ivy League diploma—is considered a success.

Brave trailblazers I've met across the country are fighting to create that world. In these pages, you'll meet them: a pediatrician-mother who spearheaded the awakening about student stress at her daughters' high school; a principal who insisted that her kindergarteners would fare better by reading stories after school instead of filling out worksheets; a teacher whose students' work improved when he stopped grading it; a superintendent striving to offer his community something deeper than test prep; a college admissions director who's personalizing the application process despite the risk of lowering his college's ranking; and a father who gently guided his kids toward genuine curiosity and away from the Ivy League.

This book tells their stories and many others. The actions they've taken (and the mistakes they've made along the way) provide a kind of playbook for other parents, students, and educators who crave change. More than that, their successes prove what is often so hard to believe in the midst of the madness: that change is possible. Their stories will empower you to start rewriting yours.

Prologue

Out of Nowhere

M Y OWN AWAKENING to the toxicity of the achievement race came the way it does to many parents: via years of trying to keep up with it.

I sensed the problem in my home before I could name it. My daughters, Shelby and Jamey, were in middle school, and Zakary was in third grade. They were still children, in the essential sense of the word. They still played hide-and-seek, treasured their American Girl dolls, and relied on me to make their meals. But their lives had mutated into an adultlike state of busyness that gave our home the air of a corporate command center.

Twelve-year-old Jamey, for instance—who still wore braces and fit into children's clothing sizes—would wake up before seven, cram in some extra studying over breakfast, and rush off to her school day, which lasted the usual seven hours. She'd go straight from there to a violin lesson or soccer practice, return home at six, and commence a daily homework marathon that took her well into the night. I'd see her hunched at her desk past eleven p.m., washed in the yellow lamplight, her long brown hair spilling over her books. The next day, she'd get up and do it again.

Now multiply that madness by three.

In earlier years, my husband, Doug, and the kids and I had spent weekends together, relaxing in the park, exploring museums, and playing games. We whiled away long hours reading books. I watched Shelby become a budding writer, Jamey fall in love with animals, and Zak develop into a garrulous drummer and athlete who could chat amiably with strangers. On weeknights we almost always ate dinner together as a family.

Slowly, though, I began to notice that our lives were less and less our own. During the week, the children would appear for dinner and then disappear into hours of assignments. Sometimes after a night's worth of homework, our dining table would be piled so high with books and papers that it looked like the conference table at a law firm. On weekends, if the children weren't practicing piano scales or traveling to soccer matches, they were often studying. They rarely simply went out to play with kids in the neighborhood; everyone else was enslaved to a schedule, too. I could scarcely remember the last time I'd seen my kids play, tinker, daydream, relax, invent a game, write or read for pleasure, or do *anything* that wasn't assigned to them by someone. They were so busy being little professionals that they had almost no time just to be children. Likewise, Doug and I were left with no time just to be the parents we wanted to be. We were too busy being chauffeurs, homework wardens, and musical taskmasters.

Worse, I began to see the constant demands taking a toll on my children's health. Jamey started complaining about headaches, stomachaches, and sleepiness, which she attributed to the pressures of school. Though she was just twelve, Jamey sometimes went to bed later than I did. Zak, only eight years old, also started getting headaches, from worry about all the work he had to do.

Believe me, I wanted my children to shine. I wanted them to earn good grades, cultivate their interests, and build the skills to succeed in high school, college, and life beyond. But as my once-curious girls withdrew from our family life and became worker bees, producing formulaic essays and correct answers and formidable extracurricular résumés, and as my once-buoyant boy cried in frustration over his hundredth set of math problems, I started to wonder whether the relentless pressure to perform was doing more harm than good.

So many parents have told me that the madness snuck up on them the same way. You want your children to learn deeply, so you push them to study. You want to give them opportunities to develop their interests—perhaps better opportunities than you had as a child—so you enroll them in whatever sports and art lessons you can afford. You think you're doing the right thing. And then, before you realize it, your life feels like it's spun out of control.

The rat race for our family began in kindergarten. The four of us (Zak wasn't born yet) bundled into the car one morning and set off to Shelby's kindergarten talent show, for which she had nervously decided to recite a poem. Puzzlingly, the expectations around the show seemed high. Were five-year-olds these days supposed to have finely honed specialties? Apparently so: the revue included impressive gymnastics routines and piano recitals, plus one particularly dazzling violin number, all executed deftly by tiny performers. Jamey, age three, immediately asked Doug and me if she could take violin lessons. Wonderful, we thought: music is educational! We said yes.

And we kept saying yes for many years thereafter. Both girls signed up for music lessons and soccer. When Shelby was in fourth grade and struggling with math, I learned that most of her classmates were taking after-school tutorials at the private Kumon learning center, so popular that it serves students in nearly fifty countries. Instead of wondering why a fourth grade math class was too hard for fourth graders, I enrolled her at Kumon, hoping to boost her confidence. Her siblings followed.

The kids' rigorous schedules also extended into our home as their homework loads grew heavier (and their enthusiasm for learning weaker) year by year. But the work seemed important. I understood it to be my duty as a mom to oversee my children's assignments and monitor their grades. I expected straight As, even made flash cards and marked up school papers with red ink. When I felt I couldn't help, I enlisted the support of teachers and tutors. I wanted to instill in my children perseverance and a drive for excellence because I believed those skills would carry them through life's challenges. I hoped they'd have better opportunities than the modest ones I had as a child. This, it seemed, was what devoted parents do.

"Children and families do not exist in a vacuum," Arizona State University psychologist Suniya Luthar would later tell me. "We exist in communities. Children exist in schools. There is a school culture, a community culture, in which there is this reverberating message: More is always better. Do more. Accomplish more. Achieve more. The schools and communities in turn exist in American culture, which again espouses the same message, the American dream. The more you can do, the better off you are. In fact, if you don't do more, you're going to be left behind."

I should have recognized the signs of overwork sooner, given my own history. My mother raised my two younger sisters, my younger brother, and me by herself, after our parents' divorce, in a small apartment on the outskirts of Miami. Seeing our mom's financial struggles made me determined to achieve independence. So I waited tables to fund my education at the University of Miami, and went from there to law school and then to Manhattan. Aiming for professional success and financial security, I joined a law firm on Wall Street and started working harder than I ever had before. Sometimes I wouldn't leave the office for days. Finally, a job move for Doug saved me. I transitioned to consulting, which allowed flexible hours, and we settled in Lafayette, a leafy San Francisco suburb where I imagined a healthier life for my family than the one we'd left behind. Never did I imagine that the frenzy of Wall Street would follow us there.

The upshot was that by the time my daughters entered middle school, our family had become enslaved to achievement. Jamey's violin studies had ballooned into a four-day-a-week gauntlet of lessons, group practices, and recitals. Her soccer team, which began as a cute exercise for second graders just striving to kick the ball straight, had morphed into a five-day-a-week commitment to practices and treks to tournaments hours from home. Even eight-year-old Zak had started soccer, piano, and Little League. We often ate meals in the car as we zoomed from one practice or recital to another. And always awaiting my kids when we returned was more homework. It seemed that anything a child did—every hobby, every interest, every lesson—had to be done at a near-professional level of commitment. Coaches and instructors expected no less. There was no room to dabble or just explore.

More and more, as I walked up the stairs to check on my children and saw Jamey through the crack in her bedroom door, she looked like my former self—hunched over her desk, joyless.

For my part, I woke up early and stayed up late to get my own work done, finding my days consumed with coordinating children's activities and studies. The expectations for parents seemed just as impossible as those for kids. How could we possibly manage all this and still have time to mind our own well-being?

"We're just really busy" was the answer I gave, reflexively, to grocery-aisle inquiries about how we were doing. Were everyone else's children handling it better? No one ever said otherwise. So we went about our busyness.

The saddest part for me is that we scarcely had to tell our children what "success" should look like. The prescription was plainly written: great grades and test scores, athletic and artistic awards, admission to a prestigious university, and, ultimately, a well-paid job in one of a handful of respected fields. Though I came to see that my husband and I had inadvertently pushed our kids too hard, they also pushed themselves. The extravagant expectations were all around them: In the impressive examples set by their friends. In the standards set by the schools, which increasingly expect all students to read fluently in kindergarten and perform feats of algebra by age thirteen. In the anxious questions overheard from other parents wondering how many AP classes their child should take for college applications. And in the shiny images of affluent lives on TV: the executives and stars in swanky New York apartments and Los Angeles mansions who appear to have reached the pinnacle of achievement.

This was the air we were breathing. And our young children, still searching for their identities, were breathing it, too.

In the spring of 2007, our family went away for Memorial Day weekend on the California coast. Shelby, whose seventh grade final exams were imminent, stayed inside studying the entire weekend. I'd never worked this hard—not in law school, not as an overburdened young associate in my first law job. Neither had Doug, who had survived the rigors of medical school. I thought: *This is nuts.*

———

Every parent who arrives at this realization immediately runs into a new set of vexing questions. Do we quit the sports and arts that our children seem to enjoy? Allow them to skip their homework? Abandon the tutoring that seems, at least in part, supportive of their confidence and progress? Pull them out of school? Each of these possibilities seems at first extreme. On top of the practical dilemmas, we confront deeper questions about the culture we are a part of. How in the world did we reach a place where school and enrichment activities, of all things, could literally be making our children sick? And how many other kids are struggling, too?

Searching for answers, I read books and attended lectures by experts in education, pediatrics, and child psychology. I started asking more people about their own experiences. What I found was staggering. The achievement-centered childhood that my kids were living was not a product of our particular family or town. It characterizes the lives of millions of children in diverse communities across the country. Nearly every parent and student I met understood the issue immediately and intimately. Everyone had a story—at least in private. Few parents wanted to publicly say that their children were being pushed beyond their limits. The kids didn't want to admit it either, having internalized the expectations of easy perfection.

Over the last couple of decades, I discovered, childhood has transformed into a performance. Not limited to the classroom or the ball field or the talent show stage, and knowing no socioeconomic or geographic boundaries, our collective focus on scores and numbers, awards and trophies, is robbing our kids of their childhoods, their health, and their happiness. This early experience with life-as-competition is shaping their nascent identities. Paradoxically, it's also swindling them out of their inborn enthusiasm for learning, challenge, and growth, thus dimming the brightness of their futures.

The deeper I dug, the more I became convinced: The pressure to perform—and its shadow, the fear of failure—represented a silent epidemic. Our competitive, high-stakes culture was the culprit. Our children were the victims.

At first I assumed that this pressure cooker was a perverse product of privilege, confined to upper-middle-class communities like mine in which success is often narrowly defined by high-status careers and elite college admissions. In some such neighborhoods there were epidemics of stealth tutoring, where every child had a tutor but no one admitted it. Yet I quickly found that students in working-class and impoverished communities suffer, too. In neighborhoods across the socioeconomic spectrum, I discovered that all students suffer in the impersonal contest that education has become, whether it be a race to ace an AP exam or to cover a year's worth of bloated content.

"I want to get into the best colleges I can," Isaiah, a high school senior in a low-income neighborhood in Oakland, told me. He was struggling in an AP government class that he took to fatten his transcript, staying up until midnight with the work. What for? He said, "Being an African American and taking AP classes is what people are looking for."

In many communities, even the nonoverachievers—the majority of kids—are afflicted. Children like my Jamey, a hardworking B student, feel marginalized by their school's limiting view of success. Meanwhile, *all* children in a system that mainly values bookwork miss chances to learn and express themselves in multidimensional ways. From the time they are toddlers, it thrills kids to count, sing their ABCs, observe bugs and birds, and build block towers. They have a natural drive to gain skills and achieve mastery, including and perhaps especially in areas where they are not yet proficient. But in too many cases, our impossible expectations for them after toddlerhood—expectations out of sync with their natural development— have made it too fraught or too frightening to continue. As our children get older, our cultural obsession with only one measurable version of intelligence—good grades, awesome test scores—discounts the value of diverse smarts and experimentation, leaving budding young poets, carpenters, and designers who don't test well to neglect their talents and doubt their self-worth.

Think of what we are losing.

And for what purpose, all this pressure? The presumed holy grail of a K-12 education in the United States is hardly a love for learning or an authentically engaged citizen. It is, against all odds, a "yes" message from one of a handful of expensive, brand-name universities that only a fraction of each year's three million high school graduates will be invited to attend. (And, it should be said, even that treasured invitation itself comes with no guarantee of lifelong happiness.) Whipped into a panic by hypercompetitive admissions practices and by hype, kids, parents, and educators pursuing that holy grail sacrifice terribly important things: time, money, health, happiness, and childhood itself. Without our even realizing it, our driving goal has become all about preparing for the college *application*, not preparing for the college *experience* or life beyond. Performing, not learning. Amassing credentials, not growing. Not even really living.

So, while it's true that resilient children need to cope with risk and failure as a part of life, we've set up their childhoods as a destructive march to likely defeat. "Success" equates to attending the most prestigious college and then netting the big house and the high-paying job. Winning the education race, we're told, is the way to get there. Rather than building their resilience, such a high-stakes education drives our children to chronic insecurity. Fear. Anxiety. Disconnection. Loneliness. Record rates of depression. And, as they get older, binge drinking, eating disorders, cutting, and even suicide. The clear message they hear from their environments is to produce, produce, produce at all costs, even if it means cheating, taking drugs, or working through the night to keep up.

The most painful irony is how badly out of step our frenzied educational practices are with science. Psychology and neuroscience journals abound with studies about how children learn and thrive, and how their brains grow, and none of it bears a remote resemblance to the spirit-crushing contest we're putting our kids through.

There's a "Goldilocks and the Three Bears" aspect to fruitful learning, explains Laurence Steinberg, Temple University neuroscientist and author of the book *Age of Opportunity: Lessons from the New Science of Adolescence.* In order to develop optimally, the brain needs just the right amount of challenge: enough to stimulate neuronal growth, but not so much as to overwhelm it. Our educational system today tends to "miss the sweet spot," he says, because "it confuses the quantity of work with the quality of the challenge."

The result? "Children are born curious, and it's pretty easy to facilitate that, to groom it," says Vassar College neuropsychologist Abigail Baird. "We're doing the opposite. We're squishing their desire to learn new things. And I think that's a crisis."

Two incidents, one small and one large, pushed me over the edge into making my first film. The subtler event was a parent forum I attended at our school on the subject of student stress. As the guidance counselor ticked off symptoms, the parents and teachers in the audience nodded their heads; it all sounded too familiar. They asked what they could do. The unhelpful answer was that overwrought parents had to stop pressuring their kids. Besides, nothing more could be done until Congress and college admissions officers changed their policies. In other words, this was the fault of misguided individuals and policies beyond our control, not a cultural sickness or a responsibility shared by all. At the end of the evening, we left feeling as helpless as ever. No one, neither parents nor educators, had taken—or even envisioned—a step to actually *do* anything about it.

I came home feeling frustrated, even desperate, went upstairs, and found my daughter still doing homework at ten thirty p.m. Something flipped in me. Here before us was another inconvenient truth: a problem too many children and families were suffering from but no one was doing much to stop. This story needed to be told.

Soon after that night came the second, more potent catalyst: a friend called to tell me that a thirteen-year-old girl in our community, Devon Marvin, had killed herself. No one had ever guessed that this star student and budding musician felt so unhappy. Nobody, not even teachers or friends, had spotted warning signs; in fact, she'd been one of the success stories, one of the kids who had seemed to have it all. When I met her mom, Jane, she told me she had torn through her memories and Devon's emails and text messages, searching desperately for a sign as to why her daughter would end her life. The only clues she found pointed to a recent algebra exam, which Devon, previously a math ace, had flunked. "She was torn up about this math," Jane told me. "Here's a child who had always been so successful on so many fronts—and a stupid math grade."

I decided then that I'd do everything I could to make a difference, to tell this story so that people didn't feel alone. I read up on filmmaking, raised money, hired cinematographers, and in early 2008 started traveling the country, capturing stories. Our filmmaking team set out to give a voice to the young people on the front lines of this battle. Many of the students and parents I met had kept silent about their struggles until then, feeling pressure to make their exhausting achievements appear effortless. Once they were asked, though, many were surprisingly open.

"Kids are told that they need to be 'special,' that they need to stand out of the crowd," explained Samantha, a fifteen-year-old from San Diego. "Without that trophy, you are just another kid who plays soccer, or plays an instrument, or gets average grades, bound for community college."

Jeanine M., a mother in Newport Beach, California, wrote to me that as her kids grew older and became stressed and unkind to one another, she "felt my family slipping away."

Eighteen-year-old Emily wasn't afraid to recount how she slipped into a deep depression her junior year, and even considered suicide, as other swimmers surpassed her in water polo and it became harder and harder to maintain her once-perfect grades. She recalled, unflinchingly:

> Junior year is supposedly the most important in high school and my effort just wasn't going to cut it, not if I wanted to go to a decent college, and without a degree from a top university I was not going to be successful. . . . I had failed. All those years of late nights studying for AP classes followed by 5 a.m. water polo or swim practices, what would they come to? Nothing, just like me. In a world where we must excel in not one but many areas, I had not done so in any. I would rather be dead than face the years to come, sure to be filled with constant reminders of my failure. In my mind, there was only one way out.

Teachers, for their part, reported that they felt helpless, hemmed in by the curricular directives of their school districts, the pressures of preparing students for standardized tests over which they had no pedagogical control. "I wanted to really . . . change these kid's lives, and get them to see learning as a lifetime skill," said Emma Batten-Bowman, who taught English in a low-income community in Oakland. "But it's gotten harder and harder to feel like I could teach the things I believe in. . . . Things that actually get our students to think, and work together and care, are pushed aside."

In the end, the film's very title came from a teenager who pointed out on camera that his life had become a kind of treadmill: an endless competition with only vague and spurious rewards promised at the end. A Race to Nowhere. He was right.

———

Race to Nowhere premiered at the Mill Valley Film Festival in October 2009. Little did I know that afternoon that it would be the beginning of a whole new journey—a quest for solutions—that would ultimately lead me to this book.

I watched the film anxiously, unsure how it would be received. The moment the lights went up, I knew I'd struck a nerve. No one moved. The entire crowd remained in their seats, rapt, hungry for discussion. Hands flew up for the Q&A session. In the emotional conversation that ensued, concerns that parents had previously kept secret tumbled out. It was as if I'd stood up and shouted, "The emperor has no clothes!" Now the illness their families had been silently living with had a name. Now they knew that they were not alone.

Since then more than a million people have seen the film at seven-thousand-plus screenings in all fifty states and more than forty countries. Audiences in all kinds of communities, from leafy suburbs to remote towns to gritty cities, have responded much like that first crowd did. I have attended hundreds of these screenings and heard thousands of students and parents describe sadness, frustration, and something like grief about what the Race to Nowhere has stolen.

A father at a screening in Hinsdale, Illinois, stood up and said he felt like a failure as a parent for not giving his teenage son and daughter a different sense of accountability—an after-school job instead of a couple of those advanced classes, time together as a family instead of time glued to homework on the computer. "They need to have a broader experience of life, which is: it isn't all about studying," he exclaimed. "Getting an A in a class does not equal success in life. It just doesn't."

A high school student from Buffalo Grove, Illinois, wrote to me that she no longer had time to paint or walk her dog because of all her schoolwork. "I cry almost every day due to stress and anxiety," she said. "Please help end this race to nowhere so kids like me can get our lives back."

Everywhere I went, teachers, parents, and students of all stripes echoed the same wish: we all craved change. Yet inevitably, near the end of each discussion, we came to a question like the one I received from Cara Natterson, a Los Angeles pediatrician, author, and mom of two children in elementary school. She watched the film with friends and wrote to me, "The overwhelming response at the end was: Now what?! We who have children in grammar school can see what they are facing down the road. So how do parents step off the crazy treadmill and buck society?"

Natterson was right: It isn't enough just to identify the problem. We have to act to fix it. And we can't do it alone.

Yes, we as individuals can work to ease the pressures on students in our own homes and classrooms, to show them a broader vision of genuine success. That is crucial. But ultimately it won't be enough. We and our children still must answer to the pressures beyond our own four walls: the hypercompetitive college applications, the mountains of state-mandated curricula, the high-stakes standardized tests and rigid AP exams, the schedules set by club leaders and coaches, the constant well-meaning questions ("Where are you thinking of going to college?"). The crisis our children face calls for a whole movement—a radically altered vision for childhood and education and a groundswell of cultural change. Unless we build that, we'll just be erecting little storm shelters in a hurricane.

But here and there among the worried faces in the audience, I found daring people ready to make change—students, parents, and teachers presenting a fresh set of values and pressing their communities to uphold them. Some of these everyday revolutionaries live in wealthy, urban enclaves. Others live in middle-income suburbs, and still others on farms or in densely packed urban apartments. Their neighborhoods are dispersed from California to Kentucky, Montana to Manhattan. They send their children to, or teach in, public, private, charter, and parochial schools. Some of their victories are small; others are more extraordinary.

Every one of these revolutionaries has had the courage to stand up—sometimes against a tide of skepticism—and say out loud what our best intuition already tells us: that education is not a race. That busyness does not equal betterment. That a perfect transcript is not worth the cost of a lost childhood. And that no battery of tests can assess what most matters in life: Integrity. Determination. Empathy. Resourcefulness. Connectedness. A thirst for knowledge. Passion. Creativity. Adaptability. The aptitude to read not just books but also faces. Confidence and kindness. Respect. These are the qualities that adults who are truly prepared and engaged possess. They are beyond measure. And they are what we must actively cultivate in our children.

The Race to Nowhere movement that grew from those screenings proved to have a unique power. That is because it brings *whole communities* together in a new conversation about what those closest to our children—parents, educators, physicians, clergy members, coaches, and students themselves— actually want for them. Once the veil of silence is lifted, diverse stakeholders can become unified teams. And it is in the collective wisdom of each community that the solutions lie. This movement is not about promoting a standardized prescription; it is about healing from within.

Yet so many film viewers at first felt stuck on how to move beyond tiny fixes to big transformations. They couldn't imagine how education would look if it looked different. So I made my second film, *Beyond Measure*, to highlight innovative schools that are already showing how much healthier, more inventive, and more effective education can be. This book traces the stories of such change makers, including some who appear in the film as well as many others who appear only in these pages and who richly deserve recognition. In the chapters that follow, I chart their journeys—their determination, missteps, and victories—and I urge you to take heart in their triumphs and take up their charge. Each community's story is linked to one of the key ingredients in the Race to Nowhere, such as homework or testing, college admissions or overbooked time, though the truth is that everyone is working on multiple fronts, as we must do. In these pages I also spell out the scientific research that underpins our efforts. Years of psychology and brain studies clearly show that children learn best when they're supported, not constantly stressed, and when they're given the chance to grapple with deep questions that have no fixed answers. Something that, as parents and educators, in our guts we already know.

Let's make this clear: This movement is not about lowering standards. It's not about protecting our children from the inevitable stress and challenge of an engaged life. It's not about coddling or helicoptering or making excuses. Rather, it's about elevating the essentials. It's about questioning our spoon-fed definition of success and remembering what we truly want for our children: wellness, independence, purpose, and the spark of excitement in their eyes. It's about recognizing that it doesn't matter what college an unhealthy, insecure teen gets into—not if she's too stressed to learn or too anxious to grow. And it's about reclaiming for children and families the precious time that's rightfully theirs.

We can't wait for state or national policies to shift, or for the College

Board (maker of the SAT) to relinquish the keys to the college gates. That could take an eternity; our children need our help now. We must start immediately, joining together to launch change in our homes, schools, and our communities. This problem requires no technology or money to fix, only will. The will of each person to implement small changes as well as sweeping ones. We all create this culture—the current one and, starting now, the new one—by taking actions from right where we are. Call it the barn raising of a new American educational culture. Many layers of change will add up to an overall cultural shift that could quite literally save our children's lives.

In this shared effort, we will establish new markers of educational success and reprioritize what matters most to us, as parents and as Americans, for our kids and our future. We will insist upon raising a generation that can create, think, and thrive—not just produce. In our new vision, the reward sought for our kids will not be the trinkets of international test supremacy or name-brand college sweatpants. Rather, it will be the best gift we can give our children: the support and preparation necessary to enter the world ready to make it better.

Whenever I feel frustrated by the inertia we face and my energy flags (which it does), I think about my hopes for my own children, and for children like Samantha, the fifteen-year-old from San Diego. She wrote to me that kids' lives now are so scheduled that "it isn't until we have a shred of free time that we realize we don't even know who we really are." Though her peers tend to hide their problems, she wrote, "If you look closely, you can see how stress and the pressure to perform affect children and teenagers, even on a physical level: stomachaches, headaches, breakouts, delayed menstrual cycles, anxiety attacks, weight gain, weight loss, depression, even suicide."

Samantha concluded: "Something is very, very wrong, and it is up to us to fix it."

She is right. And we can. Courageous individuals and communities around the country are showing us how. Let's begin.

CHAPTER 1

Sicker, Not Smarter

I N LATE 2010 I received an email from Saint Louis University School of Medicine professor and pediatrician Stuart Slavin, who was concerned about the health effects of excessive performance pressure on children. One passage in it sticks with me to this day:

> My personal feeling is that we are conducting an enormous and un-precedented social experiment on an entire generation of American children, and the evidence of a negative impact on adolescent mental health is overwhelming. This is particularly disturbing given the fact that having mental health problems in the teen years predisposes to mental health problems in adulthood. It is even more profoundly disturbing when one considers that there is absolutely no evidence that this educational approach actually leads to better educational outcomes.

The science shows that Slavin is right: Our children are paying a high price for our cultural misdirection. Thousands of students are suffering from withering anxiety, depression, eating disorders, insecurity, dangerous sleep deprivation, and even thoughts of suicide. And it's not just our children's mental health that's in jeopardy (which would be worrisome enough by itself); it's their physical health, too. The result of the Race to Nowhere is a public health crisis on a scale that we have yet to fully recognize.

Before we turn to solutions, which are the heart of this book, it's important to take a chapter to demonstrate that students' stories are backed up by hard data—to take stock of the science of just what we're fighting for. In fact, the price of the achieve-at-all-costs approach includes more than sickness. It produces a drill-like mode of education that deadens lessons and narrows students' chances to explore broadly or think creatively. We see even young students disengaging from school experiences that feel impersonal and irrelevant, high school grads arriving at college in need of remediation, and rampant cheating among students of all ages. Ironically, the constant pressure also physiologically impairs children's capacity for learning. In other words, it backfires, undermining the very achievement that it's meant to promote.

All told, the outcome is a school environment that deprives children of both sound health and vibrant learning. These grave consequences are at the heart of what makes our work to transform childhood so urgent. What's at stake is no less than raising healthy, thriving kids and—as they become adults—a healthy, thriving society.

Fremont, California: A Crisis Visible

Irvington High School is a sprawling, single-story beige building wrapped around a central courtyard with picnic tables and a few redwood trees. The city of Fremont spreads out around it, pancake flat and pasted with strip malls and small ranch houses, the bare brown hills of California rising in the background.

Over the past five years, Assistant Principal Jay Jackson has watched this school community transform. He taught world history and sports psychology here for eight years before becoming an administrator. With close-cropped hair and the compact build of a lightweight wrestler, Jackson is the kind of compassionate teacher whom students instinctively trust. He has an Elvis Presley shrine in his office—replete with Elvis figurines, Elvis clocks, Elvis PEZ dispensers, and even a life-size Elvis cardboard cutout—made up of gifts from past students, who kept giving him the knickknacks as a kind of joke, even though he insists he's not *that* big of a fan. During his teaching years in the 2000s, Jackson recalls, the student population here was mixed:

about half of them were academically oriented and intent on college, the other half not. When, in 2010, the auto plant that had employed many of the students' parents shut down, taking nearly five thousand mostly blue-collar jobs away with it, the demographics of the school district began to shift. Around the same time, the district redrew neighborhood boundaries, delivering to Irvington a flood of students from a more affluent part of town. Many of these new students' parents were immigrants, drawn to the technology industry in nearby San Jose with high hopes for their children's futures in this land of opportunity.

The school's standardized test scores shot up—as did its rates of student anxiety, sleep deprivation, and stress-induced illnesses. When Jackson became assistant principal in 2012, the change was already under way.

"Two or three weeks into the school year, you start seeing students coming into the office with these issues, with stress, breaking down crying," even cutting themselves, he remembers. The problem hadn't been as obvious from the vantage point of his classroom, where students put their best face on and their late nights spent laboring over piles of do-or-die assignments weren't so visible. But you go to work in the school office, the crossroads of students' difficulties, and, he says, "You see enough."

Enough, that is, to deeply alarm Jackson, who's also a father of two boys in elementary school. It convinced him that Irvington has a serious health crisis on its hands. Jackson organized an online survey of students in fall 2013, to see if his instincts matched the teens' own experiences. The measure wasn't perfect—only about one in six students completed the survey. But this much was clear: if even a small percentage of Irvington students overall felt the same way as those who answered the questionnaire did, the situation was dire.

More than four in five of the teens who responded said they felt moderate or high stress about school. They reported doing hours of homework a night and sleeping too little. A majority were taking multiple AP and honors classes, and the most common reason they gave for enrolling in those classes (cited by 61 percent of students) was that it would help them get into a better college; trailing far behind, the next reason (cited by just 42 percent) was that they were actually interested in the subject matter. Nearly half of the teens admitted to cheating on tests or homework in the past year, primarily because they didn't have enough time to study or finish the assignment. Perhaps saddest of all, when asked, "What is your main purpose for being in high school?" more students checked "To get into a good college" than "To learn."

Stress levels were high when I visited Irvington in the fall of 2014. Sitting with a classroom full of juniors, I casually asked, "How stressed are you, on a scale of one to ten?" The teens replied with a chorus of groans: "Ten!" One said eleven.

I went on: "Who gets seven hours of sleep a night? Raise your hand." A couple of hands went up. "Six hours?" A few more. "Five?" And there the bulk of the class raised their hands. Growing ever more incredulous, I asked: "Four?" Up went the last couple of hands. Even as the discussion continued, many students were scribbling in their notebooks, not sparing a moment that could be spent on schoolwork. Finally, I put the critical question to them: "Is it worth it?" They mumbled yes. "Why?" One boy with a blondish mop of hair answered for his peers: "To better your future."

Afterward, Jackson strode down the hall away from the classroom, his frustration showing in his gait. "It pains me to go into those classes because they're really stressed, and my assumption is we're doing this to them," he said. "They're all messed up."

A student had died by suicide the previous spring. And just the day before my visit, Jackson said, he'd checked a student into the home-and-hospital program. That's an alternative education program for students who are too sick to come to school. What was this girl's ailment? The doctor couldn't diagnose the precise cause of her bodily pains and ulcers, but mysteriously, they went away during the summer and returned two weeks before the start of school. "It's driving me crazy," said Jackson, "because what's going on is flawed, but we're not brave enough to change it."

The fact is that he and his colleagues at Irvington actually *are* taking courageous steps to change the school's high-stakes culture and rebuild student health—most notably by restraining students from overloading on AP classes and working with Dr. Slavin to research what kind of support they most need, as we'll learn more about later. The progress is just slower than Jackson would like.

The questions I didn't ask in that classroom at Irvington were these: What makes you *so sure* it's worth it? Is this sprint to achieve a certain version of "success" (reaching the top of the class, the top college, the top job, and the top life) really helping? Or is it actually making you sicker, not smarter—the kind of sick that will likely last through your adulthood—and causing you to miss opportunities to build the real-life skills that really matter?

———

Let's examine the facts about what is happening to children's health. The implications are long-lasting, as there is an avalanche of evidence that an unhealthy youth sets the stage for an unhealthy life. I'll begin with the effects that we can see right now: the current frayed state of our children's and teens' health.

Unhealthy Hearts and Minds

Students these days are incredibly stressed. On the American Psychological Association's Stress in America survey, teens rate their stress levels during the school year higher than adults rate their own. Nearly one in three teens says the stress drives them to sadness or depression. And what are the top sources of their stress? Eighty-three percent of the thousand teens surveyed named school, and 69 percent named getting into a good college or deciding what to do after high school. Meanwhile, 30 percent of high schoolers said on a government survey that they had felt sad or hopeless almost every day for two weeks or more within the past year.

Young Americans' mental health has deteriorated dramatically since the postwar days of the 1950s. Jean Twenge, a psychology professor at San Diego State University and author of the book *Generation Me*, has scoured and crunched decades' worth of data to illuminate these trends. By her calculations, five to eight times more college students today report serious mental health problems than did students at midcentury. This doesn't bode well for their future health, as depression raises a person's risk of heart disease, diabetes, and other illnesses, and having depression early in life significantly increases the risk of having it again as an adult.

Federal data also show that suicide rates more than doubled among youth age fifteen to twenty-four between 1950 and 2010 and more than tripled (though the rate is still much lower) among younger children. What's less well known but equally worrisome is how many kids *consider* taking their own lives. In a Centers for Disease Control and Prevention (CDC) survey of high school students—children as young as fourteen—nearly one in six said they had seriously thought about suicide. Half that many had made an attempt within the past year.

It makes me wonder: How much torment happens below the surface, beneath the game faces that adults can see? And how much is hidden behind the airbrushed lives today's teens present on Twitter and Instagram, where one kid's seemingly effortless achievements only make the next kid feel she must do more?

Behind these numbers are stories like that of an alarmed mother in Orange County, California, whose seventeen-year-old son had once ranked first in his high school out of a class of 764, taking six AP classes (out of seven total) in his junior year and sleeping only five hours a night. His worried mother wrote:

> I discouraged him from taking on this load, but he insisted and continued this into his senior year by taking the International Baccalaureate, and now the chronic stress and lack of sleep has taken its toll. . . .
>
> Prior to high school my son was a secure, outgoing well-liked person with many friends. He likes to surf and would design and paint patterns on his boards. He organized camping trips, booking at state parks and organizing his friends without any help from me. He would not be able to do this today. . . . He is now in his senior year and was diagnosed last month with major depression. He has a terror of going to school and has only attended school for about six days in the past two months. . . . We are working with a doctor, a counselor (who brought your film to our community) and the school to try and salvage what we can for him to graduate in June.

What happened to this young man is sadly not uncommon. And unfortunately, our kids' poor health outcomes are anything but temporary. The unhealthy, unhappy patterns laid down in the grade school years stay with teens as they enter the nation's universities, where officials are battling binge-drinking episodes and reporting a rising mental health crisis, as well.

"They work their tails off to get here, and then reach the finish line and are accepted and get here, and then realize that there is no finish line," says Kevin Wehmhoefer, a Harvard University clinician and coordinator of outreach, counseling, and mental health services. "I got here and I was blown away by the level of acuity that kids were presenting with." Wehmhoefer observed extreme anxiety or depression in many students who came to his clinic—and counselors from the University of California to Appalachian State University in North Carolina report the same trend. Surprisingly, though, after final exams ended, Wehmhoefer saw the symptoms for some students resolve within days. That's not typical of clinical depression. The problem, he says, reflects "kids who have been measuring themselves by a lone metric for a long time," who have no tolerance for failure. And who, crucially, have never learned the emotional skills to manage the acute stress that results.

The scale of the problem is huge. In the latest National Survey of College Counseling Centers, 94 percent of counseling directors said they were seeing rising numbers of students with severe psychological problems. Indeed, more than half of college students in a recent survey reported that they'd felt overwhelmed by anxiety within the past year. One in three said they'd felt so depressed it was hard to function. Tulane University, particularly hard hit in fall 2014, lost three students to suicide by Thanksgiving.

"The increased need for mental health services on our campuses is outstripping our ability to provide those services," John Stobo, an executive vice president for the University of California system, told the *California Report* radio program that same fall. The number of students seeking help at UC counseling centers had jumped by more than a third in the previous six years. Reduced stigma around seeking mental health counseling could account for some of that rise. But the increased incidence of emotional distress among college students is dramatic nonetheless: UCLA has surveyed entering freshmen at four-year colleges and universities around the country about their own mental health since 1985. In 2014, these students' ratings hit a record low.

Unhealthy Bodies

Beyond the kinds of mental and emotional pains the college psychologists describe, the health consequences of the childhood rat race are also frequently physical. Many of the pediatricians I've met around the country have told me, with grave concern, that they're seeing physiological impacts of this stress among their patients. And not just among high schoolers: many report symptoms in children as early as elementary school, just like I saw in Zak in third grade.

Lawrence Rosen, a pediatrician in northern New Jersey, told me that over the past fifteen years he's seen more and more children diagnosed with depression, anxiety, and physical symptoms of stress such as motor tics and panic attacks. "Kids are coming here with migraine headaches, ulcers. I'm talking about five-, six-, seven-year-olds who are coming in with these conditions. We never used to see that," Rosen said. "I do a lot of work nationally with other pediatric groups and pediatricians and I'm hearing this from my colleagues everywhere."

From Highland Park, Illinois, pediatrician Susan Sirota emailed me the following: "Every day I see children with some condition that is a direct result of the stress they experience related to school. Interestingly, when I started practice we used to figure this out by asking about what happened to the pain on the weekend—it would go away; now there is no difference since so many children are continuing to 'do extra school' or just not able to relax on the weekends."

This is how extreme the physical symptoms of childhood stress can get. Edin Randall is a psychologist at a pediatric pain rehabilitation center at Boston Children's Hospital. Her clinic specializes in a poorly understood and severe illness called complex regional pain syndrome—which she describes as commonly associated with high-pressure educational and extracurricular settings. This rare disease was described as early as the American Civil War and affects youth and adults in various countries, but its rates are rising, probably due to increased awareness and diagnosis. Randall says a typical case starts with an injury, such as an ankle sprain in a dance recital. The acute pain persists beyond the normal tissue healing process and then becomes chronic. Then, for reasons doctors don't yet understand, the child's nerves become irritated such that "a light touch will feel like stabbing pain," Randall explains. Normal treatments don't work for some patients. The pain is so severe that the child stops using that limb, which becomes waxy and stiff from disuse. Many sufferers stop going to school or participating in other activities.

There's been no research done yet to identify a causal link between high-stakes education and such pain disorders, but Randall sees a connection. Many of the children she treats tell her they come from stereotypically high-achieving communities with intense competition and pressure to perform. "It's a common denominator for a lot of our patients," she told me. Randall is careful to point out that, though stress seems to make the syndrome worse, it's not the cause. Rather, the physical and emotional distress work in tandem: the pain heightens a patient's anxiety, and the anxiety, in turn, makes it harder to cope with the pain. "Pain turns out to be a good communicator," Randall explains. Many of her patients put great effort into appearing fine even when they're incredibly stressed. So, Randall says, "Oftentimes pain is an indicator that there's something else going on." That *something else* may include the extreme expectations of an achievement culture gone crazy.

The Young and the Sleepless

At every screening I've attended, without fail, a bewildered, exasperated parent takes the mic and says his teen is staying up until the wee hours, night after night, then pounding coffee or going through her days in a sleepy haze, and no matter how this parent tries, he just can't convince his kid to close the books and go to bed. I couldn't sympathize more. When my girls were in middle and high school, I lost count of the number of times I'd tell them to go to bed, only to find them hours later awake at their desks, afraid to show up at school with work incomplete. Finally, I started insisting: interceding when they reached for lattes to power through piles of homework and emphasizing that life would go on if they didn't get an A.

Studies demonstrate that chronic lack of sleep is practically an epidemic among American teens. This is one of the causes of greatest concern for parents and pediatricians alike. Not only can sleep loss make our children surly at the breakfast table, it also can spell serious consequences for their health—and for their learning itself.

Researchers from the CDC have reported that the vast majority of American teens get at least two hours less sleep each night than what's recommended for their age. In a national survey published in 2010, the researchers found that fully one-third of high school students sleep only five or six hours on an average school night. Contrast that with the National Sleep Foundation's determination that, for teens, nine hours is optimal, eight is borderline, and anything less is insufficient. And it gets worse in eleventh and twelfth grades, as college application pressures mount. The rise of sleeplessness has even spawned a whole new category of pricey specialists that some parents hire: sleep coaches, who provide individualized step-by-step plans for sufficient slumber. As Cornell University sleep expert James Maas has put it, "Every single high school student I have ever measured in terms of their alertness is a walking zombie."

Skeptics will be quick to blame video games, text messaging, and the like for the teen sleep crisis, and there's no doubt technology is among the many culprits. But don't mistake it for the main one. In a National Sleep Foundation poll, more than one in three parents said that *scheduled activities* make it harder for their child to get a good night's sleep. More than one in four said *homework* had been a sleep thief within just the past week. And among the surveyed students at Irvington High School, far and away the most common reason for getting fewer than seven hours' sleep (cited by 77 percent) was homework and studying. Social networking was cited by just 28 percent. A 2014 report on teen sleep by the American Academy of Pediatrics named all of these factors—homework, extracurriculars, and social networking—as significant contributors to the crisis.

Homework's impact on sleep is sadly ironic, given the clear evidence that sleep deprivation harms the very process schoolwork is supposed to foster. Sleep plays a key role in attention and consolidation of new information in the brain, reports Harvard Medical School, and thus "the quantity and quality of sleep have a profound effect on learning and memory."

Just how foggy does a lack of sleep make children? As reported in *New*

York magazine, Tel Aviv University's Avi Sadeh tested this by instructing fourth and sixth graders to go to bed earlier or stay up later for three nights. The later-to-bed group ended up getting about an hour less sleep per night, compared to the others. When, after the third night, a researcher went to school to test the children's neurobiological functioning, the difference was stark. "The performance gap caused by an hour's difference in sleep was bigger than the normal gap between a fourth-grader and a sixth-grader," the magazine recounted. "Which is another way of saying that a slightly sleepy sixth-grader will perform in class like a mere fourth-grader."

Clearly, chronic late-night study sessions are not a pathway to mental growth; on the contrary, they are a symptom of a system that broadly encourages children to complete tasks and fulfill expectations without considering the consequences. Insufficient sleep is known to lead to ill health effects such as depressed mood, headaches, and drowsy driving. And it nearly killed Hayley Eaton, now a graduate student at the University of Oklahoma, who shared her story of how dangerously far sleep deprivation can go:

My world finally came to a screeching halt when I fell asleep at the wheel of my vehicle and crashed into a tree in the fall of my senior year of high school. Until that October day, I had assumed that I could keep pushing myself without consequence. I was taking all the available AP and Honors courses at my school, leading various school clubs, participating in an internship, volunteering, earning awards, and really anything that would make a nice addition to my college applications. I was allowing myself an average of 5-6 hours of shut-eye a night before waking up and repeating the cycle of school, then after-school activities, then oodles of homework. Spending quality time with family was a rare occurrence and hanging out with friends even more rare. Time to exercise or even just relax was simply unheard of. . . . I joked that I would "sleep when I'm dead" without realizing just how close I would come to fulfilling that prophecy at an incredibly young age.

The day of my crash was like any other: school, club meetings after school, run an errand or two, head home. I was driving care-

fully, under the speed limit, wearing my seat belt. Like any other day,
I was exhausted—this was simply a part of my reality. . . . Five and
a half hours of sleep the night before—and the previous night, and
the night before that—just wasn't sustaining me, like the ice on a
frozen lake that finally starts to crack under pressure.

People say that their eyelids feel heavy when they are tired, but I
was way past that: my entire body felt heavy, as if gravity was work-
ing extra hard on me, willing me to lie down and rest. I turned up
the volume on my CD player a bit more, in the hope that it could
keep me awake for about twenty more minutes of driving. . . . I was
getting further and further away from the present moment until
I finally fell asleep only a few miles from my house. I have a very
brief memory of the ground under my vehicle changing from smooth
pavement to shaky gravel and grass. I opened my eyes slightly and
saw for a split second the tree in front of me, but my mind didn't even
have time to register what I was seeing before the collision. I didn't
have time to brake or scream out or shield my face or react whatso-
ever before the truck went from forty miles an hour directly to zero,
and everything went black.

Hayley walked away, miraculously, with minor cuts and bruises and the
determination to change her life. "Today I pay much more attention to my
health and get plenty of sleep," she wrote. "The demanding course load and
high academic expectations for myself are a significant part of my life, but
nothing will come before my personal needs: healthy foods; sleep; exercise;
and time to reflect, to relax, and to spend with family and friends are all vital
to my well-being. Too few students have this perspective, however, and it is
easy to see why."

Self-Medicated for "Success"

It's also easy to see why more and more young students these days are turning to prescription drugs for energy and focus. With the expectations that
have been placed on them far exceeding what their minds and bodies can

naturally sustain, they're using unnatural means to keep up. *New York Times* reporter Alan Schwarz has researched the problem extensively. For his 2012 story "Risky Rise of the Good-Grade Pill," Schwarz interviewed students and doctors in more than fifteen academically intense high school communities across the country and concluded that pressure for top grades and college admissions is encouraging students to abuse prescription stimulants such as Adderall. Schwarz wrote:

> *Pills that have been a staple in some college and graduate school circles are going from rare to routine in many academically competitive high schools, where teenagers say they get them from friends, buy them from student dealers or fake symptoms to their parents and doctors to get prescriptions.*

The availability of prescription ADHD medications is skyrocketing, with the number of stimulants such as Ritalin and Adderall dispensed having shot up more than eightfold since the early 1990s. Prescription rates for teens alone more than doubled in just over a decade. The medications do help bring calm and ease symptoms for people who have a genuine disorder, Schwarz points out—yet for those who don't, a pill can provide laser-like focus and the energy to jam through late-night study sessions and final exams. In many communities, the drugs are practically de rigueur for students taking the SAT and ACT—perceived to be as essential a supply as a No. 2 pencil.

A young woman named Taylor, by then a student at Northern Arizona University, confessed to me that she first took Adderall as a high school junior. "I knew a lot of people who took it and I would ask them for it every once in a while," she said. "It's hard to be the vice president of your class, play on the soccer team, and do homework. It made me feel focused and almost better because, 'Look, I can keep up with everyone now. I come to school and my homework's done.'" Her story underscores the irony that kids are taking the drugs to compete with other kids, who are in turn taking the drugs to compete with *them*. Taylor started using the pills more frequently her senior year, until they backfired, ultimately sending her to the emergency room. "All of a sudden, I couldn't breathe as well," she recalled. "It was scary. I'd be sitting there trying to catch my breath. I couldn't fall asleep at night."

There aren't solid numbers on just how many teens such as Taylor are taking stimulants as a study aid, not out of medical need. As one might guess, studies that rely on teens' self-reporting don't provide a full picture of the problem. In the national 2013 Monitoring the Future survey, 15 percent of high school seniors said they'd taken a prescription drug for nonmedical reasons in the past year, and about half of those named Adderall. Yet the teens and doctors Schwarz interviewed would call those rates low: they estimated the real number as anywhere from 15 to 40 percent.

The short-term boost young students are after comes at a cost. What kids may think of as a harmless "study drug" is actually a DEA Schedule II controlled substance, so designated because of its potential for abuse. The misuse of stimulants can result in loss of appetite, insomnia, anxiety, heightened blood pressure, and, at high doses, an irregular heartbeat. If a child or young adult becomes addicted, the problems can get still worse. Most students who misuse the drugs don't suffer serious harm—Schwarz's research indicates that about 10 percent of those who use these stimulants will develop an addiction—but it's hardly a risk we want our children to take for the sake of their studies. The mere fact that our kids feel they need to self-medicate just to meet expectations, like pro athletes propped up by steroids, is a sign that something's wrong.

Alas, this sign of distress, too, continues into college, where substances can serve not only as study aids but also as a form of stress release. Jarreau, who runs alcohol education programs at Stanford, sums up the general mental health status of students at the university in a word: "Anxious." (He emphasizes that he speaks mainly from his own experience as a Stanford undergrad, not as a university representative.) He observes that many of them have spent their young lives so focused on academics that they haven't fully developed their social skills. They turn to hard alcohol as a social lubricant and a stress reliever, but they don't have the experience to handle it. The results—getting sick, getting injured, damaging property, injuring others—are dangerous. It's not that students today actually drink *more* than students past, he says; they just drink *differently*. "It's about something different. I don't think it was as much about the social anxiety and about using alcohol as a coping mechanism in the past."

In the radio report on the surging demand for mental health services on UC campuses, Elizabeth Gong-Guy, director of Counseling and Psychological Services at UCLA, described the situation thus: "Increasingly, we find that many of the students who make their way to our counseling centers are seasoned perfectionists who've driven themselves to unsustainable positions in which their lives lack any semblance of balance or self-compassion. These are students with eating disorders, crippling obsessive-compulsive disorders, cutting histories, addictions, and illicit stimulant abuse."

That is not how I, or any parent I know, would define success for my child.

The Tidal Wave of Illness to Come

These are the immediate health effects of the chronic, extreme expectations we have placed on our students. And if these were the only consequences of our pressure-cooker educational culture, that alone would be enough for us to act. But it's likely there are consequences we can't yet see—domino effects that could undermine our children's physical and mental health well into the future.

The science on this is just emerging, and there is little awareness of it outside the scientific community. Research over the past decade or so has clearly shown that childhood trauma affects a person's health throughout adulthood. This work, originating with the landmark Adverse Childhood Experiences Study in San Diego in the late 1990s, demonstrates unequivocally that unchecked stress in the early years is linked not only with adult mental health troubles but also with disruptions of brain development, higher rates of illness, and even altered gene expression. The more trauma a person experiences in childhood, the more likely he or she is to suffer later from depression and alcohol abuse. More surprisingly, survivors of early trauma are also more likely to suffer *physical* ailments including heart, lung, liver, and autoimmune diseases.

To be clear, most studies have focused on childhood problems that go far beyond academic anxiety, such as parental drug addiction, abuse, and neglect. It should go without saying that one cannot compare such a trauma

with excessive academic pressure. What's new, though, and what researchers are just starting to flesh out, is the realization that the constant presence
of less severe stressors could take a similar toll. No study I know of—yet—
has *directly* examined whether the excessive pressure to perform in and out
of school could be the kind of chronic stress that becomes toxic. But every
scientist I've spoken to expects that that is what we'll find as research continues. That's because stress exerts the same effects on the body no matter what
the cause. In children, any kind of stress "can really impact how the structure
and architecture of the brain forms," says Andrew Garner, a pediatrician at
University Hospitals Medical Practices in Ohio and associate professor at
Case Western Reserve University. Garner cowrote the American Academy
of Pediatrics' 2012 paper on the lifelong effects of childhood adversity, and
he adds, "It doesn't really matter what the stressor is, whether it's poverty or
chronic abuse or the bully on the bus."

Stress begins its spread throughout the body in a part of the brain called
the amygdala, which triggers a cascading release of hormones that reach our
every cell. This hormonal jolt is calibrated to help us spring into action to
avoid an immediate threat such as a forest fire (or, in modern student life, to
avoid flubbing the SAT). But it is ill suited to see us through chronic, long-
term worries. In fact, when the stress response does drag on, unrelenting, it
creates a physiological strain that scientists call allostatic load. That burden
feeds inflammation in the body, suppresses the immune system, and even
enlarges the amygdala itself, making it more volatile and reactive to future
stress. In other words, by subjecting young students to excessive and constant stress in their formative years, we may be making them more vulnerable to stress for the rest of their lives. "The brain is like a muscle," Garner
says. "The parts you use get stronger."

It's critical to understand the difference between good stress and bad, lest
we mistakenly try to protect our kids from every little thing. A little bit of
the right kind of stress can actually be essential. Donna Jackson Nakazawa,
journalist and author of the book *Childhood Disrupted: How Your Biography
Becomes Your Biology, and How You Can Heal*, explains it like this: "Of course
we don't want a childhood in which nothing bad happens, because we have
to learn adversity and learn grit and resilience and determination, and those
things take a little bit of failure and hard knocks." The critical difference, she

says, is between the bumps in the road that we might expect in life—you miss the bus, you're unprepared for an exam, or your grandmother dies— and "chronic stress that keeps coming, doesn't let up, is unpredictable, and a child isn't getting the support they need from adults." These two kinds of stress hit our brains and affect our immune systems very differently, Naka- zawa says, "and we sometimes confuse the two."

With temporary, predictable stress, we have a chance to recuperate and grow new neural connections in response to the problems we've encoun- tered, learning to arrive at the bus stop early, study better, and cope with normal loss. It's chronic, unpredictable stress from sources beyond our con- trol that gets toxic. And that is a pretty good description of what today's most pressured, overscheduled, underslept kids go through in the name of education. There's a perception that constant high demands will make kids stronger, says Nakazawa, "but biologically that is not the case; it's actually breaking down the brain rather than creating resilience."

In fact, a survey of the existing science in the 2013 *Annual Review of Public Health* concluded that "repeated exposure to less severe, but often chronic stressors is likely to play as large, if not larger, of a role in forecast- ing children's future mental and physical health," compared to extreme adversity.

What this means, in sum, is that we as a nation are not only making our kids miserable in the moment; we may actually be building a ticking time bomb of illness that will someday turn this generation of overstressed chil- dren into a generation of unhealthy adults. Research is under way that may show that bringing them up on a diet of unchecked stress is setting them up not for a happy, flourishing adulthood but for later waves of depression, anxiety, and even heart disease and cancer. And UC Berkeley health econo- mist Richard Scheffler expects this ill health will come with both a human and a financial cost to society. "Many of the health effects are apparent now but many more will echo through the lives of our children," Scheffler says. "We will all pay the cost of treating them and suffer the loss of their produc- tive contributions. Seeing these hidden costs now gives us a chance to avoid them."

Distribution of Health

By now you may be thinking, and not without good reason, that the pressure-fueled health problems described here only afflict children in upper-middle-class communities. Let me address that common perception head-on. Communities like mine, filled as they are with highly educated, financially comfortable parents who expect their children will attain the same, are undoubtedly hubs of the educational stress epidemic. And no one has made the case that children in upwardly mobile communities are suffering more vividly than has Suniya Luthar.

A psychology professor at Arizona State University and a native of India, Luthar has demonstrated over and over, in urban and rural communities and public and private schools from coast to coast, that the children of white-collar, well-educated parents in upper-middle-class communities are more likely than the average American youth to show "serious disturbance," manifested in mental health and behavior problems and substance abuse. These kids have higher rates of anxiety and depressive symptoms—sometimes at twice the national rate. Luthar's studies show that they are also significantly more likely to use cigarettes, alcohol, marijuana, and other drugs than are those from low-income settings (especially, it turns out, the girls). These youth don't appear particularly troubled as young children, Luthar reports, but—in a disturbing echo of what I saw in my own home—problems begin to emerge around seventh grade.

"Our sons and daughters are sort of living with this runaway train of who they're supposed to be," Luthar explains. Their aspirations for themselves mirror the status and accomplishments they see around them, in parents and community members and *especially* their peers, and thus they feel compelled to do everything at a peak level of performance. "The adage by which these children live is 'I can, therefore I must,'" she says. "You've got this mad rush to achieve, and that's sort of interspersed with this mad rush to relax, with whatever substances, and back to a mad rush to achieve." When a child defines herself and her self-worth by her accomplishments, Luthar adds, "That's a very tenuous way to live."

It's possible to take a cursory look at Luthar's work and the realities of inequity in America and dismiss academic stress as a rich kid's problem, an issue confined to kids with ample resources and one therefore not worthy of our alarm—or at least less worrisome than other social ills. Yet the causes for concern are manyfold. As Luthar herself notes, any population of children who are at risk, whether or not they fit our common perceptions of need, deserve to be protected. The pain these young people are experiencing is too excruciating—and the implications for our society's future are too real—to be ignored.

Besides, the knee-jerk assumption that academic stress is confined to privileged kids itself isn't true. The pressure to perform, while it pools within privileged neighborhoods, doesn't stay contained there. The troubling trends we've seen in depression and anxiety affect children from all kinds of schools and communities: affluent, middle class, impoverished, urban, suburban. School counselors widely report that the emotional distress they see in young people crosses socioeconomic lines and impacts children across the spectrum of academic ability. And they say it's worsening at a pace with which national surveys of adolescent mental health can't keep up.

Roy Wade Jr., a pediatrician at the Children's Hospital of Philadelphia, has seen the evidence. In interviews with Philadelphia youth from diverse socioeconomic strata, he has found that, though their external circumstances differ, they all describe feeling unsupported—an experience which is itself a stressor. In one study, Wade assessed stress levels in clients of five youth organizations, ranging from a homeless shelter to a running club that serves many kids from the affluent suburbs. "What we found is that if you took away the names of the organizations from the top of the report, you couldn't tell whose kids were whose," he said. "They all endorsed the same levels of stress."

No matter where we grow up, we are all inundated from birth with media messages about what makes success. Hint: it's not a modest job with a small house and a happy life; it's something at once much glossier and more limited. Perhaps it's the spacious suburban home with a smiling child eating Cheerios at the granite kitchen counter and a power-suited dad pulling his Lexus into the driveway. Or perhaps it's the übermodern city condo outfitted with slick Apple products and designer lighting. Our culture no longer celebrates the everyday travails of the blue-collar men who inhabited the bar on *Cheers*. Instead we idolize the urbanites of *Mad Men* and *Scandal*, their personal dysfunctions as grand as their lifestyles. Everywhere we look, someone is telling us to go bigger, to strive for more. Even a recently introduced line of Dreyer's frozen fruit bars (they're just Popsicles!) is named with a command: "Outshine!" All together, the glittering images that surround us fuel a status anxiety that's hard to shake.

Plus, the fierce competition for college admission among upper-middle-class students only raises the bar to entry for all students who hope to get in. For example, Mayra Valle, the daughter of Mexican immigrants in Houston, missed her last chance to see her dying grandmother because of school obligations. Her devotion to school came from years of watching her parents push their bodies to the limit. She'd seen her dad come home with white sweat stains on his green shirt from twelve hours working in the sun, and noticed her mom's calloused hands and chronic headaches from full days of childcare and cleaning. Mayra admired their strength but worried about their health, and wanted a solid education and career so she could relieve them from that labor. So, while not surrounded day to day by the trappings and expectations of affluence, she was nonetheless racing to compete academically. Mayra, vivacious and diligent, ultimately ended up at bucolic Connecticut College, in classes among peers who, by and large, faced far fewer challenges in getting there.

McKenzie Charlene Morrow, a student from a small town in western North Carolina, offers another example. As a high school junior, McKenzie wrote:

> I have lived my whole life stressing, worrying, focused on school. . . .
> I come from a family where neither my father nor mother graduated
> from high school. My parents always told me I needed to graduate
> and I needed to make something of myself. . . .

In eighth grade, McKenzie was thrilled to be accepted at a local early college high school, where students could take college and high school classes and graduate with both a high school diploma and an associate's degree. She felt as if all her hard work in middle school was finally paying off. Because her parents couldn't afford to pay for college, she felt excelling in school was her only path to a scholarship to a good college. McKenzie was determined not to squander the opportunity:

> My freshman year I focused solely on school, no other activities, I spent 4 to 5 hours after school on homework. . . . If I made a 95 on a test, it wasn't good enough for me. . . . I would study all night, and run on 3 or 4 hours of sleep daily.

She spent the summer after her freshman year reviewing SAT test prep instead of hanging out with her friends. Eventually, all that stress caught up to her.

> My sophomore year was when it all changed. I pushed myself so much, I was at the breaking point. I wasn't getting enough sleep, I was worrying too much, I was stressing over school so much that it affected me physically. I became sick more easily, my hands would break out in eczema flares. It got so bad my doctor was going to put me on medication. He thought maybe I was OCD. That was when my dad told me to just stop stressing. It was going to be okay, I needed to just relax.
>
> So when spring break arrived, I spent it with some old friends from middle school. They were all so happy and so carefree. I wanted that. I made up my mind I wanted to transfer to the regular high school. . . . I wanted to go to pep rallies, to prom, to be able to relax and enjoy things. . . . I am now enjoying every day, and yes I still stress a little about my classes even though there is no need. . . . I have enjoyed knowing I can achieve, but now I am learning something I never knew how to do before and that is just to relax and let go!

McKenzie ultimately graduated from the local high school with honors. Now she's studying at community college while working full time as a day-care teacher—a job she calls "the best thing ever"—and aiming to become an early childhood education director.

Edin Randall also sees evidence of suffering across the socioeconomic spectrum at the Boston Children's Hospital pain clinic, where many of the patients are affluent but a handful are also from lower-income families. "Interestingly, a lot of them are in the same situation," she says. "This is the good child. This is the child who's going to break out because they're such a good student."

That's just what I've heard from teachers, students, and researchers nationwide: kids in upper-middle-class communities may get a particular, potent dose of performance pressure, but children from many settings feel it. It's the precise genesis of kids' stress—whether from needing to keep up with inflated expectations or needing to escape poverty—that varies with a child's individual situation.

Impaired Learning

The excessive stress isn't doing much for children's intellectual strength, either. There's plenty of evidence that stress hurts cognition. As Garner points out, "That just makes sense intuitively. When you're panicked, you're not taking in a lot of information. You're certainly not making good decisions." Research has linked chronic stress with the loss of neurons and neural connections in the hippocampus, a brain area that's crucial to memory. Loss also occurs in parts of the prefrontal cortex, which is essentially the brain's conductor, a key player in so-called executive functions such as planning, problem solving, and self-control. The prefrontal cortex is still growing in adolescence, which means it's still being intricately shaped by the effects of experience (and which also explains a lot about teens).

In fact, the brain is particularly plastic in the teen years. We think of the years from zero to three as *the* critical period for brain development, but Temple University neuroscientist Laurence Steinberg underscores that adolescence is another one. "[T]he brain's malleability makes adolescence a period of tremendous opportunity—and great risk," writes Steinberg. "If we expose our young people to positive, supportive environments, they will flourish. But if the environments are toxic, they will suffer in powerful and enduring ways."

These sensitivities could have a serious impact on our children in school. Steinberg—who says schools chronically miss the sweet spot by overloading kids with assignments—explains that the key to learning is new experiences. These help to generate new synapses, or connections between neurons, which in turn create new links between different parts of the brain. A little bit of repetition can help strengthen those connections, but beyond that, repeated drilling produces no growth. "Novelty," he says, "is required to stimulate the growth of new synapses." So, by emphasizing quantity over quality, and content over mastery of complex skills, our traditional educational model is missing crucial opportunities to enhance brain maturation at a critical time. Plus, heightened levels of the stress hormone cortisol can injure the myelin, the protective white matter that surrounds brain circuits and allows them to function efficiently, Steinberg points out. So, school communities that place intense performance pressure on students, to the point of causing chronic stress, may actually be jeopardizing healthy brain function.

The misalignment of education with kids' real needs may explain why many check out and exacerbates the problems that cause some to leave school altogether. America's high school and college completion rates, once the world's highest, now lag far behind those of other developed nations. And while the high school graduation rate is rising, one in three students entering college requires remediation. These students made it through the exhaustive high school checklist, but the learning didn't stick. This is one of the reasons why 41 percent of students who start at a four-year college do not finish within six years. Such sobering statistics remind us of the big picture: that despite the trials we put high school students through in the name of academic preparation, our education system is still operating at a major loss. The hoops our children are expected to jump through on the way to higher education are, for too many, not hoops at all, but barricades.

"There are some kids that do need . . . to be taught how to organize, structure, manage their time," says Garner. "But we also know there are kids at the other end of the curve, crashing and burning." He argues that we must do better at helping kids stay more in the middle, where they're engaging but not burning out. Through our educational efforts to push every child to the max, he says, "We've gone off the deep end, and now we're doing more harm than good."

Less Prepared for Success

A youth spent in the pressure cooker also fails our children in one final way: by eroding the nonacademic skills that they also need to succeed in life. You'd think that a straight-A student who can manage four AP classes, run varsity track, and dominate the debate team with seeming ease would be perfectly poised to surmount challenges. In fact, we're seeing the opposite. College professors increasingly report that freshmen arrive on their campuses with the creativity strained out of them. Trained to color inside the lines, these students are afraid to take intellectual risks; they just want to know what it takes to make the grade. Then, as this stressed generation leaves college and enters the workforce, their employers report similarly troubling trends. Give them a discrete task, and yes, they can execute it like nobody's business. But more and more, surveys show, managers find young workers lacking in leadership, self-direction, critical thought, and collaboration skills—those essential, if immeasurable, qualities that truly determine success in today's world.

"Businesses often lament the lack of work readiness by recent college graduates" yet don't do enough to encourage change, says Bil Corry, a senior solutions engineer in information security at PayPal. "How can one expect innovative, creative thinkers that work well with others if the system they exclusively hire from does not value nor endorse those traits?"

We have, without really meaning to, transmitted to young people the idea that academic achievement is the most important way to measure their value as people, and that success in school exclusively assures success in life. Yet the Nobel Prize–winning economist James Heckman has decisively put that notion to rest. Analyzing thirty-five years of data that chronicled children's lives from preschool into adulthood, Heckman and colleagues demonstrated that character makes more difference than IQ for economic and social success. Improved character even boosted kids' standardized test scores, if that's what you care to measure.

The achievement-driven life appears even to be subverting our children's values. A 2011 analysis at the University of Michigan, which combined the results of dozens of personality studies of American college students over the course of thirty years, found that today's college kids rated about 40 percent lower on empathy than students in the late 1970s. Current students were comparatively less likely to agree with statements such as "I sometimes try to understand my friends better by imagining how things look from their perspective." Why? Researcher Edward O'Brien named "the hypercompetitive atmosphere and inflated expectations of success," and surmised that it all adds up to "a social environment that works against slowing down and listening to someone who needs a bit of sympathy."

A Harvard Graduate School of Education survey of ten thousand middle and high school students from diverse communities around the country found a similar distortion. When the researchers asked students to rank what was most important to them—achieving at a high level, happiness (feeling good most of the time), or caring for others—almost 50 percent picked high achievement as their top choice. Thirty percent chose happiness, and about 20 percent chose caring for others. When lead researcher Richard Weissbourd and colleagues compared the rankings head-to-head, they found that 60 percent of youth put achievement above caring. These values aren't mutually exclusive, Weissbourd explains. "We think you can be very happy and very caring and achieve at high levels. The concern we were raising is how out of balance they appear to be."

Evidence from the Josephson Institute of Ethics also reveals a disconnect. As you'd hope, 95 percent of the high school students the institute surveyed nationwide said trust and honesty are essential in the workplace. Yet, revealingly, more than half agreed with this statement: "In the real world, successful people do what they have to do to win, even if others consider it cheating." Similar to the students in Jay Jackson's survey at Irvington High School, more than 50 percent said they'd cheated during a test in school.

Even the so-called winners in the race may not ultimately gain. Daniel Kahneman and his colleagues have demonstrated that rich people don't actually feel any happier day to day than those with lower incomes. To be sure, it helps to have enough money to escape the pain of deprivation. But above an annual income of about $75,000, Kahneman and colleagues report, the link between wealth and happiness disappears.

"The irony here is all this focus on kids achieving may result in them achieving less, not more, because they're not developing certain skills that are going to be essential for their success" once they get out of the academic environment, says Weissbourd. Not to mention the skills essential for being good friends, romantic partners, and mentors, he adds, "and those relationships are probably the most important and durable sources of happiness that we have."

Cause for Action

Call upon all of this evidence when skeptics suggest that a healthy, sane education that's mostly free of anxiety is a soft one. I've encountered such resistance countless times. I've even encountered outright denial.

One screening of *Race to Nowhere* that I attended in Millburn, New Jersey, is seared into my mind. This came soon after the film's release, before it had been widely viewed and frank discussions about students' stress disrupted our national complacence. The moderator made audience members write their questions on notecards rather than speak them out loud, thereby silencing parents and students who had so much to say. Meanwhile, the evening's panelists (teachers and counselors from the local middle and high schools) said essentially that the schools weren't demanding too much of students, and that if there were problems with stress it was because of parental pressure and student procrastination. Afterward, in the lobby of the school auditorium, parents and students mobbed me to tell me just how acutely they disagreed with the panel. As one boy named Max put it to me, "I really feel that this movie is my life, and that the system truly needs change."

Change is hard. Even those who face the problem honestly still struggle to act—as I have myself, at times. Suggest to a coach that she take Wednesday nights off, and she'll say she can't because then her team will be less competitive. Ask a teacher to assign less homework, and he'll say his class might not then complete all the required content. Tell a student to ease up on her honors classes, and she'll say she might not get into Princeton. Everyone is afraid to be the first—or the only one—to change.

But those fears are unfounded. Change is already happening. And as the facts make plain, we must build on it; our children's health and preparation for the future are on the line. Even the gatekeepers at Harvard University say so. The dean and director of admissions coauthored an open letter imploring incoming freshmen to slow down their "fast-lane childhoods" and take a gap year before arriving, burned out and sapped of their souls, upon the vaunted campus. "The fact remains that there is something very different about growing up today," they wrote. "Some students and families are suffering from the frenetic pace, while others are coping but enjoying their lives less than they would like. Even those who are doing extraordinarily well, the 'happy warriors' of today's ultra-competitive landscape, are in danger of emerging a bit less human as they try to keep up with what may be increasingly unrealistic expectations." In other words, the price of maintaining the status quo is simply too high.

So "to better your future," to borrow the Irvington High School student's phrase, is actually to *stop* the automatic, unquestioned race we're all running and to redefine goals all our own. This is what the families and schools in this book have begun to do. They are not blaming each other, because they understand that the race is not the exclusive fault of any single group. It is the culture. Which is to say: it is everyone. We collectively create the culture, and it's up to us to change it.

That's what is so inspiring about the attitude of Irvington's Jay Jackson. He knows that change begins on the ground, in each community, with teams of people who believe in it. He knows this work will be hard, yet he insists upon pursuing it anyway, unflinching. "Let's try some things out," Jackson said the day of my visit after sitting with the roomful of exhausted teens. He knew his initiatives to ease students' stress and limit their overscheduling wouldn't work overnight, he said, ready for the challenges that inevitably come with change, "but let's see if we can tweak them and *make* them work."

When we look into our children's eyes and ask ourselves whether their "better future" should be the unhealthy one they're now marching toward, every parent and educator will offer the same answer: no. Instead we wish for them health, happiness, and the contentment that comes from being a good citizen of the world. We need to act *now* to preserve that better future for our children, and to protect them from the false ideals that threaten to take it away.

CHAPTER 2

It's About Time

T HE WAY to reclaim a childhood stuck in overdrive has a lot to do with time.

I recognized this when the film crew and I went to interview Kelly, a close friend of Devon, the girl in my community who'd committed suicide. We found her saddened yet thoughtful, open to talking honestly about the pressures that beset her and her peers. Kelly, an eighth grader, had just one surprising request: we had to schedule the interview at eleven p.m. on a weeknight, after all her assignments, sports practice, and piano lessons were done.

The episode illustrated a key insight into the causes of the health crisis our children are suffering and the competitiveness that's diminishing their educations. At the root of all these ills, there is a universal pattern: our collective misuse of time. The problem is visible in the child falling asleep on her books or the parent spending all afternoon driving kids around, and visceral in the sense that our children's school years are speeding by. Time is at the heart of every single problem we will address in this book: poor health, runaway homework, excessive testing, narrow learning, and unchecked college competition. But it is also at the heart of every solution. Revolutionize the way we think about and use our time—and our children's—and we transform the way they grow and learn.

In our culture's manic mindset, often bent on one version of "success," we're constantly encouraged to "use our time well." And time used well is understood to mean one thing only: time used productively. Minutes spent at rest or at leisure, playing with friends or dreaming up stories, are considered frittered away. And so we stack our days with productive obligations, pursuing the achievement we understand to be primary, and then wonder why no time remains to do the simple things that make us whole. Schools, similarly misguided, grab huge chunks of children's time *outside of school*, commanding so many hours that our kids' school-to-life balance grows horribly lopsided. Meanwhile, the misuse of time *during the school day* keeps educators locked in old and unproductive modes of teaching.

Our children's treadmill schedules—which leave little room for deep learning, daydreaming, quietude, healthy habits, or human connections—are a symptom of this. And our collective misuse of time amounts to a societal disease.

"This disease of being 'busy' (and let's call it what it is, the dis-ease of being busy, when we are never at ease) is spiritually destructive to our health and wellbeing," writes Omid Safi, the director of Duke University's Islamic Studies Center. "It saps our ability to be fully present with those we love the most in our families, and keeps us from forming the kind of community that we all so desperately crave." It also steals the fleeting time we have to grow confident, considerate, creative kids with inquisitive, inventive minds.

The problems of the Race to Nowhere call for a total time redesign. It can be tough to imagine alternate ways to use our time—the task requires us to scrutinize not only the external structures and policies that frame our lives but also our own everyday choices. Yet some smart schools and families are already doing it, and the rest of us must follow their lead. Because time is not only a prime victim of our culture's distorted priorities, it can also serve as the most tangible and immediate tool with which to start setting those priorities right. If we examine which activities actually occupy a child's hours, then compare that accounting to the list of priorities we most value, we'll quickly see where values and realities misalign.

It is by reclaiming time that we begin to rebalance our children's lives and learning—and, as adults, our own lives, too. It's how we wipe clean the slate of *how things have always been done* and liberate ourselves to imagine how they can be done now.

In this chapter we examine some of the most conspicuous thieves of children's time, and we describe a variety of solutions that schools and families have created. These examples are not exhaustive; in your own schools and lives, you could surely find many more. What they all illustrate, though, is that *time* itself it is the most powerful lens through which to view our Race to Nowhere—and through which to see our way clear to something better.

Time and Values

Let's start by turning the lens on the daily life of one student: Tira Okamoto, the author of this book's opening poem.

We see her, a junior at San Francisco's Lowell High School, dragging herself sleepily out of bed at 6:10 a.m. She carpools in and arrives at school by the bell, barely, at 7:35, and then proceeds to lurch through seven straight classes. Precalculus: turn in homework, then zone out, wondering if this material will be on the SAT. AP English: beautiful books to discuss, though they were chosen by state policy makers, not this brilliant teacher. College and career seminar: daydream again, as the content is review for Tira. At 10:35, it's lunchtime—the only time slot where she could fit lunch given the courses she needed. Not yet hungry, Tira nips over to Starbucks, already reliant on caffeine to get through her long days and nights at age seventeen.

Next: Spanish (memorizing verb tenses), AP US history, and physics. Each forty-five-minute period contains perhaps enough time to check homework and attendance, introduce one new topic, and answer a couple of questions about it. Then—ring!—Tira moves on to the next class and does it again. A few classes a day are fifteen minutes longer, which in history today means the students have time to discuss current events. Otherwise, there's little time to consider what this math formula means in real life, or to delve beyond vocabulary into the cultural richness of Spain or Mexico. The content of one class is completely isolated from the next, and the amount of time devoted to each lesson is determined not by its complexity or potential to engage and inspire a student but rather by a soulless and inflexible warden: the clock.

Tira cares about physics, where the teacher is passionate and dynamic, but by that point, her sixth class of the day, with the coffee wearing off, she struggles to stay alert. Finally, her last class, advanced dance, awakens her.

She gets to finish the day doing something she loves, before the final bell rings at three thirty p.m.

Few adults in schools experience this churn themselves. But one veteran teacher and instructional coach from the Northeast, Alexis Wiggins, decided to try it firsthand. Before starting a new job, she followed a tenth grader around for a day, and then a twelfth grader for another day. Wiggins was shocked by what a passive, silent learner the regimen made her, and how exhausted she felt by all that sitting and listening by the afternoon. The experience startled her so much that she wished she could go back and change ten things about every class she had ever taught.

"By the end of the day, I could not stop yawning and I was desperate to move or stretch," Wiggins wrote in a blog post about the experience. "I was drained, and not in a good, long, productive-day kind of way. No, it was that icky, lethargic tired feeling. . . . It was not just the sitting that was draining but that so much of the day was spent absorbing information but not often grappling with it." She had planned to do more work that afternoon, but she was tired. She went home and watched TV, and went to bed at eight thirty.

So if the way we spend our time is a clear expression of what we value, what does a student's daily schedule tell us about what we value in school? A few words spring to mind: *Speed. Uniformity. Quantity.*

Certain other words—*depth, individuality, quality*—do not.

"If you were running a business with a thousand employees, and every forty minutes everybody had to stop what they were doing, go to a different room entirely, and do something else for forty minutes that they weren't so interested in, and then rinse and repeat six times a day, you'd be out of business in a week," Ken Robinson, the international education expert and author of *The Element: How Finding Your Passion Changes Everything*, said to me. "You would get nothing done, and people would become disaffected."

But the school day itself isn't even the whole picture for most students. Factor in the way schoolwork, sports, band, theater, and other school-sponsored activities extend ever deeper into afternoons, evenings, and weekends, and you see that, as imbalanced as adults' work-to-life ratio has become, children's school-to-life ratio is often worse.

Let's return to Tira's schedule in the hours after the final bell has rung.

She dashes to her locker, still in her dance clothes, to grab books and snack. Rehearsal for the school dance company lasts until six. Lugging her heavy backpack, Tira takes an hour-long bus trip home, showers, eats, and starts her homework at eight. She nods off sometimes while reading her textbooks. At midnight, bleary-eyed, she rushes through her last precalculus problems and goes to bed, setting her alarm early to get up and do it all again.

And this is a student participating in an unusually modest number of extracurricular activities: one.

So, what does a child's daily schedule tell us about what matters beyond school? Answer: productivity and performance. Clearly not reflection, connection, or rest. Certainly not family. Nor passion. Nor joy. When I think about children today, I often picture a dozen adults gripping each of them by their limbs, pulling them in all directions with demands on their time, pulling them to pieces.

Downtime Is Up Time

The result is that our children's balance—between rest and attention, compliance and exploration, self and work—is wildly out of whack. Time and again, I have shaken my head at how little resemblance my children's youth bears to mine. As a kid, I got all my homework done and still had time to read books, play with neighborhood friends, and even work an after-school job. Young people these days barely have time to blink. Even activities that appear recreational, such as softball practice, are scheduled, orchestrated, and directed by adults. Seduced by society into thinking that children must be filled with educational enrichment lest they lie idle and amount to nothing, we feel compelled toward what sociologists call "concerted cultivation." In other words, *Washington Post* reporter Brigid Schulte says, "You're trying to grow this hothouse flower," instead of a child with the natural inclination to find her own pursuits. Then, as our kids grow older, they absorb this idea from society and start overscheduling themselves, even when we parents sense it's gone too far.

"As parents, we want what's best for our kids but we've abdicated our parental rights and duties to the new societal norm," writes Ron Turker, a pediatric orthopedic surgeon in Portland, Oregon, who sees more and more overpracticed young athletes with repetitive-stress injuries that used to be rare. "We give in to the herd mentality along with our confounded friends so that our kids won't be seen as outliers."

What we parents, educators, and coaches may forget amid all the racing around is that this modern childhood time suck comes with a huge opportunity cost. All the hours our children spend dutifully taking direction are hours they don't spend imagining, experimenting, inventing, connecting, or creating and solving problems all their own. They're missing a critical window to develop the skills that come with organic exploration and spontaneous play. While we all know intellectually that each day, every day, only has twenty-four hours in it, we often fail to note that our children's schedules are a zero-sum game. Gain an hour of piano lessons and you'll lose an hour of outdoor play. Lose an hour of homework, and you get that playtime back. It's that simple, and yet it's that hard.

Research confirms that children's downtime is dwindling. A team at the University of Michigan found that over just the two-plus decades between 1981 and 2003, American children ages six to seventeen came to spend significantly more time in school and studying. Probably not coincidentally, over the same period, children's time outdoors dropped precipitously—nearly in half. University of Washington researchers found in 2015 that even kids in preschool are given only forty-eight minutes a day for free and active play.

Boston College psychologist Peter Gray has found evidence showing a continuous decline in children's outdoor play since the 1950s. The realization really hit him on a trip about a dozen years ago to the Dominican Republic, where he saw lots of kids freely playing outdoors: "I realized: this is how I used to play. And wait a minute, I don't see that anymore back home. When I see kids outdoors they're in uniforms. They're on manicured soccer fields doing what the coaches are telling them to do. They're not playing. They're doing something that's adult directed. They may be enjoying it, but it's not play." Our lives are so scheduled, Gray laments, that "even those kids whose parents let them go out to play, there aren't other kids to play with."

We forget in the push for productivity that much of what is lost is what happens below the surface of free time. Building a fort, daydreaming, or inventing a game might seem like dreamy luxuries—but these idylls of childhood are far from idle. It's in these unstructured moments that children develop essential capacities for reflective thought, creativity, social skills, and self-control. And these opportunities, which now grow ever more rare, are irreplaceable.

"Downtime actually isn't down time," said the Harvard Innovation Lab's Tony Wagner when we met. "Downtime is up time. The research is very clear that the brain needs time off to synthesize, to integrate. Why is it that so often many of us get some of our best ideas when we are shaving or in the shower, or taking a walk or doing yoga?"

An explanation of what makes downtime—true downtime, not staged recreation—so important comes from University of Southern California neuroscientist Mary Helen Immordino-Yang and colleagues in the journal *Perspectives on Psychological Science*. Reviving an old John Lubbock quote that "rest is not idleness," they cite evidence that "wakeful rest" (daydreaming, reflection, what researchers call the brain's "default mode," with no task at hand) is essential for healthy psychological functioning. In that state, you develop stronger memory, cognitive skills, divergent thinking, and social-emotional skills such as weighing the moral and emotional effects of your actions. The researchers argue that our ceaseless demands for kids' externally focused attention, in and out of school, may be harming their growth. They write, "Safely indulging mind wandering may be critical for healthy development and learning in the longer term."

The author Tim Kreider, deploring our constant hurry, puts it this way:

> Idleness is not just a vacation, an indulgence or a vice; it is as indispensable to the brain as vitamin D is to the body, and deprived of it we suffer a mental affliction as disfiguring as rickets. The space and quiet that idleness provides is a necessary condition for standing back from life and seeing it whole, for making unexpected connections and waiting for the wild summer lightning strikes of inspiration—it is, paradoxically, necessary to getting any work done. . . . Archimedes' "Eureka" in the bath, Newton's apple, Jekyll & Hyde and the benzene ring: history is full of stories of inspirations that come in idle moments and dreams.

It follows, then, that some researchers also blame the dearth of downtime for our nation's growing creativity crisis. Kyung-Hee Kim, a professor of creativity and innovation at the College of William & Mary, published a bombshell study on this in 2011. She examined the scores of more than 250,000 children and adults on a widely respected creativity test, the Torrance Tests of Creative Thinking, from 1966 to 2009. Children's scores on this test are powerfully linked to their later life accomplishments, far more so than IQ. The data showed that indicators of creativity had flatlined or declined during that time. Looking just at the years since 1990, the picture was worse: even as Americans' IQ scores generally rose, creativity scores significantly dropped, especially in kindergarten through third grade. Breaking the creativity measure down into its component parts, Kim wrote that over the last twenty years:

> Children have become less emotionally expressive, less energetic, less talkative and verbally expressive, less humorous, less imaginative, less unconventional, less lively and passionate, less perceptive, less apt to connect seemingly irrelevant things, less synthesizing, and less likely to see things from a different angle.

That's not exactly what I wish for my children. Nor does it bode well for American ingenuity. And it may help explain why high-tech universities are doing more educational gymnastics to get incoming students to think outside the box. One MIT undergraduate dean told science journalist Annie Murphy Paul, "We scour the country looking for young builders and inventors. They're getting harder and harder to find." So MIT now offers classes and activities "devoted to taking things apart and putting them together," Paul writes, "an effort to teach students the skills their fathers and grandfathers learned curbside on weekend afternoons."

Alongside creativity, there's still another endangered species in our children's minds: a critical capacity called executive function. This is your child's basic tool kit for functioning in life, and it includes the ability to set goals, make plans, manage one's time, and control one's impulses and emotions. "When you're playing with other kids and working on your own projects, it calls for a lot of self-regulation and executive functioning," explains Paul, who's also the author of *Brilliant: The New Science of Smart.* "When you're being ferried from one activity to another, and always told what to do, that capacity for executive function doesn't have the opportunity to develop."

Indeed, a 2014 study from researchers at the University of Colorado at Boulder found that children who spent more time engaged in less structured activities were far better at setting and accomplishing goals than peers who participated in more formal, structured pursuits. The bottom line: in constantly pushing our children to do more, we may be setting them up to pursue and achieve less. "It's strangely, ironically, unproductive to over-schedule kids," says Paul. "For parents who think they're giving their kids a leg up by having every moment of their day structured, it's having the opposite effect."

Productivity does not necessarily equal good growth for older kids or teens, either. Abigail Baird, the Vassar College neuropsychologist, explains that chatting and hanging out is some of the essential work of adolescence. Just like the most critical—and easiest—window for learning a language is eighteen to twenty-four months, she told me, "The adolescent years are the prime time for social experience, to learn everything you need to about yourself and how you relate to your community. That's the perfect time." So you may do okay learning your social skills later in life, she said, "but in the same way that learning a language late in life leaves you with an accent, you'll never sound exactly like a native."

The Youth Sports Vortex

Take, as a time-thief example, the great maw of recreational sports. These seem like an unlikely bad guy. They provide opportunities for physical exercise, perseverance, discipline, and teamwork—all good things for our kids' growth. But over the past few decades, youth sports have gone off the deep end, requiring way too much time, exertion, and specialization at an ever-younger age. Practices and games engulf fifteen or twenty hours a week, while travel teams for nine-year-olds drag families across the state, gobbling up their budgets and weekends. (My extended family hasn't gathered for Thanksgiving in years because my nephews always have obligations to hockey.) It's not unusual to drive past a soccer field at eight p.m. and see eight-year-olds at practice. In my childhood, we were in bed by then.

Because everyone else is doing it, parents feel they have to do it to keep up. *Start training hard at age five, or your kid will never be a ready enough competitor to play high school sports* is the implicit or even explicit message we get from well-meaning fellow parents and coaches. Or: *Top performance in sports is your ticket into an elite college.* ("Fear-based sports marketing" is what one sports mom I know calls it.) Children themselves notice that their peers are attending summer soccer camps or slotting in extra private lessons in between team practices. So we accept these excessive schedules rather than organize for change. The consequences, besides lost time and opportunities, include high rates of repetitive-use injuries (as Dr. Turker has seen) and many kids who utterly burn out on sports and quit by the time they reach high school.

"Many parents have come to believe that more (more teams, more practices, more intense and competitive games) and earlier (travel teams at age seven!) is somehow better," reports the youth sports website MomsTeam. But "the majority of studies suggest that early specialization can have 'significant negative consequences on the development of an athlete over time.'" Many parents, including me, simply want our kids to have the chance to play sports but find the only opportunities are all-or-nothing rec teams that demand Total Commitment. Whatever happened to a bunch of kids playing informal baseball in someone's front yard with an old sweatshirt used as second base?

Even unsuspecting recreational players get swept up in the sports machine. Stacked against their overtrained peers, they often don't feel "good enough" and quit because they sense there's little value placed on having fun. Or they try so hard to catch up that they end up with the same overuse injuries or overscheduled days as their more competitive friends. This kind of overdrive is part of what drove Zak out of adult-organized sports. After a few years of soccer and Little League, he decided he preferred skateboarding, snowboarding, and surfing, where he could stretch his own limits without having to answer to coaches' and parents' ambitions.

Emily Cohen, a Berkeley mom of two and host of the youth sports podcast

TeamSnap, recalls when her daughter had finally had enough. She'd played A-level club soccer through seventh grade, but when practices were set to increase to four times a week, leaving her no time to play tennis, she declined and joined rec soccer instead. "What do you mean, she's not all in on soccer?" fellow parents asked her mom. "Your daughter's not going to get a college scholarship," said the coach, echoing a sports-can-get-you-scholarships perception (sometimes oversold) that also drives many hopeful families to pursue athletics to extreme degrees. Cohen replied, "I don't care, this is about her, what she wants." And she considers it one of the best decisions her daughter has made.

School-Life Balance

Yet the imbalance in kids' lives is hardly all due to overzealous soccer leagues. Nor can it mainly be chalked up to parents' and kids' overeager scheduling. In fact, by the time students reach middle school, if not earlier, the demands dictated *by schools themselves* account for by far the most sizable part of the problem.

Start with the thirty-five hours a week a typical student spends in school and commuting there. Add in a very conservative ten hours for one sport or school-sponsored activity, and you've already exceeded the demands of a full-time job. Beyond that, assignments, additional activities, required community service, and recommended tutoring encroach ever further beyond the last bell and even into the evening, appropriating the personal and family time that schools do not own and cannot see. Outside of abandoning academic responsibilities and quitting activities that they care about, kids and families feel like they have little say. Homework is, of course, among the most egregious means of these time grabs, so much so that I devote the entire next chapter to its origins and solutions. Here, I'll focus on the numerous other ways schools reach across the school-home line—through sports and activities that are inherently valuable but have been taken too far.

Emily Cohen remembers how high school sports teams, for instance, simply picked up the baton of extreme scheduling from the youth leagues. One day her daughter got a list of expectations from her high school soccer coach. It said: *You are a student first.* Then it said: *All doctor's appoint-*

ments and family commitments should be scheduled outside of practice and games. "I nearly threw up," Cohen recalls. "Family commitments should be scheduled around the games? What world are we living in? When it's my mother's ninety-second birthday, no, we're not going to the game." Even when coaches say schoolwork comes first, she's observed, the kid who skips practice to study for two finals the next day may get benched, "so there's a punishment for it."

The expectations have grown so out-of-control that in 2014 the California Interscholastic Federation capped high school sports practices at eighteen hours a week or four hours a day. As if even those limits were reasonable. In my own home, I found that when my older daughter decided to play high school softball, she had to head to practice the moment the last bell rang, five days a week, and then didn't get home until after seven, delaying our family dinner.

Plus, sports are only part of the broader problem of extracurriculars going overboard. School debate teams, yearbook staffs, dance troupes, and other activities can command at least as many hours as athletics. These are wonderful experiences that contribute greatly to kids' growth, but they've become professionalized to such a degree that participating in even one of them now allows a child little chance to try anything else.

Science has a lesson for us here. Psychologist Edin Randall, whom we met in the last chapter for her work with pediatric pain patients, also specializes in research on extracurricular activities. One study of hers revealed that students at a diverse, urban high school who participated in more than about ten hours of activities per week saw diminishing returns. They enjoyed benefits from moderate participation, including social confidence and connectedness. But those benefits leveled off around five to seven hours per week and started dropping around ten. Randall's subsequent research reveals an important wrinkle: it matters not only *how much time* you spend in activities, but also *why* you do them—whether for enjoyment or a sense of obligation. Children who spend oodles of hours in activities they adore, purely for the fun of it, tend to be happy and well adjusted. Those who participate because they sense pressure to do it may fare worse. The essential question for the kids, Randall concludes, is: "Why are you doing this? Because you're enjoying it, or because you feel like you have to?"

TeamSnap's Cohen has tried some rebellious tactics to spare her own children from being caught amid competing demands from authority figures they respect and trust. "Adults like to use the word *mandatory* to make the kids feel like they have to do something," Cohen says. Once she got back-to-back emails about two of her daughter's activities, both claiming to be mandatory, at times that conflicted. Since then, she says, "I have a ban on the word *mandatory* in my house."

Even spiritual leaders are joining the ranks of those concerned about overscheduling. Pastors and rabbis frequently tell me they're finding kids and families losing touch with their faith and community because they simply don't have time, just as I saw happen with my children. "Youth ministry has become extremely difficult," says pastor Doug Burford, who leads a small church in Overland Park, a Kansas City suburb high on the performance-pressure scale. Youth group meetings, Bible study, service projects—it all takes a back pew to other obligations, he says. "It's almost impossible to schedule anything."

Burford once saw a kid at church in a soccer uniform at ten on a Sunday morning. He asked if the boy had a game later, and the boy said no, he'd had one at six thirty a.m. because that's when the field was available. "In the morning?!" the shocked pastor asked him. "If I as a pastor asked for that kind of meeting time, people would look at me incredulous that I had the audacity to request that."

Without the time for cultivation of the soul, Burford senses a void in kids—a hunger that they can't quite name. "An idol can be anything that takes first place over God," he says. "And to me, frankly, sports has become that."

Too Early to Rise

It's worth noting one more important way in which school schedules are poorly aligned with our children's needs: the indecent and science-defying hours at which they roust our teens out of bed. Alarm clocks across the country go off at six a.m. or earlier to get kids up in time to stumble blearily into class as early as 7:20 a.m., poorly rested and unready for learning. School start times are determined by a host of factors—competing bus schedules, interscholastic sports, tradition. But too often missing from that list is an essential one: medical evidence.

"We're starting to see schools change their schedules to accommodate the fact, and it is a fact, that circadian rhythms change in adolescence, and making them get up at six is really dumb," says Abigail Baird. "Adolescents can only physically grow when they sleep, so disrupting their sleep cycles is really not smart."

The reason is that adolescents' natural sleep-wake cycles, governed by the timed release of hormones throughout the day, begin to shift by up to two hours as puberty begins. Teens are naturally driven to stay up later and sleep later, and our traditional school schedules directly contradict their bodies' needs. The American Academy of Pediatrics cites strong evidence that early school start times are a critical contributor to chronic sleep deprivation among American teens. Its official recommendation is that middle and high schools start at eight thirty or later—but an AAP report in fall 2014 noted that 85 percent of American high schools do not.

We saw in the last chapter that teen sleep deprivation is linked to anxiety, depression, and other ill health effects, as well as a marked drop in mental functioning. So it stands to reason that studies have found schools with later start times see fewer tardies and absences, improved student attention, and higher grades and standardized test scores. One alarming study in Virginia even found a connection between teen sleep and car accidents. The neighboring cities of Virginia Beach and Chesapeake are demographically similar, researchers reported in 2008 in the *Journal of Clinical Sleep Medicine*. The major difference for students is that the cities' high school start times are seventy-five to eighty minutes apart. Perhaps as a result, the research team found that earlier-to-rise Virginia Beach saw significantly higher rates of weekday car crashes among teen drivers than Chesapeake did.

So what our school start times tell us about our values is that, until now, logistics and traditions have trumped health and learning. Thankfully, that is starting to change. Two high schools in Boulder, Colorado, for example, pushed their first bells back from seven thirty to eight or later. Fairfax County, Virginia, high schools and the Minneapolis school district have delayed their starts. The Emery/Weiner School in Houston reset its start time by forty-five minutes after a *Race to Nowhere* screening. Rock Bridge High

School in Columbia, Missouri, pressed by a sophomore and A student who told the *New York Times* she had to set three alarms to get to class at 7:50, changed its start time to the adult-work hour of nine a.m. Other schools across the country are following this lead.

Enslaved by the Bell

And what happens when students, sleepy or not, arrive on campus? As the glimpse at Tira's schedule showed us, the hurried pace of learning during the school day only quickens the spin cycle. Overcrowded schedules fragment our kids' learning time, thus crowding out opportunities for deep consideration. The inefficient use of the school day is also part of what pushes school obligations, such as assignments and tutoring, past the last bell.

Teachers are not to blame for the mind-numbing march that school days often become. Even the most inventive among them must work within the inflexible constraints of a system created in the Industrial Age, when factory schedules framed the zeitgeist and influenced the design of public schools. The stubbornness of that system came home to me in a head-spinning story told to me by Larry Rosenstock, cofounder and CEO of San Diego's High Tech High, one of the most vibrant and innovative schools I've seen. He considers the traditional school schedule, regimented into fixed chunks of time, the single greatest impediment to educational innovation. While explaining what drove him to exit the public school system and start a charter school, Rosenstock recalled a moment working in Cambridge, Massachusetts:

> We had a schedule that really was designed for adult convenience, not for students' convenience. It made no sense to a lot of us. So, I met with sixteen teachers. I said, "We need to change the schedule," and they all sat there very somberly, and one of them said, "Well, we can't change the schedule. The schedule won't let us," as if it were sitting at the table. And it took me six years to realize that that person was right. The schedule wouldn't let us.

In other words, Rosenstock said, the schedule had been rigidly fixed for so long that people assumed it could not be disrupted—yet those very assumptions prevented them from exploring avenues for change. It was a self-fulfilling prophecy. On top of such tunnel vision, schools trying to reshape their schedules run up against practical obstacles: bus schedules, sports schedules, objections from teachers unions, and the organization of high-stakes tests and teachers' credentials around narrow subjects. Many states still have antiquated "seat time" requirements for public schools, based literally on how many hours students have spent sitting in class, regardless of how much they've learned. The resulting rigidity reflects another misalignment of our actual use of time and our values.

A number of schools across the country have successfully upturned tradition, redesigning school time around a new set of priorities—depth, personalization, creativity, connection, meaning—and restoring some of the after-school time that rightfully belongs to students and families.

Walter Payton College Preparatory High School, for example, has used several smart tactics to shake the schedule monkey off its back. The downtown Chicago magnet school draws academically high-achieving students from all socioeconomic strata from across the city. The foundation on which Payton's layered strategies are built is the block schedule, where students spread their classes out over two days, attending only four classes a day instead of sprinting quickly through all eight. The classes come in big ninety-minute blocks, which allow teachers and students to settle down and dig in—tackling more complex lessons and deeper questions. Plus, with students only having to prepare for half their classes each night, Principal Tim Devine explains, "That allows focus."

Block schedules are not uncommon in American high schools and represent a good, if basic, starting point. Research confirms their benefits. In 2001, Michael Rettig and Robert Lynn Canady, then professors at James Madison University and the University of Virginia, respectively, took stock of a decade's worth of science and found evidence that block schedules can bring a host of improvements: better student and teacher attendance, fewer discipline referrals, and higher grades.

Payton puts some unique twists on its block schedule. First, it devotes the last forty-nine minutes of each day to a period called Enrichment. This is, essentially, flex time: Payton students' all-in-one tool for addressing whatever they need on the day when they need it. Those who need one-on-one tutoring with a teacher can go to that teacher's classroom and get it. Athletes can start practice or set off for away games without missing class. Others might work together on group projects, hold meetings of academic clubs, exercise, or just get a jump start on homework. (Personally, I could use an Enrichment period every day.)

Second, Payton devotes every other Wednesday to ungraded seminars: deep dives into decidedly nonacademic subjects that expand students' minds and worlds. Teachers, who get to invent seminars based on their own interests, enjoy them, too. The subjects range from the gritty to the goofy— recent seminars include the basics of stocks and trading with researchers from Morningstar, improv comedy with performers from the sketch comedy company Second City, belly dancing, beginning guitar, and elementary astronomy.

Making these time-shifts at Payton involved clearing some common hurdles—especially skepticism about changing the status quo. In spring 2012, when the whole city of Chicago was poised to lengthen its school day, Principal Devine seized the chance to explore how to use all school time better. Payton hosted dozens of conversations with students, faculty, and parents, closely examining the benefits of potential approaches. A majority of people in all those groups ultimately embraced block scheduling, enrichment periods, and seminars—and that broad-based support helped Devine convince reluctant district officials to let Payton break the mold.

For recent Payton grad Lucian, the net effect was to create a more relaxed learning environment and deeper lessons. He says the seminar days, in particular, "allowed me to explore how to understand a new concept, idea, solution, or entire world without the stresses of a regular academic course" and "kept us excited about our other classes since there isn't the constant drain of being in the same class every day." Rising senior Daniela finds the enrichment periods especially important, "because when a chunk of school time is devoted to extracurriculars, there is more time after school to finish homework, spend time with family, and, of course, sleep."

Devine, meanwhile, is watching closely to see how Payton's reforms affect all students. So far, so good: three years after implementation, the school's impressive student outcomes remain strong. About four in ten Payton students live in poverty (and counting those who are just "a snowball's throw away from poverty," says Devine, it's closer to six in ten). Yet 98.5 percent of them go on to college. And more than 95 percent of Payton students attend school daily, on regular class days and seminar days alike, a sign that they find it worthwhile to be there.

Far west from Chicago, Saint Mary's College High School, in Berkeley, took a different approach to allowing more time for deep study and restoring balance to students' lives. As the Catholic school began looking several years ago at how to shift its focus from breadth to depth, Principal Peter Imperial realized: "The schedule sets the RPM of the school. . . . You can't go into depth if you have seven classes at night to go home and study for." He and his staff discussed it and determined that there had to be a better way. The solution they settled on: trimesters. By switching from semesters to trimesters, Saint Mary's reduced the number of courses students take at one time from seven to five—only four of which are typically academic. "It also reduced the number of classes teachers teach," noted Imperial, "because they, too, are on this wheel."

And at High Tech High, a charter school free from some of the standard constraints, Rosenstock and colleagues abolished schedules entirely. Instead of segregating lessons by subject, they give each group of about fifty freshmen just two core teachers: one for science, one for humanities. Each pair of teachers decides together on the best way to use each school day, working with students as a whole or in smaller groups, expanding or contracting different parts of the day depending on their purpose.

Radical schedule changes are possible at the elementary school level, too. After screening Race to Nowhere, the community of Potomac, Montana, a sleepy hamlet outside Missoula, created a task force and ultimately decided on a change that was nothing short of extraordinary. The K-8 Potomac School shifted to a four-day week, holding class from eight a.m. to four thirty p.m. Mondays through Thursdays. The extra ninety minutes a day became time for children to study what they most needed, get extra help from their teachers, and complete what would otherwise have been homework—not unlike Payton's Enrichment time. With this time built into the school day, Potomac eliminated homework for the elementary grades, thus evening out some inequities, enabling students to get just-in-time help from the experts (their teachers), and honoring children's time at home.

The four-day week was a true break from America's educational convention. But what it enabled Potomac to do on Fridays was even more uncommon. Every Friday, families may choose to send their children to school or not. Those who come are treated to the Potomac Explorers program, aptly described by the local newspaper as a kind of math, science, and art camp for experiential learning. The 2014–2015 calendar included rock climbing and snowshoeing trips, a robotics lesson, a visit from a mechanical engineer, geocaching, a pinewood derby, kids creating their own stop-motion movies, designing and building sets for the school's holiday show, and a "spooky science" day on Halloween. Alicia Vanderhyden, a mom of one son, said the schedule change was scary at first. But ultimately she saw it as a chance for kids to escape the everyday churn, to experience "the process of joyful learning . . . so that they carry that with them through the rest of their life, so that they don't give up."

As at Payton, Potomac's dramatic transformation came through a careful process of research and discussion involving all kinds of constituents—and it started because several people in the school community dared to question our educational habits and to put students' real needs at the heart of the answer. Taking the time to bring a majority of the community on board, and to make structural changes rather than just slapping on extra programs, really matters. "Because this was built into the culture of the school," says then-superintendent Tim Johnson, "these ideas last."

At the end of Potomac's first year under its new schedule, the school surveyed families on their opinions. More than 90 percent said the four-day week and the Friday field-learning program should go on.

Just One Night

Hundreds of schools have tried a simple experiment to counteract the over-commitment of kids' *after-school* time: a night off. This strategy has parallels in the business world, where even the elite Boston Consulting Group has made efforts to ease the 24/7 demands that were leading burned-out employees to leave the firm. Working with a Harvard Business School professor, BCG moved to make sure each employee had at least one night off per week, while fellow team members covered for that person. Relieved employees, who could at last plan a family dinner or outing that wasn't at risk of last-minute cancellation, embraced the reform.

Nights off for schools are a starting point for change. There's no way a single night could really ease our kids' overstretched lives, but it can provide a snapshot of the many other valuable things children might do with their time, a glimpse of what we're missing. These evenings fit into a broader national movement to encourage communities to schedule regular times to reset their health, such as Meatless Mondays and Wind-Down Wednesdays (the latter being a Race to Nowhere call for schools to pilot a midweek night off). And if a work-crazy consulting firm can try it, so can a school community.

Irvington High School's first-ever Community Night Off took place on a Monday in fall 2014. Assistant Principal Jay Jackson sent the whole school community a letter explaining the night's purpose—to spend quality time with family and friends—and urging everyone to follow three guidelines: no homework, no extracurricular activities, and no electronics. He encouraged teachers to take the night off from grading, too.

You would think that a single free night would be an easy sell, but Jackson had to fight for it at a faculty meeting. In the end, 80 percent of the faculty voted to approve it. "That's the 80/20 rule," Jackson told me: anytime you try to make a healthy change, 80 percent of people will support it and 20 percent will object. "But I find that 20 percent is very vocal."

The results were positive. Not every teacher honored the no-homework rule (was one night really too much to ask?), and not every student truly took the night off. But those who did embrace the evening described it as "great" and "wonderful." Some families played cards or went out to dinner. The girls' volleyball team replaced practice with a parent-student scrimmage, followed by a potluck. Aneesha, a sunny-tempered sophomore who leads the school's Edjoycation Task Force, assisting Jackson with health promotion, went to a movie with her mom.

By spring, Jackson and the Edjoycation students were collaborating to plan another, improved night off and expecting even stronger participation the second time. Dozens of other schools have made their nights off monthly, and Aneesha planned to take it upon herself to contact the elementary and middle school principals in town and ask them to participate, too, so that whole families could truly enjoy a night together.

Retaking the Reins

Nowhere does the lens of time reveal a more topsy-turvy picture than when we turn it to the realm of family. And looking at that picture can be hard. Because whenever I write about the pace at which my children live—their ceaseless sprint from obligation to obligation, distraction to distraction— I start to get the uncomfortable feeling that they remind me of someone: myself. I realize, with chagrin, that I model the marathon for them. And our respective rat races have a multiplier effect. It is not simply that the kids are busy and I am busy. *We* are busy. Our family together forms an interconnected system of busyness, a constellation of ever-spinning whirligigs, helping to propel one another.

In families, "You have a whole system that is formed and predicated on the notion that we are busy, that busyness is good," says the *Washington Post*'s Brigid Schulte, who wrote the book *Overwhelmed: Work, Love, and Play When No One Has the Time*. "It's how we show our status, it's how we derive value, it is what we do as a family. You get so busy that you never have time to stop and think about *why* you're so busy, what is all the busyness for."

If you, too, cringe as you recognize your children's mad dash as your own, take comfort in the fact that it's not entirely our fault as individuals. Overscheduling has deep societal roots. American workers clock on average 10 percent more hours per week now than we did in 1979. Schulte notes that extreme hours also afflict people at the lower end of the socioeconomic spectrum, who take on multiple jobs because it's no longer possible to support a family with just one. And stubborn gender norms take an especially high time-toll on mothers, who, on average, still do twice the housework and child care as fathers.

As a result, many of the physicians and psychologists I've met in researching my films speak about their concern for parents' health as well as that of students. We are an overworked, underslept, overscheduled bunch constantly expecting ourselves to excel at everything (work, parenting, fitness, marriage). We harbor profound anxieties about our own success and our children's futures, and those anxieties seep out of us and into our children without our even realizing it. Our kids see and absorb it all.

"A lot of times parents will bring their kids to me because I'm a pediatrician," says Lawrence Rosen, who practices in northern New Jersey. "But what we realize when we ask questions about family life is that the same issues we're seeing in the kids, the physical symptoms of stress, the depression, the anxiety, we're seeing in parents, too. . . . Nobody's taking the time to take care of themselves."

It's painfully clear that we adults need a remedy for our "dis-ease of being busy," too. I know this as well as anyone. I removed from my car the school supplies that my kids had used for on-the-go studies—but when they're not there I still make my work calls from behind the wheel. My colleagues often comment, with a shake of their heads, that they've received one email from me at midnight and the next one at five a.m. It's hard to shake the compulsion to busyness once it's in you—which is why we must work to wean our children and our families off of it as early as possible.

Breaking the habit can be hard. Zak started ninth grade with no commitments outside of school, which I supported. But as I watched his classmates practicing with their sports and debate teams, while Zak skateboarded and played with our dogs, I worried that I was failing him as a parent, letting him miss important opportunities. What if he literally did nothing?

A couple of months into the year, though, Zak and a friend started tinkering with hand planes (wooden paddles for bodysurfing), invented their own, and explored turning this into a business. The next year, he spontaneously took up cooking; I came home one evening to find him sitting at the table with two friends for whom he'd made dinner. When I doubt my better instincts now, I remind myself that downtime is a catalyst for self-discovery and autonomy. To survive as an underscheduler in an always-busy world, you have to keep faith in the value of space and time, of allowing a child to explore the new interests to which an unplanned afternoon may lead.

What about children with the opposite tendency, who will voluntarily run themselves into the ground unless you restrain them? Ridgewood, New Jersey, pediatrician Anne Robinson says that's where we parents need to step in. "The parent's primary role is to be the balance keeper," she explains. "Just the way you prepare a meal with the idea of balancing out their nutritional requirements, and you think, 'I want to have a little bit of meat, a little vegetable, a little bit of starch,' you have to think about a child's day that way."

Or, if a day is too short a horizon, think about your child's balance over the course of a week. "Have they had some academic work, but also had time for their friends and family?" Robinson asks. "Have they had time for fresh air and exercise? Have they had time for adequate sleep, time for activities that they enjoy and that enrich their lives? If you think of that balance all the time, when you start to see the balance tipping, figure out how to get it back on track."

As we will see in the ensuing chapters, some of the remedies for restoring our misspent family time lie in actions we can take as individuals in our own homes. Yet many of the important steps for resetting the balance involve advocating for school change.

To do this well, it is critical that we come together to build support networks. If we are going to shake off society's norms and define ourselves by something other than our productivity, we need backup. Your wingmen and -women might be neighbors, friends, or an organized group like the McLean, Virginia, PTSA. Past PTSA president Wilma Bowers is campaigning, alongside local clergy and the high school's college counselor, to convince parents and school officials to place more value on "authentic success," which naturally entails a redesign on the use of time. So far they've succeeded at moving the high school start time back forty minutes, organizing an annual summit on teen stress, and persuading school administrators to discourage students from taking more than three AP classes at once.

I believe that each of us who undertakes this work has the same ultimate hope: that we'll look back on our lives someday with satisfaction, seeing that we have spent our time and energy on what most matters—and that our children will someday be able to do the same. What most matters, of course, is not the number of credentials we've earned or competitors bested or records broken. Not what columnist David Brooks calls "the résumé virtues."

But rather "the eulogy virtues," the kindness, honesty, courage, and love that grow from a life lived in concert with our values.

Each person will define his or her truest priorities a little differently. Whatever they are, there should be just a few of them. And these are the pursuits to which we should devote most of our time. Success, to me, means making just a little bit of progress each day in the movement to end the Race to Nowhere, keeping a strong connection with my family and friends, and maintaining a healthy mind and body.

Everything else is optional.

CHAPTER 3

Homework:
Take Back Our Nights

NOW WE come to the Big Three—the trio of forces that demand the most of kids' time and do the most to disrupt their health and learning: homework, testing, and college admissions. These are also the ripest areas for reinvention. I'll take the first one first.

———

Stephanie Brant started seeing the ills of homework in her students during her first year as principal of Maryland's Gaithersburg Elementary School. She spotted it on her morning rounds, in the look of gloom on children's faces. "I started noticing students that came into school very discouraged," she said. "So often our students would be confused or feel bad about what they didn't get done at home."

Brant, a chipper dynamo who started her career as a teacher and literacy specialist, raised the concern with her staff. The Gaithersburg faculty read the research on homework and examined its effects on the young children they served. Ultimately, their investigation led them to a stunning fact: there is no scientific evidence to support the value of most of the homework our children are assigned. This supposedly wholesome practice—which has spiraled to such extremes that it shreds family life, steals children's chances to explore and play, and deprives growing minds and bodies of essential rest—does not even help students learn. So the teachers sought a better way to enrich the kids' learning instead of squashing their enthusiasm for it. And in so doing, they upturned this toxic old educational tradition that has typically gone unquestioned.

Homework holds a special place in the American psyche. This insistent, uninvited guest possesses a mythology all its own. We have long considered homework a rite of passage, a necessary evil, part of the training required for success in college and life beyond. Idiomatically, someone who "does his homework" is a diligent, well-prepared person. And at one time, I myself was a believer, even directing my young children to spend weekend time studying instead of playing if their grades were down. Like most of my friends, I accepted my children's ceaseless nighttime slog as the hallmark of a strong education, a vehicle for learning the value of self-discipline and persistence. This idea of developing a fierce work ethic felt especially important to me, as someone who grew up amid financial insecurity and saw education as the way out.

Yet our devotion to the myth—and a myth it is—has reached the absurd. We have confused quantity with quality, busywork with challenge, conformity with discipline. We consistently ask our still fragile and growing children to put in second and third shifts, logging more hours in a day than many adults I know. As parents, we give up our authority over the afterschool hours, allowing schools to claim as much of our family time as they desire. Combining their time in school with school-sponsored activities and homework, many children's work hours today remind me chillingly of the unhealthy way I worked while on Wall Street. Aren't seven hours of school, plus perhaps a sport or a music lesson, enough for a child?

The Intruder

As *Race to Nowhere* screened in communities across the country, parent after parent stood up and identified homework as one of the most malignant aspects of the race. They worried about how to get their teens to go to bed before one a.m., or grew heartsick watching the spark of curiosity fade from their kindergarteners' eyes. Instead of playing board games or reading books together with their children, parents were engaging in nightly

battles with eight-year-olds who (understandably) didn't want to do a lifeless worksheet after a full day at school. It was clear that the truckloads of
assignments being dumped on children today are nothing like the modest
homework our generation had as kids, when we could finish our work, get
to bed on time, and still hold an after-school job and ride bikes with friends.
Homework has become an act of home invasion.

"Now that my daughter's in fifth grade, three hours of schoolwork comes
in the door with her," said a mom and professional therapist at a screening on
the Stanford University campus. "I'd rather she come to this movie, or go to
my music group with me, or work on just making pasta the way she likes it or
making a musical instrument out of rubber bands. That's what counts to us."

In working-class Castro Valley, California, a grandmother who had also
trained as a psychologist worried about the anxiety she saw homework
causing children in her hometown.

And a girl named Amanda, from Miami, who said she consistently misses
her nine o'clock bedtime and goes to sleep at eleven thirty, wrote:

> Now, when I have just started the sixth grade, I have been piled
> up with homework to high heaven! ... I only partake in one after-
> school activity, which is on a Friday so I can complete homework
> from that day over the weekend. I have literally no time to be a kid
> anymore. I am a writer in my very sparse free time, and I have barely
> written anything for myself this school year. To tell you I'm angry
> would be an understatement.

One father of three—a sitting school superintendent, no less—said to
me bluntly: "Homework is destroying my family."

I saw the same problems in my own home. Every day, including weekends, was cast under homework's shadow; every errand, family outing, and
gathering with friends had to be shoehorned into the few hours of space
that remained. If I convinced my children to meet friends for lunch, they'd
be studying in the car en route, asking for vocabulary help instead of chatting. Even over holidays the kids spent long weekends and winter breaks
bent over their books, trying to keep up. And this was *after* Doug and I had
made deliberate efforts to lighten their course loads and reduce their com-

mitments! Jamey had quit violin and soccer, Shelby stopped ice skating and playing piano, and Zak left his soccer and Little League teams. Instead, Jamey took up cheerleading, Shelby studied for her Bat Mitzvah, and Zak zoomed around on his skateboard. Yet no amount of cutting back felt like enough. The race seemed inescapable, even for a family that no longer believed in it, and homework was a primary culprit.

This has got to stop—and it *can*. I know because I've seen it done, by pioneering schools and families across America.

In the wake of screening *Race to Nowhere* and reviewing the research showing that homework does not improve learning, the public K-8 Hillcrest School in Oakland courageously abolished homework entirely for the primary grades. The superintendent of schools in Swampscott, Massachusetts, declared a monthly homework-free night. Galloway, New Jersey, banned weekend homework for children in grades K-6. Mango Elementary School in Fontana, California, replaced homework with "goal work" tailored to individual children's needs and completed on a flexible schedule. At the Brooklyn School of Inquiry, a public "gifted and talented" program, homework is optional.

These changes might seem radical, yet the sky has not fallen. Indeed, it seems brighter than ever for the children in these districts.

Meanwhile, parents have secured similar reforms in hundreds of communities by banding together and insisting that teachers, schools, and districts provide relief. In their own homes, many individual parents now simply say no, opting their child out of homework when sleep, health, and other life lessons and experiences are more important.

Of all the aspects of the race that need changing, homework is actually the easiest place to start. Change can begin with individual parents, teachers, administrators, and students. From there, it grows, as families and schools work together to take back our nights.

A Short History of Homework

It is not your imagination. Children today actually *are* being asked to do vastly more than we did as kids. Here's a bit of history:

Homework has played a central role in American family life for centuries.

It was standard issue at the colonies' first public school, Boston Latin, where the Puritan notion that "practice makes perfect"—the precursor to "drill and kill"—reigned supreme. Complaints cropped up in the mid-1800s, when some citizens worried about the effect on pupils' health. By the turn of the twentieth century, organized objections to take-home assignments were taking hold. Assignments of that era tended toward rote memorization, including notoriously awful spelling drills of obscure words. In 1900, *Ladies' Home Journal* magazine campaigned with the support of the country's pediatricians to abolish homework in favor of fresh air and exercise. The campaign fueled the rise of a national antihomework movement, which convinced numerous cities to place limits on after-school assignments for young children.

But the resistance couldn't hold for long. In the competitive frenzy following the Russians' launch of Sputnik in 1957, the pediatricians' philosophy was eclipsed by a "more is better" maxim. Homework loads increased (though not yet to the levels seen today). Amid worries that other countries would outrace our economy, outbuild our bombs, and outeducate our students, homework became—and remains—a symptom of our fear that our children will be left behind.

The freer-thinking 1970s (when I grew up) offered a brief respite, when afternoons were reserved again for child's play—but then the modern age of homework madness began with the 1983 publication of *A Nation at Risk*, a report by the Reagan administration that once again amped up the fear of global competition. The report noted the substandard test scores of US students in relation to their peers internationally, and identified the preceding decrease in the amount of homework as one culprit. As a result, the commission recommended "students in high schools should be assigned far more homework than is now the case."

We all know where that has led. A University of Michigan study found that between 1981 and 1997 the amount of homework done by children aged six to eight more than doubled. A later Michigan study that looked at the average homework load across all ages from six to seventeen found it rose by 50 percent between the early 1980s and 2003. And that was largely *before* President Bush's No Child Left Behind Act and President Obama's Race to the Top fund—federal initiatives that applied carrots and sticks to students' standardized test scores—further upped the ante. Now teachers are under increased pressure to plow through an impossibly long list of state-required content. As a result, many of them send home what can't be covered in school. The mounting college arms race also fuels the misguided notion that children should do more, faster, sooner, so as to be prepared to do more, faster, later.

By 2005, parents surveyed by the Lucile Packard Foundation for Children's Health named homework as the greatest cause of their kids' stress, far more frequently even than divorce or family financial troubles. And the burden has only grown heavier in the decade since then. (Some news stories have proclaimed that homework levels are unchanged, but that's based on data from an exam called the National Assessment of Educational Progress, which asks test takers how much homework they did the night before—yet teachers typically lighten the load the night before a standardized exam.)

The problem is not that *every* assignment in this mounting pile is meaningless; amid the busywork, my kids have also written thoughtful essays and completed substantive science projects. The intentions behind these assignments are undoubtedly good. The trouble is that attending school alone is a full-time job for a child. Even meaningful assignments are overtime.

So deep is our ingrained faith in the virtues of homework, though, that we've developed a punitive attitude about kids who don't do it. It's not just about learning—it's about character. Children who don't complete their assignments receive a collective *cluck-cluck* from society; they must be slackers. There's little recognition of the countless other important needs and activities that command kids' time. Even when a child is sick, she's often required to do her homework or, impossibly, to make up days of backlogged work once she recovers. That's what happened when my daughter missed eight days of school in seventh grade. The school demanded that she complete all eight days of schoolwork and homework, while continuing to do new assignments, even when she still needed energy to fully heal. I said no.

A brush with such rigidity was also part of what convinced Etta Kralovec to become a homework researcher. The University of Arizona education professor and coauthor of *The End of Homework* had, earlier in her career, conducted a study for the Maine Department of Education in which she interviewed dozens of high school dropouts who had enrolled in alternative schools around the state, asking them, "When did you know you weren't going to make it through school?" These teens, most of them from poor, rural homes, contended with health, transportation, and family problems. But although it was far from the only factor, homework became a decisive one: the inability to keep up had helped to push all of them over the edge. "We were stunned," Kralovec says. "I'd never seen homework discussed as a contributing factor to dropping out of school."

The prevailing attitude is that there can be no exceptions. It's not about the learning; the fixation is on completion of the assignments themselves. Once, at a screening in New York's Westchester County, students admitted to the crowd they'd be up until two a.m. doing homework to make up for time lost to attend the event. I was shocked that their principal, in the audience, offered them no flexibility. To heck with sleep, health, and the value of participating in a discussion of important issues with their community— the Almighty Homework God had to be appeased.

No doubt some parents exacerbate the pressure on schools to assign homework by buying into the idea that homework equals learning—as I used to. Now we even have software programs like School Loop that allow parents to watch, hawklike, how their child fares on every single assignment every single day. Schools encourage this in the name of parental engagement. Yet this can transform a loving parent into yet another adult who's constantly measuring and micromanaging them. I avoid logging into these systems, finding that my children will share more with me about their school experience, and will gain a stronger sense of responsibility and autonomy, when they don't feel I'm looking over their shoulders. But many parents, with the best intentions, do just that.

Still, the vast majority of parents I've spoken to believe homework has gone way too far, and they are exasperated and baffled about what to do. Rick and Casey Sasner wrote a letter to the school superintendent after their son fell asleep at his desk at eleven thirty one night, then woke up two hours later and tried to keep studying. The letter was so candid that it still moves me. Rick and Casey agreed to let me share excerpts:

> *We are at a breaking point in terms of frustration with the over-*
> *load of junior year. It's surreal that our child is BEGGING US to*

entirely cancel our family's spring break—a four-day trip that was
originally a six-day trip but was cut back because of his workload.

Over the past three weeks, our son has had nine math tests,
three history tests and a string of other quizzes, tests, projects and
papers. . . . He is trying to operate consistently on five hours of sleep
a night and being forced to skip classes in order to prepare for other
classes. His physical and mental health are in jeopardy and there's
not a thing we can do about it except to say, "if you fail a test or a
class or get a C, it will be okay!" We are saying that, but you can
imagine how any high school student would receive that.

The Sasners described "feelings of sadness and hopelessness for our own child because we honestly believe he's being robbed of a life." For Kralovec's part, though her own children are now grown, she recalls, "I hated homework because it interfered with my family life. I didn't have a lot of time with my kids, and I didn't want to use it fighting with them over homework. . . . I don't want the state telling me how to spend my evening with my kids."

Kralovec and the Sasners, to their credit, had the clarity to realize that the system—not their child—is broken. Yet as I know from personal experience, many parents whose children strain under the weight of so many assignments are less certain; with no clear norms to guide them, they wonder if the teachers are assigning too much or if it's simply too much for their one kid. And schools often confirm those fears. For students who aren't advancing in lockstep with everyone else, I've found, the school typically suggests tutoring. The message is: the problem is you.

Why do we tolerate this? Homework is such an entrenched part of the modern idea of school that many families rarely question it. I have asked myself, as I look back and cringe at the thought of all the time lost with my children, how I let it go on so long. But that is because we as a culture consider it normal. Because homework is tradition. It is a child's educational pill to swallow. And objecting to it makes you, the parent, also seem lazy, indulgent, or unduly freewheeling. Simply put, homework is assumed to be virtuous: it is what we did (in smaller quantities) and what our parents took for granted was good for us, too. We do this because this is what is done.

Homework Doesn't Work

Luckily, this irrational, unquestioned acceptance of homework is starting to change—slowly—in schools and families across the country, as more research shows that excessive homework does more harm than good. Indeed, there is now a growing movement of schools, particularly in the elementary grades, putting the brakes on the runaway train.

Scientific research demonstrates that in many cases, homework does nothing to improve students' academic performance, as we have always assumed it does. In fact, those hours of assignments can hurt both health and learning.

On the homework-doesn't-work score, here's what the science tells us. In 2006, Duke University's Harris Cooper surveyed fifteen years' worth of homework studies conducted across the country. The conclusion: homework was found to have *little to no benefit* before high school and diminishing returns for high school students as the hours spent doing it increased. Another study in 2011 reinforced this finding. In that experiment, a pair of economists crunched numbers from 25,000 eighth graders and found that a little extra math homework (amounting to about fifteen minutes per weekday) did boost students' math scores slightly (just over 3 percent). But piling on an extra weekly hour of English, science, or history assignments, beyond average levels, made *no impact whatsoever* on scores in those subjects. So even if you believe that high test scores are the hallmark of a high-quality education—which I don't—after-school assignments aren't getting us there.

As for that bit of daily math practice that does help with mastery, students can do that best *in school*, Etta Kralovec explains. "The work of *good* homework, what we think is important"—that is, a little practice and making the learning one's own—"that needs to happen in the presence of a teacher who can help them with their learning. . . . Parents are not substitute teachers." Happily, once teachers aren't spending part of each class assigning and checking homework, they'll have time for that. Some schools are also capturing more time during the school day for independent work and assistance, through strategies such as Walter Payton High School's block schedules and Enrichment period. Others provide in-school study halls or use central assignment calendars to avoid overloading students with a deluge of tests and assignments from different teachers on the same day.

We get obsessed with debates over how much time kids of certain ages should spend on assignments each night, but that's the wrong question. The right question is: What is the best way for each child to grow and learn? The fact is that there are no proven standards for the "right" amount of homework time. Much is made of the oft-cited "ten-minute rule": ten minutes of homework per night per grade level—i.e., ten minutes a night in first grade, fifty minutes a night in fifth grade, and so on. It sounds sensible enough on the surface but is ultimately arbitrary. There is no research establishing the magic of those ten minutes; rather, the guideline is grounded in the questionable (but often unquestioned) premise that homework must be assigned each day, and therefore must be limited. Furthermore, the guideline fails to recognize that time spent on a given homework assignment can vary substantially from one child to the next. And it ceases to work entirely once students hit middle and high school and have six different classes per day, with each teacher assigning homework, unaware of what other teachers are also requiring. (Imagine if you had five to seven bosses, each sending you home with separate assignments every night and weekend, entirely beyond your control.)

There's an even more pernicious problem: homework exacerbates inequality between families. Some children go home to high-speed Internet connections and private bedrooms and parents with advanced degrees who can serve as at-home teachers. Others go home to cramped quarters and parents who lack the time, education, or English-language skills to help them. These children may also hold jobs or care for younger siblings to support their families. Still others spend their after-school hours on violent streets and in drug-infested apartments with scarcely a stable adult around. Our public education system strives toward equality—yet when it comes to homework, we expect all children to perform the same with vastly unequal resources. As Isaiah, the Oakland Tech High School student, said to me, "Academics has become a new way to test a person's character: whether they can handle the rigorous classes, the pressures of holding both a job and going to school on time, whether they can, you know, watch their little sister and write an essay at the same time." (These same inequalities prompted

French president François Hollande to propose banning elementary and middle school homework for his entire country in 2012.)

A classic counterargument to reducing homework, a favorite of politicians, is about global competition. It is the same argument that was effective in the Sputnik 1950s: Why are hours of at-home drill essential? Because children in the world's other advanced economies are doing it. *Just think of how hard the Chinese are studying while your little Johnny fritters away his time and gets left behind!* Aside from the deep flaws in our measures of "achievement" (which I'll lay out in the next chapter), there's an even more fundamental error in that statement: it's not universally true. Homework is not the key to success in these other countries. Indeed, its use varies widely. Many of the countries that score highest on international tests assign the *least* amount of homework. For instance, the PISA, the international exam that's given by the Organization for Economic Cooperation and Development, is more respected than most as a means of gauging good thinking skills. One of the consistent superstars on this test, Finland, logs the least homework time—an average of less than three hours a week for fifteen-year-olds (and Finnish students spend fewer days and hours each day in school than their American counterparts).

Precise numbers for the US are hard to pin down. OECD researchers put the US homework average at more than double that of Finland, and among the highest of the thirty-eight countries studied. Depending on whom you ask (teachers, students, or parents) and when and how you ask them, other estimates of the weekly hours an average American high school student spends on homework range from seven to nearly eighteen. In some communities, homework time can climb to five hours per *night.* More salient than the exact number is the matter of what all this desk time means for the quality of our kids' lives and learning. When OECD researchers looked at average homework loads for fifteen-year-olds in each country, they concluded that "after around four hours of homework per week, the additional time invested in homework has a negligible impact on performance." That is frustrating news when your kid is sitting inside studying chemistry equations on a lovely Saturday afternoon and you'd rather take her hiking.

What's more, our little night-and-weekend warriors rarely get assignments that are tailored to their individual strengths and needs, or that afford them the opportunity to direct their own learning. Often, all thirty kids in a class get the same to-do list, no matter who they are. The only time I saw homework stimulate my kids' appetite for learning was when they were guiding the work. In fourth grade, Jamey's class was given optional "go-getter" projects on subjects of the students' choosing, and she and her friends would spend hours together researching questions that excited them. Opportunities to engage with the world outside of school, such as interviewing a family member or a local historian, can also extend learning beyond the classroom. But alas, teachers are spread so thin that creative and personalized work is the rare exception. Too often, homework assignments are a reflex, not a rich learning experience.

The writer Karl Taro Greenfeld famously did all his daughter's homework for a week for a story in *The Atlantic* in 2013. Greenfeld struggled through consecutive late nights of algebra problems, readings from a deadly earth sciences textbook, Spanish verb conjugations, and assignments to read as much as seventy-nine pages of a novel per night. "Memorization, not rationalization," his thirteen-year-old instructed him. Barely able to sustain his energy or interest through Thursday, he asked: "Are these many hours of homework the only way to achieve this metamorphosis of child into virtuous citizen? . . . I have my doubts."

But wait—doesn't homework at least instill a sense of organization and discipline? Americans have long clung to that idea, too. Yet here there is even *less* evidence to support that assumption, as it has never been tested. Kralovec explains, in her characteristically spirited tone: "If there were one shred of evidence to prove that, I would be very compelled by those arguments, but there has never, ever been research done about any of that. That's a blind faith. That's akin to religion."

Her advice instead, issued with a note of irony: "If you want a kid to learn time management, get them four dogs and make them walk the dogs after school." Human beings learn perseverance well by taking on challenges that matter to them. Meanwhile, we have imbued homework with all kinds of powers it doesn't truly have.

One thing that we know actually *does* reinforce rich learning is—of all neglected things—rest. We've already seen how downtime supports creativity and psychological growth. It is also essential for our brains to process and remember what we've learned. So if a kid goes out skateboarding after school, that is not wasted time, according to pediatrician Anne Robinson: "He's processing the information of the day. He's using math and physics to navigate that board around. And he's using the skills that he'll need for the rest of his life to navigate the world. This is the piece that our students are missing out on, when they're spending so much time with a book."

In fact, the more challenging the work we expect our students to do, the more rest they need. In a seminal 1993 study, a trio of European psychologists examined how experts learn. Studying violinists at various skill levels, they determined that the most elite performers slept substantially more than the middling ones. They even took regular afternoon naps! All told, the experts engaged in intensive practice (what you might liken to studying) only around thirty hours a week, or a little over four hours a day. They typically spread that work out into short, manageable chunks of about ninety minutes each—not unlike a block schedule in school. Experts in other fields are frequently the same; the researchers cited evidence of similar work patterns among professional athletes, famous authors, and prominent scientists. Creativity and genius spring only from well-rested minds.

"If you look at adults, there's four or five hours in the day that you can actually do really serious, creative work," says UC Berkeley psychology professor Alison Gopnik. "You can do kind of make-work for the rest of the time, but there's only a limited period of actually being able to do really serious, intellectual work, and then you need downtime" to consolidate it.

All of which is to say: driving students to slave away over their books almost every spare minute of the day is not doing much for their education. For those who want to truly reinforce learning, the best practice is to prescribe as little as possible—only occasional, personalized assignments that involve experiences that can't happen at school—and to allow the student's brain ample time to explore fresh ideas and absorb and process what it has learned that day.

Opportunity Cost

What troubles me most as a parent is not just homework's lack of utility. It is the harm that excessive, unrelenting hours of assignments do to children's health—with all the lasting physical and emotional consequences we traced in the first chapter. And it is, less conspicuously but quite importantly, what homework takes away. All those hours *not* spent making up games, peering under rocks, talking with friends, tinkering with tools, looking up at the sky and puzzling out the constellations, or putting a nose in a book for long, lost hours—the many nonacademic pursuits that can shape a child's personality, aspirations, and dreams. Since when is *school* the only source through which children learn and grow? These lost experiences amount to numberless childhood hours that can never be recovered, even a loss of childhood itself.

Homework is responsible, first of all, for countless hours of stolen sleep, lost at a phase of life when children acutely need rest for healthy development. More than four in ten parents in a 2014 National Sleep Foundation poll said homework had made it hard for their child to get a good night's sleep within the past week. And researchers at Northwestern University who asked teens to keep a time diary discovered, unsurprisingly, that more hours spent doing homework predicted fewer hours of sleep. Exercise, too, is so often supplanted by homework that Sara Bennett and Nancy Kalish, authors of the book *The Case Against Homework*, coined the term *homework potato*. That effect is especially worrisome in light of the research linking too much everyday sitting with a higher risk of obesity, depression, heart disease, and cancer.

Yet homework steals many valuable things that are harder to recover than sleep and exercise. It's difficult to count them all. There is, first and foremost, family time. We parents have a very short period with our children, all things considered, to share daily meals and provide them with all the lessons and experiences that we consider important. Time outdoors also has dwindled to such a rarity for kids that we now talk about "nature-deficit disorder," an utterly modern ailment that journalist Richard Louv links to rising rates of obesity, attention disorders, and depression. Moreover, reading for pleasure drops off just as homework loads ramp up. A 2006 Scholastic study of five hundred children and their parents found that reading for pleasure decreased dramatically after age eight (after which only 29 percent of students read every day). Parents identified homework as the number one reason their children didn't read for fun.

Our communities suffer from our children's absence, too, as young students step back from unassigned community service in order to study. Participation in religious communities also goes by the wayside (both of my girls' attendance at Hebrew school waned and eventually ended when their homework loads got too heavy). Youth ministers across the country, from all kinds of denominations, have told me they can scarcely get young people to show up for anything after sixth grade.

Even after-school jobs—once the all-American training ground for traits like responsibility and financial prudence—are becoming nothing but a quaint historical notion for kids who don't have to work to support their families. I recall the jobs I had when I was a teen, working as a candy striper and a cashier in a grocery store, where I learned how to manage my time and be responsible to others who were relying on me, in addition to earning income to support my education. Now many teens get such first-job experiences only as college students, when the combined burden of class time and homework becomes, ironically, more manageable than it was in high school. "Contemporary children have very little experience with the kinds of tasks that they'll have to perform as grown-ups," even basic skills like cooking and caregiving, says Gopnik, the UC Berkeley psychologist. "We give them this very specialized, strange thing, which is: we teach them how to go to school."

Homework is obviously not the only reason for these growing gaps in modern childhood, but it is a substantial factor in all. It crowds out the kinds of experiences that help kids develop the very qualities we say they need, such as creativity, communication, and collaboration. And the cultural expectation that school assignments trump all other commitments gives homework cover. Instead, we parents should trust our instincts when homework starts to supplant other healthy experiences and insist that academics are not the only way to learn. We can be the whistle-blowers.

Extracurricular activities are a favorite scapegoat for homework apologists: *It's not his homework that's the problem; it's his frivolous softball practice and saxophone playing!* But extracurriculars should not be cut out of kids' lives to make way for more studying. As long as activities are done for genuine interest, not résumé padding, and their hours are kept moderate, a balance of exercise and fun is essential to healthy, happy growth. They're also a chance to cultivate a whole world of interests and intelligences beyond strict academics. Kelly, a senior at Ridgewood High School in New Jersey, grew exasperated when teachers suggested she and her peers cut activities after they complained of too much homework. Kelly said: "I do my extracurriculars because it's a way to break free from the academic stress. I do them because I'm passionate about them and I love doing them, and the fact that they want us to cut down so that we have more time to do the homework is counterproductive in and of itself."

Research backs up Kelly's perspective. William Damon, education professor and director of the Stanford Center on Adolescence, has spent decades investigating the importance of one overlooked ingredient in young lives: purpose. "The biggest problem growing up today is not actually stress," Damon told his local Palo Alto newspaper as the town reeled from a cluster of teen suicides. "It's meaninglessness." Damon's research has demonstrated that a strong sense of purpose is critical for building resilience, vigor, self-esteem, and determination, whereas a lack of it can be linked with self-absorption, depression, addictions, low productivity, and unstable relationships. Alarmingly, Damon finds, the chance to develop purpose is too often missing from modern kids' lives. His studies show that nearly one in three adolescents falls into a pattern of "high activity, low purpose," and the implications aren't good.

Extracurriculars can be one key step in that direction. As Damon explains, the path to finding purpose requires that young people have the chance to explore various pursuits, to risk failure, to play, and to work hard at things *they choose themselves*—not to be consumed by tasks chosen for them by others. In that context, kids are more likely to persevere through setbacks and find in them opportunities to grow. Simply working hard on an external goal like getting into Stanford isn't enough to cultivate purpose; the work has to mean something to the person doing it and to the community at large. "We all need a purpose," Damon told the paper. "But at the formative period of life, when you don't even know who you are, you really need it."

Another significant casualty of too much homework (and another favorite scapegoat for students' scant free time) is socializing. Critics tend to cast it as a lazy frivolity, but that couldn't be further from the truth. For young children, a huge raft of evidence shows how important play is for developing everything from self-control to creativity. The United Nations Convention on the Rights of the Child even names "time to rest and play" among the essential rights of all children. For teens, socializing is some of the primary work of adolescence, a crucial way they develop as social beings and define their identities. I can see clearly how Zak, for example, becomes invigorated, more content, and more productive after spending time with friends. Yet in 2014, UCLA's annual survey of incoming college freshmen revealed that they'd hit a record low in high school social time. In the 1980s, some 38 percent of freshmen said they'd spent at least sixteen hours a week with friends. By 2014, the percentage had plunged to just 18 percent.

Anne Robinson, the pediatrician, underscored to me how essential it is to restore kids' social time. In our youth, kids of Robinson's and my era chatted for hours with friends on the phone. This new generation does some of that socializing on Twitter and Snapchat. Whatever the medium, online or in-person, social time matters. "The fact is that's a requirement, too, just like drinking water or eating their vegetables," she explained. "They have a social requirement."

Finally, and perhaps saddest of all, I have seen over and over again that homework overload steals from young minds the desire to learn. Putting in a second shift after seven hours in school does not help a child become a confident, lifelong learner with an intrinsic sense of curiosity and joy in discovery. Excessive hours hunched over assignments—too many of which amount to pointless practice of what one student already knows, or what another student still doesn't understand—actually kill kids' natural motivation for and excitement about learning. No expert on child development is surprised by this.

Danielle Allphin, a mother and former Los Angeles elementary school principal with a doctorate in education, wrote this to me in late 2014 about her daughter:

> *Today, homework broke her spirit. . . . On this 54th day of kindergarten, homework sucked the inquisitive, eager-to-work-and-learn soul out of my child. On this 54th day of school, I find myself heartbroken. . . . I have a smart, funny, creative, sensitive child who*

went to bed in tears, with knots in her stomach over "three more boring pages" yet to be done in her kindergarten homework packet.

I found myself and my husband launching into the rite-of-passage lecture about the fact of life that is doing things we find boring— laundry, dishes, taking out the trash, reports for work, etc. . . . But why should a five-year-old who loves learning and has a solid grasp on all things one through ten have to spend her evenings repetitively drawing and/or circling sets of various items in groups of 1 through 10?

Allphin's daughter had already demonstrated mastery of those skills on a kindergarten entrance assessment the previous spring. "Yet she has now completed 37 pages of review," Allphin wrote. "And there it is, folks, the moment that learning stopped being fun. Day 54, page 37. Such a tragedy."

Students themselves can articulate the pain of the dying flame. Alexandra, a middle schooler in Redondo Beach, California, sent me this in a letter:

I used to be a very happy tomboy. I picked up water polo three years ago and I was always playing football with the boys at lunch. I loved to play and learn. As I always describe it, I had more questions than people had answers for. I dreamed of going to medical school. I spent hours just thinking of all the wonderful things I could do with that one piece of paper . . . be an army surgeon, a doctor on a cruise ship, or the team physician for the national water polo team. Now, I am an extremely stressed-out student, suffering from depression and anxiety. Even if I finish my homework in time for practice, I sometimes don't have the energy for it. Medical school is still a dream, but it's also four more years of school I'll have to go through. I am a completely different person.

In my home, the difference between frenzied overwork and joyful learning was obvious years ago, between the hair-pulling anxiety experienced by a second grader racing the clock to scratch out twenty timed addition problems and in the way that same second grader's face lit up with joy when he could accurately add the number of dogs he'd seen on a neighborhood walk.

If, in our devotion to the busy-worker ideal, we are actually raising a generation of children who lack purpose and creativity, who have missed formative real-world experience, and who are sick, sleepless, joyless, and disengaged, then I have to ask: What kind of "success" is that?

Gaithersburg and Menlo Park: Free to Learn

Homework is the low-hanging fruit of Race to Nowhere reform. Even that may sound daunting—how could decades of this entrenched habit be overcome? But it's possible, and it's already being done by forward-thinking parents, teachers, and schools nationwide.

First, there are examples of educators who have done it themselves. Stephanie Brant, in Gaithersburg, started with a concern about homework's effect on equity. The vast majority of Brant's students come from immigrant families and live below the poverty line, often with multiple families squeezing into a single apartment. Their parents, many of whom clean houses or do construction in other suburban towns around Washington, DC, frequently work two or three jobs to get by. Many speak limited English. So when one of those young students takes home a history research project or a set of tough math problems, she's on her own. She might not get through the work, or, without guidance, she might spend hours doing it wrong.

Once they came to this realization, Brant and her staff "started looking at the quality of the work we were sending home, and it was really just rote worksheets," she told me. Sometimes the assignments involved useful practice, but mostly, the staff realized, they were just sending something home to send something home. "It's not worth it," staff-development teacher Laura McCutcheon explained. "The kids are not getting enough out of this to take away from what little time they do have with their parents between jobs. We wanted kids to enjoy their time at home and come back to school the next day feeling good about themselves and not feeling really badly because they didn't do a math worksheet that research tells us probably isn't doing much for them anyway."

Now, in place of traditional homework assignments, Gaithersburg Elementary asks students simply to read a book—any book they like—for thirty minutes a day. The focus has shifted from rote practice to an attempt to "*extend* what students know," Brant said. Through reading, "We can increase their vocabulary and their background knowledge." Plus, "it gives students the opportunity to get lost in a book and become that character for a while." In the summers, the indefatigable Brant personally drives a "bookmobile" (a.k.a. her own Acura RDX) around the community, giving away books to her students.

Three years later, the new program is still humming along smoothly. In addition to changing the rules on homework, Gaithersburg had simultaneously made a major change to *in-class* work, as well, shifting to an emphasis on creative problem solving and personalized lessons that it calls "Curriculum 2.0." So, in Patricia McCaffrey's fifth grade class the day I visited, there was no lockstep lesson with the teacher lecturing at the front of the room. Instead, McCaffrey was in a corner doing a reading assessment with one small group, while the other students sat at clusters of desks working on various tasks amid a soft murmur of voices. Each child's particular assignment depended on what he or she most needed to work on.

At one set of desks, a cheerful ten-year-old named Victoria explained that she lives alone with her mom since her dad stayed behind in his native El Salvador. She often goes to a friend's house after school while her mother works at McDonald's. "We normally play in the snow or play outside or ride bikes, or anything like that," Victoria said, giving me visions of childhoods in days gone by, before homework took over. "We always do our thirty minutes of reading before anything else." When Victoria's mom gets home, the day's work is done for both of them. "We usually cook dinner, we clean the dishes, sometimes we even do games," said Victoria. "It's really fun."

Sitting opposite her, Ezra, who sported intellectual-hip black glasses and a ready opinion on everything, said, "I have a lot of better things to do than homework." Like what? "Like, where do I start?" he exclaimed, with a slight note of exasperation. Ezra likes writing and not being told what to write. He finds homework too easy. On the merits of homework overall, though, he added, "I'm kind of in the middle. It depends on the homework and it depends on the kid. Some kids learn from homework, some kids learn from reading, some kids learn more from not having homework." To set one system for all kids, he concluded, would be "irresponsible."

Brant recalls that some parents were resistant to the change at first. Without daily assignments, they understandably feared they wouldn't know what their children were studying in class. Other educator-reformers have encountered similar obstacles. When Manhattan's P.S. 116, an elementary school, eliminated homework in early 2015, some parents were outraged, with the mother of one third grader complaining that besides watching more TV, her daughter was also spending more time in her room—gasp!—playing. Meanwhile, across the country, Principal David Ackerman said he, too, had to invest a lot of time in reassuring parents when he dramatically reduced homework at Menlo Park's Oak Knoll Elementary in 2006. In the affluent heart of Silicon Valley, Ackerman observed, "There's a solid set of parents who believe that homework and a rigorous program are the same thing."

So Ackerman penned a now-famous letter to parents explaining that research shows otherwise. He wrote that "large amounts of homework stifle motivation, diminish a child's love of learning, turn reading into a chore, negatively affect the quality of family time, diminish creativity, and turn learning to drudgery." To the oft-aired fear that children who don't practice homework in elementary school will be unprepared for homework in middle school, Ackerman retorts, "You don't prepare them for torture by torturing them early." Students who graduate fifth grade with strong skills and confidence, he reasons, will readily adapt.

Ackerman had to convince skeptical teachers, too, who feared students' test scores would drop if they trimmed homework. But as time went on, and teachers experimented with new methods, he said, "They found they were just as successful as they had been before." The school's standardized test scores continued to rise.

Brant assuages parents with a weekly newsletter that suggests what kinds of questions they might ask a child, by grade level, based on what they're studying that week. Gaithersburg also hosts community learning nights; I attended a math night where teachers led parents and kids through math games that they could play together, and each family took home a gift bag of dice, cards, and other playing pieces they might need. Teachers here also offer families optional projects that they can try at home, such as creating a tennis-ball catapult or building a tower out of household supplies— exercises based on some of the reading and science that students have done.

What ultimately won over parents in both schools were simply the results themselves. Over time, it became apparent that their kids were still doing just fine (as of spring 2015, the number of Gaithersburg students reading at or above grade level was up 8 percent over the year before). That, and having their family time back. Milagros Flores, a mother of three boys who has volunteered in Gaithersburg classrooms for six years, said she misses having little homework packets that showed her what was going on in class. But now the atmosphere at home "is calmer, there's less pressure," she said. She and her kids can go for walks without worrying about the time.

Flores has also found her boys developing more independence, now that they're given more control over how they use their study time in and out of class. That's one of Brant's key selling points for her reforms: showing parents how confident children can become as leaders of their own learning when schoolwork is personal and meaningful. "When parents see their children motivated to do more and to extend their own learning through a book or a blog or just getting information from the environment or the Internet," Brant said, "it's those sparks, it's those goose bump moments for parents that we want to create."

Ridgewood: Homework Change for Health

Often the instigators of homework reform are not educators but parents and students. This is especially true in high schools, where homework is a tougher nut to crack than in elementary grades. So it was fitting that the leader of the charge in Ridgewood, New Jersey, was both a parent and a pediatrician. Anne Robinson, energetic and approachable, could make her case not only as the mother of two daughters at Ridgewood High but also as a medical professional with a clear view of the physical and mental damage that excessive homework was wreaking on teens.

Ridgewood is a leafy New York City suburb and an academic pressure cooker. When Robinson's campaign began, her message about health was one that many in the community were already anxious to hear. A junior named Laura confessed that, after five or six hours of sleep, "I'm basically asleep the first three periods of school." Even Assistant Principal Jeff Nyhuis—himself a father of a third grader, able to see firsthand how intrusive homework is in a child's day—knew most of his students were staying up studying until one or two o'clock in the morning, a statistic that upset him.

Robinson organized a few other parents to meet with school administrators in an attempt to get them to address student stress. Finding an ally in Nyhuis, she joined forces with him to make presentations at PTA meetings and faculty meetings. The reformers had to contend with many common fallacies, and they had to be ready to answer the perennial skeptical questions from parents and teachers who did truly care: How is this going to affect student achievement? How can we get through an AP curriculum if students have only two hours of homework, total, per night? Are you sure it's not just that students have too many extracurricular activities? If we free them from homework, won't they just waste their time on social networks all night?

"Practices from the past just kept rearing their ugly heads," Robinson recalled when we met. "We are stuck in a system that is used to doing things a certain way." The biggest challenge, she said, was convincing people that achievement and wellness can coexist, that they're even complementary, "that well-rested, well-balanced students will perform better academically and in every aspect of their life."

(On the fear about social media, I have a special note to add, as I've heard that ill-conceived reason for keeping up homework so many times. "But they'll just spend all that time on Twitter!" someone inevitably says when I suggest at film screenings that schools curtail homework. Many parents think homework is what "protects" kids from technology's pull. Perversely, however, those students who become addicted to Twitter, TV, or video games are often, in fact, the product of an education system that has stifled a love of learning, a curiosity for new hobbies and ideas, and an impulse to play outdoors, volunteer in the community, or bond with friends and family. Reducing homework loads and restructuring assignments to those that promote such goals could arguably reduce the hours most students spend in escapist screen time by empowering students and parents to exercise more control over their afternoons and keeping them more engaged in their physical world. Parents do indeed face a tough challenge in trying to regulate their children's technology use, but piling on mind-numbing bookwork is not the answer.)

The Ridgewood organizers named their campaign the Smart Balance Initiative, underscoring that it's possible—and wise—to strike a balance. They continually emphasized the research on what is actually healthy for kids. And when they asked a number of students to use time diaries to record what they did in a twenty-four-hour day, the resulting diagrams proved to be a game changer. "What shall we eliminate to make time for more homework?" Robinson asked at a faculty meeting, displaying the data they'd gathered. "Do we want to X out the time they need for sleep? Do we want to X out the time they need for family and friends? Is it fresh air and exercise? Which thing are we willing to sacrifice in order to add more academic work?"

It took patience and persistence, but eventually the resistance started to crack. The first change the school made was to institute homework-free holiday breaks (which should be a given). "These breaks are specifically placed into the academic calendar for the purpose of providing relief to students and their families," Robinson explained. "Just like you rest the muscles to come back a stronger athlete, you're resting your brain to come back a stronger thinker. . . . Burned-out students are not good students." Although homework-free holidays are a relatively small reform, Robinson quickly found that they were a powerful conversation starter.

That change, which began at the high school, was eventually adopted by all the schools in town. Then hundreds of schools across the country followed suit as Ridgewood became the launching point for a 2011 Race to Nowhere campaign to ban holiday homework. The swiftness with which the change spread contains a lesson for anyone working to transform any aspect of school: you can try anything for a short period of time. Homework bans, flexible deadlines, qualitative grading—try it for a week and see what kind of perspective it opens up. Or, as in the case of Irvington High's midweek community night off, try it for a day. The limited time frame makes the experiment more palatable to skeptics, and whatever the outcome, the experience is guaranteed to open eyes.

Some secondary schools have taken their homework restrictions still further. In Potomac, Montana, for example, when the K-8 school there transformed its weekly schedule, it also stopped grading homework in the middle school grades (while ending assignments entirely for the primary grades). The educators effectively made homework optional: to be done only when it fits a family's priorities and helps a particular child learn. And Potomac students continue to fare well.

In tackling homework, Ridgewood instituted another inspiring and widely applicable reform. Administrators created the Principal's Advisory Group, a set of students who meet regularly with Nyhuis to discuss issues of student well-being. This reform starts to address the widespread problem of disenfranchising young people from decisions about their own education; students, who know best how well our educational practices are working and have the most at stake, are often the last to be consulted. Olivia, a junior and lacrosse player in the advisory group, felt empowered by the change: "We have such a greater voice than we had before. . . . We see differences being made after we've told Mr. Nyhuis problems or things that upset us." Students in the group also invite their teachers to meetings and describe best practices that they've seen in other classes. For example, they lauded one math teacher who experimented with giving an "exit question" at the end of class: if students could successfully complete that problem, then they didn't need additional practice at home.

Despite all this progress, everyone at Ridgewood acknowledges that they still have a long way to go. Students still have much too much homework. Assignments tend even to creep into the homework-free breaks, when kids continue to study for tests and work on long-term projects due a few days after the holiday. I've seen the same happen with Zak, who had to read and annotate *The Great Gatsby* during a supposedly no-homework weekend. This is a reflection of how hard it is to break our entrenched educational habits. For this reason, schools would be wise to appoint a homework ombudsman to field students' and parents' concerns and ensure that policies are truly followed.

Ridgewood students also told me they want to see more flexibility on homework—a bit of understanding from teachers that some days there is simply more to do than they can get done. Nonetheless, Ridgewood has taken that all-important first step, and now stands as a model of what can happen when parents, students, and educators work together to make kids' health the highest priority.

Drawing the Line

Ultimately, the homework equation comes down to this: Just as adults increasingly find their work following them home, the boundary between school and home has blurred, almost to the point of vanishing. Somewhere along the line, we parents began letting schools decide how our children will spend their out-of-school hours and how our families will use our precious time together. It is time to reclaim that authority.

According to both scientific and anecdotal research, it is clear that homework should be the exception, not the rule. Even the most inventive or meaningful assignments still infringe on the time that belongs to families. Making this change will not only improve our children's physical and mental health, level the playing field for rich and poor students, and make more time for exploration and enrichment beyond academics, it will also be a huge step forward in eliminating our cultural misperception that education is a race, and our children competitors.

To help guide families and educators who want to restore homework sanity, I've worked with Kralovec and other education experts to create Race to Nowhere's **Healthy Homework Guidelines**, inspired by the parents and faculty who ended homework at Hillcrest School in Oakland:

- *Homework should advance a spirit of learning.* Forget the old assumption that homework will be assigned each night in certain quantities. Educators should send home an assignment only when there's a compelling reason to do so, when it advances curiosity and inquiry, and when it provides a unique learning opportunity that cannot be had within the confines of the school setting. (This might include experiential activities like asking children to take an inventory of the bugs in one square meter of their neighborhood park and catalog the findings.) There should never be homework for homework's sake.

- *Homework should be student-directed.* Educators at all levels, but particularly in the elementary and middle grades, when children need ample room to explore, should limit homework assignments to projects chosen by students themselves. For example, send a child home to read a book of his or her choosing. End the practice of sending home standard-issue homework packets that require the same exercises of all children regardless of their individual strengths, needs, or interests. For equity's sake, all homework should also be reasonable for students to complete without a parent's or tutor's help.

- *Homework should honor a balanced schedule.* Educators at all levels should avoid assigning homework on weekends, holidays, school breaks, or on the days of major all-school events when at-home time is scarce for most children. Even on regular school nights, parents should be given the flexibility to opt their child out of assignments when they judge that to be best, such as when the child is sick or when take-home assignments conflict with family, religious, or community obligations.

If schools are too worried about their competitive status to try optional assignments, we parents can do it ourselves, making homework opt-in by simply opting out. Other parents may give their child homework if they like, but their preferences are not a reason to force homework on mine. If enough of us enact this bit of civil disobedience together, the system will be forced to change.

School communities are likely to resist reform at first, often by trying to pass the buck. "It's a situation where everybody believes they don't have any power," explains Ackerman, the veteran principal from Menlo Park. "Teachers believe the principal has all the power, and the principal believes the teachers have all the power. The superintendent believes the principals have all the power. And parents are the same way." Ackerman's advice is to keep at it: "Schools respond to pressure, they really do. School boards respond, superintendents respond. It goes slowly because, like any bureaucracy, the first thing they do is put up a wall and give you all the reasons why they're doing the right thing and can't change—but they are responding. They are talking about it, and if you keep the pressure up, institutions change."

Don't discount the impact you can make, even as just one person. In my neighboring community of Danville, a mother of two, Kerry Dickinson, made the local paper for taking action. After reading Alfie Kohn's book *The Homework Myth*, she got ten friends to read it. The writings and advice of homework activist and author Sara Bennett further informed her. Then, instead of just settling for the usual parent gripe session, Dickinson teamed up with another mom and lobbied the district to form a homework task force. The task force ultimately created a new policy that discourages weekend and holiday homework and spells out teachers' responsibilities to prevent homework overload and test stacking.

In spring 2015, some of the schools in Dickinson's community took her work a daring step further. They declared an entire week in May free of homework, for all grades (another example of testing out a reform for one nonthreatening week). The explanatory letter to parents, signed by the principals of all seven schools in the Dougherty Valley region, proposed that we "encourage our children to spend a significant portion of the free time outside . . . something that will allow the sun to warm their soul and rekindle a love for outdoor play." Kirby Hoy, the district's director of instruction, told me the week off was symbolic, a conversation starter about the best uses of families' time and a way to show that the world doesn't fall apart without homework. Delightfully, he said, the parent response has been entirely positive.

Educators themselves can make a big impact—even when they have to go it alone. Mike Miller, an English teacher at Thomas Jefferson High School for Science and Technology in Fairfax County, Virginia, entirely reversed his stance on homework in 2013 after nearly two decades of teaching. "As a younger teacher, I used to think, 'What will I assign for homework?'" he recalls. "I needed to concoct something for homework, because if I wasn't assigning homework then I wasn't doing my job."

Then Miller became a father of twins, and he started reading books on both sides of the homework debate. He was swayed. Miller found a forgotten regulation on the Fairfax County books that limits high school homework to two hours a night, total. (When he tells students about this, they think he's kidding.) On the academic integrity committee he serves on, he pointed out that homework overload encourages cheating (in fact, a Josephson Institute of Ethics survey of tens of thousands of US teens found that three in four had copied someone else's homework). The committee is now working to bring assignments to a reasonable level, but in an intensely performance-oriented community, it's slow going.

So Miller decided to do what he could in his own classroom. "I haven't waited for the school to do anything. I've seen the research," he says. It used to be that Miller would automatically assign half an hour of homework a night, not really doing the math that thirty minutes for each of six classes amounts to three hours. Teachers "tend to think in isolation," he says. Now he needs "a very compelling reason to assign outside homework." And when he does, he frames assignments in terms of time, not quantity. Instead of asking for a page of analysis, he asks students to write for about forty minutes over the course of two nights. This way, they can write at their own pace.

Around the same time, Miller made the bold move of eliminating letter grades on everyday assignments. Instead of grades, he gives narrative feedback, sometimes as much as six hundred words on a single student's essay. At the end of the quarter, each student assembles a portfolio and discusses her work one-on-one with Miller, and he converts that assessment into a letter grade. The net result of Miller's single-handed reforms is not that his students have become lazy Twitter-heads with nothing better to do in the evenings. What he's found is that his students, relieved of daily drudgery and the threat of constant judgment, are more engaged and willing to take creative risks. "I don't see a decrease in the quality of what they're producing," Miller observes. "If anything I see an increase. They're writing better. They're reading more deeply."

For him as a teacher, the transformation has breathed new life into his job. "It's been a shift from more of a learning factory to a place where we talk about books and write some interesting stuff," he says. "It's begun to blur the lines between play and work."

———

As parents, of course, the most immediate thing we can do is to support our children. In my home, I stopped asking my kids reflexively about homework the moment they walked in the door. Instead, I focused on taking the time for conversation and reflection. "How did your day go?" I would ask. "Who did you have lunch with? Did anything surprising happen today?" I eventually learned, by the time Zak was in elementary school, to say "Lights out" at bedtime, whether his homework was done or not. When he couldn't complete his assignments and also honor his needs for exercise, family dinner, and sleep, I wrote an explanatory note to his teachers. This is a small but important act of resistance, one that I'd encourage other parents to try. Many teachers, to their credit, were accommodating. Even when they disagreed, at least Zak was learning where my priorities lay.

Our children need our understanding. Sometimes they need us to help them talk with teachers and principals about overwork. They need to hear us say "Your grades are not you" and "It's okay to do less," and to emphasize as early as possible, before other ideas set in, that there's no shame in failing. Sometimes our kids simply need us to tell them that they're not crazy. A New York mom named Diane posted the following example on our Facebook page:

> When, after six months of struggling in her senior year to complete all the requirements of her IB program, my daughter finally said, "Enough!" we were able to listen, and advocated on her behalf with her school to scale back the requirements. Recognizing your limits is not the same as quitting—it's the mature response to an impossible situation. We are proud of our daughter for standing up for what she needed, and grateful we were able to hear her.

Millions of young students, entrenched in a system that tells them they must sacrifice sleep, health, hobbies, and joy in order to succeed, also need to be supported and heard. Start by requesting a meeting with your child's teacher or principal, or by encouraging your student, if she's old enough, to join you in taking up the cause. Start by talking honestly with other parents about your concerns, finding allies among them, and requesting an agenda item at the next PTA or school board meeting. Start by considering which everyday activities are most important to your family. Or start just by telling your children you care more about their health than their homework.

Whatever you do, start tonight.

CHAPTER 4

Testing:
Learning Beyond the Bubble

O N A cold, rainy morning in February 2011, I stood with three hundred students outside the brick facade of Briarcliff High School in the New York City suburbs. The young people around me held umbrellas and hand-lettered signs asking: Where is *learning* in our budget? The teens had arrived on campus at least an hour early that morning to protest a school board vote that condensed their schedules from nine periods to eight. The change was intended to provide the students more instructional time in core subjects—those in which they would be tested. But the shift came at a cost: the students would be squeezed out of study periods and electives they cared about.

As yellow school buses rolled by, a skinny sixteen-year-old organizer named Philip took to the megaphone. For too long the school system had thought of students "as merely numbers and statistics," he proclaimed. "Today's system doesn't think of any of us as the boy who loves music, but instead the boy who has a 1600 SAT score and a good amount of extracurriculars. Are we not the leaders of tomorrow?"

The outrage at Briarcliff was a symptom of a growing nationwide discontent. The cause: the blind quantification of our entire education system. We are suffering from a slavish devotion to numbers—tests, and the scores and rankings they produce—that's dehumanizing our schools, increasing homework loads, and enshrining the belief that canned questions asked on paper are the ultimate measure of educational "success."

Our young students spend weeks a year regurgitating information onto computer screens and Scantron forms instead of learning. There are the annual state tests, the pretests, the practice tests, the district tests to check readiness for the state tests, and the field-test tests. Combine those with the extra deluge that comes in high school—the AP exams, SAT, PSAT, and ACT—and children take as many as twenty standardized tests a year, averaging ten tests a year in the tender grades of three through eight. Even when they're not being tested, students are frequently being subjected to deadening test prep. All the while, our testing obsession earns billions of dollars a year for the private companies that write, administer, score, and tutor for these exams.

The testing machine is massive, but here again, there is much that we parents, students, and educators can do about it, and that many are already doing. The Briarcliff protest was an early glimpse of that. It did not stop the students from losing their beloved art classes to the tightening grip of testing, but it did earn Philip (a guitar player who does indeed love music) an appearance on the *Today* show. More important, that morning signaled the beginnings of something far bigger. The Briarcliff students were early voices in a chorus of protest that soon erupted from coast to coast.

At Castle Bridge elementary school in New York City's Washington Heights, so many parents refused to let their young children (kindergarteners and first and second graders!) take a multiple-choice test that authorities canceled the whole exam. The teachers at Seattle's Garfield High School outright refused to give their students the district-mandated Measures of Academic Progress test, which they contend is misaligned with the state curriculum they must teach and wastes precious instructional time. In doing so, they put their jobs on the line. In Providence, a crowd of students in zombie costumes, complete with green skin and blood-spattered clothes, staggered up to the doors of the Rhode Island Department of Education, protesting what they called the "zombifying effects" state testing was having on young people. (The Providence group later administered a set of sample problems from Rhode Island's high school graduation exam to fifty accomplished professionals, including lawyers, state senators, city council members, nonprofit directors, and college professors. Only 40 percent passed.)

The protests reached a fever pitch in spring 2015, when the parents of more than 175,000 New York State students had their children sit out state tests, more than double the number the year before. Opt-out groups cropped up in Florida, Iowa, Colorado, and more. The previous fall, nearly five thousand high school seniors in the Denver area refused to take state science and social studies tests, contending that the exams were out of sync with what they'd learned and wasted valuable educational time. According to the national organization FairTest, eight states have laws granting parents the right to keep their children out of standardized tests: Utah, Colorado, Wisconsin, Pennsylvania, Minnesota, Oregon, Washington, and California. Everywhere else, opting out is an act of civil disobedience.

Meanwhile, signatures on the National Resolution on High-Stakes Testing mounted into the tens of thousands, and the National Education Association, the nation's largest teachers union, launched a campaign against what it calls "toxic testing." The campaign aimed to "end the abuse and overuse of high-stakes standardized tests" and "put the focus of assessments and accountability back on student learning."

Such actions now constitute nothing short of a national movement, and the protesters have very good cause. Standardized testing may have originally been based on the sensible idea that we should make sure all schools are doing a comparable job of teaching kids what they need to know. But America's devotion to exams has spun out of control. The occasional fill-in-the-bubble tests of my youth—which were dull but low-stress for students and used only as a temperature check for schools—now sound like a dream. In their place we have a nightmare, a national testing obsession of monstrous proportions.

The outcome is *not*, as the tests intended, a good education for all. In fact, it is nearly the opposite. Standardized tests have driven American education into a vise grip of regimentation. Now there is one narrow set of things to learn and one way to learn them—all at one uniform pace. Stressed teachers race to get through reams of content, any of which might be tested, at the expense of depth and personalization. Students, for their part, are demoralized by the constant judgment and competition. Young people whose minds don't fit the one-size-fits-all mold disengage from school and doubt their own worth. Even those who do fit miss the chance to plumb their own ingenuity or to nurture a lifelong love of learning.

Policy makers made matters even worse when they attached powerful consequences to standardized test scores—teachers' job evaluations, schools' funding, and students' high school diplomas and college admissions—thereby plunging the entire American education system into a stultifying culture of fear. The product of an education system that judges success through narrow, fearsome exams is not a nation of geniuses; it is a nation schooled in narrow, fearful thinking. This is not the way for our country to cultivate the curious spirits and creative minds that will thrive in a dynamic global economy—or in life.

Zombie Nation

I don't believe that the authors of the No Child Left Behind law in 2001 understood the monster they were creating. They saw a society in which massive gaps in education and achievement persisted between rich and poor, and between whites and Asians on one side and other minority groups on the other. They wanted to insist that our education system attend to those inequities—an important and laudable goal. The lawmakers also (mistakenly) saw high-stakes testing as a key weapon in a contest among nations to produce the smartest, most successful workers.

So they mandated a national exam regime in which every child in the country would be tested on reading and math every year from grades three through eight, plus once in high school. The idea was to hold kids from both affluent and less privileged communities to the same high standards, to try to level the playing field. Scores would be public, and schools would be penalized for poor results. Then, in 2009, President Obama and Education Secretary Arne Duncan doubled down with their educational initiative Race to the Top, a $4 billion competition for states. In order to get a slice of the federal funding pie, states had to agree to evaluate teachers in part on their students' scores, to adopt "college and career-ready standards" that would become the hotly debated Common Core curriculum, and to test kids on those standards every year. Teachers and principals in schools that weren't performing would be fired. What began as an effort to raise standards became a punitive accounting strategy.

At the same time (as I'll address more in the next chapter), the pressure on students to take ever more Advanced Placement and SAT and ACT tests, and to score ever higher on each of them, was mounting.

The sum total of these developments is that today's kids are the most tested generation in history. This has not translated to greater success. Indeed, the negative consequences are so numerous it would be hard to list them all. Yet two are particularly important to address: the deadening effect of excessive high-stakes testing on the character of education and the sickening stress and self-doubt it causes in kids, who are misled by the twisted message it sends about what matters.

To the first point, test worship is squeezing the life out of our children's learning, both in *what* schools teach and *how* they teach it. Within the first few years of No Child Left Behind, schools scrambling to boost math and reading scores on the annual tests started cutting back on all kinds of other classes. The nonpartisan Center on Education Policy found that, by 2007, more than 40 percent of the nation's school districts had trimmed time from nontested subjects to make way for more reading and math in elementary schools. The cutbacks included such throwaway subjects (ahem) as science, social studies, art, music, and physical education. Many schools had even shortened recess and lunch. All told, the decreases amounted to an average of nearly thirty minutes a day lost from those other important subjects. And the trend has continued: more than half of the teachers in a 2011 national survey said that the extra focus on math and reading was resulting in "disappearing curriculum" in other areas, with the cutbacks at their worst in elementary school.

"When you look at the force of standardized testing, what they're testing pretty much is mathematics and reading comprehension," says Tim Devine, principal of Chicago's innovative Walter Payton College Prep High School. "So where does that leave science and social studies and arts and music programs? They become afterthoughts. They become the stepchildren of education, and that's not where they should be. Our kids are much more dynamic than that."

Ironically, the distorting of priorities plays especially heavily on children in schools in low-income communities with generally lower test scores— precisely those whom No Child Left Behind was intended to help. In the CEP study, these districts reported cutting elementary school recess alone by fifty minutes a week (not to mention other academic subjects). That's especially counterproductive when you consider the ample evidence that physical activity is essential for brain function.

Zoom the lens in closer on the *way* students are actually studying those subjects that remain, and you'll see that our sledgehammer approach to accountability is incentivizing what Harvard educator and author Tony Wagner calls "stunningly mediocre" teaching and learning. "And that's not the teachers' fault," Wagner says. "That's what they have to do to get kids to pass multiple-choice, factual-recall tests."

Sadly, it's true: most standardized tests really are shallow tests of basic skills. And that's partly by necessity, since the tests are annual and universal—it would be awfully hard to design and score a deep and personal assessment that elicits complex thought and individual talent for every single American child every single year. Researchers at the RAND Corporation looked at seventeen states whose tests are regarded as the most thoughtful and demanding. Even among these supposedly standout states, the researchers found the cognitive sophistication of their math and English tests was low. Using a range of criteria, they concluded that a mere 1 to 20 percent of state reading tests, and around 30 percent of state writing tests, tapped truly deep thinking. None of the math tests did.

Teachers know that they and their students will be judged mainly on their ability to regurgitate content or produce cookie-cutter written responses for these tests. So lectures, textbooks, and problem sets become the default vehicles for teaching, and in-class tests remain the main way to gauge learning along the way (recall that the Sasners' son suffered through more than a dozen teacher-given tests in just three weeks!). The testing obsession perpetuates an obsolete and unscientific vision of learning that's focused on facts. Moreover, the high stakes of failure scare schools away from trying new innovations. Glance into many modern classrooms and you'll still see students regimented into rows of desks, staring blankly and miserably as the teacher drones—looking, indeed, very much like zombies. In this staid system, the *product* of children's learning—an expected answer to a prescribed question—becomes more important than the *process*. And in the inexorable forward march to cover it all, there's little time left for kids to pursue original questions, take risks, or explore anything that's not on the exam.

"Go down the assembly line, get some math. Go down the assembly line, get some social studies," quips Walter Payton High's Devine. "And out comes a perfect Model T Ford."

Obviously certain schools and classrooms succumb to the drumbeat more than others—but the fixation on soulless metrics is alarmingly pervasive. And this drill-and-kill method tends to squash deep thought, creative collaboration, and sometimes the possibility of a trusting relationship between teachers and students, since it discourages students from asking questions and leaves less time to develop that essential rapport. The effect of this mindset extends even beyond standardized testing and the prep that precedes it, as it shapes everyday lessons and activities that remain stuck in stale old methods of evaluating student learning. Quizzes, worksheets, short-answer exams—even "fun" activities like spelling bees—all treat students' minds as merely inert receptacles for information.

Our everyday reliance on easily quantifiable tests and grades also flies in the face of everything we know about human motivation. Daniel Pink, author of *Drive*, explains that schools are mired in methods that tap a shallower, *extrinsic* kind of motivation rather than students' *intrinsic* drive to think and discover. They rely heavily on "if, then" rewards—if I memorize these Civil War facts, then I will get an A on the history test. "Those kinds of rewards are very effective for simple, straightforward routine . . . adding up columns of figures, turning the same screw the same way on an assembly line," says Pink. Yet fifty years of social science tells us they don't work well for motivating original thought. "If you want people to come up with the next iPad mini, a solution to the climate crisis, new medicines to fight diseases," Pink adds, "they do it better under conditions of autonomy. We can't 'if, then' people into creativity. It just doesn't work." The result in schools, he says, is that you find some students who are compliant and some who are defiant, but few who are truly engaged.

Nicole, a high school student in Oakland, knows the feeling. She told me her Spanish classes had never been presented as relevant to her real life, despite the obvious applicability of speaking Spanish in heavily Hispanic California. Instead, the lessons were just part of the foreign language admission requirement for the University of California system. "You think, 'Oh, all right, I'll take it. I'll get an A,'" Nicole said. "I took three years of Spanish and I can't put a sentence together. You memorize, you spit it out, and once you do you move on to the next chapter."

Research echoes Nicole's experience. In one study, Clark University psychologist Wendy Grolnick gave kids a passage to read about the history of medicine. She told some that they'd be tested on it and told others just to see if they found it interesting. Afterward, she asked all of them to repeat all the information they could remember from the passage, and to say what they thought the main point of it was. Those who expected a test could cough up just as much rote information as the others, "but they were worse in terms of their conceptual understanding," Grolnick told me. "They would focus on some detail and not on the main point." Two weeks later, she saw the students again and asked them to repeat all they could remember. Those who'd read the passage purely for interest had retained a lot more.

"So when we are focused on grades, focused on outcomes, whether in the learning environment or the home environment, it narrows kids' attention," Grolnick said. "It makes them focus on specific details, prevents them from getting the larger picture or other things that weren't specifically supposed to be learned."

Scared Sick

Tests are also a huge source of unhealthy stress on children. Kids as young as six or seven understand that their performance on a certain test on a certain day at a certain time can have big implications for their teachers, whom they don't want to let down. Children internalize the message that a test says something significant about who they are: smart or not, good or not, worthy or not. Our testing obsession fuels the notion that every individual can be weighed, measured, tallied, categorized, and ranked against others—and that each one should be.

Parents and students in nearly every state have told me how the specter of an upcoming test can turn even very young kids into anxious insomniacs, crying or yelling or even pulling their hair out with worry. California, in fact, has a protocol for what to do when a child vomits on a test—put the test paper in a sealed Ziploc bag and mail it in. The irony is that anxiety triggers a cascade of chemicals in the brain that interfere with clear thinking and memory. Eleven-year-old Becca, a fifth grader in Radnor, Pennsylvania, sent me this letter describing how testing affects her:

> It's always test after test after test: math, social studies, spelling, spelling pretest, science, health, music. Then there are the standardized tests . . .
>
> I feel so tense when I take these [standardized] tests. The teachers tell us to get a good sleep and have a good breakfast. They don't say that on normal test days. That makes me worry more and sleep less. The "what ifs" start running in my mind at night and I can't sleep. "What if I get stuck?" "What if I don't finish on time?" "What if I don't know an answer?" "What if I don't do well?" "What if I don't get in the best class?" "What if I don't get enough sleep?" And then I don't get enough sleep. . . .
>
> I had a conversation with some of my friends a little while ago. They say that if you don't get into a good class, you won't do as well in school and you won't get into a good college.
>
> It's just worrying, worrying, worrying.

In the case of math, for example, Stanford University professor Jo Boaler notes that we know from neuroscience "that speed is extremely detrimental to math. . . . Timed tests are the early onset of math anxiety for kids. Yet speed is emphasized in every math classroom. The one who gets the right answer first is the one who's valued. . . . What's interesting about that is mathematicians are some of the slowest thinkers of all."

The pressure of the exams also prompts schools to push advanced content into ever-lower grades. A University of Virginia study found that even in kindergarten, teachers in 2010 spent more time than those in 1998 on advanced literacy and math, and substantially less time on art, music, science, and activities chosen by children themselves. Schools now routinely press all kindergarteners to read, despite scant evidence on the educational advantages of that practice. (In fact, evidence suggests the opposite: children in less academic kindergartens perform *better* in school years later.) And algebra, once sensibly situated in ninth grade, now starts in seventh grade for any student who wants to appear "advanced." This is not the universal norm in countries with the strongest education systems; Finland, for example, doesn't even start compulsory school until age seven.

At a film screening in Castro Valley, California, a teacher of thirteen years stood up and called upon the entire audience to mobilize and ask Congress to quit its unrealistic expectations. "This was my son's latest third grade math problem," she told the crowd. A bar graph showed twenty lunches of various types. The question was: *What number times three, minus sixteen, equals the number of lunches on the graph?* In other words: an algebra problem assigned to eight- and nine-year-olds! "Now, you tell me what eight-year-old on their own is going to figure that out?" the teacher and mother exclaimed, incredulous. She said her son, a strong student, cried over the problem and said to his dad, "I'm afraid you're going to be mad at me because I didn't figure this out by myself." The woman went on: "What curriculum writer would do this? Piaget must be turning over in his grave." The audience applauded.

This march for more-sooner-faster may also be partly fueling the dizzying rise in ADHD diagnoses in recent years. To illuminate the link, professors Brent Fulton, Richard Scheffler, and Stephen Hinshaw at UC Berkeley looked in 2015 at ADHD rates among children from low-income families attending elementary and middle school in the years after NCLB began. They compared states that had already issued rewards and punishments for standardized test scores *before* NCLB was enacted with states that only started issuing consequences *after* the law was passed. Their striking finding was that while ADHD diagnoses rose everywhere, rates shot up far faster in states where the testing pressure was new. Writing in the journal *Psychiatric Services*, the researchers concluded that high-stakes tests "provide incentives for teachers to address and refer children having academic difficulties" for treatment.

For teens, the pressure only intensifies as AP and college admission tests—and, in some states, exams required for high school graduation—loom. The stakes of the tests are so high and the pace so relentless that many students are tempted to cheat. A case on Long Island in 2011 made headlines when the Nassau County district attorney actually criminally charged more than a dozen teens with paying other, high-performing students as much as $3,600 to take the SAT or ACT for them. At Middleton High School in Wisconsin in 2013, administrators made nearly 250 seniors retake a calculus test after finding that some had stolen copies of it and sold photos of questions. Beyond the punishment, the incident served as a wake-up call for school staff, prompting them to consider what kind of learning environment makes it seem okay to cheat—or so important to do well that stealing a test seems like a reasonable risk. To their credit, they decided to change their system by crediting students more for the skills they demonstrate throughout their learning process and less for a single examination at the end.

Besides cheating the old-fashioned way, a distressing number of teens now turn to chemical aids for an advantage. "I used Adderall before taking the SAT so that I would be able to stay focused for the whole time," one eighteen-year-old from the Northwest told me. "I actually don't regret taking it because I wouldn't have gotten as high of a score without it. . . . Most kids I know took Adderall or some type of performance drug for the SAT just because it's so long and rigorous."

How serious is the stress? Lawrence Rosen, the New Jersey pediatrician, said he sees more children come to his office in the spring testing season with headaches, stomachaches, and other stress-related symptoms than at any other time of year. "I have kids as young as first grade, second grade, who are being subjected to these tests, who are coming in with migraine headaches and ulcers, and not eating well," he said, "to the point where parents are really thinking about pulling their kids out of school for that week and just saying, 'Enough. I'm not going to engage in this.'"

So let me make this clear: protecting kids from excessive test pressure is not coddling. It's not the equivalent of insisting that every child needs to get a trophy. It is a critical mission to preserve our children's health and provide a kind of education that truly nurtures their minds. And it's a call to arms that's backed by research, which consistently tells us that testing does a very poor job of measuring or encouraging the learning that matters most.

The Blunt Instrument

Susan Engel, an education psychologist at Williams College, recently reviewed more than three hundred studies of K-12 academic tests and came to this startling conclusion: "Most tests used to evaluate students, teachers, and school districts predict almost nothing except the likelihood of achieving similar scores on subsequent tests. I have found virtually no research demonstrating a relationship between those tests and measures of thinking or life outcomes."

You would think that kind of decisive science would end the debate; research shows the tests are a red herring. What's tricky about standardized testing, though, is that the principle of it sounds so simple: teach kids some stuff, then ask them to repeat it, and that'll tell you what they learned. What could be wrong with that? Yet the reality is incredibly more complex, and so boiling it all down to a single measure can do tremendous harm. Psychometricians—the scientists who make and study tests—themselves will tell you so. Daniel Koretz, a Harvard psychometrician and author of *Measuring Up: What Educational Testing Really Tells Us*, explains that for tests to serve a useful purpose in education, they have to honor a fundamental principle: "Don't treat 'her score on the test' as a synonym for 'what she has learned.' A test score is just one indicator of what a student has learned—an exceptionally useful one in many ways, but nonetheless one that is unavoidably incomplete and somewhat error prone."

That's because, scientifically speaking, a test is merely a small snapshot of one particular kind of performance, gauged in one particular kind of way, taken from a vastly bigger picture of knowledge, behavior, and skill. It is a blunt instrument, not a surgical tool. So can a state achievement test tell you approximately how well a new curriculum is working across several cities? Sure. Can a set of AP exams indicate whether the classes are generally covering the material the College Board assigned? Most likely. But neither can really tell you whether *this* school or teacher did a good job, or whether *that* student is well prepared to thrive. Unfortunately, that's what we're using them for.

Even if the exams *could* show us everything a child understands about reading or math or AP biology or AP history, that still would be only a fraction of what counts. We all know that persistence, adaptability, creativity, and charm account for just as much of a person's success as his or her book smarts do. And experiments such as those by Nobel Prize–winning economist James Heckman have demonstrated that those noncognitive traits have just as much, if not more, to do with a person's accomplishments in work and life as the kinds of cognitive abilities covered by tests. Yet that's not what our education system communicates to kids.

"Formal education systems tend to confuse academic ability with intelligence," says British educator and author Ken Robinson. Plenty of people who aren't that comfortable with writing or numbers are actually brilliant with music, dance, craftwork, or gardening, or they're intuitively skilled at caring for people or animals, Robinson says. "These aren't mindless activities; they're different ways in which human intelligence expresses itself."

Erin, a high school junior, actress, and writer in California, knows just how confining schools' narrow definition of smarts can be. "Art is my release, my hallelujah, my break," she says. But in schools, "art is the first thing to go. . . . There's a specific thing the school wants you to shine in, and if you don't shine in it, then you don't [shine at all]. . . . I feel like they're trying to make us into one person."

Character and creativity also have a whole lot to do with the success of nations. "Innovation comes from innovative people," writes Yong Zhao, chair of educational methodology, policy, and leadership at the University of Oregon. The countries that will flourish in the modern age will be those whose people burst with original ideas and readily adapt to change. Yet those aren't the qualities our test culture is cultivating or rewarding.

In his book, *Catching Up or Leading the Way*, Zhao has chronicled one of the great paradoxes of American education: we are pushing ever more narrow-minded testing in an attempt to compete with the likes of high-scoring China, while at the same time the Chinese are trying to create a more flexible and creative kind of schooling that they see as more American.

The Chinese, coming from a long tradition of rigid examination, have learned from experience that test worship is the enemy of innovation. Zhao underscores his point with a cautionary tale. China's historical devotion to testing, he writes, has produced huge numbers of students "who score well on tests but have few skills that are usable in society." This is such a big concern for the Chinese that they even have a name for that sort of academically stunted person, *gaofen dineng*. The flourishing of Chinese labor and the floundering of its invention so worries authorities there that in 1997, the national education ministry issued a screed against what it called "test-oriented education." This "tendency to simply prepare for tests" and "blindly pursue admission rates while ignoring the real needs of the student," the ministry wrote, "emphasizes knowledge transmission but neglects moral, physical, aesthetic, and labor education" and "relies on rote memorization and mechanical drills as the primary approach." The upshot is trampled motivation and squelched creativity.

Sound familiar?

The Chinese authorities concluded that test-oriented education violated Chinese education law and must be replaced with "quality education"—a goal they're still pursuing, even as America moves in the opposite direction.

By contrast, Finnish children, whose performance on international exams is the perennial envy of other nations, undergo almost no standardized testing. The Finns' dominance instead seems to stem from educational practices far different from our own. In place of punitive, top-down mandates, Finland recruits and pays teachers well, grants them respect and autonomy in their classrooms, and both prepares and trusts them to design their own curricula. Teachers assess students' individual progress in the classroom, not en masse on external tests, and provide personalized lessons without tracking kids into separate groups by ability. Plus, young children are given minimal homework and more playtime, while high school students also have more opportunities to choose electives than peers in the United States.

There are obvious differences between tiny Finland and the massive melting pot of the United States. But this much is clear: even if stellar scores on international tests are your goal (they're not mine), you don't have to enslave children and their teachers to an endless run-up of standardized exams to get there.

America now faces a choice. We can break the chains of standardization and embrace a kind of education that nourishes the creative thinkers and compassionate leaders of tomorrow. Or we can keep insisting on the same outmoded protocol, trying to quantify all knowledge and churn out "educated youth" like uniform items on an assembly line. One California college professor told me about the day he assigned his students—a generation groomed on multiple-choice education—to examine the facts of a Supreme Court decision on church and state and reach their own conclusion. One asked: "What's the right answer?" The professor was aghast. "There is no right answer," he said. His highly educated students had been tested to the point where they were unable to think for themselves.

New York City: Learning Goes Deep

None of this is to say that we should not be evaluating students' skills and knowledge. Assessment is an essential part of education and, if used wisely, can actually help to drive deep and powerful learning. The proof is in the schools that are doing it well.

The Institute for Collaborative Education, a public school in the Gramercy neighborhood of lower Manhattan, occupies two floors of a stately, century-old school building with a columned cement facade. Just under five hundred students, in grades six through twelve, are enrolled here.

Mike Hills's sunlit classroom is on the fifth floor, at the top of the building. The classroom isn't fancy—wood floors, high ceilings, whiteboards, and twenty-some of those terrible plastic chairs with attached desks arranged in two concentric semicircles. But the educational activity going on there is impressive. When I visited, Hills was leading his eighth grade humanities students through a discussion on juvenile crime, to kick off their monthlong unit on the US justice system. A simple enough assignment, except for the caliber of the conversation.

A reserved-looking girl with dark hair hanging in her face (who turned out to be not reserved in her opinions at all) was countering a classmate's argument that juveniles are more vulnerable than adults to peer pressure. "I don't think peer pressure for adults is nonexistent. I just think for adults, they use a different word, and it's more about competitiveness," she said. She cited the example of a friend in another school where many of the kids live in elegant brownstones, making her friend's mom feel they need a brownstone, too. "Your parents are also bragging about your grades to their friends, so it's the exact same thing, they're just older and taller than you," the girl said. A couple of her classmates nodded vigorously.

Hills, with his long red beard and calm demeanor, listened attentively to his students' points and interjected now and then to steer the conversation toward challenging questions. "So when should a person legally become an adult?" he asked them. A skinny boy, who looked young for eighth grade, said confidently that it should depend on the crime, as kids at different ages have different understanding of the wrongness of certain offenses. Even an eleven-year-old knows killing is wrong, he said—but he or she may not understand the consequences.

Every time there was the hint of a lull, at least four hands shot up from students keen to talk. "Self-awareness really determines how you can judge or grade a person," argued another boy, who spoke eagerly and sported a Yankees shirt. "What makes somebody an adult is they're very aware of what they're doing and are intentionally trying to hurt a community."

These were eighth graders? When my kids were in eighth grade, I don't remember them having many assignments this profound. No one asked them to deeply challenge their opinions, to publicly defend their beliefs, or to listen intently to differing viewpoints from their peers. And they certainly never showed this kind of verve for their course material. Yet in fifteen minutes of constant discussion in Hills's class, not a single student spoke twice. When Hills cut off the conversation, five hands were still up high.

Meanwhile, down the hall, eighth graders in a science class were designing their own hydroponic systems to grow lettuce. They'd studied different types of systems and nutrient mixes, and they were working to see which group's design would produce the biggest yield. (Try to put that kind of collaboration and inventiveness on a test.)

What makes Hills and his fellow teachers at ICE feel free to invest time in deep inquiry is that the school is exempt from New York State's standardized Regents exams, the subject-area tests required to graduate from high school. (Technically, the middle schoolers there are still supposed to take state tests, but many of their parents opt them out, and the school makes clear when parents visit that test prep is not on the program.) ICE is a member of the New York Performance Standards Consortium, a group of more than two dozen public schools that possess a little piece of educational gold: a waiver. The only Regents exam their high schoolers take is in English. The consortium was founded in 1997, before high school seniors had to pass the

Regents as a graduation requirement, and it has fought to keep its test-free status. It has succeeded—so far—in part because of its impressive results. Students in the consortium come from comparable socioeconomic backgrounds as those in New York City's other public schools. Yet they graduate from high school and go on to college at substantially higher rates. Of those who enter a four-year college, more than 93 percent return the second year, far more than the national average of 75 percent.

Don't think, though, that just because consortium students skip the standardized tests they go unevaluated. Far from it. In place of multiple-choice and short-answer questions, the consortium schools use performance assessments: meaningful tasks that challenge students to think and demonstrate their skills *while they're doing them*, not by proxy on paper at the end. Students take on these kinds of learning tasks daily and weekly, in place of traditional tests. Rather than receiving a single, onetime grade on each assignment, they engage in a deep revision process with their teachers' help. Plus, students must complete four larger performance assessments— one in each core academic subject area—to graduate. And they are grueling. "They're really hard," said Erica, an ICE senior. "We're not talking about Googling your topic. We're talking about reading pages and pages and pages of journal articles."

The assessments range from conducting an original science experiment to writing a social studies research paper: a deep and lengthy work of scholarly quality on a subject of your choice. ICE senior Joya, for instance, wrote a whopping thirty-two pages on post–World War II economics and its effect on minorities. When students complete larger projects, they don't just hand in their work to a teacher to get a grade; they have to present and defend it to a panel of judges, including teachers, peers, and members of the broader community—similar to a graduate thesis defense. How can the school be sure students are getting the essential math and reading skills the state requires? The mastery shows in the students' work—along with equally important skills such as analysis, persistence, organization, communication, and original creative thought.

"Our school really teaches us how to think, instead of telling us, 'This is correct,' and, 'This is what you need to know,' and, 'This is what you need to know two months from now on the test,'" Erica said. Teachers still give students quizzes to check for understanding, but the quizzes don't count toward their grades. Most consortium schools don't offer any Advanced Placement classes, either; they feel they can educate students better when they're not simply driving toward a factual exam. And the lack of APs doesn't hurt their graduates' college applications; colleges know the consortium's policy and simply consider what students did with the offerings they had.

The ICE students talked about one particular aspect of their education that means a lot to them: choice. This is a refrain I've heard from students across the country. As Ridgewood High School recognized by creating its student advisory group, education becomes a far more engaging experience when you have a voice in what and how you study. Yet student choice is utterly lacking in traditional, overstandardized schools, where teachers feel they have only enough time to stick with the program. At ICE, choice *is* part of the program.

Erica, Joya, and their friend Jordan told me about their recent study unit on new journalism—the long-form, literary nonfiction pioneered by writers like Tom Wolfe and Truman Capote. After reading and analyzing Capote's *In Cold Blood*, each student wrote his or her own true-to-life story. Erica, a stylish dresser who wants to go into fashion, wrote her story on attending New York's Fashion Week. Jordan described a day in the life of her family, which she said helped her notice small details she never had before. And Joya did a sociological exposé of Macy's at Christmastime, a setting she detests.

Joya said coming to ICE and being allowed to make choices and asked to think for herself changed her whole experience of school. "It's a shift in emphasis," she said. "It's learning for yourself instead of learning for someone else."

Experiments actually show Joya's experience to be broadly true—people of all ages thrive when they have some independence. Wendy Grolnick, the Clark University professor, explains, "What we know is that kids feel most engaged in school when they have a sense of autonomy, when they have some volition or some choice. That doesn't mean that we can't give kids tasks to do sometimes that aren't things they would spontaneously do. But to have that sense of autonomy is really important to sustaining motivation. We don't value that as much in schools as we could."

That same week in New York, farther uptown, I met a student at a consortium school called Urban Academy for whom deep inquiry and choice had made an especially big difference. Jameel came to Urban Academy as a sophomore after flunking and repeating ninth grade at another school. He'd earned straight As in middle school, "but that wasn't saying much, because they didn't really challenge us," he said. High school was a whole different ballgame. Jameel went to an elite college-prep high school reputed for its high standards, aiming to be the first in his family (he's the youngest of four siblings) to go to college. But he quickly found he could not keep up with the school's huge quantities of hard work—most of it geared toward textbook answers. His teachers cared but seemed unaware of what he was struggling with, and he didn't feel free to ask for assistance.

The Jameel I met that day at Urban Academy was worlds happier. Now an eighteen-year-old senior, he was rehearsing for the school musical and interning weekly with a small film director. He shook my hand firmly, spoke in a resonant voice, and frequently flashed a smile that pushed his cheeks up high. He told me he'd found that at Urban Academy, where the teachers weren't caught up in the march through tested material, they made the time to really get to know him. They provided reading materials at his own level and helped him improve. Then, the chance to choose subjects for deeper study made him suddenly care more about his learning. The idea for his graduation project in history, for instance, came from a discussion in his gender studies class that he wanted to explore more deeply.

"It really makes a difference, when you're learning something, to focus on something you really care about," he said. "It's really weird because before you know it you have this ten-page essay and you're like, 'Whoa, I wrote that?'"

Even the fact that Jameel got to take a gender studies class owes to Urban Academy's exemption from state testing. The consortium schools still teach history, but since they're not being tested on the mile-wide, inch-deep details the state requires, they can explore. Other options students can choose from there include a full semester on the civil rights movement. The range of subjects helped Jameel find what he wants to study in college: gender studies and Africana studies. And, with his grades much improved since freshman year, he had been admitted to Goucher and Hampshire colleges.

This time, he felt ready for the transition. "This school has really prepared me for college," he said. "The rigor of the performance assessments we do alone prepares you."

As we wrapped up, I asked Jameel and the students at ICE which learning experiences had made the most impact on them. They all named the work they did for their graduation requirements. Whoever said that about a standardized test?

Danville, Kentucky: A Challenge for Every Child

The New York consortium schools are hardly the only ones using performance assessments to support richer learning. There are other schools that use this practice even though their students still have to take standardized tests. Educators at these schools generally don't even try to cram in every piece of content that might be tested. Instead, they more or less ignore the state exams (though some still prepare kids for the SAT and ACT) and just keep the faith that, if students are learning deeply, they'll score okay.

The school district in rural Danville, Kentucky, is one such setting. In 2011, under the leadership of then superintendent Carmen Coleman, the district had lifted its dismal test scores and shot up to twenty-fourth in the state. "We were celebrating," Coleman recalled when I visited her a few years later, "but at the same time, less than 30 percent of our students were even meeting the minimum bar on the ACT. Those that were going to college were having to take remedial classes and were certainly not equipped for success."

So Coleman, along with several teachers and Bate Middle School Principal Amy Swann, traveled to New York to see what the consortium schools were doing. They came away amazed by what the New York kids could do, and they wanted their own students—70 percent of whom live in poverty— to have the same opportunities. Within a couple of years, they had Danville seventh graders doing original research projects, writing fifteen-page papers, and giving twenty-minute presentations to panels of judges that included university graduate students. One girl who loves swimming tested how two different types of pools, saltwater and chlorine, affected her timing.

Students with special needs (who often really struggle on fill-in-the-bubble tests) were able to do experiments, too, each one at a level of complexity that matched her abilities.

"The reason that we love the performance-based assessments is because they require kids to show what they know in different ways," Coleman explained. "Maybe with a public presentation. Maybe having to respond to questions just as they would in a defense of a dissertation. They might have to work in groups to solve a problem. So, not only can we assess content, but we can assess skills like perseverance, like leadership, like adaptability."

After Danville initiated the change, behavior incidents at the middle school dropped by 50 percent. Pointing to their success, the Danville schools boldly applied to the state for a waiver to opt out of state tests, even though no legal avenue for such a waiver existed. They were denied.

Danville has done another thing differently than most other districts. Not satisfied with the basic standards, Coleman and her colleagues created the "Danville Diploma," a set of aptitudes that each child should master by high school graduation. These include the ability to exercise creativity, persevere in the face of challenges, find reliable and accurate information, function well on a team, manage time, think critically across disciplines, and take initiative. (I'd note, again, that none of these essential skills could appear on a paper exam.) Starting in kindergarten, Danville students keep a digital portfolio of work that shows they're mastering those competencies. The children will show these portfolios to their panels of assessors at the end of fifth and eighth grades. When they graduate from high school, they'll be able to send their portfolio link to colleges and potential employers to show what they can do beyond a transcript.

In one girl's portfolio, Principal Swann told me, will be a series of dazzling animated videos on dance. This girl, socially isolated and withdrawn, was a poor test taker who hadn't particularly distinguished herself until she proposed an independent study to create the animations. "She can already talk about camera angles and physics and all kinds of things that we never would have known had we not said, 'Okay, follow your interests and let's see what you can do,' " Swann said. "We would have just thought she was an average student."

There's one more benefit to *nonstandardized* evaluation that's important to understand. Assessing students as the Danville and New York educators do—through a variety of modes and through personalized projects with real meaning—helps to shape kids' mindset about learning.

The reigning expert on this science is psychologist Carol Dweck, whose 2007 book *Mindset: The New Psychology of Success* became a surprise bestseller that shook up the status quo in schools, businesses, and family dinner-table conversations. Some of the schools I've visited have had their entire staff read it. Dweck's book distills decades of research down into a dichotomy between two visions of intelligence and learning: *fixed mindset* or *growth mindset*. When I met her in her office at Stanford University, she explained it like this:

> In a fixed mindset, students believe their abilities are just these fixed traits. You have a certain amount and that's that. Some of us got a lot of math ability and some of us did not. But in a growth mindset, students understand that abilities can be developed. Everyone can improve, can cultivate their abilities through hard work and mentoring.

The concept sounds simple enough, but it's actually incredibly powerful. "When you have a fixed mindset, as soon as you encounter something difficult, your interest wanes," Dweck said. "If the whole point is to look smart and feel smart and you're not, how much fun can that be? So we find students dropping majors or turning off to something they loved before as soon as they hit difficulty or have to struggle." In contrast, "Students with a growth mindset tell us they feel smart when they're working hard on something and finally making progress."

Dweck's research also upends the way many of us thought we were supposed to praise our children. She found that praising a child's innate qualities, such as intelligence ("Oh, look what you did, you're so smart!"), backfires. "It puts kids into a fixed mindset," Dweck says. "It tells them that deep trait of intelligence is fixed, and that's what we value in them." Instead, she urges parents and teachers to praise children's effort, progress, and thought process, and to place value on struggle, not just success.

Unfortunately, our traditional education system is stuck in a fixed mindset. It's common for children as young as six to be tracked according to an assessment of their aptitudes—placed in reading groups or math groups by ability, for example. These students quickly learn to identify themselves as "fast" or "slow," "smart" or "dumb."

Our test-driven methods make this kind of labeling worse. This institutionally fixed mindset celebrates academically adept students, rewarding them for their high scores and good grades and making them feel smart without ever really challenging them. And it leaves students for whom conventional testing is difficult feeling inadequate, which hardly encourages them to keep forging ahead.

It's hard to get kids to adopt a growth mindset when they spend their young lives in a fixed-mindset system. Yet it's crucial that parents and educators try, because—while our children's mindsets may partly be rooted in their natural temperaments—research shows that the experiences they have at home and in school also play a significant role. Performance assessments can make a big difference. They place the emphasis on a student's creative and analytical process instead of a one-shot display of a narrow set of skills. They're especially beneficial when paired with a school-wide attitude that failures are useful lessons, not defeats. In Danville, for instance, when students' work for a performance assessment isn't up to snuff, they're expected to keep revising until it is.

Dweck also recommends that schools and parents explicitly teach kids about the mindsets. "Kids are fascinated by the brain," she observed to me. "And teaching them that the brain actually forms new connections when they learn, especially when they learn hard new things or even struggle with new material, it's thrilling for the child."

Ending the Obsession

There's no sense waiting for the zombie apocalypse. Every child in America should have access now to the sort of stimulating, personalized learning that's going on in Danville and New York City.

One antidote to our testing affliction will ultimately be policy change. It is urgent that each of us who cares about children's health and quality education press our school board members, state lawmakers, and representatives in Washington, DC, to eradicate the creativity-crushing regime and instead adopt a program that encourages deep thinking and honors children's diverse strengths. The high stakes placed on exams have to go; no one's job or graduation should depend on a single measure. And instead of fixating on a single written test, we could evaluate schools on a host of outcomes with more meaning, such as college entrance and persistence rates, improved student health, and student engagement.

There are little glimmers of movement now. FairTest reports that by fall 2014, at least seven states had repealed or delayed their graduation testing requirements. (Rhode Island, finding itself under student-zombie attack, was one of them.) That same fall, state education secretaries and district superintendents from across the country got together and pledged to cut back on testing. The officials insisted that some testing is necessary, but told news outlets that many currents tests "are poorly designed, take too much time, [and] don't measure what schools really need to know." On a smaller scale, the whole district of Windsor Locks, Connecticut, is phasing out letter grades and instead using rubrics, which allow students to track their progress toward the skills they need to master. And high schools in Glastonbury, Connecticut, and Acton-Boxborough, Massachusetts, stopped publishing their honor rolls to relieve competition among students for grades and class rank.

As we undertake the campaign for change, we'll hear some skeptics contend that the new Common Core standards are already making things better. My answer: maybe. The standards were intended to replace eclectic and voluminous state requirements with a more streamlined national set that encourages critical thinking. Whether they actually improve learning remains to be seen; it will depend entirely on how they're implemented. "The Common Core, however dressed, shares the fundamental spirit with NCLB: standardization of curriculum enforced with high-stakes testing," writes Yong Zhao. Even if the learning goals are better, students' experiences will only improve if the means are better, too. Naysayers may also argue that doing deeper assessments on a national scale would be too time-consuming and expensive. That argument is a distraction. The fact is we *could* assess schools with better measures if we tested a smaller, representative sampling of students instead of every single one—which is the way science is normally done.

But—reality check. We all know how slowly the wheels of politics turn. It will take years to reform the testing regime in statehouses and in Washington. Fortunately, we can start to change children's experiences immediately by taking matters in our homes and communities into our own hands. We can begin, of course, by pressing districts to reduce standardized tests; some districts require double or even triple the number of standardized exams that states do. Beyond that, we should ask teachers to assess their students' daily learning in far more diverse and deep ways: through such endeavors as hands-on projects, public presentations, debates, and digital portfolios—the kind of work that actually resembles what students will someday do in the real world. If resistance is stiff, consider starting these innovations in a single classroom, where skeptics can see for themselves how students thrive.

"Whatever we do repeatedly is how we wire ourselves neurologically," explains Mariale Hardiman, director of the Neuro-Education Initiative at Johns Hopkins University. That's why it's crucial to give children a wide variety of experiences in school, she says, rather than "always teaching them and testing them in the same way."

Much of our work at the local level is not procedural but cultural. We need to teach our kids and our communities a growth mindset, and to broaden our shared definition of what learning looks like and what success in school can be. It starts with each of us shedding the belief that good test scores equal a good education. Without standardized tests, we'll still have ample evidence to gauge whether our students are learning well—just look at the essays they've written, the presentations they've made, the science experiments they've conducted, or the thoughtful discussions they're able to have. Yong Zhao also advocates for measuring a school's quality by the resources and opportunities it provides to every student, such as fair and equitable funding, a safe physical environment, well-trained teachers, personalized lessons, a broad curriculum including the arts, and support for innovation. In other words, assessing inputs, not just outputs.

Do not believe, either, in the "best high school" rankings that are invented by commercial magazines, and do not participate in the stampede to buy ever more excessively priced homes in "top-ranked" districts. Test scores are well known to parallel children's parents' income and education levels, so those rankings may not tell you any more about school quality than they do about local property values. (Dozens of high schools have already asked to be removed from such rankings, calling them "simplistic and misleading" and arguing that "communities deserve better.") As long as parents buy into these false measures, our schools will remain stuck in traditional education practices and test prep. Rankings keep schools focused on the wrong things.

Some of the cultural shift can start as simply as parents and teachers changing the tone of conversations at home and in the classroom. Allison Nelson, a mother of two in Potomac, Montana, says she and her husband have deliberately shifted the importance they place on their elementary-age daughter's test grades. They still urge her to do her best, but they don't pass judgment if a bad score comes home. "We just say, 'You know what? Maybe it was a bad day,'" says Nelson. And they look for a lesson to learn from it.

Changing our conversations with children sounds like a tiny tweak, but don't underestimate its power. I always think back to a particularly tough precalculus test my older daughter took. She got a D but took it in stride, knowing the test was tough and using the opportunity to see which concepts she'd missed. In earlier years, I had fueled her anxiety by fretting over every B and C, once even keeping her indoors all weekend to study for a fourth grade biology test. By this point, though, I'd learned to stay calm and just listen, to ask her what mattered to her and how she wanted to respond. Shelby, who loved math, decided that she wanted to learn what she'd missed, so she asked the teacher for extra help and worked hard to deepen her understanding.

Opting your children out of standardized tests can also send them an important message about what you value—in them, in their education, and in life. This is a message worth spreading to other parents, as well, to galvanize the community. Michele Gray, a mom of two boys in State College, Pennsylvania, was distraught when her third grader became so anxious about the state test that he started scratching his legs in his sleep. He knew his performance could have consequences for his school, yet Gray saw no educational benefit to the exams. So she called the state education department and learned that she could have her sons skip the tests based on a religious objection. She took it. Her boys did independent study during the two weeks (two weeks!) their classmates were undergoing exams. When Gray wrote a column in the local paper telling parents how and why to opt out, CNN aired a story about her. Suddenly, Gray was getting phone calls from as far away as Georgia from parents who hated the tests but never knew there was anything they could do.

Students, too, can take steps to reclaim their own educational lives and those of others from single-minded measurement. Zak Malamed, a student body president at Great Neck North High School on Long Island, had an epiphany sophomore year when he burned out after months of attempting to devote himself fully to everything—the school newspaper, student government, and a tough slate of AP and honors classes. Zak scaled down, still getting his work done but not trying to ace every test. In exchange for his well-being, he decided, a B-plus instead of an A-plus was fine. Friends started telling him he seemed happier. "As long as I do it my way and do my way really well," he believes, "I don't have to do everything, and I don't have to be good at everything."

The following fall, several of Zak's schoolmates were arrested in the Nassau County cheating scandal. He began to see how, even at his highly regarded, high-scoring school, our madness for measurement was hurting the whole system. His school sorely needed improvements, he believed. But as long as the scores were high and the college admissions were golden, everyone seemed content with the status quo. Frustrated, Zak and others formed a student organization to give voice to their concerns. Later, the group was formalized as a nonprofit organization called Student Voice, which aims to place students' input at the center of education debates around the globe. Zak is now a junior at the University of Maryland, pursuing an "engagement and media" major that he created, and Student Voice is still going strong.

Lillian Van Cleve came by her epiphany even more unexpectedly. She is a warm, open college student who grew up in San Francisco attending elite schools that put a premium on test scores. These schools required copious quantities of uncreative work—which took Lillian, a girl with ADHD, hours longer each day than her peers. By the time she reached high school, exhausted and uninspired, she was asking herself, "Where am I going to get the stamina? When is this going to end?"

One experience saved her. In the fall of her ninth grade year, Lillian's mom took her to Florida for a few weeks to work on Barack Obama's presidential campaign. She worked in the field office and became the de facto assistant to the local director. Handling phone calls, helping volunteers, and arranging logistics, she found something astonishing: her own value. "That experience was transformational," Lillian says. "It was the first time in my life that I can remember feeling good about myself, and feeling good at something. And I *was*." Suddenly, Lillian could see a world beyond the rigid confines of school, and she could see herself in it.

Back in San Francisco, she joined the Parents Education Network, an organization for parents of children with learning challenges, as a student adviser. And she transferred to a school that placed greater value on deeply exploring ideas. Now Lillian is a junior at a small liberal arts college in the Midwest. Some people treat her diagnosis with the gentle phrase *learning difference*, but she prefers the blunter term *disability*. "It is a learning disability not because of the way my brain works, but because of the system that I'm in," Lillian argues. "I'm disabled by the system, and if you think about it, everybody is, because it's set for a very narrow definition of a learner, and everybody's different whether they have a learning disability or not."

———

Since my own awakening I have struggled to help my children step back from society's measures of success and define their own. I've been opting my own Zak out of standardized tests since he was in fourth grade. Jamey opted herself out in tenth grade—and I understood why. I saw the need starkly one particular day, her first day of school that year. Here was Jamey standing in front of me, sweaty from cheerleading tryouts, flush with excitement for the new friendships she was making with teammates, full of determination to master the tumbling techniques she'd need to make the squad. And here, also, in that afternoon's mail, were the results of her California-mandated standardized tests. A row of good-but-not-great numbers, decontextualized and soulless on a sheet of paper in my hands. This is the vast divide our kids have to negotiate daily, between their *selves* and their *scores*. Will they or will someone else determine how their worth is defined?

Nowhere in those cold numbers will you see Zak Malamed's knack for leadership, Lillian's skillful activism, or Jamey's adeptness with animal science, which is now so apparent in the thriving preveterinary college student she has become. Let us join forces to end the testing madness and make it possible for every child to reach that state of self-determined success—to discover her own value and put it to great use—without having to fight such formidable obstacles all along the way.

CHAPTER 5

College Admissions:
Break Free from The Frenzy

I T WAS an overcast evening in late February when parents, students, and educators gathered for a *Race to Nowhere* screening in the auditorium at the Academy of the Sacred Heart in suburban Michigan. The 160-year-old school sits on forty-four wooded acres and is designed to be a nurturing place that focuses on the whole child, not just the Harvard application. After the screening, a panel of model students told the crowd that yes, the film raised serious issues, but no, this wasn't such a problem at Sacred Heart. They assured the community that they didn't feel as stressed as the kids in the film.

The students were doing what they thought they should—supporting their school. But junior Elle, another model student sitting in the audience, knew the rosy picture they painted was an illusion. She was a straight-A student, a field hockey and lacrosse player, poised, and bound for the most prestigious college she could test and transcript her way into, and she couldn't take it anymore. "They didn't speak the truth," Elle would later recall to me. "So I was sitting at my seat, and I just remember I was, like, fuming. And I was shaking."

Before she even realized what she was doing, she asked for the microphone. And then, her voice amplified across an audience of her teachers and peers, Elle uncorked the pressure that had been building in her for years.

Starting in sixth grade, Elle told the audience, she'd made it her mission to maintain a perfect transcript. She believed this was the necessary cost of admission to an elite college, and that ticket was priceless. "Going to a really great college that everyone sees as a really good school, that was success," she explained. Elle managed to sustain her taxing effort through sophomore year, when a British literature class had her reading and annotating fifty pages a night. The assignments took her five hours daily, on top of sports practice. She was so stressed that she started losing her hair; her ponytail shrank to half its normal width. But she didn't consider stopping.

Finally, junior year, an AP US history class pushed Elle over the edge. "It rocked my world," she said. "I had so much homework. I lived in my room, and a lot of times I would cry myself to sleep." She spiraled into a deep depression. "I would be driving down the road, and I would just be like: if only I could just turn the wheel a little, go a little faster, and just crash into something, it would be that easy." Elle confessed all of this, right down to her wish to die, to the assembled audience. Even her mother, sitting in the crowd, had never heard it before.

"I couldn't breathe," recalls Sister Bridget Bearss, the head of school. A devoted educator who believes deeply in the "heart" part of Sacred Heart's mission, she thought to herself: *This can't be happening.*

Elle's courageous act would trigger changes small and large, immediate and long-lasting, in the school community and in her own life. Right away, one of the girls on the panel "burst into tears onstage and started talking about how stressed she was," Elle recounts. Bearss convened a team of teachers that same night, staying at school until nearly midnight to discuss what they would do to make things better for their students. Bearss remembers asking herself, *Who else are the hidden Elles in our community?*

For Elle's part, she heard herself say out loud for the first time that her obsession with building the perfect college résumé was destroying her. "It woke me up," she says. "I realized that something had to change."

Many students and families I've met have taken the college admissions race to equal or greater extremes. What Elle realized that night—and what we as a society must recognize and embrace—is that the holy grail we're after is a mirage. A good life does not depend on a brand-name alma mater, nor is one guaranteed by an Ivy League acceptance letter. Either way, we're losing too much in its pursuit.

A Frenzied Nation

The Frenzy—capital *T*, capital *F*—is what Jon Reider, director of college counseling at San Francisco University High School, calls it. The college admissions process is a Darwinian and soul-bruising contest that represents nothing of the great leap toward autonomy, independence, and adventure that it should. The drive to *get in* spurs students to spend precious time on résumé-building activities that don't interest them, and their parents to spend precious money on test-prep courses that don't build meaningful knowledge. It demands that kids see their community of peers not as their safety net but as their competition. Perhaps worst of all, The Frenzy convinces many kids (and some parents) that admission to an elite college defines them; without an Ivy League acceptance or its equivalent, they are failures.

Eva Dodds, an independent college counselor in Michigan and board member of the Michigan Association of College Admission Counselors, sees the madness daily. From August through November, she says, "one of my lambs loses it almost every night." Intuitive and down-to-earth, Dodds tries to calm them; she does this work because she believes in her students, not in the system. Yet even outside the office, parents of her six-year-old son's classmates ask her what she thinks of certain schools, saying, "I know it's a little early, but . . ." and inquiring, "Is there anything we should be doing now to help our kids get into college?" Her answer is an emphatic, and rather horrified, no.

Yet Dodds understands where their worry is coming from. Acceptance rates at the most prestigious schools do indeed appear to be growing infinitesimal. For the class of 2018, for example, Wesleyan University admitted just 23 percent of applicants, Notre Dame 21 percent, Williams 18, Cornell 14, Vanderbilt 12, MIT 8, Harvard and Yale 6, and Stanford a mere 5 percent. Those odds may not be quite as impossible as they appear—more students are being courted to apply to elite colleges for which they're not qualified, effectively inflating rejections—but the numbers spread fear nonetheless. One client of Dodds's was so panicked that she came up with the idea of applying to her choice college via the art program, though she was not an artist, and using her friend's portfolio in the application. Plenty of others,

Dodds says, commit the less conspicuous fraud of pursuing nongenuine interests, cheating themselves above all.

Dodds's charges are suffering from the ailment that Philadelphia clinical psychologist Jeff Mitchell terms "Harvard-or-Walmart syndrome." On his website, he published a withering critique of the "academic extremism" driving the college race:

> This is a societal disease, a virus of an idea that has spread through the LinkedIn generation and its children. It is a conviction, stark and unforgiving, that one's children will either (1) get into Harvard or (2) spend their lives working for Walmart. Infected with this idea, parents and children drive themselves far past the point of healthy ambition. Believing the odds are so poor, the stakes so high, and the degree of control over the outcome so tenuous, parents and children take extreme actions. No amount of pressure, no expense, no degree of sleeplessness or risk of humiliation is too high. And frankly, if one believes the choices are Harvard=success=security or Walmart=Dickensian=poverty, this extremism seems sensible and the only right course.

The great fallacy is the belief that those ivory towers are the *only* place a student can adequately learn, grow, and embark on a good life. There's no certainty that those elite institutions are even the *best* place for every kid to do so. The *New York Times*'s Frank Bruni reported recently that he looked up the undergraduate alma maters of the CEOs of the top ten companies in the Fortune 500 and found only one Ivy (Dartmouth) among them. The remaining nine attended such universities as Arkansas, Texas, Nebraska, Kansas, Missouri, Auburn, and Saint Louis.

Eva Dodds herself attended the little-known College of Wooster in Ohio, where she honed her writing, research, and leadership and got what she considers a better education than she did later, in a master's program at the Harvard Graduate School of Education. "The reality of the situation is there are three thousand awesome, awesome, awesome colleges out there," she says. "And as cheesy as it sounds, there is a match for everyone." That match is a school whose offerings fit your particular academic and extracurricular interests, and whose campus culture is suited to help a student like you succeed.

But the status anxiety fueled by American culture—not to mention the genuinely fearful vise grip of rising income inequality—makes an alternate path invisible to those in the throes of The Frenzy. "The stress is there," Dodds says, "because the culture says you're only successful if you go to these fifty colleges." The truth is that there is no surefire formula: some star students don't get in, while some students do get in with lower scores but unique qualities that help a college build a diverse class. Above a certain level of academic achievement, getting into elite schools is akin to a lottery. Nonetheless, many families mortgage the high school years trying to fatten applications and read admissions officers' minds. This panicked sense of competition even afflicts students with more modest goals as it fuels the misperception that perfect résumés are required to get into college, period, which is far from true.

Amid all the jockeying, the hurdles for low-income students can be especially hard to clear. A mom at another Michigan screening pointed out that the stakes of getting her kids into a university—and out of the cycle of poverty—were incredibly high. Yet for those whose families have no experience with college, there may be no one to tell them which high school courses to take or how to prepare for the SAT, and no one to help them with applications. Teachers in low-income communities tell me that the strain on these students tends to go unrecognized.

Meanwhile, The Frenzy has even spawned an entire sector of the economy devoted to helping both colleges and students (at least those who can afford it) play the game. The attendant army of marketing and recruitment consultants for colleges, application consultants for students, private test-prep tutors, essay coaches, and standardized test makers comprise what Reider calls "the admissions-industrial complex." Revenue among all these businesses runs well into the billions. Fear sells.

The craziest extreme I've ever seen is a hedge fund manager turned college counselor named Steven Ma. From his chain of ThinkTank Learning centers in the San Francisco Bay Area, Ma provides tutoring, test prep, and application coaching and guarantees that his clients will get into a "top" school, provided they hit certain minimum GPAs and SAT scores, or their money back. How much money? His astronomical fees are based on a proprietary algorithm that predicts each kid's chance of admission to each school, *Bloomberg Businessweek* reported. The price tag for tough cases can reach $700,000. And some parents actually pay it. "Of course we set limits on who we'll guarantee," Ma told the magazine. "We don't want to make this a casino game."

Origins of the Arms Race

Today's college application process bears not the faintest resemblance to what this generation of parents experienced a few decades ago. My own applications in the late 1970s were a straightforward documentation of my courses and grades and a thoughtful essay about the career for which I hoped my college education would ready me. My volunteering as a candy striper in the local hospital, my work on the yearbook staff, and my participation in the math club were welcome breaks from schoolwork and chances to be with my friends—not credentials for college. I remember my applications not so much as a stressful hurdle to be jumped but as an exciting and empowering step toward my adult independence and stability.

So what's happened?

The former Yale professor William Deresiewicz sketches out the history of the slippery slope in his book *Excellent Sheep*. As Deresiewicz tells it, the origins of The Frenzy lie in an effort to expand private colleges from the exclusive clubs they'd been for a century or more, the province of elite Anglo-Saxon Protestant progeny groomed in private boarding schools. In the 1930s, a Harvard University president set out to raise academic standards and broaden access to the rising classes. He chose as his primary tool a then-obscure test called the SAT. In the 1960s, the Yale president did the same, and in short order other colleges followed. Yet this move toward meritocracy sparked a new arms race. Now applicants had to boast *both* the "character" and culture of an old aristocrat and the academic excellence of a modern technocrat—and look better than the growing competition while doing it. No pressure.

Since then the contest has only accelerated. Between 1970 and 2010, the number of students enrolled in four-year colleges more than doubled.

And the more grads that entered the workforce with a bachelor's degree, the more everyone else felt that they, too, needed a diploma to compete. "What was once an opportunity has become a necessity," Deresiewicz observes. "There is only one definition of happiness, and only one way to get it." In fact, over the past forty-five years the reasons students themselves give for going to college have drastically changed; whereas most incoming freshmen once said they sought meaning in their education, most today say they seek money.

Now the obsession with this one-and-only yellow brick road extends alarmingly far backward—into preschool, in certain communities. UC Berkeley psychologist and philosopher Alison Gopnik likens the resulting distortion of our children's "learning" to the famed plight of the Irish elk. The males of the now-extinct species earned a slight evolutionary advantage if they had bigger antlers. The result, Gopnik quips, was an antler arms race that produced bucks that could barely move under the weight of their giant antlers. "We've got something like that in the American system," she says. We all think it's crazy for high schoolers to pull caffeine-fueled homework binges every other night, but as parents, when it comes to our own child, in whose future we're so deeply invested, we can't help but fret that a slightly more majestic antler might get her into a better college and on the path to a better life.

It's all been intensified by the *U.S. News & World Report* college rankings, launched in 1983. The annual lineup purports to name the "best" colleges and universities in the country on sixteen measures of "academic excellence," including admission rates, graduation rates, class sizes, per-student spending, and—in a self-referential spiral—the reputation of each institution according to other college officials' opinions. So rich is this business that other media now publish copycat rankings of their own. (*Washington Monthly* deserves note as an exception. Its rankings are based on the refreshingly meaningful criterion of how much each institution contributes to the public good in terms of research, service, and social mobility for low-income students.)

These rankings generally do nothing to help students find an educational environment that fits them. Yet the list, however suspect its criteria, stokes students' ambitions and fears and fuels the myth that there is a "best" when it comes to the complex and personal art of education. Plus, it perpetuates a growing tendency among prospective college students to see college primarily as a stepping-stone to yet more prestige and "rank," rather than an opportunity for growth and learning.

Rankings also handcuff colleges that might want to demonstrate their success another way. Arizona State University psychologist Suniya Luthar, for one, has called on schools to systematically assess students' *well-being* and include that stat among their institutional credentials. Reed College, a selective and respected school in Portland, Oregon, stopped participating in the rankings altogether in 1995, refusing to send *U.S. News* its data. Reed argued that the magazine's methodology amounts to a "statistical charade" and that its lineup "takes a one-size-fits-all approach to institutions with radically different missions and character—a bit like asking whether the Beatles are better than Beethoven." The college paid a price for its stand: *U.S. News* kept on ranking Reed anyway, gathering its data from other sources, and the following year its rank plummeted to the lowest tier.

Some of the ingredients in the college panic are even more malignant. I was shocked to learn, for instance, that a lower acceptance rate earns a college not only a higher *U.S. News* ranking but also a higher bond rating. The more applicants a school rejects, the more generously Wall Street will lend money to it. A school's ranking also rises if it enrolls more students with higher SAT and ACT scores. So the more applicants a college attracts, the better positioned it is to skim those with the best statistical profiles, thus boosting its ranking and prestige and attracting even more applicants. It's no surprise, then, that I heard admissions officials on Jamey's campus tours urge high school students to take the SAT and ACT multiple times so that the colleges could "superscore" them, taking their highest score from each section even if it meant pulling from different sittings. This expensive and grueling exercise benefits the colleges and favors kids from families who can afford to pay for the test over and over.

In part for these reasons, colleges are increasingly deploying huge marketing machines that flood students' mailboxes with glossy brochures whether or not those students are qualified. The more applications they receive, the more they can reject, puffing up their statistics. Yet this numbers game can create a cruel, false hope for families. Eva Dodds routinely hears parents say,

"I know she has a 3.2, but look at what she got from Harvard. Should she still apply?" Dodds can't always dissuade them.

Moreover, the ever-shrinking admission rates spur students to apply to an ever-expanding number of schools. Using the Common Application, it's especially easy for anxious students to tick extra college boxes and thus hedge their bets. The National Association for College Admission Counseling reports that, in 1990, just under one in ten students applied to seven or more colleges; by 2014, more than three in ten did so. Applying to a dozen or more schools is now common. Dodds sees plenty of kids throw in five or six applications to schools they won't get into, against her advice. Their parents say proudly, "My kid has applied there," Dodds says, and then other parents think their kids should, too.

And so the growing flood of applications drives down acceptance rates still further, and the vicious cycle goes on. As we've seen, all this misery does not even produce the genuine learning we want for our kids. College professors widely report that too many freshmen arrive on their campuses profoundly averse to risk, not daring to try new subjects or endeavors that they can't be sure to ace. The traditional treadmill has stripped them of their spark. At UC Berkeley, for example, Gopnik told me her most interesting students are those who've transferred in from community colleges. They have "actually gone out in the world and done things . . . and now are coming back and bringing a degree of enthusiasm and exuberance and creativity to their schooling that we don't necessarily see in these very finely honed grade-getting machines that we are creating in our high schools."

Saddest of all is the self-doubt induced by our singular, competitive vision of college success. Kathleen, a high school senior from the Midwest, wrote to me that she'd built her life around getting into the same university as her older brother did. Aiming to be perfect in high school, she took almost exclusively AP and accelerated classes, participated in ten clubs, served as cross-country and track captain, and slept an average of four hours a night. As a result, she developed extreme migraines, scoliosis, and ovarian cysts, and longed for it all to end. Kathleen wrote:

The thing is, I was never as smart as my brother and the other girls in my class. I was the dumb girl in the smart classes. I hated myself.

Whenever I looked in the mirror I wanted to punch it so hard. . . .
I was 11th in the class and not in the top 10. And worst of all, I
was rejected from [my first-choice school]. I failed. The one thing I
wanted more than anything in my life was taken away. I let down so
many people. The day I found out, I walked into traffic hoping that it
wouldn't hurt, hoping that all the pain would go away. But the cars
stopped. I'm still here.

I want people to see that we walk around every day with the
world hanging on our shoulders weighing us down. Imagine what
would happen if it gets too heavy, and we crash. What would hap-
pen then?

Steps at Sacred Heart

Bridget Bearss and the staff at Sacred Heart did not wait around to find out
what would happen if Elle and her schoolmates went on bearing that pressure without some help. Acting quickly after hearing Elle's testimony, they
launched a "curriculum think tank" to reassess what students truly needed
to learn and figure out how best to teach them. They asked, for instance,
whether summer reading really helps kids perform better. The answer, says
Bearss: "We don't really have any statistical evidence that more homework
and more summer reading equals higher achieving kids." So they eliminated
summer reading and tried to shift students' most challenging assignments
from homework to classwork.

Recognizing the importance of granting students a voice in their own
learning, the school also began building in more opportunities for children
to choose pursuits they're passionate about, culminating in a self-chosen
capstone project for seniors. Sacred Heart started a speakers series on
wellness, highlighting topics such as depression, suicide prevention, and
balance. And the staff redoubled their efforts to dissuade kids from overscheduling. "When you see a student who is just biting off way too much,
we're much more aggressive about saying no," Bearss says (though students
and parents can still override their advice).

To Elle's surprise, the school even changed the rules for what it takes to
be valedictorian. No longer did a student have to take the hardest course

load possible to become valedictorian or salutatorian. Elle stumbled on the change while looking through the student handbook at her senior year orientation. "It was kind of incredible for me," she said. "If I had just let the panel speak and say that everything was okay, nothing would have really changed because everyone would have thought that every student in our school was doing fine."

Bearss is watching to see what impact the reforms make. By fall 2014, a couple of years after the work began, Sacred Heart was seeing higher standardized test scores and fewer kids being referred for psychological evaluation, but it was too early to identify the reforms as the cause. Bearss, a onetime anti–Vietnam War activist turned educator, admits that there's some cultural quicksand her school still can't escape. "I have kindergarten parents who ask me for the college acceptance list," she told me. And for a small school that depends on its enrollees to stay in business, the pressure is real. Sacred Heart publishes the acceptance list on its website.

The Advanced Placement Illusion

Sacred Heart's move away from an insistence on the hardest possible course load is not an easy one to make. This is an issue dominated by the dreaded Advanced Placement class, one of The Frenzy's chief instruments of destruction. Originally designed to help capable students earn college credit while still in high school, the AP program is now touted as a way to prepare teens to succeed in tough college classes, expose poor and minority students to more rigorous course material, and reduce the cost of college by enabling students to graduate earlier. And the AP business is booming. *Politico* reports that the number of AP exams taken per year more than doubled in just a decade, reaching nearly three million by 2012. At the same time, revenues to the College Board, maker of the AP exams, surged to more than $600 million a year (prompting *Nonprofit Quarterly* to question whether the organization was a "nonprofit in name only").

Yet in 2012, students failed nearly half of the AP exams they took. The passing rates were even lower for Latino and African American students. The educators and students I've met across the country typically tell me the demands of AP classes leave them rushing through reams of rote content at the expense of rich, in-depth learning. Burned-out students cram before exams and quickly forget what they've learned. Rarely does teaching to the test leave time to cultivate the critical thinking skills that colleges claim to want.

Take the example cited by Jay Chugh, who teaches both AP biology and an elective, non-AP biotechnology class in the Acalanes Union High School District in California. In the elective course several years ago he started allowing more time for authentic research and open-ended exploration. As a result, two of his students went on to win the top prize at the Intel International Science and Engineering Fair. Ironically, the AP biology students would never have had time to do that—they often didn't even have time for labs because they were trying to cover so much content before the test in May. "Where is the time to do authentic science?" Chugh exclaimed. "It's not there."

The AP program doesn't necessarily, in fact, bolster college performance. A Harvard and University of Virginia survey of eighteen thousand college students in introductory science classes found that having taken AP science classes did not significantly boost their grades. And a study of more than eighty thousand University of California students found that once you factor in students' academic and socioeconomic backgrounds, AP courses had no significant relationship to how well they perform in the early college years. Middlebury College math professor Priscilla Bremser complained publicly in 2011 that more and more of her students who scored well on the AP calculus exam hadn't actually contemplated the important theories on which calculus is based. After hurrying through high school math to reach AP calculus, Bremser wrote, "a number of bright, hard-working students have shockingly weak algebra skills. At some point along the way the A.P. program has shifted from a way to meet the needs of a few students who are ready for a challenge to a de facto admissions requirement for many who may not be."

Besides, some private colleges—Dartmouth, for one—no longer offer credit for these exams because they are not seen as true equivalents to the college's own courses. As for the touted cost savings, it is possible for some students to enter college (at public institutions that *do* give AP credit) as second-semester freshmen, saving themselves a sizable chunk of tuition.

However, many private colleges charge by the semester for four full years, not by the course. So students there pay the same tuition no matter how many AP exams they aced. This is, ironically, the case at some of the nation's most prestigious institutions, whose students are most likely to have taken tons of AP tests (at more than ninety dollars a pop).

Still, frantic students are flocking to AP classes, and many high schools encourage this. Unfortunately, it actually boosts high schools' reputations to push more kids into AP classes, ready or not. The *U.S. News & World Report* "Best High Schools" rankings score schools entirely based on how many of their students take and pass at least one AP or IB exam. And schools whose students take the most AP and IB exams, regardless of whether or not they pass, rank highest on the *Washington Post*'s annual "America's Most Challenging High Schools" list. So we end up with sixteen-year-olds taking four "college equivalent" AP classes plus three regular classes simultaneously, whereas actual college students typically take just four courses at a time.

This is not to say that APs are all bad. There are some brilliantly taught AP classes out there, and some students who feel genuinely challenged and engaged by them. But that caliber of teaching and learning is possible in any class, perhaps more so in a course not driven by a standardized exam. What we lack above all in our AP mania, as in The Frenzy overall, is any shred of balance.

The pressure even gets to those who don't believe in it. Jon Reider, the San Francisco University High School college counseling director, is a self-confessed "curmudgeon" and "rebel" who spent much of our conversation deploring colleges' role in the admissions madness. (As a former Stanford admissions officer himself, he has the credentials to be a critic.) Reider complained that the hundred-plus college reps who visit his campus each year always tell students to take the hardest course load possible, leaving out the important phrase: *within reason.* Yet in the same phone call, he had to step away for a few moments to explain to a student who was considering dropping an AP class that it could hurt her college chances. "I hate that I have to do that," he said. "Maybe I'm a hypocrite."

At Irvington High, Assistant Principal Jay Jackson and the guidance counselors set out several years ago to discourage students from signing up for too many Advanced Placement and honors classes in their quest for a collegiate edge. Some kids were registering for courses far beyond their academic capacity, simply because they felt they should, and then struggling and failing. The counselors were starting to see serious psychological disorders among students as young as ninth grade, and the school's 5150s—police code for forcibly committing someone to a mental hospital, typically because of suicidal plans—seemed to be growing more frequent.

Wendi Bennett, an Irvington counselor with dirty-blond bangs and a tell-it-like-it-is demeanor, believes there are a few students who can genuinely handle all that work. The problem comes from the large number "who *think* they can do this, and they're the ones falling apart." Worse, she says, there are just as many beyond that who take the classes because their parents expect them to.

So the counselors created a special registration form for students to complete before they can register for an AP or honors class. Students had to fill out a table estimating all the time in their day, including homework, family time, free time, and necessities such as eating and showering, with eight hours already tabulated for sleep, and a maximum of twenty-four hours (yes, the school actually had to underscore that limit). They had to factor in added time for advanced classes. And the students and their parents had to sign statements including:

> I understand that an AP class is extensive in content and requires additional time and work. The course load I am registering for is balanced and suits my ability level.

And:

> I understand that I should base my course choices on genuine interest and should NOT register for an AP course(s) because my friends/peers are registering for it or for the sole purpose of impressing a college.

The form was a good effort, but it was no match for the achievement machine. The counselors found that when they sent the form home, students weren't giving it serious consideration. Bennett would laugh when students penciled in fifteen minutes for family time. "I had a couple that put zero for necessities," she recalls. "I'm like: please shower."

So, in a stunning act of commitment, in spring 2014 the counselors sat down individually with every single freshman, sophomore, and junior (about 1,700 students total) as they registered, to urge them to think carefully about their course choices. They pulled students out, one by one, during their English classes. The entire process took all four of Irvington's counselors a whopping one and a half months, every day, most of the day.

The school also put in place prerequisites for AP and honors classes. Students have to get good grades in the fall in a given subject area in order to register for an advanced class in the same discipline the next year. And, though it's not mandatory, the counselors enforce a very strong recommendation that students reach a certain GPA before they decide to increase their load.

Within a single semester, the Irvington counselors' intervention cut the AP class failure rate in half. Whereas the counselors used to be routinely called to tend to overwhelmed students having emotional meltdowns in class, only one student had that crisis the following year. There's still a long way to go to change the community's achieve-at-all-costs mentality—to get students, parents, and even some pressure-pushing teachers to reexamine their priorities. But students are clearly feeling some relief. And though it was too early to have comprehensive data on college admissions, the counselors were already seeing students accepted at great schools, such as Purdue, UC Davis, and UC San Diego, with only one or two APs. So Irvington made the decision to continue the one-on-one course registration again the next spring, despite the incredible investment it took. Imagine if every school did.

AP classes are, in fact, not critical to a college application. The Cranbrook Kingswood School in Bloomfield Hills, Michigan, restricts students to two or three AP classes a year yet remains a highly regarded prep school. Some of the country's most respected schools offer no AP classes at all. The Independent Curriculum Group, for example, includes about seventy-five schools nationwide that have chosen to liberate their teachers to create rigorous, deep, and challenging advanced courses instead of AP. Its participants have included many private schools, such as the Crossroads School in Santa

Monica and the Park School of Baltimore, as well as public high schools in performance-driven communities: Scarsdale, New York, and Marblehead, Massachusetts, to name two. In place of prescribed curricula these schools focus on fostering curiosity, creativity, and genuine engagement. The Carolina Friends School in Durham, for example, puts the money it might spend on APs into diverse opportunities to develop critical thinking, such as senior seminars in neuroethics and immigration and an entire semester course on the fall 2008 presidential election.

What happens when AP-less Carolina Friends grads go up against college applicants from elsewhere with oodles of APs? Nothing. Colleges know about the ICG schools' approach and thus don't penalize their students for it at application time. Having zero AP classes hasn't harmed their admissions. Nor has it hurt graduates of the New York Performance Standards Consortium schools. Nor of San Diego's highly regarded High Tech High, which worked directly with the University of California to develop an honors curriculum with more depth and flexibility than the AP regimen. The school offers the option for honors credit in any class instead of segregating students into separate AP courses.

It is possible for individual kids attending schools that are stuck on AP to opt out of those classes and distinguish themselves in other ways. Jamey took not a single AP class in high school but distinguished herself through community service that she cared about. She also chose certain courses to which to devote extra effort, once studying so hard that she set the curve on a math exam. Ultimately, she had multiple colleges to choose from. However, it's harder to convince colleges of the value of your choices when you have to go it alone, as Jamey did. Here again, our greatest power to end the race comes when whole communities work together to redefine what matters—and the success of groups like the ICG and schools like Cranbrook Kingswood and High Tech High is proof of that.

Colleges, for their part, must cop to their role in fueling the madness and cap the number of APs they'll consider on a student's application. The Ivies, especially, should recognize their powerful influence and limit the advanced courses that applicants may list. That would be a simple, responsible step, and other colleges would follow suit. High schools, too, should follow the courageous lead of those I've described in this chapter. Sacred Heart of-

His case in point is the program at Emory's Oxford College, a two-year residential college with automatic enrollment at Emory in junior year. At Oxford, Wagner explained, "We gamble more," admitting students with lower grades and SAT scores a hundred points below those at the main campus. Placed in small classes and taught partly through collaborative projects, these students flourish as well as or better than peers in the regular Emory program, and more of them go on to pursue doctoral degrees. "So I know for a fact that we're admitting students that we and our peers would otherwise reject, who are fabulous students," he said. "I don't know how to get that message out: Universities will not suffer [if we change our admission criteria]. We'll actually thrive. We'll be relieved, in fact, in many ways."

Plenty of admissions officers make their decisions just fine *without* those all-powerful scores, anyway. FairTest, a Boston-based organization that advocates for fairer measures in education, keeps a comprehensive list of all the colleges and universities that admit at least some freshmen without SAT or ACT scores—and it numbers well into the hundreds, and growing. The list includes more than 160 such schools ranked in the "top tiers" by *U.S. News*, including Wesleyan, Bowdoin, Bryn Mawr, Connecticut College, Wake Forest, and the California state universities. And how do their students fare? A 2014 study backed by NACAC and conducted by a former Bates College dean of admissions looked at a huge sample: more than a hundred thousand students at nearly three dozen of the colleges and universities that make standardized tests optional. The researchers compared the college grades and graduation rates of students who did and did not submit an SAT or ACT score with their application, and found no significant difference in their success.

Why does the reliance on standardized test scores persist despite so much evidence against it? David Hawkins, NACAC's executive director of educational content and policy, explains that it's partly because of history—"It was the very most elite institutions that were using these tests to begin with," he says, and where the prestigious schools lead, others tend to follow—and partly because there's a misperception that the tests provide what Hawkins calls "a common yardstick," an efficient way of sorting applicants and transcending variations in grading from high school to high school.

More universities must follow the test-optional schools' sensible lead. In place of standardized exams, they could allow applicants to submit digital portfolios, papers, videos, and other more personal demonstrations of skill. In a few places, this change is already starting. In 2014, Goucher College, outside Baltimore, began accepting a two-minute video, plus two high school work samples, *in place of* the Common Application. That is how Jameel, the student from New York's Urban Academy, applied. Bennington College in Vermont started offering applicants an even more flexible option: they can send in a portfolio of any material they want, including or not including grades and scores. This "dimensional" application is an invitation for creativity and independent thought. Admissions officers use the portfolios to gauge applicants' academic readiness and understand what each will bring to the college community.

Colleges that have made such changes say they're looking to capture more applicants with unique résumés who might be deterred by conventional measures. Since 2013 Bard College has been accepting what it calls the Bard Entrance Examination from those who don't want to take the traditional route. The instructions are to write four 2,500-word essays, chosen from twenty-one topics, to be graded by Bard faculty. Get at least a B-plus combined grade, and you're in—no tests scores, transcripts, or résumés required. Bard president Leon Botstein told the *New York Times* the new application was "declaring war on the whole rigmarole of college admissions," which is "loaded with a lot of nonsense that has nothing to do with learning."

Privately, admissions officers elsewhere admit they, too, want the system reformed. But colleges are infected with a Frenzy of their own—a senseless cultural panic about outcompeting other schools for applicants, stoked by the well-paid college marketing industry that makes it possible. Up against the juggernaut of the rankings, the other colleges' recruitment machines, and the directives of boards of trustees, individual officers don't see how they can be among the first to change.

Michael Beseda, the vice president for enrollment and communications at Willamette University in Salem, Oregon, is trying to buck the trend. After arriving at Willamette in 2013, he canceled the school's contract with Royall & Company, the enrollment-consulting behemoth that sells students on easy, quick, and free applications, and set about doing recruitment and admissions his own way. Every message sent to prospective students came not from the marketing machine but from Beseda's own email address, and was written by Beseda himself to emphasize Willamette's particular offerings instead of the ease of application. Each acceptance letter contained a personal note about the candidate's qualities. In short, he cast Willamette as a unique school that suited particular students instead of a commodity.

The result: Applications, which had tripled to nine thousand under Royall, dropped to six thousand in a single year. But Beseda says the school got "a larger class, a much better class," because accepted students were more likely to actually attend. Wasn't Willamette afraid of losing rank as its admission rate ballooned? A little, but not much. Beseda's explanation centered on a startling fact: it turns out that a college's admission rate—one of the factors in the *U.S. News* rankings to which institutions seem most slavishly devoted—actually makes up a barely consequential 1.25 percent of its overall score. In other words, a school could theoretically admit every single student who applies and still score a 98.75 percent overall in *U.S. News*. (The portion determined by incoming students' SAT and ACT scores is more substantial, at over 8 percent.)

So why does the race for the ever more infinitesimal acceptance rate go on? Partly because extreme selectivity boosts the aforementioned bond ratings and conveys prestige in news stories, alumni reports, and other realms beyond the rankings. And partly, Beseda says, because the popular misperception about the rates' importance is self-perpetuating. Plus, both public and private colleges have grown more financially dependent on undergraduate tuition, driving them to recruit more "full pay" students who don't need aid and more out-of-state and international students who pay higher rates. "So both reputation and revenue really come down to who's in your entering class," says Beseda. "Those are the realities that have created this pressure, and educators haven't kept their wits about them."

So college officials, like young college applicants, seem to be sweating under some artificially created pressures. Yet as long as everyone else is doing it, it's scary to break away. Beseda hopes that by doing things his own way at Willamette, he can say, "There's nothing to be afraid of."

Reclaiming Success

The rest of us must not wait around who knows how long for more colleges to see the light. There is a lot we can do now. And most of it comes down to facing *our own* fears.

We need to remind ourselves, our students, and our children, as often as necessary, that education is not a badge to be worn. It is a deep and personal journey whose conclusion you cannot foresee, and the substance of that journey is far more important than the brand name in which it's packaged. Besides, it doesn't actually make *that* much difference where you go to college. Plenty of Yale students feel adrift and get little out of their time in New Haven; plenty of community college students are able to explore and grow along the way to their diplomas. The 2013 Chegg Student Skill Index, a survey of college students and hiring managers across the country, found that while 45 percent of students believed a degree from a prestigious college is "very" or "extremely" important to make them attractive to employers, only 28 percent of hiring managers thought so. The hirers cared far more about leadership.

So cast aside the rankings, the kid-to-kid comparisons, and the false gods of prestige. The greatest myth of all is that only a tiny handful of colleges are worth attending. And once you stop believing that, you can also stop believing that you have to kill yourself to get there—because the vast majority of schools out there truly want a diverse set of students, including interesting kids with Bs and Cs. Instead of competing for the same standard résumé builders as everyone else, focus on cultivating your own skills and passions. "Stop asking the question 'What do I have to do to get into <u>blank</u>?'" college counselor Eva Dodds advises. "Start asking: 'Where can I learn about <u>blank</u> and what will it prepare me to do?'"

Also frequently forgotten in the midst of the madness is that most students have to contend with practical questions, too. Outside of a very small, affluent minority of college-bound students, most future freshmen have to consider not only their own aspirations or passions but also family economics and geography. For them, a simplistic fixation on finding the "right" or "best" college obscures the more nuanced reality: that the "best" college may be, after all, the school that offers the biggest financial aid package or is close enough to home for them to help their family.

Sometimes, the answer to Dodds's question "Where can I learn about blank?" isn't even college. Abigail Baird, the Vassar professor, chuckles as she describes how she horrified her mother at Thanksgiving dinner by insisting that she didn't know if her six-year-old twins would go to college. "They're six!" she exclaims. "I don't know if they're going to go to college because I don't know what they're going to want to do." They might end up like Skylar Bird, who apprenticed himself to a local chef and opened his own restaurant in Buckingham, Pennsylvania, while still a teen. Or like the growing tribe of young college opt-outs working in tech in San Francisco.

There are important steps that each of us who plays a role in the college admissions race can take to escape. Here is where I urge you to begin:

Students, you can help yourselves by casting off convention and choosing learning over maximal prestige. Take advanced classes and join extracurriculars if they interest you, not because you think you should. Limit the number of times you take the SAT and ACT—or even opt out entirely, taking inspiration from Seattle high schooler Sylvie Baldwin, who refused to take the test because she didn't want to be boiled down to a number. Sylvie planned to apply to test-optional colleges as well as those that require scores, explaining her test choice in her applications. With the fifty-plus hours that Sylvie would have spent studying for the exams, she decided instead to write proposed state legislation to require drivers' education courses to address the environmental impact of driving.

It's also helpful to consider taking a gap year before enrolling in college to work, travel, or try something totally different; you'll benefit more from the education if you've first had time away from the academic race to reflect on your goals.

And relax: remember that there are hundreds of good colleges for all kinds of students. Consider, for example, the confident, blond-haired boy, clearly a student leader, who captivated the audience at a California *Race to Nowhere* screening by recounting how he'd forgone AP classes to spend time with his family and then listing the multiple four-year colleges he'd been admitted to with his 2.4 GPA. Alison DeFiore, who grew up in suburban Massachusetts, is working full-time while earning her degree at the Woods College of Advancing Studies, Boston College's night school. She's enjoying the depth of life experience that her classmates bring and looking forward to graduating with minimal debt. And Elle, who, after her epiphany, took no more AP classes at Sacred Heart, enrolled at the University of Vermont. She planned to study psychology so that, as a therapist, she can help young people who struggle as she once did. More than seven million other students each year enroll in community colleges, where they can save substantial sums of money and potentially take more time to discover their interests.

"Just learn for the sake of learning," Elle advises. "Learn about what you're interested in and not what other people are interested in. That's what's really inspired me. . . . I focus on asking questions that are going to help quench my curiosity and things that are really going to help me understand the world better, as opposed to just get an A on the next test."

High schools hold plenty of power to defuse the race, too. And we parents, students, educators, and PTA groups can press them to do so. To displace competition and restore learning as the central aim of high school, they can limit the number of AP classes students may take and stop ranking students by GPA. Schools can encourage students to pursue classes and activities that truly interest them, and to apply only to colleges they genuinely wish to attend. They should also, like colleges, eliminate the GPA boost for AP classes and request to be excluded from the high school rankings. As the ICG schools demonstrate, it's possible for high schools to make dramatic changes and, by communicating their policy to admissions offices, not harm their students' applications at all.

Campus culture counts, too. High schools can ease their atmosphere by avoiding "college days," where students wear attire from the schools they plan to attend. Holding information sessions for parents that reframe college applications around personalized goals, not brand names, as Irvington High has done, can also help to lessen collective anxiety.

When it comes to equity, high schools should invest in more college and career counseling to help level the playing field between students with family resources and those without. San Diego's High Tech High, for example, serves its diverse students by hiring only college counselors who have worked in college admissions and who themselves are the first in their family to earn bachelor's degrees—thus ensuring that the counselors understand what some kids are up against.

And **individual educators** can take a cue from Esther Wojcicki, a legendary journalism teacher at Palo Alto High School. Every year on the day admissions decisions arrive, she makes sure to reassure her worried students with stories about kids who thrived at less fancy colleges. She underscores that acceptance or rejection letters neither seal anyone's fate nor represent their success or failure in life.

Parents, of course, probably hold the heaviest sway of all. Parental pressure can get bad: one Michigan dad made his fifteen-year-old daughter a "bible," a binder titled "Carly's Future" that listed the top-tier schools she should aim for, including his alma mater, Princeton. Eva Dodds routinely sees parents pushing their kids toward prestige and even writing college essays for them (which is perfectly visible to admissions committees). Most of us don't take it that far. But we still unintentionally influence our kids through the worried questions we ask or the kind of praise we bestow—or simply by failing to give our children a different vision of success from the overwhelming one that surrounds them.

If college is the right choice for your child, help her look for schools whose programs and campus activities actually suit her interests. Remind your child that college is what you make of it; the skills and lessons she gains by getting to know professors and engaging in the campus community will benefit her far more than the school name on her diploma.

One western Massachusetts dad named Jonathan Baum, a hedge fund lawyer, says he's seen enough of the fast lane to become "highly skeptical that the traditional path through law and finance bred anything more than the desire for more, a grinding inherent dissatisfaction." He made it a priority to frequently talk to his two kids about the importance of learning broadly and deeply, of meeting some basic standards but then pursuing what you enjoy. When it came time for his son to look at colleges, Jonathan underscored these priorities with a clever trick: he created a spreadsheet listing key qualities about each school, such as its size, its setting (urban or rural), its athletic options, its majors, and campus photos. The only thing he didn't include was the school's name. "To remove the name and prestige or lack thereof, and to really look at a school for what it is," he says, "I think that was the best thing that really happened in my choosing a college." He went to Bard.

What worked in my home was avoiding incessant dinner-table conversation about college applications. I let my kids take the lead in researching and applying to colleges because it was their journey, not mine. Our house was free of magazines that rank colleges, and our kids waited until junior year to take the SAT. The lessened pressure freed up Jamey to pursue what she loved, volunteering in a local veterinary clinic instead of loading up on activities. She searched for a school that would offer what she wanted: individual support, access to professors, and opportunities to learn the way she learns best, through hands-on experience and small-group discussions.

As I drove away at 1 a.m. after moving Jamey into her dorm at Denver University, I felt the pang of setting my second child free. The automated Bluetooth voice in my car kept repeating, like an echo of my heart, "searching for Jamey's phone, searching for Jamey's phone." But I had the comfort of knowing that Jamey was in the right place *for her*, a decision she'd made free from anyone else's expectations or definitions of success. And that she'd spent her precious years in my home building the real knowledge of herself, and the real-life skills, to thrive there.

———

Getting free of The Frenzy is fundamentally about defining your own values. Or, as college counselor Reider advises, "Refuse to get rattled. Be comfortable in your own skin. Don't listen to what other people think you should want. Realize that the most important thing about your education is what you put into it. The most important things that happen to you in college are the things that you could not have anticipated. A friend you made. A course you never expected to take. A professor you connected with. An activity. Some lead on life."

And finally, prepare yourself for the possibility that college will not be a life-changing climax after all. It might simply be a blend of fun, frustrating, interesting, and educational—one of many such learning experiences that our lives will hold.

CHAPTER 6

Teaching and Learning:
This Way Up

IT'S TIME to think bigger.

That became clear in the hundreds of *Race to Nowhere* screenings I attended, which at first left me feeling hopeful. In every audience, I found a growing awareness of the ills that undercut our kids' health and learning, the very ills we've identified in this book so far. The despotic grip of homework with questionable benefit. The depersonalizing pursuit of meaningless scores. The college admissions casino game, the padding of résumés, the deprioritizing of personal and family time, the perversion of values. And from that awareness sprang a new set of revolutionaries who refused to let themselves, their families, or their students get swept up in it all.

Still, something seemed missing. Our progress was piecemeal. Finally it dawned on me: we were trying to mend cracks when we needed to rebuild the foundation. All our discussions were based on the assumption that we were stuck with the current model, and we had to work around it. What we needed was a fresh vision of what education could look like if we cast aside outmoded practices and believe in our collective power to change the *system*, not just the symptoms.

So I set out to find schools in the United States that weren't just valiantly fixing the problems with the old model of education—reducing homework, dethroning tests, and defusing competition—but also pioneering something totally different.

What would the ideal school look like? A kind of school that goes deep instead of wide, that capitalizes on children's particular strengths and tends to their weaknesses rather than putting them all through the same paces, and that asks every student to cultivate truly original ideas instead of mere right answers? A school like that would value quality over quantity, encouraging students to persevere through challenging work that actually means something important to them. It would show high- and low-performing students alike that they can accomplish feats of intellect and creativity they never knew they could. It would frame learning as a rich and varied experience, not a transactional equation. Ultimately, a school focused on learning through vigorous, genuine inquiry would grow the kind of inventive thinkers and keen communicators that our children's futures will demand.

Such schools do exist in America. They are not, as you might guess, confined to wealthy enclaves where ample taxpayer contributions fund tiny class sizes and lavish enrichment programs. In fact, the reality is sometimes the reverse. Many schools in the affluent suburbs are constrained to conventional methods and perfectly content to remain that way, delivering their graduates to the doorsteps of Dartmouth and a formulaic life, few questions asked. The pioneers, it turns out, are found in a wide range of communities and include public schools serving diverse populations. These schools are led by teachers and administrators, and supported by communities of parents, who understand that the old ways of education don't work for most kids and that the modern world demands something different. Their methods are driven by the belief that our educational system should modernize its purpose and work to unleash the true potential of every child.

I have spent countless days in these groundbreaking schools, marveling at the excitement on kids' faces, the near-professional quality of their creative work, and the confidence and pride with which they described their learning to me. Every time, I've wished my family lived nearby so that my own kids could go there. And every time, I've asked myself: Why can't every child have an education like this?

———

That is what superintendent Travis Hamby was asking himself when he took the helm of the Trigg County Public Schools in 2010. The entire K-12 district is housed on a single campus in rural Cadiz, Kentucky, three hours southwest of Louisville and more than an hour northwest of Nashville. Cadiz (locals say *KAY-deez*) is a sparse, sleepy place where the whole community comes out to cheer on the high school football team on Friday nights. It has a two-block downtown of brick storefronts, including a salon, a bank, the county courthouse, and a disproportionate number of antique shops. A big draw to town is the annual Country Ham Festival.

Hamby, a chatty former math teacher with a cheerful Kentucky twang, took the job in the midst of a tough time for Trigg County. A car seat factory that employed hundreds of residents had shut down, sending many into unemployment. More than half of the district's two thousand students already qualified for free or reduced-price school lunches based on their families' low incomes; the plant closure only pushed that number higher. And though Trigg students' test scores were good—at one point the district ranked twentieth out of the 170-plus districts in the state—the outcomes for graduates were not. More than 20 percent of the Trigg grads who entered a four-year college were not returning for their second year. Among those who went to a two-year college, the rate of those not returning was nearly 30 percent. For Hamby, the writing was on the wall: the former factories weren't coming back, and his students weren't well prepared to thrive in a new kind of economy. In this new world, he understood, good old reading, writing, and 'rithmetic aren't nearly enough skills to succeed.

Plus, when he peered into classrooms, Hamby saw students sitting inertly and unhappily at their desks, bored and disengaged. As a father of three, Hamby could see in his own home how traditional schooling was extinguishing creativity and passion instead of sparking it. In the early years, all three of his boys were curious, imaginative, and enthusiastic about learning, as most children tend to be. His kindergartener would still come home and immediately open his backpack to show his mom what he'd created that day. But the older two had stopped showing that kind of excitement years ago. Every night in the Hamby home became a homework battle, unraveling the family's cohesion. "I want our school district to continue to tap a child's curiosity, imagination, their creativity," Hamby said. "I want my kids to come home with that enthusiasm every single day, because they've been engaged, because someone's cared about them, because someone's really tried to pull out the greatness that lies within my child."

When I met Hamby in early 2013, he was preparing to make a dramatic change in the way teachers taught in his district. A courageous change, in fact, for someone working within a system that still prizes conformity. He knew he'd have to take a hundred risks to create the kind of inspiring education that he wanted for his own children—but he was ready. "We've got to do something different for the sake of our kids," he said to me. "The greater risk is that we do nothing."

The Greatness Within

Hamby was entirely right. We are the inheritors of an outmoded education system, designed for an age when most decent students could anticipate a lifetime of reliable industrial or agricultural work. The world that today's graduates enter is entirely different, demanding not regimentation but invention. To thrive in the modern (and unknown future) economy, where work is increasingly creative and service-oriented, today's students need to develop the kinds of adaptive skills that can make them successful in any role. Besides, the old ways have *always* confined kids to narrow modes of learning and narrow opportunities to find success. There's no evidence that that traditional model was great for our generation, either.

The technological revolution in the world economy has, at last, focused public attention on this problem. "What was considered a good education 50 years ago is no longer enough for success in college, career, and citizenship in the 21st century," wrote the National Education Association, the country's largest teachers union, in 2012. "The new social contract is different: only people who have the knowledge and skills to negotiate constant change and reinvent themselves for new situations will succeed."

You'll find all kinds of different names for these evergreen skills. A group of leaders in education, business, and government joined together in 2002 to define them as "twenty-first-century skills" and work to position them at the center of American education. The partnership included executives from Apple, Cisco, the National Education Association, the US Department of Education, and more. They interviewed leaders across diverse industries and found broad consensus on the most crucial skills. And they summed up these core aptitudes as the Four C's: critical thinking, collaboration, communication, and creativity. Tony Wagner, an educator at Harvard University's Innovation Lab and author of *The Global Achievement Gap*, then traveled the world conducting interviews and expanded and adapted the list to seven:

- critical thinking and problem solving

- collaboration and leadership

- agility and adaptability

- initiative and entrepreneurialism

- effective oral and written communication

- accessing and analyzing information

- curiosity and imagination

"Literally, from Taiwan to Singapore to Thailand to Bahrain to Finland, Spain, England, from West Point to Wall Street," Wagner told me, "I've seen total agreement about the importance of these skills."

However you count them, it's evident that these kinds of creative and collaborative abilities—and the vibrant learning experiences that foster them—are what people have always needed to succeed. They form the foundation of an engaging life. Yet when the American Management Association in 2012 surveyed hundreds of managers, directors, and executives across a wide range of public and private industries, more than half said their workers needed to improve on the Four C's. The bosses called their workers' competency average, at best. Three out of four predicted these skills would become even more important in the near future. "In the world of business, you see a premium on novelty, nuance, customization, experimentation," says Daniel Pink, author of *Drive* and *A Whole New Mind*. "In our schools, we see a premium on routines, right answers, and standardization. That ought to alarm us very deeply."

Our schools, steeped in tenacious traditions, have been far too slow to adapt. Walk into a classroom today, and it's likely to look pretty much the same as when Hamby was a student himself in Hopkins County, Kentucky, in the 1980s. He earned good grades but never felt especially challenged or engaged, and he's frustrated that so little has changed. "Students are still primarily sitting in rows," he observed. "They are primarily listening to a teacher, for much of their day, talk. There's a lot of rote types of learning still going on."

One study published in the journal *Science* states the problem in hard numbers:

Researchers observed elementary classrooms across four hundred US school districts and found that fifth graders spent more than 90 percent of their school day in their seats, either listening to the teacher instruct the whole class or doing seat work on their own. They spent a negligible amount of time learning in small groups, and received five times more instruction on basic skills than on problem solving or reasoning. No ten-year-old is going to be inspired to creative leaps by this kind of system.

No one I know—not Hamby, or Pink, or Wagner, or me, or any of the hundreds of folks I've interviewed—blames teachers alone for this stagnation. It's natural to teach the way one was taught. Besides, the education system itself is inflexible. Teachers are tethered to a heavy bureaucracy, stacked up all the way from the principal's office to the halls of Congress, which insists they cover more material each year than is humanly possible. Then it tests their students on this, and publicly praises or shames their schools on the results. Teachers of English, for example, "are often asked to teach 120 or more students a day a simplistic formula style of writing that will enable the students to pass standardized tests," writes Wagner, a former teacher and school principal himself. "And they have very little time to do anything more." Even the new national Common Core standards, much touted for reducing the number of required bullet points and emphasizing skills along with facts, may prove too wide, too tested, or too standardized to fix the problem.

As educator, author, and speaker Ken Robinson points out, this stifling paradigm has even infiltrated our language, in which educators widely describe teaching lessons as "'delivering the curriculum,' like dropping it off like FedEx," he says. Instead, learning should be seen as an active process, a form of growth fueled by experience. This is true for learners of all ages. A 2014 study at the Universities of Washington and Maine compared undergraduate college courses in science, technology, engineering, and math that were taught through traditional lectures or through more participatory learning. In an analysis of more than two hundred studies on the subject, the researchers found that students in active-learning classes scored higher on exams. Students receiving lectures, in contrast, were one and a half times more likely to fail the class. To break those unhelpful old traditions, Robinson suggests excising the word *delivery* from our educational vocabulary entirely.

To be sure, students still need some basic knowledge: strong literacy, numeracy, and an essential understanding of our social and scientific world. But the great realm of granular information is now available at their fingertips, through technology. What they will need to succeed as adults in this century is not piles of information in isolation, but rather practice in how to use it well. They need to understand how to access information and apply it to new situations, and how to be good citizens of an interconnected global world (essential life skills that are, in truth, long neglected but not really new). The continued fixation on informational knowledge to the exclusion of genuinely meaningful experiences produces disengagement and narrow thinking, even among star students.

"I'm a straight-A student, but I think a lot of my As in the past have been because I did my homework. I don't think I retained all the information," says Alexandra Carr, a poised and confident recent graduate of Trigg. "A lot of teachers would be surprised to know how bored I was in their classes sometimes." What actually prepared her for her mechanical engineering studies at the University of Kentucky, Alexandra says, was a hands-on high school engineering class where teams of students created their own original product and built it, setting their own deadlines, over the course of a year. (Alexandra's group made an award-winning safety latch for a cattle gate.) Outside of that, she said, her traditional high school classes gave her no major challenges that students had to solve without hand-holding by teachers, "and that's a huge part of what college is."

What pains me most as a parent is how much raw talent and passion we are losing in our devotion to such limited—and limiting—modes of learning. The students who drop out, or who spend their school years feeling bored or unsuccessful, or who simply never realize there are broader ways to think than the tests demand: theirs are bright minds squandered. The same is true for straight-A students like Alexandra, whose other talents languish in a system stuck on right answers. There are inventors, artists, craftsmen, and entrepreneurs among them. Some will eventually find their way despite their schooling, and some, discouraged and disillusioned, will not. "Typically what you see in schools is a preoccupation with a certain conception of intelligence," Robinson observes. "It's a capacity for a certain type of propositional knowledge, a certain type of deductive reasoning. It's very important, but there's much more to human consciousness than that."

As this generation of children grows up in a world grappling with a booming population, a changing climate, a widening income gap, and an ever-evolving technological revolution, the stakes are too high to cast the whole universe of indispensable other human capacities aside. The stakes are too high for even a single schoolchild, one whose experience might help her discover the power of her own imagination or, conversely, determine early on that she's a dud with little to contribute. Says Robinson:

> If you incarcerate kids for eight hours a day, if you give teachers no creative freedom, if you treat them like data points or points on an assembly line, don't be surprised if they don't enjoy it very much. You wouldn't either. . . . If we start to treat students as human beings and schools as living centers of imagination and creativity, then you get a completely different result.

In Students We Trust

When Hamby looked around the Trigg County schools in his first years there, they didn't look anything like "living centers of imagination and creativity." So he and a handful of other administrators and teachers went looking for more innovative models.

The Trigg team's quest ultimately led them to an inspiring, innovative charter school half a country away in California. High Tech High occupies a sprawling campus of old US Navy training buildings near the San Diego airport. What started as a single high school of two hundred students in the year 2000 has been so successful that it's grown to a network of twelve schools spanning grades K-12 and serving five thousand students. Co-founders Larry Rosenstock and Rob Riordan opened High Tech High with one primary mission: to improve equity in education. So the school has no tracking system and groups students in mixed-ability classrooms. The teaching here is based on the philosophy that students (actually, all people) learn best by working collaboratively on real-world projects with impact beyond the classroom, coached but not spoon-fed by mentors who know them well.

When you walk into the original high school, you see students working together in clusters, both in classrooms and around couches and tables in the wide halls. The warehouselike space is filled with light from skylights. The walls between classrooms are actually windows, creating a feeling of openness and fluidity (there's nothing strange about collaborating widely when you can literally see one another). And as in the real world, the disciplines here blend: social studies is not separate from English, nor English from science, nor science from math. The atmosphere conveys something akin to a thriving office: calm but not quiet, focused but not constrained. There are no textbooks or bells. Kids are working mostly under their own direction, with guidance when they need it. No one is riding or haranguing them. If they need to go to the bathroom, they go, like adults do, no need to ask permission. And by and large, given genuine responsibility for their time and an engaging purpose, the teens put it to good use.

Some of the projects that students here have produced will defy the imagination of almost anyone who's spent most of his or her time in traditional schools (which is almost everyone). A biotechnology class worked with the Port of San Diego and the San Diego Zoo to research, write, design, illustrate, and publish an absolutely professional guidebook to biomimicry and sustainability around the San Diego Bay. Following the massacre at Sandy Hook Elementary and the shooting deaths of two boys in San Diego, eleventh graders ran a successful Kickstarter campaign to produce a documentary film on the causes of gun violence in America and what young people can do about it. And, on a day when the Trigg team and I visited, a ninth grade class showed us a visual and intellectual gem: Apocalypto, a huge, beautiful wooden diorama, suspended on the wall, combining mechanical gears, artistic carvings, and the principles of physics to visually represent the social, environmental, and political reasons for the cyclic rise and fall of civilizations.

So, rather than generating formulaic assignments (what Ken Robinson calls "low-grade clerical work") or writing research papers only ever to be seen by their teacher, these kids are asking original questions and producing projects that mean something to the world. They present and defend their work to classmates, teachers, parents, and community members at periodic exhibition nights. Knowing their work will face a real audience, students feel motivated to do their best. If their product isn't polished enough, a teacher coaches them to revise it until it is. Students still learn lots of content, but they acquire it as needed while they're passionately pursuing important projects. The ultimate assessment of their learning is the quality of their work itself.

"We have found that the more we trust young people," says cofounder and CEO Larry Rosenstock, "the more trustworthy they become."

What most struck Hamby on his early visits to High Tech High was the students' confidence in explaining their work to adults. When they showed Apocalypto to the Trigg team and me, a self-assured freshman named Sharon explained, "In humanities, we started out by studying ancient civilizations and how they rise and fall, and every individual group created a theory. And then in physics, we had to take our theories and create a mechanical representation." A boy in her work group continued, describing how his group's theory hinged on five different states: "The first one is trust, which was represented by this cam, which slowly declines over time, and the last one is rebellion, and we represented this with civil unrest, which slowly rises over time." We had to work to keep our jaws from dropping.

"It was evident through that conversation that there was a really deep level of learning that had occurred, which was in every conversation," Hamby said. There was no "'Okay, I've taken a test, and now I can forget it,'" he observed. "It meant something to them."

Visitors to High Tech High tend to assume that these are exceptional students enjoying the benefits of a school with deep pockets, but that's not true. Admission is by random lottery. More than one in three students qualify for free or reduced-price lunch. Moneywise, nearly all of the schools' operational funding comes from California's per-pupil allocation, the same budget given to every public school in the state. Much of the dazzling work the school achieves is facilitated by collaborations with local businesses and organizations, and by the passion of a faculty that is, unlike teachers in so many schools, given true freedom to teach. The outcome: 98 percent of graduates of all the High Tech schools go to college, and 86 percent graduate from college (compared to a national rate of just 59 percent). About one in three High Tech grads are the first in their families to go to college.

"You walk away from visiting this high school and you think, why can't we do this?" Hamby said out loud after one trip there. "Why can't a public school in western Kentucky do this for our kids?"

Learning by Doing

What's happening at High Tech High is called project-based learning (or problem-based learning), and it's not really new—it's based on the sort of educational inquiry pioneered by Socrates. It is, fundamentally, *learning by doing*, and doing so with provocative questions and appropriate supports in place. Project-based learning is only one model of personalized, inquiry-based learning; there are many. But it's the one I'll focus on here because it's well established and documented, and because it's what I've seen practiced most clearly.

"Imagine if we taught baseball the way that we teach science," says UC Berkeley psychologist Alison Gopnik. "We would tell kids about baseball in the first couple of years. By the time they got to be in junior high, maybe we'd give them a drill where they could throw the ball to second base, over and over and over again. In college, they'd get to reproduce great, famous baseball plays, and then they'd never actually get to play the game until they were in graduate school." High-quality project-based learning is, essentially, playing ball.

There are also some important things that project-based learning is *not*: It's not total unstructured anarchy. Nor is it a recipe with an expected outcome. It is, significantly, not the shoebox diorama or poster-board "project" or canned science experiment that you and I probably did in school. Daniel

Pink calls these sorts of assignments "terrarium problems," self-contained and clearly defined and thus wholly unlike the real world.

Another thing innovation in learning is not: technology for its own sake. Digital technology is a tremendous tool, and one that kids need ample guidance and practice to use well. But it's not a panacea, and it doesn't replace the human relationship in education. (Don't let High Tech High's name fool you: technology enables some of the work kids do there, but the machines themselves are not the point.) I've seen students use computers to create captivating videos and conduct complex data research, and I've seen rooms full of students staring at screens doing math practice problems in a kind of robotic test prep. Like any tool, digital technology can be used for exciting invention or mind-numbing monotony—in other words, for good or ill. As Hamby said to me once, voicing lessons learned firsthand, "Technology plays a critical role in supporting twenty-first-century learning, but you can have twenty-first-century learning in the absence of a lot of technology. . . . Don't mistake that we're doing something great just by giving everybody an iPad."

Inquiry-based education is tricky to study scientifically because it's so complex. There are countless different ways to do it, plus different teachers, students, and settings, so it's hard to compare apples to apples. On the whole, though, the research shows that an inquiry approach doesn't hurt test scores, and sometimes it helps. More importantly, it reveals that test scores are not at all the point. Students learning this way build skills that are not easily tested on Scantrons—problem solving and self-reliance among them. And studies show that they have higher attendance and more excitement about learning, which naturally helps them learn better.

One study of five thousand Detroit middle schoolers in low-income communities found that those learning science through a well-developed inquiry curriculum scored higher on a standardized exam than those learning science the traditional way. A US Department of Education study tested more than four thousand high school students in Arizona and California learning economics through project-based or traditional modes. The project-based group edged out their peers on a test of economic literacy, and substantially outperformed them on problem-solving skills and application to real-world economic dilemmas. Other studies have found similar impacts in elementary school. In other words, if the projects are well designed (and that's an important *if*), students studying through inquiry still learn the facts, and they also learn essential skills for life and work beyond the classroom.

Fundamentally, this sort of learning springs from the belief that children flourish when we support them in asking open-ended questions and solving problems for themselves. Thus, they cultivate their creativity, which Ken Robinson defines as "the process of having original ideas that have value." "The argument for creativity in education is all-encompassing," says Robinson, who contends that it's just as important in science, math, and language as in art. "It's not some exotic addendum that we can squeeze in on a Friday afternoon when all the serious work's finished. It's about the whole character of education."

Trigg's First Try

Hamby and the Trigg team took what they'd seen in San Diego back to Cadiz and decided to try it. In preparation, a handful of administrators and teachers attended more trainings at High Tech High (which runs its own graduate school of education and provides professional development to teachers from around the world) and at the University of Kentucky. They visited model schools in Kentucky and Ohio, including Danville, Kentucky, where students were already blossoming in the district's first year of using performance assessments. Crucially, the school board supported them. The district formed a committee of twenty people to guide the change, including three high school students—youth input that Hamby considers essential. For the new approach to take root, it couldn't be a mandate issued from above; it had to become a part of the school culture at every level.

The change makers set the Four C's as their goals. And they braced for mistakes. "It's like jumping into the pool," said Hamby. "We're going to take a risk."

To stave off community skepticism, the high school held a meeting in the school theater before the semester started, where Principal Shannon Burcham gave a packed house of freshman students and parents this message: "We're trying to provide you with opportunities that maybe your brothers or your sisters or your mothers or fathers didn't have. We want you to start connecting school to your life and to the passions you have."

Trigg started small, in fall 2013, with just the teachers who were game to try something different, in grades five, eight, and nine. This is just what High Tech High's Rosenstock recommends: "You're going to have some horses at the gate who are ready to move, and you know who they are," he says. "Get those people running, and give them as much freedom to run as possible."

The school reworked its class schedule to give ninth graders a longer block of time for projects. The ninth graders, many of them just a year away from earning their driver's licenses, began with a project on distracted driving. Working in small groups, they were to use math to research local and national safety statistics, and then use language arts to create an awareness ad campaign for their community. The teachers started the students out with some direct instruction and then remained as guides to help them along the way. Meanwhile, the fifth graders followed a similar process to investigate why birds were congregating and nesting on campus and how to kindly encourage them to live elsewhere.

I visited that October to see how the experiment was going. In Amy Breckel's freshman class I met Summer, one of the students on the district's change committee. She was a broody teen with a bubbly voice, a puff of dark brown hair, and bright blue-green eyes. Summer didn't like the new kind of learning at first, and she wasn't shy about saying so. "The teachers pushed you," she said. "I didn't want to be pushed. So I really didn't like them." Plus, she resented being assigned to work with classmates she didn't know well.

Breckel affirmed that the experiment started shakily. When she suddenly gave kids more independence to direct their own learning, perhaps for the first time in their school careers, many of them didn't know what to do with it. "When you give them that kind of freedom, wanting them to be creative and come up with solutions to problems, they look at you like, 'Where's my rubric? Where's my step-by-step process of how I do this? How many points is this? How long does it have to be?'" Breckel said. And opening up the classroom to unscripted discussion and questions, "The first day I did that it was like crickets chirping in my room." Some of her typical "good students" struggled with the new methods.

What turned Summer's views around was the close connection she began to forge with her teachers. When the Trigg team had visited High Tech High, they saw that strong relationships were central to the school's success. The ninth grade teachers they observed there work in teams of two, one covering humanities and one covering science, and keep the same group of students most of the day. Plus, each adult in the building serves as an adviser to ten students, meeting weekly and sticking with the same kids for all four years. "What makes problem-based learning work for them is they have a system in place where they can make every kid successful in that environment," Breckel noted. "If a kid is falling, they have somebody there to catch them, to find out what's going wrong."

Each Trigg teacher had a much larger caseload of students rotating through her classroom, but even so, they had started to see deepening relationships that fall. Rather than weaving projects into the core academic classes, the high school had placed them in a separate class called Fusion, designed to draw on all the other disciplines. Over the first month of Fusion, the teachers came to know Summer better than they had before. They discovered that while Summer had been on the honor roll in sixth and seventh grades and intended to be the first in her family to go to college, she'd hit a major obstacle in eighth grade. The Saturday after Christmas that year (she remembers the day), Social Services had taken her away from her mom, split up her siblings, and sent her to live with her dad, with whom she had very little connection. Her grades crashed.

"I felt like the world was going to end," Summer told me of her eighth grade year. "I didn't take school seriously. It was boring, and I stopped caring." As teachers lectured at her and assigned what seemed like busywork, she felt she had no control over her world, neither at home nor at school.

When I visited her ninth grade class in October 2013, though, I saw what a difference a new year—and a new teaching model—had made. Summer and her project partner were busily designing a billboard to read, *If you want to survive, don't text and drive.* She was engaged and excited to make a good product. Other kids in the class, too, seemed far more alive than the glassy-eyed bunch that Breckel had sometimes seen before. As the students worked in small groups, the teachers could circulate the room and assist them one-on-one. That's what Summer says allowed her to bond with them, to feel cared for, and to reconnect with school. "School is way better this year," she said. "It's not all just sitting in the classroom listening to the teacher and doing worksheets. It's you having a voice with your fellow peers."

In early November, all the freshmen presented their work at Trigg's first-ever exhibition night. Parents, community members, and fellow students poured into the high school's halls and classrooms. They watched fourteen-year-olds, dressed in their Sunday best, describe what they'd created and why. The visitors pressed the kids with questions. The kids, bubbling with a mixture of nerves and pride, answered from the expertise they'd gained.

To be fair, the product of Trigg's first foray into a more vibrant kind of learning wasn't perfect. But it was a beginning. The teachers had struggled to let go of their typical direct instruction, ingrained over so many years, and spent too much time trying to deliver to kids everything they'd need to know before they started. Summer and her project partner had nearly come to blows over disagreements about how the product should look and how equitably the work was being shared. Many others had run into trouble just finding enough time in class to work together on such a complex endeavor. In a single semester Trigg hadn't matched the sophisticated work they'd seen at High Tech High, but neither Hamby nor anyone else expected them to.

What they *had* done was given kids a taste of a new kind of school. The experience showed Summer how reliant she and her classmates had previously been on their teachers, and she wanted more. "It's extra work, yes, but it's good work. It makes you want to try harder," she said to me. "I want the teachers to teach more interactively, not just standing in front of the room and telling you that you have to do this and this. I want it to be us coming up with the answers, and I want it to be us finding good and new ideas to put forward."

Learning Is a Process

Stanford University professor and IDEO founder David Kelley says people often ask him if today's college students are creative. At first blush, he responds, you could say they're not. But in reality, "They're wildly creative, just like they were in kindergarten. It's just been blocked. And our job is to figure out how to take those blocks away."

Fortunately, there are many variations on richer, more exploratory kinds of learning going on around the country. In the Reggio Emilia approach, for example, young children lead their own learning, with parents and teachers as collaborators, and cultivate thinking and creativity through art. The Big Picture schools, a network of more than fifty in the United States, provide teens a customized curriculum based on each student's interests and goals and reinforced by real-world internships. And, inspired by innovation hubs like IDEO, a growing number of classrooms are integrating Design Thinking—a collaborative problem solving method where student teams design products and solutions with a real-world user in mind.

Whichever kind of innovation you might try, key principles apply. Wherever I've seen schools improving students' experience, I've found that learning is:

- led by the student, with support, rather than spoon-fed by the teacher

- guided by a teacher who has the autonomy and trust of her supervisors to make critical decisions about each child's education

- personalized to tap the strengths and interests, and to address the needs, of individual students

- geared toward depth of understanding, not breadth of information

- blended across disciplines, allowing for the natural overlapping of science, math, language, history, art, technology, and other subjects

- purposeful and meaningful to students beyond the goal of a mere grade, a kind of purpose that typically derives from a connection to the real world

- strengthened by collaboration: among students, among teachers, between students and teachers, and between schools and the community

- free from the arbitrary confines of traditional school schedules

- equitable for all students, providing an appropriate challenge for each one without segregating (or "tracking") them by ability

One of the key lessons that the Trigg team took from High Tech High—and something that conventional education frequently forgets—is that deep learning is as much about the *process* as it is about the product. Ron Berger, a teacher in rural Massachusetts for forty years and chief academic officer of the nationwide network of inquiry-based Expeditionary Learning schools, explains this aptly.

"When I was in school," Berger says, "we were on a treadmill of turning in final-draft work every day, every assignment. We were given an assignment, we filled it out, we turned it in. We were given an assignment, we filled it out, we turned it in." When the assignments came back, graded, kids typically threw them away. The work didn't mean much. Though Berger attended what were considered to be good public schools, he says, "Nothing I did in the thirteen years I was in school is something that I still own today and would show you as an example of beautiful work."

The work students do at the 160-plus Expeditionary Learning schools (and High Tech High, among others) is quite a contrast. There, the first assignment that a child hands in is only a starting point. The students' work, often conducted over the course of weeks, is to reconsider, revise, solicit feedback, and improve what they've done—much like I do when polishing rough cuts of a film, or editing drafts of this book. The teachers' job is to provide the resources and supports that individual students need and to show them how much more they can actually achieve. Children learn to give one another rigorous, constructive critiques—and to take them. They might make half a dozen drafts or more. The final product, as Berger has seen over and over again, is a work of "extraordinary quality, something of beauty and value for their community and for themselves."

Why go through this laborious process instead of just churning through worksheets? Because it's more meaningful and motivating for everyone, adults included, and because human beings learn so much better this way. Since school is an experience that shapes a child's identity, a process like this can even shape how she learns and works for life. "High-quality work is transformational for kids," Berger says. "When a student does a piece of work that's way better than he or she thought they could do, they're never the same person again. It changes their sense of who they are and what they're capable of." Simply put, it's the growth mindset set in motion.

Psychologists support Berger's observation. "Piaget, the father of child development, was super clear: people learn from their own experience," says Vassar College neuropsychology professor Abigail Baird. "Think about the stuff you know really well. You know it from trial and error, from your own experience, not from being told."

When implemented well, this approach allows all kinds of students to find success. One boy had grown frustrated with the repetitive lessons in elementary and middle school. He felt apathetic. He didn't shine. Then, in ninth grade at High Tech High, he undertook a project on the history of rock music posters. Preparing for his presentation, he researched the history of twentieth-century America, found the connections between the music and the culture, read books, and regaled his family with all he learned. "It was the first time where he did something of that magnitude all by himself, and the outcome was just gorgeous," said his mom. "That is the project he looks back on and says, 'Wow, if I've done this, I can do whatever the next challenge is.' . . . He discovered his capabilities in a way that he hadn't before."

Berger, who works as a carpenter outside of class, offers further examples of what happens when you turn schoolwork into an act of craftsmanship. His own classroom is constructed like a workshop, with movable project tables instead of desks. There, seventh graders once collaborated with a local college laboratory to collect samples and test the town's homes for radon gas. Students prepared surveys, kits, and information packets for residents, learned to use Microsoft Excel to analyze their results, responded to press inquiries, and made a final report to the town government. The state and federal radon commissions ultimately requested copies of the students' report. And in Portland, Maine, Berger recounted to me, King Middle School students studied the civil rights movement by finding local residents who'd been active, but unsung, participants in that history. The children interviewed these people and told their stories in a four-volume book, *Small Acts of Courage*, which they presented at a public ceremony alongside their interviewees.

If the Portland students had been told to study the civil rights movement for a test, some would have done so and some would not. Most wouldn't have remembered many of the details for long. This way, though, Berger noted, "They all studied it deeply because they knew that pretty soon they would be going out and meeting with a person whose story was never told by anyone, and they would be interviewing that person, an unsung hero, and it would be their job as a journalist and an historian to really tell their story in a way that would honor them." As he wrote in his book *An Ethic of Excellence*, "As every teacher knows, you can mandate tests and standards and curricula all you want, but it means nothing if you can't inspire kids to care."

Starting Small

Let me pause for a moment to acknowledge that the prospect of wholesale, whole-school change might look a little daunting to many communities. The Herculean effort and humility required of the change makers in Trigg County is evidence of the challenge. Yet there are many examples of communities that have made an impact with more bite-size (which is not to say *easy*) reforms.

David Ackerman, principal of Oak Knoll Elementary School in Menlo Park (whom we met in chapter 3), has made bold moves to reduce homework. He's also taken some unusual steps to deepen teachers' relationships with their students and provide more personalized attention.

In 2008, having pulled off his homework revolution with relatively few scars, Ackerman decided to try looping—keeping children with the same teacher for more than one year. Without looping, he explains, school ends each spring "and everything you've learned about that kid . . . it doesn't pass easily to the next teacher. The new teacher spends the entire month of September figuring out who the students are as learners and how to approach them. That seems so inefficient." Moreover, when teachers keep the same students for longer, he says, "The accountability for their progress is much deeper."

Ackerman pointed out to me that looping should hardly be considered revolutionary. The practice is at least a hundred years old and is commonly used in Europe. However, he took the change a step further by combining it with two more innovations: multiage classrooms and team teaching. In his new program, children in kindergarten through second grade would share the same classroom, and they'd stay with the same group of peers for all three years. Their kindergarten, first, and second grade teachers would teach the whole group together. This one-room-schoolhouse kind of setting would help students learn at their own pace. An advanced kindergartener could read with second graders, or a struggling first grader could pair up with a younger reader. (Some experts advocate for looping or multiage approaches in middle and high school, too.)

For an administrator like Ackerman, making the change wasn't so complex. He was a seasoned principal with a solid track record, so he simply decided to do it. But he also employed some wise strategies to help his innovation work well. First, he gave teachers a choice, starting his reform only with those who were enthused about it. Second, he presented scientific research to parents and staff showing how looping helps. Third (and most uncommonly), he gave *parents* a choice. They could pick whether their child would be in the multiage, looped class or a traditional class.

When I saw Ackerman several years later, he told me the program had grown so popular that it had twice as many applicants as spots, and the school had to hold a lottery to determine who got in. Plus, Oak Knoll had added a second multiage program for grades three through five. All told, 260 of the school's 760 students were in a multiage, looped group. And Ackerman had instituted regular looping (staying with the same teacher for two years, though not combining multiple ages in one classroom) for the rest of the school in grades four and five. Starting innovations as opt-ins "is a way to get what you want," Ackerman told me. "Give people the choice, and if they're skeptical then prove it to them."

At Monument Mountain Regional High School in Great Barrington, Massachusetts, an innovative solution for student engagement came from the most important (and obvious) source: a student. In his junior year, Sam Levin was growing frustrated with what he saw around him. "I felt my friends weren't engaged, that they weren't learning, that they weren't happy," he recalled. His mom issued him a challenge: to start his own school.

Sam thought about this, and realized he'd seen the same classmates who fell asleep in class and begrudged homework get up at six a.m. on a Saturday to tend to the school's student garden. They earned no grades or extra credit for this work. But students themselves had created the garden, so they cared about it. Sam proposed to school leaders that they bring that level of passion and ownership to the classroom by creating a school-within-a-school led by the students themselves. Principal Marianne Young, who recognized the same problems with traditional methods that Sam did, went for it.

The high school's Independent Project is now in its fifth year. Students who choose to participate spend an entire semester in a class with no periods or bells. Instead of following a prescribed curriculum, students come up with their most burning questions in English, history, science, and math and spend their mornings researching them and presenting their findings to classmates. They discuss, debate, and offer one another critical feedback. A teacher is there to guide, support, and challenge them. In the afternoon, students work on a semester-long project of their own design. One boy composed his own portfolio of musical pieces. A group of students collaboratively filmed and edited an original documentary. A girl who had previously pushed herself to a near breaking point to earn top grades studied photography and produced a book of images illustrating human connection.

Matt Whalan, who was diagnosed with ADHD and had long hated school but loved creative writing, wrote his own short novel. Before the Independent Project, Matt would write for hours every day after class, but "most of that work went unrecognized by anyone at school," he said. Besides giving him the opportunity to apply his passion in school, Matt says the experience helped him focus and taught him to see "what was important to me . . . and the ways in which I can be important in the world."

Some teachers and parents worried at first that the program's unconventional model would harm students' college applications. But so far, participating has only served to distinguish them. Matt, for one, enrolled at Marlboro College with a generous merit scholarship. Since the Independent Project started, schools across the country have approached Principal Young for guidance in creating their own.

Successes and Setbacks at Trigg

I keep going back to Cadiz, though, because I feel so compelled by the courage of their efforts—the sweeping scale of the change they're seeking and the persistence they're applying to it, despite obstacles. Change takes time. As Trigg expands its reforms, piece by piece—it extended projects to more grade levels and added performance assessments in its second year—it continues to straddle two systems. The educators are pursuing inquiry-based learning on the one hand, while still having to serve the master of standardized testing on the other hand. Teachers don't yet have the time built into the day for the collaboration and planning that complex projects require. And the state, like many others, still credits the school based on the old metric of "seat time" (literally the number of hours students have spent in each subject, not what they've learned). Trigg could choose to switch to a competency-based credit system, but then it would lose funding for every student who fails the competency assessment.

Still, Trigg soldiers on. By year two, in the fall of 2014, the tenth graders were now doing project-based learning, too, working on a cross-disciplinary assignment to solve a water-quality problem at Land Between the Lakes, a forested National Recreation Area straddling the Kentucky-Tennessee border nearby. The students had visited the park, where each small group had chosen its own problem to tackle: some investigated how to combat invasive mussel or lotus species, others how to tame algal blooms from agricultural runoff.

This was a much meatier, more effective project than the year before, where the effort looked at times like an arts and crafts exercise, with final products that didn't reflect all the research students had done. One exceptional group of three students, Autumn, Kaylin, and Brayden, had decided to address beaver dams that were flooding a road in the park, where cars contaminated the water that then flowed back into the watershed from which residents drink. "We visited there and we saw that this was a huge problem, and so we immediately said, 'How are we going to fix this?'" explained Autumn, her round face framed by brown hair spooled into a wide bun. The three teens described, with obvious depth of knowledge, how they'd interviewed park staff about previous failed solutions, tested water samples for contaminants, and considered local laws. They'd divided the labor according to each kid's strengths: Autumn writing, Kaylin designing, Brayden building. Their solution: beaver pipes, the ends covered with metal mesh to prevent beavers climbing in, set up to drain water quickly from the road back into the waterways. The group said Land Between the Lakes staff liked their idea and might implement it.

That was the high point of my visit. Low points were in evidence, too. It felt a bit scary, as a parent, to see the semichaos of students who weren't yet used to this method working on their own with only occasional guidance. I could tell that teachers hadn't yet mastered how to guide kids through the iteration process that Ron Berger described. And understandably so: Breckel still had to handle a caseload of nearly 150 students at a time, compared to the High Tech High teaching teams' fifty. Consequently, the teachers themselves were unsatisfied with the quality of some kids' creations. Breckel said, "I had one student say to me, 'Ms. Breckel, this is the most work I've ever done in my whole life, and you're still telling me I need to do more.'"

Summer, for her part, was taking two math classes, playing clarinet a dozen or more hours a week in the marching band, and trying to earn the straight As she felt she'd need for a college scholarship. She said Fusion class this year was "way better" than the year before. They were getting the hang of it. Outside of Fusion, however, most of her classes remained the same as ever.

Hamby would be the first to admit that Trigg still has a long way to go. "We might have a failure or two or three or four in our experiences in implementing this change, but we're going to pick up the pieces," he said. "We're going to figure it out, regroup, and go back to the drawing board, and we're going to implement again."

He, Breckel, and others had visited High Tech High again that fall to get more help (pursuing their own process of iteration and improvement). As Hamby ambled in and out of classrooms there, he exclaimed in frustration about how the trappings of tradition—especially school schedules and physical spaces—constrain innovation. He'd like to literally move walls in Trigg County, to carve out a "makerspace" for group project work in the library. And he's doing it—but it took him eighteen months and an expensive engineering contract to finally get the approval. He's also trying to convince his high school site council to obliterate the traditional bell schedule, which keeps students cycling from one isolated subject area to another (English happens over here, science over there). "Just throw it out the freakin' window," he exclaimed while exiting one High Tech classroom. "I mean, there's no reason." His ideal schedule would give half the freshman class over to four teachers (English, science, social studies, math) and let the teaching team use the day as they see fit. In other words, he would trust teachers— which our educational bureaucracy rarely does.

The Trigg team toured High Tech's elementary school, as well. Inquiry-based learning can fit fairly naturally into the early grades, with simpler projects tailored to children's ages (Montessori and Waldorf methods are, after all, based on inquiry). Honestly, what we saw there didn't look as dramatically different from a regular school as the high school does. The teachers at High Tech Elementary still spend the mornings on direct instruction in reading and math, then turn to projects in the afternoons. But the work was of excellent quality, and the kids weren't afraid to describe their learning.

The day we visited, students in a fourth grade class had just received copies of a book of adventure stories that they wrote. They'd researched their stories by rock climbing, kayaking on a local bay, and hiking up a nearby mountain, while holding bake sales and other fund-raisers to cover the cost. They planned to sell the books at the next exhibition night and donate the proceeds to charity. Hamby asked the children how they felt when they saw their books. "I was yelling," said Andreas, a small boy in a backward cap, excitedly. "And I felt so happy. Like: I'm an author!" Meanwhile, in a nearby room, fifth graders were using Chromebooks to write proposals for the robots they would create.

For all their dazzle, the High Tech schools also have their imperfections. A handful of students each year find that the student-driven format doesn't work well for them, and they leave. Some parents of conventionally "successful" students worry that the hands-on work at High Tech High will derail their kids from the traditional track to college. Yet one mom, an engineer, expressed great gratitude that both her creative, unconventional son and her book-smart daughter got to go there. All schools talk about putting individual children's needs at the center of their work, she said, but this one actually does it. "They are learning to work in a group environment, which is very important," she observed. As in the real world of work, "They're learning to plan, they're learning to scope, and I think they're learning more from their mistakes than they're learning from their successes. . . . It's pretty awesome when a kid at ninth grade experiences this."

Pick Your Metric

Foremost in Hamby's mind that day at High Tech High was one big worry: test scores. His district's scores on state tests (which are not given to ninth graders, one of the classes piloting project-based learning) had dropped slightly the first year of the change. Hamby had a firm faith that deepening students' engagement and understanding through meaningful projects would ultimately translate into better test scores. But he worried his teachers might defect if the marks didn't go back up. "They fear that somebody's going to take out a big stick and beat them over the head if they take this risk," he said. Besides, he told me, the school board has been supportive so far, "but after this year I have three years left on my contract, and then it's one election away for me." If Hamby goes, so, too, could the momentum for change. All the more reason to make a whole set of students and teachers, not only the superintendent, the leaders.

Larry Rosenstock, the High Tech High CEO, answered Hamby's concern by arguing that just because you can measure a thing doesn't mean that it's what matters. He urged the Trigg team to pick a metric that they *do* believe matters and stick with it. "We pretty much ignore standardized tests, and we get away with it because our four-year college graduation rates, for the population we have, are very high," Rosenstock said. "So I urge people who want cover to pick your metric. Don't assume the metric they gave you is the right metric." (High Tech High also gets away with it, it should be noted, because its students test in the 80th percentile statewide, which is pretty good for a school that does no test prep.)

Rosenstock's argument might be harder to sell in Cadiz, where the accomplishments in San Diego are half a continent away. So Hamby hoped, at least, that the exhibition nights would demonstrate what sophisticated skills this effort is all for. "Come in and see," he pronounced. "The scores might not show it yet, but look at what our kids can do."

By the second year of Trigg's transformation, the exhibition nights had indeed come closer to convincing one skeptic: Trigg County High's own PE and health teacher, James Shelton. A towering man in a blue Fellowship of Christian Anglers Society sweatshirt, he told me he worried about whether the students were really learning all the required content in the midst of the projects. Shelton had skin in the game. His daughter was one of the sharply dressed students lined up along the hallways beside their posters and dioramas, ready to explain their work. Fewer than ten freshmen were absent that night—a level of attendance matched only by athletic events.

Despite his concerns, though, Shelton indicated that he wouldn't ask his school to turn back. "I saw [students] presenting in front of a group, public speaking, research, standing up for your position, and then trying to explain it," he said. And he expects those skills to bolster them in college and beyond.

I have deep admiration for the brave change the Trigg team is undertaking, flaws and all. Shelton had said, "We're going to get there, I have no doubt," and I fervently hoped that he was right—that they would ultimately arrive at the kind of transformation they were aiming for, despite the hurdles.

If we are going to grow more schools as creative as High Tech High, as engaging as the Expeditionary Learning schools, and as courageous as Trigg, the change will happen at the local level. We needn't (and shouldn't) wait for shortsighted politicians in Washington or misguided college admissions gatekeepers to recognize that they're leading a generation of youth in the wrong direction. Starting now, we can begin to change children's everyday experience in school. Teachers can experiment with inquiry-based projects and invite students to pursue their own questions, gauging their learning through the quality of their work. "You are, for [your] students, the education system," says Ken Robinson. "And if you change your practice, you have changed the education system for your students."

Parents can inform educators about alternate models, advocate for local change, and support schools that are willing to do it. Principals and superintendents can create the conditions that facilitate deeper learning: assessments that support diverse, hands-on lessons; schedules that allow time for teachers and students to collaborate; a culture of experimentation that gives teachers freedom to innovate and students the space to make mistakes; and flexibility in the way the school day runs and the classrooms are arranged.

Students, too, can make an impact by speaking up for what they want and how they learn best. Everyone has the power to help tear down some (literal and figurative) walls.

As I left Trigg and turned south toward Nashville, the nagging question on my mind was the same one Tony Wagner, the high school teacher turned Harvard professor, had put to me when we met. We were discussing the ways that education can (and can't) cultivate young innovators. "The best and brightest of this generation are succeeding in spite of, not because of, their schooling," Wagner said. "We should not leave the future success of our kids and our schools up to what I would call random acts of excellence. We need to create a system that is about intellectual and moral excellence, a system that is humane and vibrant and exciting. And we know how to do that. The question is, *will* we do that?"

CHAPTER 7

First, Be Well

ZOOM OUT.

We've seen that fixing the runaway stressors that are sickening our kids is essential. It's imperative that we revolutionize our approach to homework and testing, reimagine success, and reclaim our families' frayed time. We must invent new school policies and practices, local and national, that encourage risk and innovation. And we must collectively decide, as stakeholders in our school communities, to meet children where they are, instead of prodding them continually toward a prescribed credential. As the preceding chapters have illustrated, all of these changes—attacked singly *and* taken together—are crucial to safeguarding our children's health and fostering true learning.

Which brings us to one final, important piece of our work: the deliberate promotion of children's total well-being—extending beyond the realm of academics—above all. Just as the new vision for great schools casts them as hubs of deep and personal learning, it must also frame them as centers for fostering lifelong wellness. Unless we place that priority first, all of the practical and policy changes will not be quite enough. Nor is simply ensuring our children's basic health a sufficiently high bar. Beyond healthy, we need to strive toward happy. Stable. Self-possessed. Equipped to embrace meaningful challenges, forge strong relationships, tap inner resources, and make good decisions. These are the hallmarks of true success: the qualities that will empower young people to become thriving students and, later, thriving adults, and that will enable them to flourish in any realm they enter, long after they have left our care. And these are the skills cultivated by schools, families, and communities that support the whole child—social, emotional, physical, spiritual, and cognitive—and not just the one-dimensional student.

This is, in the end, what this entire book is about: rising to the challenge of raising and teaching children to become whole people, ready to genuinely thrive. This essential aim calls on schools and communities not only to immediately address the issues we've examined in this book but also to proactively place children's well-being at the center of every decision they make. The cultivation of resilient hearts and bodies must be as much a part of our core mission as cultivating lively minds. This is an especially profound responsibility when we consider the tremendous physical and emotional growth that takes place during childhood and adolescence, which sets the stage for a child's whole life. When we truly put wellness first, the question "How will this affect students' well-being?" becomes inseparable from the question "How will this affect students' learning?"

The task is considerable. Many times, as both a parent and filmmaker, I've found that wellness ranks last among considerations in school. Historically, the demands of athletic leagues, bus companies, testing regimes, teachers unions, and traditions—calcified by our fear of questioning the status quo—have come before the goal of nurturing happy, healthy students. Health, as a discipline, is merely a one-semester high school class. Balance is absent from the syllabus entirely. Wellness is too often addressed only when something goes wrong.

"It's very strange not having any acknowledgment that we're human beings in this," says Erin, a California high schooler who stayed home nearly her entire freshman year with severe depression. Erin remembers ruefully how, even as her family and friends supported her, the school made recovery hard. There was no letup on the amount of work sent home to her, despite her fragile state. A biology teacher flunked her on several assignments because she couldn't attend labs. When Erin finally felt ready to return to school, she was forced, despite doctors' notes, to take an anxiety-provoking test to prove that she needed accommodations (extra time, a calm space in the library) to, of all things, take tests. In the contest between Erin's well-being and the inflexible demands of that system, the system won.

And yet the value of structuring schools to support holistic well-being is obvious to most of us. The skeptic will insist that schools' focus should be academic alone, or that all nonacademic skills are "soft." But most of us know implicitly that wellness is no fluffy frivolity; it is a necessary ingredient for other good things. Our children can do their best only when they are physically and emotionally well.

Science backs up our instincts. Studies have found that the brain actually works better when it's in a good mood. In a positive state of mind, doctors make more accurate diagnoses. Happy job candidates are more likely to get a second interview. Optimistic businesspeople make more sales. And students who were told to think about the happiest day of their lives before taking a math test scored higher than their peers. Shawn Achor, a researcher and author, calls this the "happiness advantage." In his much-watched TED Talk, he explains, "Your brain at positive performs slightly better than at negative, neutral, or stressed. Your intelligence rises, your creativity rises, your energy levels rise. In fact, we've found that every single business outcome improves."

So, too, do outcomes in other realms of life, such as friendship, marriage, and health. One study, published in *Psychological Bulletin* in 2005, synthesized more than two hundred scientific papers on the link between happiness and success. The authors' conclusion: that positive emotions don't simply happen in concert with successful life outcomes—they come before. They wrote: "Study after study shows that happiness precedes important outcomes and indicators of thriving, including fulfilling and productive work, satisfying relationships, and superior mental and physical health and longevity."

I find it telling that the best businesses are already figuring this out. Silicon Valley firms routinely offer mindfulness lessons. A new management book by international business leader Margaret Heffernan touts the great benefits of learning to listen, of avoiding mind-numbing overtime, and of treating employees humanely, letting them leave the office and take a walk. The data analytics firm SAS Institute even caps its employees' workweek at thirty-five hours. And as we learned in chapter 3, years of research on human expertise shows that people who excel in all kinds of fields typically devote themselves to highly focused work no more than about four and a half hours a day. For health, productivity, and creativity alike, less is more. It's striking that billion-dollar corporations, the very destinations some hope their kids can reach someday, have recognized this before our education system has.

Our kids' miserable state is not some inevitable modern norm. UNICEF, in a 2013 report, ranked the United States twenty-fifth out of twenty-nine affluent countries on overall child well-being. Poverty and income inequality account for some of this dismal record, but not all. American adolescents rated their own life satisfaction lower than their peers did in two-thirds of the other countries. And the United States came in second to worst on children's ratings of their own relationships; kids in most of the other countries were more likely to say that their classmates were helpful and kind, and that their parents were easy to talk to. I'm reminded of the many times students at film screenings have said they can't turn to one another for support because they are in competition.

The moral is not that we should spare our children from the least discomfort or displeasure—that's unrealistic and unhelpful. It's that we must provide them with the environment, in school and at home, that will teach them to find satisfaction in their everyday lives. In place of exaggerated demands out of step with children's natural development, we must provide the support and learning experiences that give kids the skills to cope with life's challenges and to reset their moods to positive once the trouble is gone.

An entire field of research and educational practice has arisen around the cultivation of resilience. What makes one child bounce back from disappointments and setbacks while another child crumbles? Researchers have found that, even in the most terrible circumstances, beset by poverty and neglect and violence, at least 50 percent of children rebound and succeed. Children with the capacity to tap into their resilience possess certain essential strengths—empathy, communication skills, problem-solving skills, confidence in their ability to affect their own circumstances, and a sense of identity and purpose. They are typically flexible, optimistic, self-regulated, and internally motivated. The potential to embody these strengths lives within all of us.

"The question of whether we believe an individual possesses the capacity for resilience is no longer appropriate," says Sara Truebridge, author of *Resilience Begins with Beliefs: Building on Student Strengths for Success in School*. "Everyone has the capacity for resilience. The appropriate question is whether it has been tapped—and if not, what can we do to tap it?"

That challenge is ours. Research has clearly established that a child's capacity to access her resilience often hinges on three main supports from the adults around her, Truebridge notes: caring relationships; opportunities to contribute and participate; and high expectations that are not about the end product but rather about the qualities that sustain learning and growth, such as effort. Ed Hallowell, psychiatrist and author of *The Childhood Roots of Adult Happiness*, explains: "If parents and schools would promote these qualities"—such as optimism, self-esteem, a feeling of control over one's life—"with the verve and ingenuity they promote getting good grades, the emotional health of children (and the adults they become) would skyrocket."

A Strategy from Saint Louis

So how do we do that? How do we, in the midst of the competitive firestorm that childhood has become, cultivate in kids a sense of joy and worthiness and the capacity to cope with hardship?

These were among the questions troubling Stuart Slavin when he witnessed the simultaneous undoing of two groups of people he cared about deeply: his medical students at Saint Louis University and his own two teenage daughters. Slavin is the pediatrician and medical professor who emailed me after seeing my first film. He has become one of Jay Jackson's close collaborators in the campaign for wellness at Irvington High. But before I introduced him to Jackson, Slavin had already carried out his own quest to restore young people's well-being.

About eight years ago, he saw some articles on medical students' poor mental health. "I really was struck by how awful the statistics were," he recalls. "It was not just one study. It was multiple studies that showed a serious problem." Yet all his students at SLU appeared to be happy, so he thought perhaps his school didn't have the same problem. Or were they just good at hiding it? To make sure, he anonymously surveyed students. "The results were just as bad as everyone else's," he says. "We had very high levels of depression, very high levels of anxiety." So Slavin did the right thing, the thing we all must do when facing the reality of our students' distress; he put health first. He said to himself and to his colleagues: "This can't be. We can't allow this to stand."

Like a good scientist, Slavin went back to the medical literature to see what solutions had been tried. "And again I was kind of shocked by how little had been done," he recalls. So he and his colleagues at SLU, a Jesuit school, undertook their own kind of mission. Their first action was improving students' access to mental health care, which is critical. Then they launched a variety of wellness initiatives, including team-building activities and optional seminars on how to eat, sleep, and exercise well—which "was nice but didn't seem to fundamentally address the issue," Slavin observes. The meat of their work came next. SLU took twin approaches: one, change the academic environment to reduce stress, and two, build students' capacity to cope (because, as Slavin says, we can't control their environment forever).

To reduce the fuel for unnecessary stress, SLU gave students a half-day off every other Wednesday and converted preclinical classes for students in their first two years to pass/fail grading. The school strengthened its social fabric by creating student-led learning communities that convene students with common interests and plan activities. These learning communities, in turn, sponsored new electives that would bring students a deeper sense of meaning, on subjects such as violence prevention, global women's health, music therapy, and the intersection of spirituality and medicine. And, in the second year of the effort, the school began requiring a course of resilience training.

"The results have been unbelievable," Slavin says. Depression rates among first-year medical students, which hit 27 percent when Slavin first measured them in 2009, have plunged to 8 percent. The portion of students suffering from anxiety plummeted from 55 percent to 23 percent during the same time. Simultaneously, students reported that they felt more connected to each other. And their scores on early medical boards exams improved. (After seeing those statistics, can you doubt that schools exert powerful influence over students' mental health?) "The cost is virtually nonexistent, and academic performance has gone up," says Slavin, rather amazed himself by the results. "So you kind of go, 'Oh my God, why isn't anybody doing this?'"

We might go further and ask: If a medical school can do this, why can't our high schools and middle schools?

Slavin wondered the same thing. As his daughters entered middle school and then high school, their homework loads became ever more absurd. His older daughter began showing signs of anxiety and distress, breaking down crying, staying up until midnight finishing assignments when she was already exhausted. The stress spilled over onto the whole family, as Slavin, his wife, and both girls became edgy and short-tempered with one another and could no longer find time to do fun activities as a family. "Ninth grade," he recalls, "felt like just a complete breakdown of our family's structure." As a pediatrician and educator, he could clearly see the harm being done to his daughter's mental health and well-being.

So Slavin, who sat on the board of his older daughter's high school, gave his fellow board members a detailed presentation showing all the relevant research on teen health, the limited effectiveness of homework, and more. He got nowhere. He kept pressing, but the board made no movement toward meaningful change. As is so often the shameful case, all kinds of other concerns came before health. Finally, exasperated, Slavin pulled his daughter out of that school. "It was really frustrating," he remembers. "This is my work. I'm a pediatrician. I know more about child development than 99 percent of the people in the country, and that's not because I'm smart, that's because I've studied it. And I have this mountain of evidence. But ultimately I couldn't get the evidence to win."

Slavin is hoping to have better luck at Irvington, where he has a devoted ally in the main office. And his successful strategy at SLU provides a kind of blueprint for other schools working to improve students' mental health. His lessons for reformers are fairly simple: prioritize wellness by (a) resetting policies and practices, both academic and extracurricular, to relieve excessive stress, (b) directly caring for students' mental and physical health, and (c) teaching them how to care for themselves. These primary actions, in turn, promote a general *culture of wellness*: a shared belief among educators, students, and parents that health and balance are the first priority and are a prerequisite to true success and learning.

Tackling part (a)—the tweaking or even overhauling of polices—entails everything this book has addressed so far. This is the work of taming runaway homework and testing, defusing college admissions anxiety, and reclaiming the shared definition of what makes a person a success. A key aspect of part (b)—the direct care of children's well-being—is ensuring that our schools have enough counselors to give adequate individual attention to the students who need it. In Slavin's case, this was SLU's first priority. Irvington High, as well, expanded its counseling staff in fall 2014 through a partnership with the local youth and family services department. The new counselor devoted all her time to ninth graders who were struggling in their classes, meeting with families, providing extra supports, and trying to help them stabilize before sophomore year. This was an improvement over most American high schools, where the average ratio of students to guidance counselors is nearly 500 to 1, and where those counselors are disproportionately occupied with college applications rather than genuine psychological care.

Another essential element of part (b) is, of course, physical. A slew of scientific studies establish the importance of exercise for physical and mental health and optimal brain functioning. That's why the wisest schools are making time for it during the school day. A high school in Naperville, Illinois, bucked the trend to cut back on every subject that's not tested and made PE a daily requirement. Naperville Central High even arranged for struggling students to have PE immediately before their most challenging classes. And it helped: students showed dramatic improvements in those subjects. Bishop O'Dowd High School in Oakland created space during lunch for games like Ping-Pong and Frisbee, to promote play and socializing rather than working through lunch. And at the college level, Berklee College of Music professor Kathleen Howland, who teaches neuroscience and music therapy, pauses in the middle of her classes for a dance break. Howland turns on music, and she and her students dance and laugh, "which allows us to decompress from the curriculum and oxygenate," she says. The exercise also contains a lesson: afterward, Howland prompts her students to reflect on how the dancing affects their attention, mental processing, and energy, and how that compares to drinking coffee or eating a candy bar.

The Power of Connection

It's important to recognize one critical part of caring for children's wellness that requires no new staff or special programs and costs next to nothing. The approach is simply to create more opportunities for kids to forge deep personal *connections*—with adults at school, with other adults in the community, and with one another. (This is what Slavin achieved with his medical school learning communities.) Research demonstrates that connections are critical both at home and at school. In fact, studies have shown that strong relationships with caring adults are among the most powerful forces for building resilience in children. One study in New Zealand monitored a thousand residents over more than thirty years and revealed that social connectedness in adolescence was more closely linked with adult well-being than was getting great test scores and doing well in school.

"In resilience research, the biggest predictor of doing well in the face of adversity or pressure is good relationships, love, feeling connected, feeling warm support," says Suniya Luthar, the Arizona State University psychologist. "Teachers are very often cited by youth as the people who saw them through very difficult times. . . . If [you do] not feel that kind of acceptance and love, you can be the person with the most perseverance and grit and toughness, eventually we all crumble."

That kind of connection doesn't necessarily happen on its own. It's not sufficient for schools simply to leave teachers and students to their own devices and expect that they'll forge the bonds they need. The school day is busy. Teachers in high schools with traditional schedules might see 150 students in a day. In order to truly serve children, schools must make connectedness a part of their core educational practice.

Nadia Lopez, the Brooklyn principal who became suddenly famous when the Humans of New York blog featured her appreciative student, fosters connection through sheer force of energy. When I spoke with her to learn more about her approach, it was spring break, yet she was nonetheless in her office with a student who had asked for help with his studies. Her school serves middle schoolers in gritty Brownsville, a poor neighborhood rife with drugs and despair. Lopez's whatever-it-takes approach derives in part from her training as a nurse, where she learned to look at a patient's entire wellness picture instead of just diagnosing a narrow problem. Then, as a young teacher dealing with distressed, distracted children, she told me, "I found that the most powerful thing I could do was just sit and talk to kids, and once I knew about them, management wasn't an issue, because they knew I cared about them."

So Lopez, a Brooklyn native herself, arrives at Mott Hall Bridges Academy at six a.m. and stays until evening. She observes classrooms daily, and deeply reads the file for every one of her two hundred students. It's crucial to her that school be a place where each child feels seen for her unique gifts, not branded by shortcomings. So, if a child voices an interest in a particular sport or field of study, she tries to create opportunities for him to pursue it. Outside of class, Lopez calls parents and visits their homes when she has concerns about a student. "I'm just relentless," she said. When Lopez asks parents and students what's different about this school, she added, "Ninety-nine percent of the time it's: 'Someone cares about me here.'"

Lopez's superhuman dedication creates the conditions that can give rise to resiliency. It is admirable, amazing, and, in her view, necessary to serving students who face so many obstacles in the rest of their lives. It is also hard to replicate Lopez's energy. She's an outlier. Yet the fundamental values that underlie her approach apply everywhere. It takes only one relationship to make a difference for a child, and it's incumbent on all of us, educators and parents alike, to help put in place the structures that support that. Any adult at school can create a culture of care.

Educators do, however, need the opportunity to foster connection with kids within the hours of a normal school day, and I see more and more schools making this possible. Block scheduling, for example, which gives teachers and students more flexible time for one-on-one interactions, can help. So can smaller class sizes. Also beneficial is team teaching, where pairs of teachers share all the same students, or looping, where students stay with the same teacher for multiple years. Creating small schools within schools can be another effective way to strengthen community.

"What resilience research offers advocates," writes Bonnie Benard, author of *Resiliency: What We Have Learned*, "is well-documented support for an educational approach based on meeting young people's basic needs—for belonging and affiliation, a sense of competence and meaning, feelings of autonomy, and safety."

Of course, the adults working in schools need the same things, too. So collaborative approaches such as team teaching are effective not only because they build bridges between students and their teachers, but also because they create a network of relationships that support *everyone* in school—including teachers and staff. Schools do well by widening the ecosystem of connection still further to include parents and neighbors. Maryland's Gaithersburg Elementary, for instance, has done this by inviting local residents in to use school computers and take adult classes, and by hosting evening events where families share meals and learn educational games. The national movement for community schools promotes this, casting schools as community centers where local kids and adults alike can find resources and opportunities on weekdays, evenings, and weekends.

The net result is a good kind of climate change—a school that becomes less like an assembly line and more like a community, where children and adults alike feel known and supported and thus able to thrive. Parents, in addition to benefiting from this kind of connectedness, can encourage it. Beyond advocating for new policies, I've urged my own kids to seek out one teacher or counselor whom they trust so they have someone to turn to with concerns at school. I've tried to build a little village of caring friends and mentors around our family, knowing that my children may sometimes need support from people besides me. Now I see Jamey building her own community and making a point of getting to know her professors in college, perhaps helped by that early experience.

A world away from Brownsville, in Palo Alto, dad and newly minted school board member Ken Dauber is trying another promising tactic to build connection. The cries for reform in his affluent community are poignant. Three local students killed themselves in the 2014–15 school year by stepping in front of commuter trains. A Palo Alto High School junior, Carolyn Walworth, wrote in March 2015 in a local paper that she and her peers are "gasping for air." Revealing that she has missed menstrual periods, had silent panic attacks in the middle of class, and landed in urgent care due to stress-induced pain, Carolyn went on: "We are not teenagers. We are lifeless bodies in a system that breeds competition, hatred, and discourages teamwork and genuine learning. We lack sincere passion. We are sick."

I heard about Dauber because of the grassroots group he started in 2011, as the community reeled from an earlier string of teen suicides. His organization, called We Can Do Better Palo Alto, champions students' mental health and proclaims to any potential skeptics: "We reject the false choice between lowering stress and high achievement. We believe that lower stress and achievement go hand in hand." For Dauber, a sociology professor turned Google software engineer, this work is a matter of principle. It is also personal; his oldest daughter, the firstborn of his five children, suffered from mental illness and took her own life at age twenty-six.

Relentless in his own way, Dauber has ruffled feathers. He used public records laws to access internal school documents and refused to take no for an answer on his reforms. He lost his first bid for a seat on the school board in 2012, then won his second run in 2014 with the endorsement of the *Palo Alto Daily News*, which wrote that he "has forced the district to take a closer look at itself." Dauber advocates loudly for reduced homework, and also wants to see the schools change their schedules, complete finals before winter break, provide lessons in social and emotional skills, and more closely align the standard curriculum to individual students' needs.

His biggest push, though, is for an advisory program. The idea couldn't be simpler: the school sets aside one period a week (or more) for a small group of students to meet with a teacher or other staff member to discuss issues of importance, academic or otherwise. Over time, the advisory group becomes a little community, where students feel known by the teacher and supported by one another. "It's a way for kids to have a connection to an adult at school," says Dauber. "Teachers are probably the most valuable connection kids can have."

I've seen advisories work beautifully at San Diego's High Tech High, where each teacher-adviser sticks with the same students for all four years. Advisers there make home visits to get to know families well. Each advisory group includes students in all grade levels so that younger teens can watch the older ones weather important milestones and learn from their experiences. The impact is powerful. I saw one High Tech High student turn to her adviser for help improving a relationship with a core teacher, and another receive great support from her adviser after the loss of a family member.

In Palo Alto, Dauber backs up his argument for advisories with evidence from student surveys at the district's two high schools, Palo Alto High (a.k.a. Paly) and Gunn. Their ratings of school counseling services differ widely. In the 2012 survey, 88 percent of students at Paly said at least one adult at school could support them if they were struggling academically, while only 57 percent said that at Gunn. And 84 percent at Paly said they'd have a supporter if they were struggling emotionally, compared to just 43 percent at Gunn. To what does Dauber attribute the disparity? To the fact that Paly has an advisory program and Gunn does not.

Of course, the success of advisories is all in the execution. They miss the mark when used for impersonal school logistics or tab keeping, becoming just another forum for herding kids along the academic track rather than an outlet for emotional support. The program must be about authentic personal connection, and teacher-advisers need solid training to respond to serious issues that may arise.

Dauber's demands for change, which ran aground on institutional inertia for years, may stand a better chance of succeeding after this second wave of tragedies. Gunn High's new principal, Denise Herrmann, is a transplant from a Wisconsin high school where she took steps to relieve excessive pressure. She is enthusiastic about advisories, observing that "students say the teachers they feel most connected to are their band teachers or their football coach, someone who they're with for four years who has really seen them grow and change." Advisories could be part of a package of reforms she's developing.

Meanwhile, Herrmann is working immediately to rein in extreme homework loads as another means of caring for students. She's also pressing for a simple little thing that's anathema to public education: flexibility. "The idea of not having four or five tests to study for the next day, the idea that they can postpone a test so when they do feel stressed there are releases that they know will be there for them," Herrmann explains. "That's the thing that students are asking for as the most immediate relief." Some teachers, schooled to think that requiring every student to turn in the same assignment on the same day is "fair," are finding it hard to shake that tradition. So Herrmann says she's working with them, sharing relevant research, and letting them know that it's okay to make time flexible because, after all, "We're after learning."

An Ounce of Prevention

As to the final aspect of Slavin's strategy—teaching students how to care for themselves—I can already hear the chorus of critics clamoring that emotions are the domain of the family and schools should keep out. Or that the responsibility for teaching greater well-being resides with physicians and counselors, not educators. Which would be fine if learning happened in a vacuum, hermetically sealed off from children's inner and outer lives. But that is not reality. "Schools have no choice but to teach character," observes educator and author Ron Berger. "Because the very experience of school imbues character in students. You either do it poorly by paying no attention to it and instilling poor character values in kids, or you do it thoughtfully and make sure that your school is making kids more respectful, more thoughtful, more kind, more studious, more courageous."

Besides, we parents need schools' support in this critical piece of child development. In our family, I strive to teach emotional and physical health, offering my kids vocabulary to talk about their feelings. I pointed out early to Zak how cheerful he was after exercising outside, yet how grouchy he got from playing video games, and he ultimately chose to avoid them. I make sleep, family dinners, and time outdoors a top priority. We take walks together, and we unplug from devices as a family at meals and certain times on the weekend. It *is* my job, as a parent, to take these kinds of proactive steps. Still, Zak still spends seven or eight hours a day at school—and more if you count band, tutoring, and other activities. Many of his life lessons occur there.

What's more, there are explicit kinds of instruction that we will examine below that can help children build the skills for happiness, wholeness, and resilience, and schools should play a role in teaching them. Before I did the research, I might not have believed that emotional intelligence can be taught—coaching kids to manage their own emotions, take setbacks in stride, and relate in healthy ways to themselves and each other—but it's true. And these emotional and social skills, once imbued, stay with kids as they grow.

Important caveat! These lessons are valuable, but they can never, ever be an excuse to avoid systemic change. Just like a business defeats its own wellness efforts if it still expects employees to clock eighty-hour workweeks, we'd be doublespeaking to say, "Our kids are breaking under the weight of our impossible demands, but they've got relaxation classes, so they'll be okay!" Equipping kids for resilience is good medicine, but we must still cure the societal sickness that ails them.

With that caution in mind, I'll describe three well-established educational practices (among many) for teaching children how to maintain healthy minds, hearts, and bodies. These work best when they're not simply an add-on—a separate program delivered in forty-minute chunks once a week—but a reflection of the way we teach children every day, putting our humanity first, whether in class, on the athletic field, in band rehearsal, or at home.

Social and emotional learning is, in essence, a set of tools and strategies for managing the self. It equips children with the skills to be good friends and collaborators, committed learners, and stable individuals—skills including self-awareness, self-regulation, empathy, communication, and thoughtful decision-making. As SEL expert Janice Toben explains, "It allows students to solve their own problems," to weather mistakes, to accept and support one another, and to manage their own moments of boredom or disappointment. "The social and emotional skills are not fluff. They're not touchy and feely; they actually create an environment so that real academic learning can happen."

At the WINGS after-school SEL program in low-income North Charleston, South Carolina, teachers weave social and emotional skills instruction into crafts, games, and homework help, five days a week. The strategies they've studied then become an integral part of teachers' discipline methods when skirmishes break out. "You're worrying about his choices when you need to be worried about your choices," they remind kids who get upset about others' behavior. "Make the choice that's best for you." These sorts of easy-to-remember sayings, echoed and enacted day after day, eventually embed themselves in students' own social and emotional tool kit.

Toben, who ran the SEL program at the Nueva School south of San Francisco for twenty-seven years, explained to me how the lessons typically evolve as children move through the grades. They'll start in the early grades by teaching children a vocabulary for emotion: this is *sad*, this is *frustrated*, this is *lonely*. Next, as children become more adept at noticing their shifting emotions, they start to learn assertive communication strategies and problem solving. By fifth grade, they're studying how conflicts escalate and how to prevent escalation. "Students tell me all the time they go home and say to their parents, 'Hey, that's escalating,'" Toben says. In fact, parents, staff, and other adults at school are very much a part of this approach. By sharing the principles of SEL with all, it becomes not just a program, but a set of values shared by a whole school community, reinforced in every arena.

Finally, in middle school and higher, kids begin to examine their own ways of interpreting setbacks and talking to themselves. Negative thinking patterns (e.g., "I failed the math test because I'm stupid, and I'll always be stupid") are powerfully linked with depression, while positive thinking patterns (e.g., "I failed the math test because I misunderstood some things, but I can learn") protect against it. Armed with these skills as they enter the cauldron of adolescence, Toben says, "They're better off at being an individual, at holding a boundary, at pushing aside groupthink and pressure."

The earliest SEL programs emerged from Yale University in the 1960s. Now SEL is practiced in thousands of schools around the United States and included in nearly a dozen states' education standards. Some entire city districts, including Austin and Nashville, are integrating SEL into their K-12 approach. A landmark 2011 study gauged the results of more than two hundred in-school SEL programs serving hundreds of thousands of students. It found that, compared to peers who got no SEL, students in these programs showed significantly better behavior, better social and emotional skills, and a substantial bump in academic test scores. Another study looking at dozens of *after-school* SEL programs found similar benefits. The WINGS after-school program, for one, has a real impact during the school day. Despite the destabilizing effects of poverty and crime in many WINGS children's lives, after two years in the program students demonstrate significantly better school attendance and higher test scores and grades. Doesn't it stand to reason that kids who feel socially happier and steadier within themselves are more able to take advantage of their studies?

For communities looking to adopt SEL, the Collaborative for Academic, Social, and Emotional Learning (CASEL) in Chicago is the online hub for resources and guides to proven programs.

Positive psychology is an entire field of science as well as an educational method. Its mastermind, University of Pennsylvania professor Martin Seligman, spent decades studying depression and helplessness before arriving at a dramatic turnabout in his thinking. Psychology "has been sidetracked," he wrote as he assumed the presidency of the American Psychological Association in 1998. Rather than focusing narrowly on fixing disorders, psychologists should also dedicate themselves to fostering strengths, he argued. "Treatment is not just fixing what is broken, it is nurturing what is best within ourselves."

The ensuing research produced a practice called positive education— a set of methods for nurturing the traits that are known to act as buffers against mental illness, such as honesty, optimism, and perseverance. In practice, positive education programs have a lot in common with SEL. They use stories, skits, and examples from students' own lives to teach healthy communication, relaxation, and other coping and problem-solving skills. The results so far are hopeful: studies of Seligman's Penn Resiliency Program, for example, have found that it reduces depression, anxiety, and behavior problems, and that its benefits last at least two years.

The skills for happiness *should* be woven into the fabric of education, Seligman and colleagues assert, because so many young people are already depressed, because wellness also leads to better learning, and because "we want our teenagers to be healthy and vibrant, not merely free of disease; optimistic and exuberant, not simply 'non-depressed'; intimately connected to others, not just part of the crowd; . . . and passionately engaged in activities that excite them, not just 'occupied.'" Amen.

Finally, there's **mindfulness**—which was trending in education even before it made a 2014 cover of *Time* magazine. The practice began in schools on a small scale a couple of decades ago and then mushroomed over the past five years into an educational movement. You can now find dozens of mindfulness programs in hundreds of schools in a majority of US states. At Saint Louis University, for instance, Stuart Slavin opted for a resilience course that includes mindfulness. Kevin Wehmhoefer, coordinator of mental health services and outreach at Harvard, started offering mindfulness classes in student dorms and found it to be the "single most effective tool" he's encountered in his work so far. At Gunn High, Principal Herrmann plans to weave the practice into her reforms.

It's clear why: not only do the lessons provide kids a little oasis of quiet and calm in the midst of the school day, but studies show the training actually improves students' behavior and attention. If your brain is abuzz with agitation over the latest playground skirmish, or anxiety about an upcoming test, or distress about a painful situation at home, you're not likely to be fully tuned into today's fractions lesson. Plus, the basics of the practice can be taught and put to use in very little time, while the benefits can be lasting. Mindfulness is often confused with a religious practice, but it's actually just a method for noticing one's own mental and emotional state and calming it down. Parents can learn it and model it for their kids, too. (As a chronic overthinker and rat racer in recovery, I've experienced the benefits firsthand.)

I had the chance recently to witness a mindfulness lesson in Richmond, California, in an impoverished neighborhood where children routinely come to school upset about neighborhood shootings. The instructor was Tim Scott Jr., a mindfulness professional and hip-hop artist who goes by the name JusTme. He stepped to the front of a fifth grade classroom, sporting short dreadlocks and a gray hoodie and exuding compassion and enthusiasm, and twenty-eight heads turned toward him. "I got my feet on the floor, my spine in a line, my hands in my lap, and my heart to the sky," the children sang together as they settled into a "mindful sit." Then, with JusTme reminding them to notice the sensations in their bodies and to let go of any judgments about themselves, the classroom fell into silence.

The sit lasted just a few minutes, but it seemed to release the frenetic energy that had buzzed among the students moments before. Afterward, they acted calmer and more focused. JusTme's lesson today was on mindful test taking. He asked the kids what changes happen in their thoughts, emotions, and bodies when they're taking a test. "I feel nervous and stressed," one boy said. Other students added on: "I feel pressure." "I feel sleepy."

What could they do about this? To keep calm, he said, they could take five mindful breaths (they all practiced one, inhaling deeply). They could send themselves and their classmates some compassion, saying things like "I'm going to give it my best" instead of "I'm not good enough." And they could notice the emotions in their bodies, in a tight stomach or a tapping foot, and "name it to tame it." When JusTme left after his twenty-five-minute lesson, he had trouble crossing the playground as every few steps a child ran up to hug him.

The Bay Area–based nonprofit that trained JusTme, Mindful Schools, also trains teachers to practice and teach mindfulness in their classrooms. Training for teachers is crucial, as the practice can sometimes surface past traumas for kids that instructors must be prepared to handle. A UC Davis study showed that Oakland elementary students who received Mindful Schools lessons demonstrated significantly improved behavior—especially in paying attention—compared to peers who didn't get the lessons. Studies of other mindfulness programs have found benefits including better attendance, lower suspension rates, and even improved grades. My favorite stat: according to a state survey, a San Francisco middle school that adopted a transcendental meditation program posted the highest happiness levels in the city.

Demand for mindfulness in schools is rising accordingly. Enrollment in Mindful Schools' online introductory class had multiplied nearly tenfold in just two years as of early 2015. The practice suits diverse students and communities, as it can help one child cope with family turmoil and another child cope with academic performance pressure. I know for myself that even simple breath work can help me untangle the tension in my mind. When I've shared this technique with my kids, it has helped them, too.

Digital Detox

Speaking of serenity, and the lack thereof, one other potential thwarter of well-being that deserves special scrutiny is digital technology. I've wrestled mightily with the merits and perils of technology for myself and my family. I've despaired whenever I've noticed that my kids just spent half an hour texting when they could have been outdoors, or that I just squandered forty minutes on email that could have been spent with my children. I've gasped upon seeing groups of teens at school sitting "together," staring at their phones. Seeking guidance, I read all the credible research and commentary on the subject that I could. And what I found is that with screen time, as with everything, the key to well-being is balance.

Some amount of tech time for kids is healthy. They need to learn to use today's tools, and to use them well. They should have the chance to unwind with digital entertainment if they like to, and to socialize in modes that match those of their peers. "It *is* the way this generation communicates, and anyone who worries that tech is isolating our kids should just look at one of the 'stories' their kids tell on Snapchat or Instagram," says Brigid Schulte, the reporter and author of *Overwhelmed*. "Some are hilarious and sweet."

Still, the growing science on screen time confirms our gut parental sense that caution and supervision are required. Digital devices can play on our brain's reward system, releasing the neurotransmitter dopamine and making it hard to resist a tweet or a text message. When we're hooked on that hit, our screen obsession sucks us away from ourselves and the people around us, and it habituates us to a distant, disembodied kind of human exchange. "Science is showing that tech works on the same brain structures as addiction—the basal ganglia—which means it's incredibly seductive, if not addictive," Schulte explains. "We as adults have a hard time managing it. I would argue it's using *us* more than we are effectively using *it*."

The danger lies in that lack of control. In an interview with journalist Bill Moyers, MIT professor Sherry Turkle argues that seeking that "neurochemical hit of constant connection" actually leaves us with a face-to-face-connection deficit. Absent are the intimate, important subtleties of a facial expression or a tone of voice, the meandering path of an in-person conversation. The loss affects all of us, but the implications are especially troublesome for children, who are still forming their social selves. Turkle, the author of *Alone Together: Why We Expect More from Technology and Less from Each Other*, explains that our smartphones and Snapchat accounts promise us that we'll never have to be alone. And this is powerful because "the capacity for solitude is terribly important to develop. I even believe that if you don't teach your children to be alone, they'll only know how to be lonely."

School communities, likewise, could use a dose of digital-communication restraint. In some schools, it is increasingly routine for teachers or coaches to email students and families about assignments late in the evening or on weekends—or vice versa. Even if it's not explicitly demanded, many kids, parents, and educators feel the pressure to promptly read and respond. This late-night communication is not malicious on anyone's part—it reflects the inherent temptation technology creates to blur the line between school and home, just as it has blurred the work-home line for businesses that reach their always-on employees at all hours. But it is nevertheless an invasion of private time. It is appropriate and important for us now to set limits, asking schools to contact students and families—and families to contact educators—only during normal business hours. Companies including Volkswagen have already done the same for their workers.

If we want to give our children all the opportunities they need to grow a full set of social skills, we need to teach them to how to resist the constant digital connection fix. And if we want to preserve the precious time our families have to be in the same room and actually engage with each other, we have to set limits. But spotting the problem is one thing, and knowing how to solve it is another. How do you safeguard your kids from the downsides of technologies that are ubiquitous and somewhat necessary, or tell them to put down a device that you yourself are holding in your hand and compulsively checking every ten minutes?

I've found that the experts' advice for parents so far generally comes down to this: pay attention. Families need to be mindful of how they use tech—taking care not to let it use them—and keep ever vigilant about maintaining a balance. "Create sacred spaces in your home," Turkle advised Moyers. "Places that are device free: kitchen, dining room, and the car. You can't introduce this idea when your child is fifteen that the car is for chatting. From the very beginning, kitchen, dining room, and the car are places where we talk." Saying "no" to phones and computers in the bedroom, while tricky to sustain in our hyper-connected world, is another sound way to set limits and safeguard children's sleep. For her part, Schulte and her family have built in a kind of autocorrect mechanism for each other. "There are some times that I look up and my husband's on his email and I'm on my email and our kids are on their phones," she says. "We say, 'Phones down! Everybody be where you are.'"

As to the confounding question of how much is too much, the American Academy of Pediatrics recommends zero screen time for children under age two and a maximum of one or two hours a day of entertainment on screen for older kids—which sounds, I confess, too permissive on some days and too restrictive on others. I take comfort in the message from the organization Common Sense Media that the *quality* of kids' media diets matters as much as the quantity. "The reality is that most families will go through periods of heavy and light media use, but, so long as there's a balance, kids should be just fine," the group writes. The sweet spot for each child and each family will look a little different. The key is to make a media-use plan that suits your family and to talk with your children about your values. And, sometimes, to join them in consuming the media they enjoy! In my house, Zak and I have lots of fun watching *Modern Family*, whose all-too-relatable characters often lead us into meaty conversations.

You Count, Too

Now we come to the trickiest part of prioritizing wellness, the part that demands we pair our dedicated advocacy with deep introspection: modeling healthy living ourselves. This is true not only of monitoring our own technology use but also of moderating the pace of the entire way we lead our lives. As someone who has at times preached better than I practice, I know how challenging, and how important, this part of our work can be. Children learn their priorities not only from the structure of their experiences in school and at home but also, quite keenly, from the role models around them. In other words: us.

When I was at my most balanced, Zak was in middle school and the girls in high school. I was making my first film and putting into practice the lessons I learned in researching it. Our family had pulled back from overcommitment. Shelby and Jamey were playing just one school sport each. Zak played in the school band but exercised on his own, always on some kind of board (skate, surf, snow). For myself, though I had film screenings to attend and a growing grassroots community to nurture, I made time to exercise almost daily. I turned off my computer in the evenings, read books, and took hikes with my friends. When the kids saw me going to yoga class every week, they asked if they could come along. My wellness set the tone for the household. And, revelation of revelations, I found that—just as research would suggest—when I felt well and rested the quality of my work improved.

Nonetheless, maintaining balance is an ongoing challenge. When I started making my second film, I slipped back into familiar patterns, sleeping too little and sending emails at eleven p.m. Old habits die hard—especially when breaking them is an act of cultural defiance.

I have come to see that this problem, like every problem we've examined in this book, stems from twin plagues: our twisted vision of success and, related, a culture of busyness that has become synonymous with success itself. In the American lexicon, "success" is defined by publicly visible achievements: career, income, property, influence. It is the man who climbs his way into the corner office, the woman who leads a high-tech design team while raising perfect kids, and the child who plays state-level soccer and earns a 4.5 GPA—all of them dashing around to do so. Nowhere on that list would we typically think to put the man who simply makes time to meditate each morning, the woman who enjoys gardening with her neighbors, the young adult who feels rewarded by mentoring a struggling kid, or the child who sleeps amply and has time to stare at clouds. Why couldn't those be the markers of a successful life?

As we begin to redefine success—for our kids and for ourselves—we must place wellness at its core. That doesn't mean we need to quit all commitments and retreat into monastic stillness—though doing just that, at least occasionally, would likely do us all good. The key is to reset the balance. When I set about reclaiming my family's own runaway schedule, I began by asking myself what mattered most to me, and by asking my children what topped the list for them. I let go of believing that peace would come when I made it through my to-do list—an eventuality that, of course, never came. Instead, peace had to take precedence.

As parents, it is also time we reclaim the definition of successful parenting, with wellness ranking first. Half a century ago, success as a parent in America meant raising responsible, respectful citizens who stayed out of trouble and grew up to be gainfully employed and start families of their own. Now it seems the measure is how well your children perform, from school to sports to sparkling alma maters to high lifetime earnings. As the culture has tilted more toward materialism, so has the definition of excellent mothering and fathering. The focus is too often on what your child does, instead of on who she is. Let's tilt it back. Success ought to be raising a healthy, wholehearted child who cares for herself and others, appreciates everyday joys, and believes in her own ability to handle life's ups and downs.

For example, as Erin, the California teen, recovered from depression, her mom started a local support group for parents of kids dealing with mental health problems—thus bolstering children's and parents' wellness at once. Her mom also became a strong advocate at the school, convincing officials to add mindfulness lessons in PE classes, distributing suicide prevention information, and pressing the administration to appoint a liaison for students with health problems. I'd call that successful.

Young people today need to see more adults acknowledge health problems openly and place them before every other concern. In fact, experts urge us to talk honestly with our kids about our own stresses and struggles, and about the roots of and treatments for anxiety and depression. Schools and parent groups can play an important role here, by organizing events and campaigns to educate the community about mental illness and the effects of toxic stress. We should even discuss the realities of suicide, and we parents should ask our teens, directly and compassionately, if they've ever thought about it. The honesty doesn't scare them; it strengthens them. It also does not put the idea of suicide in their heads; psychologists are clear on that. Rather, it empowers young people to tend to their own hearts and prioritize their inner goals. It shows them that it's okay to ask for help. Most of all, it telegraphs to them, as they strain against the impossible expectations around them, that *they* are not the problem. As Erin observes, "There's all these kids who don't know that what they're living through isn't normal."

A final word on adults' wellness: like children, we, too, need strong personal connections in order to thrive. This always reminds me of a moment related to me by psychologist Suniya Luthar. After a lecture she gave on student stress in a privileged, high-pressured community, she spoke with a mother in the audience. The woman was beautifully, impeccably turned out, but Luthar recognized a look of despair and anguish in her eyes. That conversation awakened Luthar to the loneliness and isolation that so many mothers feel. And, I would argue, many fathers, too—all kinds of parents from communities across the socioeconomic spectrum. "Why? Because there is no time," Luthar says. "You're caught up in doing so much for so many people and doing it so well that there is absolutely no time or space left over for you to be connecting."

In a study she conducted of more than two thousand mothers, Luthar told me, a single question emerged as a strong predictor of our well-being: "Do you feel seen and loved for the person you are at your core?" In the midst of all our accomplishing and achieving, we often forget to make time for those everyday moments, with family or friends or strangers, where we give and receive love. "Little exchanges where you feel a true warmth from somebody do so much to inoculate you for the next several days or even weeks," Luthar says.

So as we begin to place our own wellness first, perhaps hauling it up from fifth or sixth place, where it has languished, we need to make *connection* a part of it. We thrive best when we each take care to create our own network of supportive friends and family. Friendship, love, and companionship are essential to our well-being. Let us grant ourselves the time and space to be well. We deserve it. "Once we get there," says Luthar, "we're going to be that much better able to do it for our children."

Irvington Strides On

Irvington High School is trying to get there, too. When I checked in on the progress of the school's wellness effort in mid-2015, the status was: slow—but determined.

Jackson and the Edjoycation Task Force students were preparing to hold their second Community Night Off, ideally with local elementary and middle schools on board. The Edjoycation students had handed out leaflets on sleep and tabled at the school health fair. The action that was making the most impact at Irvington so far, though, was a structural one: the new class

registration routine, which requires a one-on-one meeting with a counselor for every student and limits overloading on honors and AP courses
(as explained in chapter 5). "Even a lot of hard teachers who you'd think
would promote taking as many as you can, they're going, 'Oh, you should
only take three,'" said Edjoycation leader Aneesha. And some of her fellow
students were voluntarily reducing their course load to have more time for
themselves. The new registration process, no longer a free-for-all, she said,
"got them thinking."

It seemed that Jackson and the Edjoycation crew had achieved an important first step: awareness. At least Irvington students, teachers, and parents
were starting to recognize the problem, even as the pressure continued to
boil around them. And boil it did. Jackson said a half dozen kids had already
forged teachers' signatures to get into more AP classes. The yearbook was
still publishing its annual "Top 10" list of seniors with the highest GPAs,
and the student newspaper was fully funded by tutoring center ads.

Jackson's hopes for further wellness reform currently center on two ongoing strategies. One: embedding happiness lessons into students' regular
classes (Jackson is delivering many of these short teachings himself, visiting
English classes to provoke students to consider the true purpose of their
learning and remind them that happiness hinges not on our accomplishments but on our relationship to our goals). And two: his work with Stuart
Slavin, modeled on the successful process at Saint Louis University.

Slavin and Jackson were nearing the moment of revelation with a tactic
they'd been working on for months: a detailed scientific survey of students'
mental health. Unlike the informal survey Jackson had run before, this
one would reach almost every student in the school. It would use scientifically verified measures to gauge the teens' anxiety, stress, and depression. It
would link their ailments with factors such as sleep deprivation, homework
loads, AP courses, parental and peer pressure, and college admissions. All
told, it would reveal precisely how unwell Irvington students were and the
likely causes of their ill health.

What could possibly be so powerful about a survey? Proof. Jackson and
Slavin were after hard evidence that the epidemic of student distress is oc-
curring right here in *this* community, with *these* children. Such proof is what
Slavin possessed at Saint Louis University, where he enacted swift and ef-

fective reforms, and what he lacked at his daughter's high school, which refused to budge. What Slavin learned from that experience is that generic stats about miserable teens across America aren't enough to conquer cultural and institutional inertia. "It has to be *your* kids," he observes. In fact, measuring students' well-being is actually a practice that all schools should do annually, whether they're considering reforms or not. It's just as important as any assessment of learning.

By the summer of 2015, after some number crunching, Slavin and Jackson expect to have a scientific analysis of the real state of Irvington students—including irrefutable data on the severity of their stress. And they intend to use that evidence to get the community's attention. Forget your traditions, assumptions, and standardized tests, they might say. Forget the *U.S. News & World Report* college rankings, the Common Core standards, and Race to the Top. *Our kids are sick.* This problem is here, and it is real. And as any parent knows, when your child is sick, nothing else matters.

The data will also help them tailor new reforms directly to Irvington students' real needs, based on the prime sources of stress that the survey reveals. If the data-first method proves effective at producing real change, and that change proves effective at improving children's health, then Slavin wants to help many more schools apply it. "As a pediatrician and educator, even though my younger daughter is now a senior in high school, this is part of who I am and what I need to fight for," he said. "That's why I'm still here."

My own hope is for all of the above. I hope that Irvington and others can restore health and wellness to their rightful place as our first priority. That our shared definition of success comes to reflect integrity and joy instead of status and frenzy. And that, even as we gather local evidence to provoke broad change, we don't wait on the data to begin.

I know personally how much courage and tenacity the task can take. My commitment to the cause has ruffled feathers at my children's schools, where I've made more than one request for a meeting. It has made for awkward conversations in the pickup line, as other parents raised eyebrows at my kids' empty schedules. It has also branded me as a bit of a renegade among my friends. I hear the same from others—the Anne Robinsons, the Stuart Slavins, and the hundreds more who contact me every year—who have taken up the daily charge against the cultural inertia that says there's little we can do to hit the emergency "stop" on the treadmill.

We continue, though, because it is precisely this multitude of persistent actions that ultimately adds up to transformation. Many of the change makers we've met in this book have already shifted policy and moved public opinion, through organized actions with their schools, school district boards, and PTAs. Less visible but just as essential is sustaining the daily churn of change: the quiet, dogged, everyday decisions that we each constantly make to champion our kids' holistic well-being and safeguard the precious few years that make up their childhoods. It is through such actions that we dare to disrupt the status quo. This effort, at once individual and communal, is ultimately about healing our culture. And we will know we are successful only when our children are truly well.

CHAPTER 8

Action:
How You Can Replace the
Race to Nowhere

T HIS IS what we've learned, in a nutshell.

Education and childhood should not be a race. Yet our achievement-obsessed culture has turned them into one. For too many children and families, the school years now feel like a sprint. Students race against what feels like a ticking clock, striving to burnish the best résumé and outcompete other kids on the path to college. From privileged enclaves to low-income communities, students, parents, and educators across the country feel relentless pressure to compete, achieve, and perform. Crowded out is time to genuinely learn, discover, and grow.

In homes across America, nightly homework marathons have replaced family dinners. High-stakes tests have turned ten-year-olds into clinical anxiety patients. Parents have converted into chauffeurs and taskmasters. And in classrooms, the mountain of content required for standardized exams keeps students and teachers in a mad scramble just to get through it, rarely pausing to consider questions deeply or develop creative skills.

Against this backdrop is the mounting expectation that children should zip through back-to-back music lessons, soccer practices, tutoring sessions, and other enrichment activities—forsaking sleep, health, family time, and play. The ironic result of it all is that our children are sadder and sicker, not smarter, and they're leaving home less prepared to thrive.

There is a better way, a way that cultivates the kind of genuine intellect, happiness, and integrity that is beyond measure. Many parents, educators, and students are already working to create it. We can all join them. Here are some simple truths and basic steps to guide us.

(Note that these tips apply to everyone. The "actions at home" are written toward parents, but students also could take the initiative and ask their parents for support. The "actions at school" could be spearheaded by anyone—student, parent, teacher, counselor, or administrator—and any community member could contribute. Suggested actions in each section appear approximately in order of difficulty, with the simplest starting points listed first.)

1. You govern your home.

Somewhere along the line, parents granted schools authority over what our kids should do *outside* of school. The result: countless hours of excessive homework and extended school activities, starting at an ever-younger age, all coming at the expense of sleep, family time, and the myriad kinds of learning that happen outside of classrooms. After-school hours belong to us. It's up to us, as guardians of our children's welfare, to gauge the healthiest, most important uses of their time. It's time to draw the line.

Actions at home

- *Look at your child's school-to-life ratio.* Keep track of the amount of combined time that homework and school activities take after the last bell, and how that affects your family. Just recognizing when the ratio is imbalanced is a first step to righting it.

- *Urge your child to go to bed at an age-appropriate hour,* regardless of homework. If homework assignments are consistently incomplete because they interfere with play, family time, or an appropriate bedtime, schedule a conference with the principal or classroom teacher to discuss the mismatch between assignments and your child's well-being. Children should be going to bed before, not after, working adults. The National Sleep Foundation recommends nine to eleven hours of sleep a night for children through age thirteen, and eight to ten hours for older teens.

- *Don't require your child to do schoolwork when she's sick.* Schools, under pressure to stick to a strict content schedule, tend to send home thick work packets to sick kids, which only mount into a homework pileup. Send your child a message that if she needs to rest, she can—and should. The work can wait. When asked, teachers are usually able to offer creative ways for students to combine or skip assignments if they've missed more than a day of class. Besides, the appropriate place for schoolwork to happen is in school.

- *Resist the push for private tutoring.* One-on-one support is worthwhile for some students and not for others. Yet in some communities, tutoring is practically standard fare, seeming necessary just to keep up with everyone else who's doing it. Ask yourself if it's really best for your child. Even better, encourage whole groups of parents to stop along with you, while calling on schools to bring lessons in line with students' actual developmental needs. Pricey private tutoring deepens inequality, extends the school day, eats up essential time for other experiences, prevents teachers and schools from truly seeing what kids understand, and sends the message to kids that we don't think they can do it themselves. Children who need extra help can ask their teachers—which also helps teachers keep better track of what students are and are not learning.

Actions at school

- *Ask your school to create a shared calendar* with teachers and coaches to track major assignments, events, and exams. This enables educators and mentors to check the combined demands on students and avoid accidental pile-ons. You can also ask your school to assign set days of the week to specific subjects for homework and tests to ease bottlenecks of out-of-school work.

- *Press your school district to set developmentally appropriate curriculum,* personalized for each child, so we can stop sucking up afternoon hours with outside tutors. There's no sense expecting all six-year-olds to read sentences and seventh graders to master algebra—or requiring those who are ready to learn more to wait. Each child reaches these kinds of milestones on her own schedule. Schools should also build time into the regular school day when teachers can offer students individual help, as Chicago's Walter Payton College Prep High School and the K-8 Potomac School in Montana have done.

- *Petition your school to set a no-homework policy on weekends* (aren't they supposed to be weekends?), holiday breaks (aren't they supposed to be breaks?), and over the summer—and to cap outside-of-school hours that may be directed to homework, sports, and clubs. Ultimately, petition for one evening each week to be free from all school obligations. Well-rested minds work better.

2. Homework doesn't work.

We tend to take it as a given that homework helps kids learn and develops their self-discipline. The trouble is, that's not necessarily true. Research shows little to no academic benefit to homework before high school, and diminishing returns in high school when take-home assignments last longer than an hour or two. Besides, homework exacerbates inequalities for students whose families don't have the resources to help them with it, or those who need to care for younger siblings or hold down after-school jobs. Moreover, once students are in departmentalized schedules with five to seven teachers assigning thirty to sixty minutes of work each, we're relegating them to a second or third daily shift. Excessive homework eats up the time kids need to grow in all the essential ways, not only academic. Exercise, socializing, downtime, and sleep all optimize children's brain functions and are essential elements of their growth. Homework shouldn't trump all.

In accordance with our Healthy Homework Guidelines—detailed in chapter 3—I recommend the following.

Actions at home

- *Let your child know your priorities from a young age* so that when she gets older she's already comfortable putting health and sleep before finishing every last assignment.

- *Avoid asking about homework the moment your child walks in the door.* A warm conversation or a bit of playtime between you and your child is more meaningful than being a taskmaster. It's important to honor the break that a kid needs after a full day at school.

- *Resist the impulse to do your child's work for her.* Doing so deepens inequities between kids and reinforces the message that kids can't handle their own education. Plus, parents' intervention keeps teachers from seeing how well students actually understand the assignment. If the work is negatively impacting your child, address that with the teacher.

- *Experiment with replicating your child's homework for a week,* as writer Karl Taro Greenfeld did for *The Atlantic,* to get a sense of what's truly expected of students and what, if any, benefits it might confer. "Memorization, not rationalization" was his thirteen-year-old daughter's advice to him. The experience left Greenfeld exhausted and doubtful about homework's merits.

- *Consider opting your child out of homework entirely in elementary and middle school.* Meet with your child's classroom teacher, guidance counselor, and principal to explain your stance at the beginning of the year, and encourage other parents to do the same. Change comes with critical mass.

- *Help your high schooler factor in homework overload when choosing classes.* It may be possible to prevent excessive after-school work by resisting the temptation to overschedule academically. Encourage your child to limit AP and honors classes to subjects she truly enjoys and wants to pursue and support her in advocating for herself if she needs to change her schedule.

Actions at school

- *Survey students school-wide to determine how much time they're actually spending on homework* and publicize the results. Ask them which kinds of work are helpful to them and which are not. It's surprising how frequently we forget to go straight to the source for feedback. Also consider surveying teachers on how much work they assign and compare their estimates to students' actual reports; teachers may be surprised by the realities.

- *Launch a community-wide initiative to have teachers and parents all do homework for a week,* as Greenfeld did in his home. Opinions may shift once adults have walked a mile in modern students' shoes.

- *Create study periods during the school day* where students can put new skills to work in the presence of a teacher who can help as needed. Doing so narrows the gap between affluent and poor students, provides teachers with valuable opportunities to offer individual attention, and supports a better school-to-life ratio.

- *Urge individual teachers and whole schools to stop grading homework.* As Virginia teacher Mike Miller found, eliminating the superficial goal of a grade can free students to think creatively and take risks. And research shows that grades diminish motivation. To grow and improve, learners need more feedback than a single letter, anyway.

- *Organize with fellow students, parents, and educators to make homework assignments at your school the exception, not the rule, and to allow any family or student to opt out.* One parent's preferences about how her child spends the after-school hours shouldn't dictate another's. It is through collective action that we can press effectively for this ultimate cultural change.

3. Just because you can measure it doesn't mean it matters.

In our test-obsessed education system, schools are under so much pressure to post good scores that they speed through tons of tested content while pushing aside deeper, more engaging ways to learn. The march toward uniformity leaves little room for attending to children's individual talents or needs. Tests now drive what and how we teach, when what we need is the other way around. When the tests are high-stakes—meaning teachers' jobs, schools' budgets, and students' diplomas are on the line—this structure does even more harm. The people in the best position to evaluate what students know and what they still need to learn are actually the teachers who know them. By placing so much weight on just one limited measure of student knowledge, we're dismissing entire other realms of important skills (creativity, cooperation, critical thought) and missing opportunities for much more meaningful learning driven by teachers and students themselves. Ironically, test scores aren't even a predictor of life success.

Actions at home

- *Remind your child that she is more than a test score.* Explain to her that standardized tests measure only one narrow set of skills in one limited way, and there is far more to human intelligence and value than that. It's important for her to hear this when even her teachers are stressed about the exam.

- *Opt your child out of standardized tests* if you find the exams are doing harm. Strengthen your action by organizing other parents to do the same. Parents have done this effectively even outside of the eight states—Utah, Wisconsin, Colorado, Pennsylvania, Minnesota, Oregon, Washington, and California—that explicitly allow it. Refer to the organizations FairTest and United Opt Out National for more information.

Actions at school

- *Remind your teachers that they are more than a test score.* Teachers, like students, need to know they're supported if they break the mold and strive for student engagement and deep learning instead of simply scores. Parents might take the time to send a positive note to school with your child thanking the teacher for a thoughtful assignment; administrators could celebrate great inquiry-based lessons at staff meetings.

- *Urge your high school to request to be removed from school rankings,* such as those published by *Newsweek* and the *Washington Post.* These rankings perpetuate the false notion that quality learning can be quantified and keep schools focused on the wrong goals.

- *Reserve more time for self-directed and open-ended projects* while spending less time on students passively listening to lectures. This is a crucial part of a shift toward making education student-centered. To develop creativity and collaborative skills that will be essential in work and life, students need time to explore complex questions without expected answers.

- *Call for an end to the publishing of student honor rolls, rankings, and test scores,* which promote the notion that scores matter most and prompt students to compare themselves to one another. Academic marks are a private matter. Experiment with ways, such as gallery shows and project exhibitions, to recognize and celebrate young people for a wide range of skills and contributions, academic and otherwise.

- *Encourage your school to use performance-based assessments* in which students demonstrate their skills by performing meaningful tasks (such as original research and design) and presenting them in various formats (such as visual depictions, oral presentations, written stories, or digital portfolios) rather than simply answering prescribed questions on paper. Capstone projects can replace final exams. Students at San Diego's High Tech High, for example, have published compilation books of their short stories, created a documentary film about gun violence prevention, and worked with the local port and zoo on sustainability for the San Diego Bay.

4. Learning is a process, not a product.

Education, likewise, is an experience and not an equation. Our educational system is stuck in churn mode: children crank out assignment after assignment, rarely getting the chance to receive deep feedback, refine their work, or reflect on what they have learned. Productivity takes precedence over improvement. The drive for perfect performance eclipses actual learning. And students often remain passive recipients of content. The classic bell schedule is another impediment; it cycles students to a different class every fifty minutes, leaving no time for depth or focus and little chance to have a say in what they learn. It also stacks up simultaneous homework assignments for as many as eight classes a day and prevents teachers of different subjects from collaborating. As a result, our children lose opportunities for rich learning daily because they're sleepy, hurried, and disengaged.

Actions at home

- *Cultivate a growth mindset in your home by praising effort, not outcomes.* A growth mindset holds that skills grow with practice and perseverance. Effort counts, and mistakes are opportunities to learn. Process and persistence are more important than perfect performance. Vocally observe your child as he tries, struggles, and improves, and don't lavish praise for specific grades or honors.

- *Change the focus of your conversations from grades and homework to interests, efforts, and discoveries.* Find opportunities to ask your child what she's interested in or excited about at school. What you talk about sends a message about what you value.

- *Allow your child to make mistakes and learn from them.* Ease performance pressure by talking with her about your own missteps and how they helped you improve.

- *Resist the temptation to constantly check grades on School Loop* or other online tracking systems. Everyday grades are not the most important part of kids' learning. And no one, including children, thrives when micromanaged.

Actions at school

- *Cultivate a growth mindset in your classroom and school.* This applies
  to adults' development, too. Make your school a safe place to innovate. Encourage teachers and students to take risks, and see the opportunities for growth in failure. Celebrate process and progress,
  not output.

- *Change the schedule to allow depth, foster relationships, and support
  personalized learning.* Block scheduling, in which classes meet for
  longer chunks of time and not all classes occur every day, is one
  model for doing this. A growing number of schools are making this
  switch and finding that it allows for deeper study.

- *Create opportunities for personalized and inquiry-based learning* in
  which students explore questions that they generate themselves
  on subjects with particular interest to them. This means creating
  flexibility in schedules and requirements so that teachers and students may shape their own experiences. Honoring students' own
  voice and choice in their studies helps to engage them. And the
  inquiry process—finding and vetting information sources, experimenting, and asking further questions—is just as educational as
  the answers students find.

- *Make constructive critique and revision an integral part of your students'
  work.* Otherwise, as educator Ron Berger says, you're just on "a
  treadmill of turning in final-draft work every day." The richer learning comes in the revision. Reducing the total number of assignments
  and projects will allow more time to go in depth on each one.

- *Provide teachers more time to work together and plan cross-disciplinary
  projects.* Old traditions keep teachers siloed in their classrooms,
  even though science, history, math, art, and language are intimately
  connected with each other in the real world. Supporting more staff
  collaboration can yield livelier projects, invigorate teachers themselves, and help students see deeper meaning in their work.

- *If it's tough to overhaul the whole school, try testing your innovations in certain classrooms where teachers, parents, and students can opt in.* Creating a little laboratory school within a school allows you to demonstrate the benefits of different methods without scaring those who are reluctant to change. The same strategy can be effective for many innovations, such as classrooms that are non-test driven or are homework free. Once they see the caliber of teaching and learning happening in this "lab," many more people may want to participate.

5. Brand names are for clothes, not colleges.

The college rankings, invented as a marketing technique to sell magazines, have mixed with other societal shifts to produce utter madness around college admissions. Your child's school years become an arms race, and their classmates become their competition. Even if your student isn't aiming for a top-ranked college, she is nonetheless swept up in the misguided sense that every school wants a superstar's résumé. It's all a shell game. There is no such thing as a "best" college—different students thrive in different settings—and colleges actually seek a diverse set of students. If you think about it, you probably know graduates of all kinds of schools who have gone on to be happy and well suited to their careers. The right college for your child might be one you've never heard of. Or a community college. Or, for some students, no college at all.

Actions at home

- *Emphasize with your child that the point of high school isn't simply to get into college.* Likewise, the point of high school and college isn't strictly to prepare for a career. Important learning happens for its own sake, and leads to paths and successes that cannot be prescribed. Discourage overscheduling and explicit résumé building. Encourage your child to make his or her choices about classes and activities with the present—and not just the future—in mind.

- *Help your child seek a "best fit"* rather than a "best" college. Your mantra: "Be yourself." No one but your child herself can determine the best path for her.

- *Boycott paid test-prep courses.* Like private tutoring, this is one of the "extras" that exacerbates social divides but that parents and students come to feel they need to do to keep up. You don't. The SAT and ACT are exams of limited value that mainly mirror family income and indicate little about a child's potential for success in college or in life. Not all colleges require them for admission. If, however, they are unavoidable, your child can prepare on her own with books and practice questions for a fraction of the cost. Then, take the exam itself no more than once or twice. Encouraging a teen to approach the tests this way will help her build self-efficacy, goal setting, and confidence. The time (and money) saved can be used for more nourishing purposes.

- *Refuse to buy magazines or read websites that rank colleges.* The rankings are a numbers game that says little about the educational experience. (Assessments such as *Washington Monthly*'s, which rates schools based on their contribution to the public good, are a notable exception.)

- *Based on your child's own priorities, help make a personal, anonymous assessment of colleges based on the schools' merits beyond brand name.* Together with your child, list the attributes of the colleges that interest her, such as campus setting, course offerings, and clubs, then compare them without the colleges' names. One Massachusetts dad I met did this with his son, who said he found it eye-opening.

- *Encourage your child to consider taking a gap year* to reflect on her goals and strengths and experience new endeavors away from school. Even the Harvard admissions office encourages this as a way to reduce stress, discover new interests, and arrive at college better prepared and ready to benefit. Information and resources are available through the American Gap Association.

Actions at school

- *Bust the myths about college admission.* All sorts of false ideas (that you need to take the SAT over and over again; that a kid with a B average can never get into a good college; that where you go to college will determine who you become) swirl around schools and add to students' and parents' anxiety. Information from the non-profit Education Conservancy can help dispel these myths. Go out of your way to spread the truth.

- *Refrain from publicizing lists of the colleges that admit students from your school.* These lists fuel the misperception that there are "best" schools and that status, not education, is the purpose of admission.

- *Invest in more college counselors* to provide personalized guidance to students seeking to scratch beneath the headlines and find the right college fit. This resource will also help level the playing field for students whose families can't afford private consultants.

- *Petition college admissions officers to cap the number* of advanced classes and extracurriculars they will consider on applications. They have the ultimate power to end the résumé arms race, and high schools (a.k.a. their recruiting centers) might influence them. High schools can also set caps of their own, as explained below.

6. Time is a mirror.

The way we use our time is the truest expression of our values. That means that, if we pay attention, our schedules can show us whether we're living our most important values or not. We need to constantly consider our children's school-to-life ratio and strive to help them keep it in balance. As the writer Annie Dillard famously said, "How we spend our days is how we spend our lives." Your child only gets one childhood.

Actions at home

- *Keep a log of your activities, and your child's activities, over the course of a few days.* The record will show you what you're truly prioritizing.

- *Safeguard time for what matters most* to your family. Sleep, exercise, family meals, and time to connect with friends and community don't come after you've checked off everything else on your to-do list. Often, much of the list can wait.

- *Choose one midweek day when your family schedules nothing.* No afternoon lessons or social engagements for kids, no evening meetings or events for adults. This is the moment in the middle of each week when your family is automatically set to pause, rest, and reconnect.

- *Model healthy use of technology.* Consider whether you own your technological devices or they own you, and ask your kids the same question. If tech is taking over, create tech-free zones for family interaction, such as the dinner table, the car, vacations, and the hour before bed, and call a regular tech-free evening (e.g., Tech-Free Tuesdays) when your family can connect in person. You might even create a weekly technology Sabbath: an entire tech-free day. Kids need our help learning to tame the tug of technology.

Actions at school

- *Keep a log of how much time in a day students spend* doing certain activities: listening passively to lectures, losing minutes to passing periods and attendance checks, using more minutes checking and assigning homework—or engaging deeply and actively in learning under their own direction. The imbalance you find may convince you to restructure your schedule and your methods (see guideline 4, above).

- *Ensure adequate breaks for kids of all ages.* Fears about high-stakes tests have prompted some schools to curtail recess, despite the mountain of evidence that rest supports learning and play is an essential part of cultivating happiness and creativity.

- *Plan community nights off* when teachers assign no homework, coaches cancel practice, and families are encouraged to turn off their technology at home. It'll give everyone a little glimpse of what it's like to rest, play, and reconnect with family without obligations hanging over our heads. If it works well, make it a monthly or even weekly occurrence.

- *Advocate for an appropriate school-life balance.* Document the daily hours your child spends on school demands and let teachers, coaches, and club directors know how all the lessons and activities assigned by many adults add up. Often they are unaware. Question how many after-school hours the school should own.

7. Less is more.

We want the best for our children, so when we see other kids loading up on Advanced Placement classes, dazzling audiences at the dance recital, or crossing the state to play soccer, we fear that ours are falling behind. In fact, we're more successful when we choose to focus on just the few things that matter most. Research shows that happiness lends itself to greater success (better work, health, and relationships), not the other way around. Even a bit of idleness itself is essential; neuroscience confirms that our most important and creative thinking and growing often happens when we're at rest.

Actions at home

- *Urge your child to limit the number of Advanced Placement and honors classes she takes at one time.* This choice affects homework, health, and everyday life in your home for the whole year. It may or may not affect her admission at the most competitive colleges, but wherever she goes, she'll be healthier when she gets there.

- *Help your child choose just a few activities that genuinely interest her,* not gobs of them that she feels obliged to stuff on her college résumé. Encourage her to fill in the blank: "Above all else, I want to do . . . with my free time." Colleges still appreciate applicants with strong character and real interests, and prioritizing her passions will help your child with time management, too.

- *Put a premium on play.* Not the structured kind, where kids appear at appointed times on soccer fields to take instructions from adults, but genuinely free and unplanned time, no adult direction allowed. Research shows it's essential for children to spend some time inventing activities for themselves.

- *Reclaim control of your family's school-to-life ratio*—and empower your child to do the same for herself. Like Berkeley sports mom Emily Cohen, try banishing the word *mandatory* from your home. Teachers and coaches are free to make requests for your kid's time. But if your child has a cold, a big exam the next day, or an important family event, you decide.

Actions at school

- *Limit the number of AP and honors classes any student can take at one time.* There's no proof that students learn more or better in AP classes; in fact, the huge quantities of required content tend to crowd out time for deeper learning. Yet students competing for college admission feel compelled to take more than everyone else, even at the expense of sleep, health, and learning. Colleges evaluate students' applications in the context of what their school offers; if there's a school-wide cap on AP classes, there's no penalty for not taking more.

- *Cap the number of mandatory hours students must spend on a sports team or school activity each week.* Research suggests that the benefits of athletics and activities diminish beyond about ten hours per week, total, for all commitments combined. Schools should set limits to preserve students' well-being and keep the proverbial playing field level among activities.

- *Consider shifting from semesters to trimesters* in which students take the same number of classes over a year but fewer each term. This schedule affords greater focus and allows more time for depth and independent work. Taking fewer, yet deeper, courses at one time also more closely resembles how students will learn in college.

8. Wellness is worth as much as academics.

Without physical and emotional well-being, no student can embark on a happy life or achieve his or her full potential. Research shows that stressed and sleep-deprived brains can't learn optimally. Yet young people's health is often an afterthought in an educational system that's sprinting to satisfy standardized-testing pressures and stubborn traditions. We need to put students' well-being in the place it deserves, as a foremost priority all its own.

Actions at home

- *Learn about the long-term effects of sustained stress on the mind and body* and share what you know with your kids and their teachers. Research shows the potential harm is profound.

- *Teach your children that their health is more important to you than their achievements.* That message too often gets lost in all our running around to meet expectations and obligations.

- *Model balance for your children.* We know the keys to well-being are sleep, good nutrition, exercise, play, purposeful work, time outdoors, and time to connect with friends and community. Make wellness a priority for yourself, as well, and explain to your kids what you're doing and why.

- *Know the signs of depression and talk with your teen about suicide.* Watch for the signs in the young people (and grown-ups) you know. California's Know the Signs campaign, available at suicideis preventable.org, is a helpful resource.

- *Start a support group for parents or families* dealing with stress and mental health concerns, as one California mom did. This way, you bolster the well-being of both kids and their caretakers at once. If the members agree, the group can also become an organization advocating for changes at school.

Actions at school

- *Campaign for later school start times.* Science has clearly established that kids' sleep chemistry changes in their teens, making them sleepier in the morning and more alert at night. The American Academy of Pediatrics recommends starting middle and high schools at eight thirty or later.

- *Elevate young people's voices by creating a student group, supported by school staff, to discuss and address excessive stress.* Irvington High's Edjoycation Task Force, which organizes fun stress-relief activities, and Ridgewood High School's Principal's Advisory Group, which works with teachers to tackle homework overload, are different examples of these. Kids need to know they'll be listened to if they speak up about the support they need.

- *Offer mindfulness lessons at school.* Besides reducing excessive stress on students, we also need to equip them with coping skills for stress they can't avoid. Mindfulness lessons for schools are rapidly growing, and research is finding that they can reduce depression and help improve children's attention, participation, and care for others. What's good for hearts and minds is good for learning.

- *Educate the school community on the signs of depression* and the ways in which our education system fuels it (e.g., marching students through repeated defeats and constant measurement, with no sense of control over their time or circumstances).

- *Measure stress, depression, and anxiety among your students.* An anonymous survey can help illuminate the real magnitude of the problem, which kids are often adept at hiding. Be sure to ask about the root causes of stress, and then design interventions to address them, as Saint Louis University Medical School has done and Irvington High School is doing.

9. Relationships are the foundation of health and learning.

Humans are social beings, and strong connections with others are critical to the healthy development of children and to happiness at any age. Connections for kids are also a key to developing resilience, that all-important capacity to navigate challenges and overcome traumas that research shows is nourished by a strong bond with a caring adult. Interpersonal connections are critical to learning and motivation, too. It's the lessons connected to our personal interests and done with guidance from a teacher we know and trust that most often light up a mind. Unfortunately, our educational tradition tends to prevent personalization and erode the chances for kids and adults to get to know each other well. Important connections exist not only between and among teachers and students, but also between what young people are studying and what they care about. We have too much content to cover, too many testing requirements, and too many changings of the guard (switching teachers every year or even every hour) to make learning personal or connections deep. Clever schools are finding ways to fix this.

Actions at home

- *Know your child.* Inquire about her genuine interests. Avoid the temptation to become another constant measurer in a kid's life, asking continually about grades and scores; this way, she knows she still has your support even when she stumbles.

- *Prioritize kids' social time.* Time with friends—play for younger children, and hanging out for teens—is as essential to healthy growth as food and water. Protect social time from the myriad other "productive" obligations that would crowd it out.

- *Develop a village of supporting adults in your child's life.* Encourage kids to interact with teachers, coaches, fellow parents, clergy, and other community members. Each adult may offer something

different: an interest, an interpersonal style, a life perspective. There
will be times when kids need to turn to someone besides you.

Actions at school

- *Urge your school to schedule a weekly advisory period* where a small
  group of students and one adult meet to support one another and
  discuss important issues in school and life. Keep the same adviser-
  student group together for as many years as possible. Besides
  teachers, school counselors, nurses, and principals can lead advisories, too.

- *Offer ample opportunities for students to exercise voice and choice in
  their school experience.* Students who have a say in how their classroom runs, and a choice about what books they read or what
  topics they study, are more engaged. Schools in the New York
  Performance Standards Consortium, for instance, typically teach
  a whole class about a general topic (e.g., World War II) but allow
  individual students to choose which aspect (e.g., war propaganda,
  Rosie the Riveter, or the roots of the military-industrial complex)
  to study deeply.

- *Encourage your school to shift its academic schedule* for the sake of
  relationships, not just academics. The classic bell schedule makes
  teachers' caseloads too large and class time too quick and impersonal. Longer, deeper classes can create stronger teacher-student
  bonds and a calmer campus.

- *Ask your elementary school to consider looping*—keeping students
  with the same teacher for more than one year. Middle schools and
  high schools can create a similar closeness through team teaching,
  keeping fifty or sixty kids together as a unified group, with just two
  teachers (typically one for English/history and one for science/
  math) sharing all the same students.

10. Cultural rebellion is better with company.

It can be lonely diverging toward sanity and humanity in your child's education when every family around you appears to be marching straight ahead.
Sometimes you wonder if *you're* the crazy one. You are not. Plenty of other
parents out there share the feeling that the Great Résumé Race has no place
in childhood. They, too, are wondering what to do about it. You'll gain crucial support—and amplify your calls for change—if you find them.

Actions at home and school

- *Talk about your values.* Talk about them anywhere (in private conversations and public forums, at birthday parties and youth sports
  meetings), with anyone who'll listen. By voicing your thoughts
  you'll empower others to listen to their instincts, too.

- *Build a support network.* When you meet others who share your
  values, stay connected with them. It's easier to break with convention when you're not the only one.

- *Arm yourself with reliable research* on the real benefits and costs of
  homework, the impact of test obsession, and the long-term effects
  of unchecked childhood stress. Solid knowledge will support your
  conversations. Understand what makes for *good* research. You'll
  find relevant studies cited throughout this book.

- *Listen to young people.* Ask kids how they're feeling and what they
  need. It's a simple but often overlooked step. Their voices matter,
  and their answers will inform your actions. Give students a real
  voice and a place at the table.

11. Society doesn't know everything about success.

When well-meaning adults ask kids the dreaded question "What do you
want to be when you grow up?" we all know there are certain acceptable answers. The same is true when a fellow parent asks, "Where does your child
go to college?" Name an unknown state university or say your child is not

in college at all, and an awkward silence is likely to ensue. There's no sense blaming these people, since the assumption that status and money are the measures of success infects us all. TV shows and advertisements only reinforce the illusion. But we don't have to believe it—or participate in it.

Actions at home and school

- *Redefine success for yourself and your family.* Challenge your own assumptions. Ask your children (or students) about their views, too. If we look deep inside, tuning out the cultural noise, most of us will find that our hopes for our children are this simple: health, happiness, and the ability to support themselves and contribute something to their community.

- *Be explicit about your values.* Your children (or students) may get the message from everywhere else that anything less than a top-ranked college admission is inadequate. They need to hear, convincingly, from *you* what really matters, and to know they will be loved, valued, and respected no matter what.

12. Children's health and preparation for the future ultimately hinge on school change.

However much we do to cultivate healthy homes and prioritize meaningful learning instead of the collection of credentials, schools still have a lot of impact. We'll be swimming upstream until we help schools undo old traditions that hurt students' health and education and adopt new practices that tap children's individual talents and fulfill their needs. And we will only effect this change through a groundswell of grassroots action that begins with you. It is by engaging everyone that we begin to spark a cultural shift in our communities—a change deep and pervasive enough that it will outlast any one leader. You, along with your fellow parents, students, educators, and community members, are the advocates the next generation needs.

This last principle is crucially important—it is the ultimate aim of this book. It is also complex and tricky to execute effectively because it entails organizing diverse stakeholders, dealing with the historic and top-heavy institution of education, and asking people to question assumptions they hold dear.

Fortunately, parent-advocates before us have found strategies for doing this effectively. I devote the rest of this chapter to presenting their advice.

How to Advocate Effectively for School Change

- *Gather your community together for a discussion of concerns and priorities.* This is what turned out to be so powerful about *Race to Nowhere*; the film screenings were an opportunity to bring communities together, raise awareness of the problems and potential solutions, spark discussion, and galvanize people to action. At screening after screening, I saw how the emotional testimonies of people in the audience shook others out of their complacency with the status quo and moved them to make change.

  "I was sitting here thinking about my son, who's only been in the first grade for, what, five or six months," said one parent in Castro Valley, California. "And he has already come home and asked me, 'Do you think I'm doing a good job? Are you proud of me?' This is my seven-year-old!" Feeling the power of her community assembled around her, this parent went on, "We need to mobilize, we need to do something. At what point are we just sick of it? What are we going to do about it? Can we join together, not just in Castro Valley, and get up there to the White House?"

- *Organize with like-minded parents and educators.* Every community possesses the power to set new priorities and organize for action—and the collective wisdom to know what it needs. All it takes to begin is to convene. "It's not a top-down change, it's a bottom-up," says High Tech High CEO Larry Rosenstock. "It's like community organizing. You go out and you individually connect with people." A parent meeting or film screening can be a starting point. Then, ask those who share your concerns to help you reach out to more people, speak out at school meetings, conduct research, propose new school policies, and orchestrate petitions.

Alicia Vanderhyden, a mom who supported reforms in Potomac, Montana, explains, "It takes a community. Change starts
with one person, but the most powerful part of any change is not
the leader, but actually the followers. It's that second and third person that have that faith that the change can happen, and that support it and practice it, that are the most critical."

• *Involve students from the get-go.* Students are, ironically, the most
ignored voice in education reform—even though they are the most
profoundly affected by school practices and the most intimately familiar with what works and what they need. You could solicit their
input through informal conversations, formal surveys, or, as Trigg
County, Kentucky, superintendent Travis Hamby did, by asking
them to sit on the committee that would guide his schools' change.
At Monument Mountain Regional High School in Massachusetts,
educators even took a student seriously when he suggested starting
a school-within-a-school for independent studies, with great results.

"It was probably the very best thing that we did, to engage our
students in the conversation," says Hamby. "If you want to think
about what you want to create, let students talk about what it is
that would more deeply engage them in learning. Students know
the kind of learning experience they would like to have."

Ron Berger, a Massachusetts teacher and chief academic officer of the Expeditionary Learning schools, adds this perspective:
"The hard thing about changing school is that what we're familiar
with is hard to step away from. We're in habits of how we teach.
We're in habits of what we think school should be, so change feels
a little scary to us, not just to parents, but to teachers, too. The only
people who aren't afraid of that change are students themselves,
because students grow up today in a changing world. They're ready
to take on those challenges."

• *Partnerships between parents and educators are especially important.*
As any mom or dad knows who has tried and failed to work through
a school bureaucracy on an important matter, disconnection be-

tween home and school leaves parents feeling disempowered. It's also a wasted opportunity for a powerful collaboration. So parents, find someone at school who shares your goals (a teacher, an assistant principal, a counselor, a curriculum director), and join forces. Educators, reach across the home-school divide and do the same. The greatest potential for change comes when parents and schools work together.

Anne Robinson, pediatrician and parent-activist in Ridgewood, New Jersey, says a key to her success at starting reforms was finding one sympathetic administrator (Assistant Principal Jeff Nyhuis) and then sticking with him. "This is how you begin to create change: through conversation," she says. "The only way to create change is to open up lines of communication."

Her collaborator, Nyhuis, agrees. "I get very busy with other tasks," he says. "If I didn't have the parents helping me in pushing me in the right direction, we wouldn't be where we are today."

- *Use social media to expand your support network and amplify your message.* Create local networks to stay connected with people within your community who share your goals. Or connect with other reform-minded parents and educators, even those across the country or across the world, to find fresh research and resources and exchange experiences and ideas with others in the movement. The Race to Nowhere pages on Facebook and Twitter can be a starting point for finding these comrades.

  It was in part through a Facebook group, for example, that New York State's testing opt-out movement mushroomed from one Long Island mother to the parents of more than 175,000 students statewide. Social media also played a central role in the Race to Nowhere network's successful campaign for homework-free holiday breaks. Ridgewood and Walter Payton took the lead. Then we shared their stories and called on everyone in our network to advocate for this symbolic change, placing a map on our website where schools could add a pin when they joined. Hundreds of schools and thousands of individuals ultimately participated.

Sometimes, the greatest benefit of participating in such communities is simply knowing you're not alone. One member of our Facebook community, Renee, wrote that the "daily doses of sanity . . . swim upstream in an onslaught of get-ahead-academically-at-all-costs-and-by-all-means messages." Another, Marianne, rallied fellow members to action with this cry: "Jump off the hamster wheel and start speaking up, there is strength in numbers!!"

- *Start with a realistic goal.* Traditions, even outdated ones, are sticky. You may need to spread awareness and win allies by starting with smaller steps that don't send skeptics away panicking. For instance, you could try homework-free holiday breaks on the way to making homework assignments the exception, not the rule. Begin with one hands-on, student-directed, cross-disciplinary project per semester. Or pilot your innovation with one class or teacher and then expand. A few small victories will fuel bigger ones. Be patient and persistent.

- *Gather data to support your case.* Resources in this book and on our website can provide general hard data. But beyond the general science on stress and school, you'll need local statistics to show that the problem affects your own community. Saint Louis University pediatrics professor Stuart Slavin found this out the hard way. He presented a host of general research on excessive homework and student health to the board of his daughter's Saint Louis school. Despite his credentials as a medical professor and pediatrician, he couldn't get the board to budge on easing students' pressure. Lesson learned: national statistics aren't enough to cut through the haze of the race to college. Says Slavin, "It has to be *your* kids."

So when he set about helping Irvington High School in California to address its stress problem, Slavin started by conducting a survey. (If it's too tricky to get approvals to survey at school, try asking local health departments or pediatricians' offices to share data.) He wanted to ask students: "Just how much homework are you doing? How much sleep are you getting? How many of you feel excessively stressed, anxious, and depressed—and why? How many of you are cheating?" The results of the survey, completed in spring 2015, will help Slavin and Irvington Assistant Principal Jay Jackson design appropriate interventions and—they hope—convince students, parents, and teachers that change is needed.

- *Start with those who are ready.* Forcing change on people who don't believe in it tends not to be fruitful. So when Trigg County was just beginning its move toward project-based learning, High Tech High's Rosenstock advised the team to get the teachers who were open to innovation started, and to give them as much support as possible. That's what Trigg did, beginning its experiment with just a few teachers who really wanted to try something new. Once parents and fellow educators see the impact the new methods are having, the Trigg team wagers it'll be easier to bring them along.

- *Be for something, not against something.* This is the strategy employed by Torri Chappell, a teacher turned parent-activist in San Anselmo, California. When the going gets tricky, remember that our work always comes down to what's best for kids. Be for health, rich learning, and family time. Those are priorities everyone can get behind.

Epilogue

I N T H E Y E A R S that I have been advocating for change, there have been times when I felt so frustrated that I nearly wanted to throw up my hands, discouraged by the incremental nature and the glacial pace of change. Even in the face of a need so urgent—our children sick, disengaged, unprepared, and grieving for their lost hours and thwarted selves—reforms still grind on maddeningly slowly.

In many communities I've visited, it takes months of task force meetings and private pleas and public forums to begin to address concerns as fundamental as health and learning. A single night off from homework, one out of 180 school days in a year, counts as a victory. Even Palo Alto, which suffered a teen suicide cluster while I was making my first film seven years ago, jumped into a flurry of discussion then but followed through on very few changes. "It was a fairly sad school for a number of years, in terms of being in crisis and then just simply marching in place," says the new Gunn High School principal, Denise Herrmann. As I was writing this book, three more Palo Alto teens took their lives. I'm convinced that Herrmann is serious about reform and optimistic about her chances—but even she must contend with the pace of bureaucracy. Before she starts a social and emotional learning program years in the making, for example, the idea will have to spend yet another year in planning.

Meanwhile, the Race to Nowhere remains as toxic as ever. I see it in news stories and statistics: cheating is rampant, childhood anxiety is epidemic, and elite colleges entice an ever more absurd number of applications, only to reject the vast majority of them. The annual survey of entering college

236

freshmen posted its worst mental health ratings ever in 2014—though who knows, this could be outdone in 2015. I also see it in communities and families I know (a friend called me recently looking for a therapist for her thirteen-year-old son, who was so overwhelmed with work that he didn't want to get out of bed).

And I still see it in my own home, where just the other day Zak put in eight hours at school, including a required math class that takes place *after* the last bell, and finished at four p.m. Then he had a doctor's appointment, and we dropped off dinner for a friend who'd just had surgery. Errands done, we arrived home at seven—at which point Zak, who thrives on physical activity, had been doing required tasks for eleven straight hours without a moment of exercise, and he still had homework to do. His life was not his own. When Zak went to bed at eleven, homework still not quite complete and no time outside, he told me he'd been having trouble falling asleep at night. Is it any wonder?

Our competitive, lockstep model of education continues to pain students in every part of the socioeconomic spectrum. Susan Engel, the Williams College psychologist and education expert, encapsulates the breadth of harm done in her new book, *The End of the Rainbow*:

> By allowing the pursuit of money to guide our educational practices, we have miseducated everyone. We are so hell-bent on teaching disadvantaged children skills (both academic ones, such as reading, and social ones, such as obeying rules) that will lead to a job that we fail to teach them the pleasure of being part of a literate community, how to make their work meaningful, or how to draw strength from the group—skills that might offer them a satisfying life. Just as bad is that middle-class and privileged children are pushed to view every stage of their schooling as a platform for some future accomplishment ending in wealth. This deprives them of the chance to figure out what they really care about, how to think about complex topics with open minds, and how to find a sense of purpose in life.

Blessedly, though, amid the great challenges of this work I have also found great reasons for hope. Some of the trailblazing schools featured here have progressed even further since my last visits. The Trigg County schools in Kentucky are now using performance assessments in their middle school, and this fall they plan to expand their project-based learning initiative, which didn't even exist two years ago, into eleven grades. Trigg County is also working with state officials to create a waiver allowing high school students who meet basic academic standards to craft their own, personalized graduation plan in place of the standard, one-size-fits-all exit exam.

Meanwhile, more than 550 New York State school principals signed a letter protesting state tests. The young and growing organization Student Voice, which aims to place young people's perspectives at the center of education debates, unveiled its Student Bill of Rights, including rights to wellness, personalized learning, fair assessment, and opportunities to participate in the world beyond the classroom. Plus, schools from all over the world continue to visit High Tech High, seeking to emulate its creative and captivating approach to learning.

Sometimes the bravery amazes me. At Monument Mountain Regional High School in Great Barrington, Massachusetts, whose innovations are featured in my new film, *Beyond Measure*, Principal Marianne Young had the courage to skip a grant opportunity worth tens of thousands of dollars. Why? Because it would have required her school to significantly shift its schedule and align its curriculum with the specifications of a private company, the College Board, so as to place a prescribed number of students in AP classes. Young's school, which just launched a student-directed civics course, and where students and teachers recently worked together to build a makerspace, had much better things to do.

In celebrating these successes, it's important to remember that, in education, every piece of progress is fragile. Every positive reform is only one new principal, one new superintendent, one school board election, or one new regulation away from reversal. In Gaithersburg, Maryland, for instance, the ouster of a supportive superintendent in spring 2014 makes the future of Principal Stephanie Brant's homework and teaching reforms uncertain. Brant said to me after she heard the news, "I'm scared." The teachers, students, and administrators who are brave enough to make change need our loud and unwavering support. Schools, likewise, need to see parents as true partners in transformation.

As I reflect upon my journey, starting from that useless student-stress forum at my children's school that sent me over the edge to make my first film, I see that our cause has come a long way. A decade ago, the race was a problem shrouded in silence. We feared that if we questioned the march to "success" we'd be left behind. We tried to keep up because everyone else appeared to be keeping up. Every child who felt crushed by the impossible standards around her and every parent who secretly thought this race seemed crazy suspected that they were the only ones.

Now we are talking about it openly—not only those of us who are living it but also school superintendents and politicians and TV pundits and columnists. We are publicly calling competitive childhood what it is: a perversion of values, a sickness, a poison. We have broken the barriers of awareness. There is still too much private suffering, denial, and shame. But now we know that we are not alone.

This is precisely the progression that Betty Friedan traced in her status-quo-shattering 1963 book, *The Feminine Mystique*. Friedan called out the toxic culture of a society that suffocated women with rigid expectations, and she explained how freedom required that we change not only institutions but also our own mindsets. We had to challenge flawed assumptions, to break the chains "of mistaken ideas and misinterpreted facts, of incomplete truths and unreal choices," she wrote. That is how I see our task for kids today: we, too, must come to see the purpose of school and the point of childhood in a whole new way. "You do have to say 'no' to the old way before you can begin to find the new 'yes' you need," wrote Friedan. "Giving a name to the problem that had no name was the necessary first step. But it wasn't enough." First: awareness. Next: revolution.

That is why we must continue trumpeting these stories of change, whether they're small or large. It's also what compelled me to make a second film spotlighting solutions. Each person, family, school, or community that dares to challenge convention shows others that it can be done. Sharing these real-life triumphs will help us bridge the second canyon, from awareness to action. Eventually, the stories will grow so ubiquitous that our movement will reach an inflection point. So many people will be calling for sanity in childhood and education that the defenders of the broken old culture will start to feel like the crazy ones. Then our children will be truly free to learn.

It is too late for my kids. It has been crushing for me at times to visit so many centers of educational innovation while my own children remained trapped in a traditional school experience. The best I could do was to make my home a completely different world for them—a place where they weren't constantly measured, where their individuality counted and their health came first.

All three of them will be okay, though they have lost much along the way. Shelby today is a much happier and healthier person, as a college junior, than she had the opportunity to be in middle school or high school. She works and pays all her own expenses except tuition, by choice, preferring to stand partly on her own. She's spending the summer working at a camp for children with serious illnesses. The old me might have worried about that, seeing all the fancy corporate internships the other kids were doing and fretting over her future. Now, I couldn't be happier. Who knows what a difference she might make to those children, or what interests of her own she might discover?

As Jamey completes her first year of college, finally empowered to choose her own classes and set her own schedule, I see her confidence blossoming. On her own volition, she applied for multiple jobs working with animals, secured a weekly internship with Colorado State University's veterinary school hospital, and figured out how to take a Zipcar to the site seventy miles away. I believe Jamey has been able to do this in large part because she arrived at college centered and balanced—much healthier than she would have been if Doug and I had pressured her to fit the mold throughout high school.

And Zak, a high school sophomore, has learned (in part due to our laying off him) to manage all his schoolwork on his own. He takes fewer academic classes than other kids, and I'm glad. He still has too much homework, but we support him in taking time each day to be outdoors, pursue hobbies, and get enough sleep. He understands the value of education but also feels confident advocating for himself and breaking away from others' expectations to chart his own path. The teamwork, sociability, and responsibility that he's learning through the pursuits he loves will serve him well in the long term, far more than bookwork alone could.

So, although my own kids are almost grown, I continue this work because I want other children to start life better. My heart is uplifted every time I hear about the success of young people who broke out of the straight and narrow race and instead took a winding path strewn with great mistakes. These are unsung heroes—living proof that there is more than one route to a meaningful life, that we can diverge from the norm and *not* be left behind. In my travels I have met and heard about many of them.

There is Claire Carroll, who grew up in a Detroit suburb and withstood odd looks and critical comments from her peers, all bound for faraway universities, when she decided to enroll in community college after high school. She wasn't sure what she wanted to do and needed time to explore. A trip to Nashville gave her a taste for the music business, so she started choosing classes that would prepare her for music public relations and took a minimum wage event-planning job with a Detroit radio station. Claire transferred into Michigan State University as a junior, joined the school's student-run public relations firm, became the president her senior year, and graduated with multiple job offers.

Jarreau, from working-class Rancho Cordova, California, believed as a kid that he wanted to be a doctor "because everybody else did." In college, he discovered that he hated studying biology but found a fascination with adolescent development. "Once I figured that out, I got to study a subject that I adored," he says. Jarreau became an alcohol abuse educator, as well as a spin instructor and life coach, and he loves it.

John Slater, another Michigander, skipped college altogether, except for a smattering of community college classes, and went to work in a lawn mower repair shop. What might have looked like a dead end was actually a beginning; he moved from there to a job as a mechanic at an auto dealership, then graduated to high-end cars, and finally went to work on Indy-style race cars. Along the way, he started his own design and fabrication business, taking custom orders. His mechanical expertise recently took him to a race in Monaco.

Finally, there is Nina Rubenstein, a onetime college dropout from rural Oregon with an irreverent wit and a taste for political debate. Nina is unabashedly honest about the ways she's stumbled. She recalls struggling to get through all the work in high school, although she found much of it useless, and spending "a lot of nights frustrated beyond function and probably crying." Her dad tried to reassure her: "This does not mean you're not smart, it means you're smart in a different way." After high school, she enrolled at Mills College in Oakland. Why did she go to college then? "Because that's what you did," she says. By her own admission, Nina wasn't ready. "I had no business being in college when I was eighteen," she says. "I was wasting time." (How many other teens who went to college on autopilot could say the same thing?)

After two years of halfhearted studying, Nina dropped out. She commenced a series of moves across the country, from city to city, working at Trader Joe's and wondering who she was. Unlike college, this was not wasted time. "I learned that work life is monotonous. I learned that school can be something you long for rather than resent," Nina remembers. Also, "I learned about being a grown-up and paying bills and being places on time."

The pivotal moment for Nina came in the unlikeliest of places. She had joined AmeriCorps and was working for the Washington Conservation Corps, where she earned so little that she qualified for food stamps, when she was invited to deploy to Alabama for a month of tornado-relief work. "I've always believed that every once in a while you should do something that scares you, and this was scary, so I did it," Nina says. Suddenly, she was dropped into the middle of devastation. She and her crewmates would arrive at a work site to find entire homes scattered across an open field, parts of them impaled on tree trunks broken off like toothpicks. They would labor all day clearing debris alongside the homeowners. Occasionally, they'd find an item intact—a daughter's favorite stuffed animal, pieces of a wedding album. The homeowners would cry, "and sometimes we would cry, too, and stop and hug, and then get back to the task of moving on," Nina recalls.

Later, she took on a role as a one-woman call center, handling calls to and from homeowners about the status of their work orders and developing relationships with them along the way. One day, a weary middle-aged man with leathered skin walked up to her in her parking-lot-turned-command-center. "Are you Nina?" he asked. "Oh my God, I recognized your voice, we've been talking on the phone for a week. Thank you *so much.*" There, in the midst of so much loss and sadness and fear and uncertainty, Nina realized she had made an impact. And, she says, "It was like I got slapped in the face with my reasons for being."

Now show me where you'd find *that* in a traditional school curriculum.

Within weeks of returning home, Nina applied to complete her bachelor's degree in disaster management and homeland security studies at the Tulane University School of Continuing Studies. She moved to New Orleans and worked full-time as an office assistant while taking classes at night, made the Dean's List for consecutive semesters, and became president of Tulane's student chapter of the International Association of Emergency Managers. As this book went to press, Nina graduated with honors—a month shy of her twenty-ninth birthday—happy, highly employable, poised to use her talents for good, and finally believing that her dad was right.

I want so many more promising young people to make discoveries like Claire, Jarreau, John, and Nina did. I want to open up more winding pathways, more socially acceptable routes to a worthy life, and to ensure that kids won't feel dumb and defective if they choose to follow them. I want bright young minds, supported by healthy bodies, to spark with excitement about the worlds opened up to them by *learning*. Our children's future and our country's future depend on it.

We can do this. We can do this if parents organize together and simply say *no*. No, my child does not need more assignments on top of a thirty-five-hour workweek. No, you may not take up two weeks of my child's school year on state tests that kill children's curiosity and teach them nothing. No, a Harvard diploma is not the only possible evidence of my child's success. And the blowback be damned: "Maybe in the end I'll lose my job because test scores go down, who knows," said Amy Swann, then a Danville, Kentucky, principal who was daring to try creative and personal project-based lessons (and who did *not* lose her job, in the end). "But it's a battle that's worth taking. There are certain hills that are worth dying on, and I think kids are that."

We can only do this if parents join forces with educators who share our vision, and if we begin our work by listening to students, who already know what they need. All of our voices together are loud enough to rise above the madness and say: "No, it's not a race." The most important lessons and qualities cannot be measured. And insisting on measuring them will never lead our kids to thrive.

When I feel exasperated and worn down by the obstacles in our way, I remember a poem written by Colin, a high school sophomore in New Jersey. His mom, Jacqueline, found it in the trash and asked his permission to share it. The poem, titled "The Kids Aren't Alright," includes these lines:

> *There are so many things to speak about,*
> *The importance of not wasting time,*
> *So that you don't let it all tick down,*
> *And wake up when you're forty,*
> *Searching for the happiness,*
> *In the corporate grind,*
> *You were promised,*
> *By the greatest lie of all time,*
> *The American dream,*
> *Or the broken education system,*
> *Not enough for the poor kids,*
> *And all the wrong things for the rich kids,*
> *Screwing our generation over,*
> *Without ever admitting that,*
> *The kids aren't alright,*
> *But that's of no concern,*
> *Because the blame can be passed around,*
> *Make us somebody else's problem,*
> *Parents blame the school,*
> *The school blames the teachers,*
> *The teachers blame the students,*
> *And the students blame the parents,*
> *Because they haven't learned a thing,*
> *Or the experience is stressing them out beyond belief,*
> *And as the numbers of use and abuse rise,*
> *The blame keeps getting passed along,*
> *Because we're the future's problem now . . .*

After finding the poem, Jacqueline wrote her son a three-page letter spelling out in thoughtful detail the changes that our schools and our society need. The letter began with the words, *I am sorry for letting you down*, and ended with a promise: *I will work to enact change to make this happen for you.*

In that spirit, I write the following to Shelby, Zak, and Jamey:

In your honor, I will work fearlessly to undo the cultural tangle that tells you your only value lies in grades, admissions, scores, and fortune. I will insist upon an education system that cherishes individual minds, nurtures healthy bodies, and opens myriad doors to students instead of shutting all but one. I will collaborate, with perseverance and integrity, with everyone who shares this goal.

You survived this trial, to your credit, with your *selves* intact. But we, the adults in society, owe you something better than that. And if we want our society to thrive when you inherit it, we must deliver. I commit my own time, strength, and energy to creating a world in which each child, fragile and hopeful as each is born, can sustain the curiosity and possibility that I saw fade from your eyes and only recently return. Childhood is no time for constant panic or pervasive self-doubt. Childhood is the *very* time for curiosity, for possibility, and for discovering who you really are in a setting that's supportive and safe.

I take up this quest so that the children who follow you will have that chance. And so that you know, beyond any doubt, what matters most to me.

Acknowledgments

Since my first days shooting *Race to Nowhere*, my work has always been an act of collaboration. This book is no exception. A chorus of voices inspired, supported, and shaped it from first concept to final copy. That chorus—loud and growing louder—is made up of the thousands of students, parents, teachers, principals, pediatricians, professors, researchers, counselors, and coaches who believe in a better way to raise and educate our children. Their letters, phone calls, and conversations have forged my thinking about the past and future of American education. Moreover, they have become the fabric of this book: the insights and examples that reflect an exciting and growing movement to revolutionize learning in the classroom and beyond. Jacqueline Rush, a student who passed away in 2014, deserves special recognition for the joy and generosity with which she lived and the determination with which she continued to participate in our work even as she battled cancer. To each of you in this movement, I offer my respect and gratitude.

Thank you, in particular, to the people whose personal and professional stories appear in these pages, and to the many more who have welcomed me into your living rooms, classrooms, and offices over the years, unafraid to stand up to the status quo and to reveal your struggles along the way. Your courage to share your lives, work toward change, and translate your concern into action is the reason I wrote this book.

I owe special thanks to my writing team, especially the formidable and speedy Grace Rubenstein, my cowriter and collaborator for the past year, whose powers of synthesis and storytelling, and whose reportorial eye, have helped mold into book form my eight-year journey through the American education landscape. Caitlin Boyle deserves huge appreciation as a thought partner and wordsmith who helped hone and polish every paragraph, from the first outline through the final draft. Thanks, too, to Sara Bernard, for stalwart research; to Mitzi Mock, for invaluable first-read feedback and fact-checking; to Sara Godley, for detailed management of our releases and critical support on deadline; to Chelsea May Bedard, for nurturing our relationships with the international Race to Nowhere community and meticulously documenting community members' trials and successes; and to Sara Truebridge, for her expertise, friendship, reading of drafts, and engagement in an ongoing dialogue about these issues. Sincere thanks, as well, go to Jess Deutsch and Donna Jackson Nakazawa for their early contributions; to Sharon Wood, Mary Ellen Hannibal, Jason Friedman, Michelle Ferber, and Sara Bennett, for the time and thoughtful feedback they offered as early readers of the manuscript; to Elizabeth Kaplan, the literary agent who believed in this story and helped shepherd it to Simon & Schuster; and to Millicent Bennett, my editor, whose careful eye and keen sense of structure guided us to a stronger book. Constructive feedback is an essential ingredient in my work, and I am grateful to everyone who has provided it.

My friends and family also played essential roles in this book's realization. My parents, sisters, and brother have been and continue to be an invaluable source of love and support. Doug encouraged me to take on this ambitious quest for change and, despite its demands, to see it through. Aunt Jackie, an author in her own right, urged me to write and provided helpful input. My mother, in particular, instilled in me a passion for learning and a respect for the power of education, while prioritizing effort over achievement. She was ahead of her time.

Finally, my deepest appreciation goes to my children, whose company, love, and spirit have made my life richer from the moment they were born. Shelby, thank you for challenging me, reading drafts, offering constructive feedback, and sharing your school memories. Jamey, thank you for allowing me to tell your stories and contributing your own wisdom and reflections about your educational path. And Zak, thank you for seeing humor in your experiences even as they shape you, cooking gourmet meals and snacks for a mother hard at work, and pulling me away from the computer to spend time outside with you. Without each of you, this book would not exist.

—Vicki Abeles

My appreciation goes to Kathleen Foote, for reading me the storybooks that inspired me to write. Donald Rubenstein, for urging me to grab life's lapels and never doubting that I could. Both parents, for never expecting any more than that I be honest, responsible, kind, and true to myself—thus sparing me from the extremes of the Race to Nowhere. Jim Daly, for the patience, advice, and entertainment during my long months on book deadline. And the San Francisco Writers Grotto, for supporting me every step of the way.

—Grace Rubenstein

Notes

Prologue: Out of Nowhere

7   *It is, against all odds*: "Fast Facts: Back to school statistics [2014]," National Center for Education Statistics, accessed May 8, 2015, http://nces.ed.gov/fastfacts/display .asp?id=372.

1. Sicker, Not Smarter

19   *On the American Psychological Association's*: American Psychological Association, *Stress in America: Are Teens Adopting Adults' Stress Habits?* (Washington, DC: February 11, 2014).

19   *Meanwhile, 30 percent of high schoolers*: "1991–2013 High School Youth Risk Behavior Survey Data," Centers for Disease Control and Prevention, accessed June 2, 2015, http://nccd.cdc.gov/youthonline.

19   *By her calculations*: Jean M. Twenge et al., "Birth cohort increases in psychopathology among young Americans, 1938–2007: A cross-temporal meta-analysis of the MMPI," *Clinical Psychology Review* 30 (2010), 145–54.

19   *This doesn't bode well*: National Institute of Mental Health, "Depression in Children and Adolescents (Fact Sheet)," accessed online June 15, 2015, http://www.nimh.nih.gov /health/publications/depression-in-children-and-adolescents/index.shtml.

       Stephanie L. Burcusa and William G. Iacono, "Risk for Recurrence in Depression," *Clinical Psychology Review* 27, no. 8 (December 2007), 959–85.

19   *Federal data also show*: "Death rates for suicide, by sex, race, Hispanic origin, and age: United States, selected years 1950–2010," Centers for Disease Control and Prevention, accessed June 2, 2015, http://www.cdc.gov/nchs/data/hus/2011/039.pdf.

19   *What's less well known*: "Suicide Prevention: Youth Suicide," Centers for Disease Control and Prevention, last modified March 10, 2015, http://www.cdc.gov/violence prevention/pub/youth_suicide.html.

21   *Wehmhoefer observed extreme anxiety*: Jan Hoffman, "Anxious Students Strain College Mental Health Centers," *New York Times*, May 27, 2015, accessed online.

21   *In the latest National Survey*: Robert P. Gallagher, *National Survey of College Counseling*

249

Centers 2014, monograph series no. 9V (Alexandria, VA: International Association of Counseling Services Inc., 2014), http://www.collegecounseling.org/wp-content/up loads/NCCCS2014_v2.pdf.

21 *Indeed, more than half*: American College Health Association, "American College Health Association–National College Health Assessment II: Reference Group Executive Summary Spring 2014" (Hanover, MD: American College Health Association, 2014), p. 15.

21 *One in three*: Ibid., p. 14.

21 *Tulane University, particularly hard hit*: Liz Goodwin, "Tulane's mental health meltdown," *Yahoo News*, April 5, 2015, http://news.yahoo.com/tulane-s-mental-health -meltdown-144028239.html.

21 *"The increased need for mental health services"*: April Dembosky, "Students Struggle to Access Mental Health Services on UC Campuses," KQED News, September 19, 2014, http://ww2.kqed.org/stateofhealth/2014/09/19/students-struggle-to-access-mental -health-services-on-uc-campuses/.

21 *In 2014, these students' ratings*: Cooperative Institutional Research Program, *The American Freshman: National Norms Fall 2014* (Higher Education Research Institute at University of California, Los Angeles, February 2015), http://www.heri.ucla.edu/briefs /TheAmericanFreshman2014-Brief.pdf.

22 *This rare disease*: R. L. Richards, "The Term 'Causalgia,'" *Medical History* 11, no. 1 (January 1967), 97–99.

"Complex Regional Pain Syndrome Fact Sheet," National Institute of Neurological Disorders and Stroke, last modified February 23, 2015, http://www.ninds.nih.gov /disorders/reflex_sympathetic_dystrophy/detail_reflex_sympathetic_dystrophy.htm.

Edin Randall, personal communication, December 3, 2014.

24 *Researchers from the CDC*: Danice K. Eaton et al., "Prevalence of Insufficient, Borderline, and Optimal Hours of Sleep Among High School Students—United States, 2007," *Journal of Adolescent Health* 46, no. 4 (April 2010), 399–401.

24 *The rise of sleeplessness*: Jennifer Moses, "Waking Up to Young Kids' Sleep Troubles," *Wall Street Journal*, November 5, 2011, http://www.wsj.com/articles/SB10001424052 9702045282045770120232998869 52.

24 *As Cornell University sleep expert*: James Mass and Rebecca Robbins, *Sleep for Success* (Bloomington, IN: Authorhouse, 2011).

24 *In a National Sleep Foundation poll*: National Sleep Foundation, *2014 Sleep in America Poll: Sleep in the Modern Family* (Arlington, VA: March 2014), http://sleepfoundation .org/sleep-polls-data/sleep-in-america-poll/2014-sleep-in-the-modern-family/.

24 *A 2014 report on teen sleep*: Adolescent Sleep Working Group, Committee on Adolescence and Council on School Health, "Policy Statement: School Start Times for Adolescents" *Pediatrics* 134, no. 3 (September 2014), 1697.

24 *Sleep plays a key role*: "Why Sleep Matters: Sleep, Learning, and Memory," Harvard Medical School, last modified December 18, 2007, http://healthysleep.med.harvard .edu/healthy/matters/benefits-of-sleep/learning-memory.

24 *Just how foggy*: Po Bronson, "Snooze or Lose," *New York*, October 7, 2007, http://nymag .com/news/features/38951/.

25 *Insufficient sleep is known*: Eaton et al., "Prevalence of Insufficient, Borderline, and Optimal Hours."

27 *For his 2012 story*: Alan Schwarz, "Risky Rise of the Good-Grade Pill," *New York Times*, June 9, 2012, http://www.nytimes.com/2012/06/10/education/seeking-academic-edge-teenagers-abuse-stimulants.html.

27 *The availability of prescription*: Nora D. Volkow, testimony to US Congress (September 22, 2010), http://www.drugabuse.gov/about-nida/legislative-activities/testimony-to-congress/2010/09/prescription-drug-abuse.

27 *Prescription rates for teens*: Samuel H. Zuvekas and Benedetto Vitiello, "Stimulant Medication Use among U.S. Children: A Twelve-Year Perspective," *American Journal of Psychiatry* 169, no. 2 (2012), 160–66.

28 *In the national 2013 Monitoring the Future*: "DrugFacts: High School and Youth Trends," National Institute on Drug Abuse, last modified December 2014, http://www.drugabuse.gov/publications/drugfacts/high-school-youth-trends.

29 *In the radio report*: Dembosky, "Students Struggle to Access Mental Health Services."

29 *This work, originating*: American Academy of Pediatrics, "The Lifelong Effects of Early Childhood Adversity and Toxic Stress," *Pediatrics* 129, no. 1 (January 1, 2012), 232–46.
    Candice L. Odgers and Sara R. Jaffee, "Routine Versus Catastrophic Influences on the Developing Child," *Annual Review of Public Health* 34 (2013), 29–48.

30 *Stress begins its spread*: American Academy of Pediatrics, "The Lifelong Effects."

31 *In fact, a survey*: Odgers and Jaffee, "Routine Versus Catastrophic Influences."

32 *A psychology professor at Arizona State University*: Suniya S. Luthar, Samuel H. Barkin, and Elizabeth J. Crossman, "'I can, therefore I must': Fragility in the upper-middle classes," *Developmental Psychopathology* 25, no. 4, pt. 2 (November 2013), 1529–49.

33 *School counselors widely report*: Sharon Noguchi, "Teen Health: Depression, Anxiety, and Social Phobias Rising in Kids, Educators Say," *San Jose Mercury-News*, February 5, 2014, accessed online, http://www.mercurynews.com/health/ci_25074044/teen-health-depression-anxiety-and-social-phobias-rising.

34 *All together, the glittering images*: Jean M. Twenge and Tim Kasser, "Generational Changes in Materialism and Work Centrality, 1976–2007," *Personality and Social Psychology Bulletin*, 39, no. 7 (May 2013), 883–97.

36 *Research has linked chronic stress*: American Academy of Pediatrics, "The Lifelong Effects of Early Childhood Adversity and Toxic Stress."

36 *Loss also occurs*: Ibid.

36 *"[T]he brain's malleability"*: Laurence Steinberg, *Age of Opportunity: Lessons from the New Science of Adolescence* (Boston: Eamon Dolan/Houghton Mifflin Harcourt, 2014), p. 9.

37 *America's high school and college graduation rates*: Henry M. Levin and Cecilia E. Rouse, "The True Cost of High School Dropouts," *New York Times*, January 25, 2012, accessed online.
    OECD, "Education at a Glance 2013: OECD Indicators," OECD Publishing (2013), http://dx.doi.org/10.1787/eag-2013-en.

37 *And while the high school graduation rate*: Janie Boschma, "A Surge in U.S. High School

Graduation Rates," *The Atlantic*, November 7, 2014, http://www.theatlantic.com/edu
cation/archive/2014/11/high-school-graduation-rates-at-an-all-time-high/382494/.

US Department of Education, "Profile of Undergraduate Students, 2011–2012,"
NCES Web Table 2015-167, October 2014.

37 *This is one of the reasons*: US Department of Education, National Center for Education
Statistics, "The Condition of Education 2014: Institutional Retention and Graduation
Rates for Undergraduate Students," NCES 2014-083 (2014).

38 *College professors increasingly*: William Deresiewicz, *Excellent Sheep: The Miseducation of
the American Elite and the Way to a Meaningful Life* (New York: Free Press, 2014).

Abigail Baird, personal communication. Alison Gopnik, personal communication.

38 *But more and more*: Chegg Inc., *Bridge That Gap: Analyzing the Student Skills Index* (Fall
2013), https://www.insidehighered.com/sites/default/server_files/files/Bridge%20
That%20Gap-v8.pdf.

Center for Professional Excellence, *2014 National Professionalism Survey: Career Development Report* (York College of Pennsylvania, 2014), http://www.ycp.edu/media/york
-website/cpe/2014-National-Professionalism-Survey—-Career-Development-Report.pdf.

Millennial Branding and American Express, *The Gen Y Workplace Expectations Study*
(Boston: September 3, 2013), http://millennialbranding.com/2013/gen-workplace
-expectations-study/.

38 *Analyzing thirty-five years of data*: James J. Heckman, Jora Stixrud, and Sergio Urzua,
"The Effects of Cognitive and Noncognitive Abilities on Labor Market Outcomes
and Social Behavior" (paper presented at the American Economic Association annual
meeting, Boston, January 2006, and six other locations).

38 *A 2011 analysis at the University of Michigan*: University of Michigan, "Empathy: College students don't have as much as they used to," news release, May 27, 2010, http://
ns.umich.edu/new/releases/7724-empathy-college-students-don-t-have-as-much-as
-they-used-to.

39 *A Harvard Graduate School of Education survey*: Rick Weissbourd et al., *The Children We
Mean to Raise: The Real Messages Adults Are Sending About Values* (Cambridge, MA:
Making Caring Common Project, Harvard Graduate School of Education, 2014),
http://sites.gse.harvard.edu/sites/default/files/making-caring-common/files/mcc_the
_children_we_mean_to_raise_0.pdf.

39 *Evidence from the Josephson*: Josephson Institute of Ethics, *2012 Report Card on the
Ethics of American Youth* (Los Angeles: 2012), http://charactercounts.org/pdf/report
card/2012/ReportCard-2012-DataTables.pdf.

39 *Daniel Kahneman and his colleagues*: Daniel Kahneman et al., "Would You Be Happier If
You Were Richer? A Focusing Illusion," *Science* 312 (2006), 1908–10.

Daniel Kahneman and Angus Deaton, "High Income Improves Evaluation of Life
But Not Emotional Well-Being," *Proceedings of the National Academy of Sciences*, 107,
38 (2010), 16489–93.

40 *The dean and director*: William Fitzsimmons, Marlyn E. McGrath, and Charles Ducey,
"Time Out or Burn Out for the Next Generation," Harvard College, 2000 (revised
2011), https://college.harvard.edu/admissions/preparing-college/should-i-take-time.

2. It's About Time

43 *"This disease of being 'busy'"*: Omid Safi, "The Disease of Being Busy," *On Being With Krista Tippett*, November 6, 2014, http://onbeing.org/blog/the-disease-of-being-busy /7023.

44 *Let's start by turning the lens*: Tira Okamoto, personal communication.

46 *Seduced by society*: Brigid Schulte, personal communication.

46 *"As parents, we want"*: Ron J. Turker, "All Played Out," *New York Times*, July 27, 2014, accessed online.

47 *A team at the University of Michigan*: F. Thomas Juster, Hiromi Ono, and Frank P. Stafford, *Changing Times of American Youth: 1981–2003* (Ann Arbor, MI: Institute for Social Research, University of Michigan, 2004).

47 *University of Washington researchers*: Pooja S. Tandon, Brian E. Saelens, and Dimitri A. Christakis, "Active Play Opportunities at Child Care," *Pediatrics* 135, no. 6 (June 2015), 1425–31.

47 *Boston College psychologist*: Peter Gray, "The Decline of Play and the Rise of Psychopathology in Children and Adolescents," *American Journal of Play* 3, no. 4 (2011), 443–63.

48 *An explanation of what makes downtime*: Mary Helen Immordino-Yang, Joanna A. Christodoulou, and Vanessa Singh, "Rest Is Not Idleness: Implications of the Brain's Default Mode for Human Development and Education," *Perspectives on Psychological Science* 7, no. 4 (July 2012), 352–64.

48 *The author Tim Kreider*: Tim Kreider, "The 'Busy' Trap," *New York Times* Opinionator, June 30, 2012, http://opinionator.blogs.nytimes.com/2012/06/30/the-busy-trap/.

49 *She examined the scores*: Kyung-Hee Kim, "The Creativity Crisis: The Decrease in Creative Thinking Scores on the Torrance Tests of Creative Thinking," *Creativity Research Journal* 23, no. 4 (2011), 285–95.

49 *One MIT undergraduate dean*: Annie Murphy Paul, "In Praise of Tinkering," TIME.com, October 19, 2011, http://ideas.time.com/2011/10/19/in-praise-of-tinkering-2/.

49 *"When you're playing with other kids"*: Annie Murphy Paul, personal communication.

50 *Indeed, a 2014 study*: Jane E. Barker, "Less-structured time in children's daily lives predicts self-directed executive functioning," *Frontiers in Psychology* 5 (June 17, 2014), 593.

51 *The consequences, besides lost time*: John P. DiFiori et al., "Overuse injuries and burnout in youth sports: A position statement from the American Medical Society for Sports Medicine," *British Journal of Sports Medicine* 48 (2014), 287–88.

University of Florida Sport Policy & Research Collaborative, "Research brief: What does the science say about athletic development in children?" prepared for the Aspen Institute Sports & Society Program's Project Play (September 13, 2013).

51 *"Many parents have come to believe"*: Brooke De Lench, "Early Specialization: Nine Reasons Why It Is a Bad Idea," MomsTeam.com, accessed June 2, 2015, http://www .momsteam.com/successful-parenting/early-specialization-in-youth-sports-supported -by-myths-and-competitive-culture-not-facts.

53 *The expectations have grown*: Michael Lingberg, "New CIF rule limits high school sports to 18 hours of practice per week," *Porterville Recorder*, May 14, 2014.

53 *One study of hers*: Edin T. Randall and Amy M. Bohnert, "Understanding threshold effects of organized activity involvement in adolescents: Sex and family income as moderators," *Journal of Adolescence* 35 (2012), 107–88.

55 *Its official recommendation*: Adolescent Sleep Working Group, "Policy Statement: School Start Times for Adolescents."

55 *One alarming study*: Robert Daniel Vorona et al., "Dissimilar Teen Crash Rates in Two Neighboring Southeastern Virginia Cities with Different High School Start Times," *Journal of Clinical Sleep Medicine* 7, no. 2 (2011), 145–51.

55 *Rock Bridge High School*: Jan Hoffman, "To Keep Teenagers Alert, Schools Let Them Sleep In," *New York Times*, March 13, 2014, http://well.blogs.nytimes.com/2014/03/13/to-keep-teenagers-alert-schools-let-them-sleep-in/.

57 *In 2001, Michael Rettig*: Michael D. Rettig and Robert Lynn Canady, "Block Scheduling: More Benefits than Challenges," *National Association of Secondary School Principals Bulletin* 85 (2001), 78–86, http://csapstaff.ednet.ns.ca/htony/cyberquete/bloc%20scheduling.pdf.

60 *This strategy has parallels*: "How to Stop Sleeping With Your Smartphone," *Bloomberg Business*, May 29, 2012, http://www.bloomberg.com/news/articles/2012-05-29/how-to-stop-sleeping-with-your-smartphone.

62 *American workers clock*: Claire Cain Miller, "The 24/7 Work Culture's Toll on Families and Gender Equality," *New York Times*, TheUpshot, May 28, 2015, http://www.nytimes.com/2015/05/31/upshot/the-24-7-work-cultures-toll-on-families-and-gender-equality.html.

62 *And stubborn gender norms*: Brigid Schulte, *Overwhelmed: Work, Love, and Play When No One Has the Time* (New York: Sarah Crichton Books, 2014).

64 *Past PTSA president*: Brigid Schulte, "In McLean, a crusade to get people to back off in the parenting arms race," *Washington Post*, March 23, 2014, http://www.washingtonpost.com/lifestyle/style/in-mclean-a-crusade-to-get-people-to-back-off-in-the-parenting-arms-race/2014/03/23/9259c6a2-a552-11e3-a5fa-55f0c77bf39c_story.html.

    Wilma Bowers, personal communication.

    Brigid Schulte, "Health experts have figured out how much time you should sit each day," *Washington Post*, June 2, 2015, http://www.washingtonpost.com/blogs/wonkblog/wp/2015/06/02/medical-researchers-have-figured-out-how-much-time-is-okay-to-spend-sitting-each-day/.

64 *Not what columnist*: David Brooks, "The Moral Bucket List," *New York Times*, April 11, 2015, http://www.nytimes.com/2015/04/12/opinion/sunday/david-brooks-the-moral-bucket-list.html.

3. Homework: Take Back Our Nights

69 *The superintendent of schools in Swampscott*: Donna Krache, "Homework: How much, how often?" CNN Schools of Thought blog, December 9, 2011, http://schoolsofthought.blogs.cnn.com/2011/12/09/homework-how-much-how-often/.

69 *Galloway, New Jersey*: Associated Press, "Galloway schools won't give homework on

weekend to K-6 students," NJ.com, August 19, 2011, http://www.nj.com/news/index
.ssf/2011/08/galloway_schools_wont_give_hom.html.

69 *Mango Elementary School in Fontana*: Winnie Hu, "New Recruit in Homework Revolt:
The Principal," *New York Times*, June 15, 2011, http://www.nytimes.com/2011/06/16
/education/16homework.html.

69 *It was standard issue*: William J. Reese, *The Origins of the American High School* (New
Haven, CT: Yale University Press, 1999), 201.

69 *Complaints cropped up*: Ibid.

70 *Assignments of that era*: Brian Gill and Steven Schlossman, "'A Sin Against Childhood':
Progressive Education and the Crusade to Abolish Homework, 1897–1491," *American
Journal of Education* 105, no. 1 (November 1996), 27–66.

Karen Bates, "The Futility of the Spelling Grind Revisited," *History of Reading
News* 26, no. 2 (Spring 2003), http://www.historyliteracy.org/scripts/search_display
.php?Article_ID=244.

70 *In 1900, Ladies'* Home Journal: Cathy Vatterott, *Rethinking Homework: Best Practices
That Support Diverse Needs* (Alexandria, VA: Association for Supervision and Curriculum Development, 2009), 1–25.

70 *The campaign fueled the rise*: Gill and Schlossman, "'A Sin Against Childhood.'"

70 *In the competitive frenzy*: Vatterott, *Rethinking Homework*.

70 *The freer-thinking 1970s*: Ibid.

70 *As a result, the commission*: David P. Gardner et al., *A Nation at Risk: The Imperative for
Educational Reform* (Washington, DC: National Commission on Excellence in Education, April 1983), 29, http://files.eric.ed.gov/fulltext/ED226006.pdf.

70 *A University of Michigan study*: Sandra L. Hofferth and John F. Sandberg, "Changes in
American Children's Time, 1981–1997," University of Michigan, Population Studies
Center Research Reports No. 00-456, September 11, 2000.

70 *A later Michigan study*: Juster, Ono, and Stafford, *Changing Times of American Youth*.

71 *By 2005, parents*: "Stress Levels High for Bay Area Kids, Parents Say," Lucile Packard
Foundation for Children's Health, October 27, 2005, http://www.lpfch.org/newsroom
/releases/parentpoll10_27_05.html.

71 *Some news stories have proclaimed*: Allie Bidwell, "Homework Loads Haven't Changed
Much in 30 Years," *U.S. News & World Report*, March 18, 2014, http://www.usnews
.com/news/articles/2014/03/18/report-students-today-have-no-more-homework-than
-30-years-ago.

74 *In 2006, Duke University's Harris Cooper*: Harris Cooper et al., "Does homework improve academic achievement: A synthesis of research, 1987–2003," *Review of Educational Research* 76, no. 1 (2006), 1–62.

74 *Another study in 2011*: Ozkan Eren and Daniel Henderson, "Are we wasting our children's time by giving them more homework?" *Economics of Education Review* 30, no. 5
(2011), 950–61

75 *There's an even more pernicious problem*: Organization for Economic Cooperation and
Development (OECD), "Does homework perpetuate inequities in education?" *PISA
in Focus*, December 2014.

75 *These same inequalities*: Valerie Strauss, "French president pushing homework ban as part of ed reforms," *Washington Post*, October 15, 2012, http://www.washingtonpost .com/blogs/answer-sheet/wp/2012/10/15/french-president-pushing-homework-ban -as-part-of-ed-reforms/.

76 *Many of the countries*: OECD, "Does homework perpetuate inequities in education?"

76 *One of the consistent superstars*: Ibid.

76 *OECD researchers put*: Ibid.

76 *Depending on whom*: National Center for Education Statistics, "Youth Indicators 2011: America's Youth: Transitions to Adulthood," US Department of Education Institute of Education Sciences, Table 35, accessed June 15, 2015, https://nces.ed.gov /pubs2012/2012026/tables/table_35.asp.

    University of Phoenix College of Education, "Homework anxiety: Survey reveals how much homework K-12 students are assigned and why teachers deem it beneficial," press release, February 24, 2014, http://www.phoenix.edu/news/releases/2014/02 /survey-reveals-how-much-homework-k-12-students-are-assigned-why-teachers-deem -it-beneficial.html.

76 *When OECD researchers looked*: OECD, "Does homework perpetuate inequities in education?"

77 *The writer Karl Taro Greenfeld*: Karl Taro Greenfeld, "My Daughter's Homework Is Killing Me," *The Atlantic*, October 2013.

77 *Yet here there is even less evidence*: Etta Kralovec, personal communication.

78 *In a seminal 1993 study*: K. Anders Ericsson, Ralf Th. Krampe, and Clemens Tesch-Romer, "The Role of Deliberate Practice in the Acquisition of Expert Performance," *Psychological Review* 100, no. 3 (1993), 363–406.

79 *In a National Sleep Foundation poll*: National Sleep Foundation, *2014 Sleep in America Poll*.

79 *And researchers at Northwestern University*: Emma K. Adam, Emily K. Snell, and Patricia Pendry, "Sleep Timing and Quantity in Ecological and Family Context: A Nationally Representative Time-Diary Study," *Journal of Family Psychology* 21, no. 1 (2007), 4–19.

79 *Exercise, too, is so often*: Sara Bennett and Nancy Kalish, *The Case Against Homework: How Homework Is Hurting Children and What Parents Can Do About It* (New York: Harmony, 2007), 81–100.

79 *Time outdoors also has dwindled*: Richard Louv, *Last Child in the Woods: Saving Our Children from Nature-Deficit Disorder* (Chapel Hill, NC: Algonquin, 2008).

79 *A 2006 Scholastic study*: Scholastic and Yankelovich, *Kids & Family Reading Report* (2006), http://www.scholastic.com/aboutscholastic/news/KFRR_0207.pdf.

81 *"The biggest problem growing up today"*: Terri Lobdell, "Getting Off the Treadmill," *Palo Alto Weekly*, November 18, 2011, 33–38.

81 *Damon's research has demonstrated*: William Damon, Jenni Menon, and Kendall Cotton Bronk, "The Development of Purpose During Adolescence," *Applied Developmental Science* 7, no. 3 (2003), 119–28.

81 *His studies show that*: Lobdell, "Getting Off the Treadmill."

81 *As Damon explains*: William Damon, "How Can We Encourage a Sense of Purpose

and Meaning Early in Life?" *Big Questions Online,* December 9, 2014, https://www.big questionsonline.com/content/how-can-we-encourage-sense-purpose-and-meaning -early-life.

81   *In that context:* Lobdell, "Getting Off the Treadmill."

82   *The United Nations Convention:* United Nations, "United Nations Convention on the Rights of the Child, Fact Sheet No. 10, Rev. 1," November 20, 1989, http://www.ohchr .org/Documents/Publications/FactSheet10rev.1en.pdf.

82   *Yet in 2014, UCLA's annual survey:* Cooperative Institutional Research Program, *The American Freshman.*

86   *When Manhattan's P.S. 116:* "Parents outraged after elementary school abolished home work," AOL News, March 6, 2015, http://www.aol.com/article/2015/03/06/parents -outraged-after-elementary-school-abolished-homework/21150479/.

86   *So Ackerman penned:* David Ackerman, letter published in *The Almanac,* March 5, 2007, http://www.almanacnews.com/news/2007/03/05/oak-knoll-principals-letter-on-home work-policy-.

4. Testing: Learning Beyond the Bubble

98   *Combine those with the extra deluge:* Melissa Lazarín, *Testing Overload in America's Schools* (Washington, DC: Center for American Progress, October 2014), https://cdn .americanprogress.org/wp-content/uploads/2014/10/LazarinOvertestingReport.pdf.

98   *At Castle Bridge elementary school:* Dao X. Tran, "Forget Teaching to the Test—Castle Bridge Boycotts It!" in *The New Uprising Against High-Stakes Testing,* ed. Jesse Hagopian (Chicago: Haymarket, 2014), 211–18.

98   *In Providence, a crowd:* Cauldierre McKay, Aaron Regunberg, and Tim Shea, "Testing Assumptions: Zombies, Flunkies, and the Providence Student Union," in *The New Uprising Against High-Stakes Testing,* ed. Jesse Hagopian (Chicago: Haymarket, 2014), 135–40.

99   *The protests reached:* Valerie Strauss, "Report: 175,000-plus N.Y. students opt out of Common Core test, more expected," *Washington Post,* April 18, 2015, http://www .washingtonpost.com/blogs/answer-sheet/wp/2015/04/18/report-175000-plus-n-y -students-opt-out-of-common-core-test-more-expected/.

99   *Opt-out groups:* Kimberly Wiggins, "'Opting out' becoming more popular option for Central Florida families," Fox 35 Orlando, November 14, 2014, http://www.myfox orlando.com/story/27387181/opting-out-becoming-more-popular-option-for-central -florida-families.

     Amy Moore, "Parents need authority to opt-out of testing," *Des Moines Register,* November 13, 2014, http://www.desmoinesregister.com/story/opinion/abetteriowa /2014/11/13/amy-moore-school-testing-opt-out/18969065/.

99   *The previous fall:* Daniel Wallis, "Thousands of high school students skip Colorado state tests," Reuters, November 14, 2014, http://www.reuters.com/article/2014/11/14/us -usa-colorado-education-idUSKCN0IY2HO20141114.

99   *According to the national organization*: Monty Neill, executive director of FairTest, personal communication.

99   *Meanwhile, signatures on*: "The State of National Rebellion Against High-Stakes Testing," *FairTest Examiner*, October 2012, http://fairtest.org/state-national-rebellion-against-highstakes-testing.

      Cindy Long and Sara Robertson, "NEA Launches Campaign to End 'Toxic Testing,'" National Education Association, accessed June 2, 2015, http://www.nea.org/home/59747.htm.

101 *The nonpartisan Center on Education Policy*: Jennifer McMurrer, "NCLB Year 5: Choices, Changes, and Challenges: Curriculum and Instruction in the NCLB Era," Center on Education Policy, July 24, 2007, http://www.cep-dc.org/displayDocument.cfm?DocumentID=312.

101 *And the trend has continued*: Tim Walker, "The Testing Obsession and the Disappearing Curriculum," *NEA Today*, September 2, 2014, http://neatoday.org/2014/09/02/the-testing-obsession-and-the-disappearing-curriculum-2/.

102 *Researchers at the RAND Corporation*: Kun Yuan and Vi-Nhuan Le, *Estimating the Percentage of Students Who Were Exposed to Deeper Learning on the State Achievement Tests* (RAND Education, February 2012), http://www.hewlett.org/uploads/documents/Estimating_Percentage_Students_Tested_on_Cognitively_Demanding_Items_Through_the_State_Achievement_Tests_RAND_3_2012.pdf.

104 *In one study, Clark University*: Wendy Grolnick, personal communication.

105 *A University of Virginia study*: Daphna Bassok, Scott Latham, and Anna Rorem, "Is Kindergarten the New First Grade?" EdPolicyWorks Working Paper Series, no. 20, http://curry.virginia.edu/uploads/resourceLibrary/20_Bassok_Is_Kindergarten_The_New_First_Grade.pdf.

105 *Schools now routinely*: Valerie Strauss, "Report: Requiring kindergarteners to read—as Common Core does—may harm some," *Washington Post*, January 13, 2015, http://www.washingtonpost.com/blogs/answer-sheet/wp/2015/01/13/report-requiring-kindergartners-to-read-as-common-core-does-may-harm-some/.

106 *In fact, evidence suggests*: David Kohn, "Let the Kids Learn Through Play," *New York Times*, May 16, 2015, http://www.nytimes.com/2015/05/17/opinion/sunday/let-the-kids-learn-through-play.html.

106 *To illuminate the link*: Brent D. Fulton, Richard M. Scheffler, and Stephen P. Hinshaw, "State Variation in Increased ADHD Prevalence: Links to NCLB School Accountability and State Medication Laws," *Psychiatric Services* (2015), provided in advance of publication.

107 *A case on Long Island*: Jenny Anderson and Winnie Hu, "20 Students Now Accused in L.I. on Cheating," *New York Times*, November 22, 2011, http://www.nytimes.com/2011/11/23/education/more-students-charged-in-long-island-sat-cheating-case.html.

107 *At Middleton High School*: Elena Kadvany and Chris Kenrick, "Wisconsin Principal Named to Head Gunn High School," *Palo Alto Weekly*, May 19, 2014, http://www.paloaltoonline.com/news/2014/05/16/wisconsin-principal-named-to-head-gunn-high-school.

      Denise Herrmann and Lisa Jondle, "Letter to Middleton HS Parents," Madison.com,

December 20, 2013, http://host.madison.com/letter-to-middleton-hs-parents/pdf_bd 7e8103-3f30-5034-899d-78cf18831471.html.

108 *Susan Engel, an education psychologist*: Susan Engel, "7 things every kid should master," *Boston Globe Magazine*, February 26, 2015, http://www.bostonglobe.com/magazine /2015/02/26/things-every-kid-should-master/uM72LGr63zeaStOp9zGyrJ/story .html.

108 *Daniel Koretz, a Harvard psychometrician*: Daniel Koretz, *Measuring Up: What Educational Testing Really Tells Us* (Cambridge, MA: Harvard University Press, 2009), 10.

108 *That's because, scientifically speaking*: Grace Rubenstein, "Reinventing the Big Test: The Challenge of Authentic Assessment," *Edutopia*, March 18, 2008, http://www.edutopia .org/testing-authentic-assessment-reform.

109 *And experiments such as those*: Heckman, Stixrud, and Urzua, "The Effects of Cognitive and Noncognitive Abilities."

109 *"Innovation comes from"*: Yong Zhao, *Catching Up or Leading the Way: American Education in the Age of Globalization* (Alexandria, VA: ASCD, 2009), 68.

109 *China's historical devotion*: Ibid., 81.

110 *The flourishing of*: Ibid., 95–96.

110 *By contrast, Finnish children*: Anu Partanen, "What We're Ignoring About Finnish Schools' Success," *The Atlantic*, December 29, 2011, http://www.theatlantic.com/na tional/archive/2011/12/what-americans-keep-ignoring-about-finlands-school-success /250564/.

Pasi Sahlberg, "Teach for Finland? Why It Won't Happen," *Washington Post*, February 12, 2015, http://www.washingtonpost.com/blogs/answer-sheet/wp/2015/02/12 /teach-for-finland-why-it-wont-happen/.

110 *Plus, young children*: Partanen, "What We're Ignoring."

113 *Students in the consortium*: Performance Standards Consortium, *Educating for the 21st Century: Data Report on the New York Performance Standards Consortium*, http://www .nyclu.org/files/releases/testing_consortium_report.pdf.

113 *Of those who enter*: Ibid.

"Retention Rates—First-Time College Freshmen Returning Their Second Year" (2008), NCHEMS Information Center, accessed June 5, 2015, http://www.higher edinfo.org/dbrowser/?year=2008&level=nation&mode=map&state=0&submeasure =223.

116 *In 2011, under the leadership*: Carmen Coleman, personal communication.

116 *Within a couple of years*: Anya Kamenetz, "In Kentucky, Moving Beyond Dependence on Tests," National Public Radio, June 1, 2014, http://www.npr.org/sections/ed/2014 /06/01/317433695/in-kentucky-students-succeed-without-tests.

117 *After Danville initiated*: Amy Swann, personal communication.

120 *FairTest reports that by fall*: Monty Neill, personal communication.

120 *That same fall*: Patrick O'Donnell, "Is student testing excessive? Is it working? National educators raise those questions today," *Cleveland Plain Dealer*, October 15, 2014, http://www.cleveland.com/metro/index.ssf/2014/10/is_student_testing_excessive _is_it_working_national_educators_raise_those_questions_today.html.

120 *On a smaller scale*: Peter Marteka, "Glastonbury Principal May Gauge Support for Publishing Honor Rolls," *The Hartford Courant*, September 12, 2011.
Margaret Smith, "Acton-Boxborough Schools Will Not Publish Honor Rolls," WickedLocal.com, December 16, 2011.

120 *the whole district of Windsor Locks*: David Desroches, "Goodbye to Grades: Windsor Locks Schools Pioneer a New Way to Assess Students," WNPR, June 8, 2015, http://wnpr.org/post/goodbye-grades-windsor-locks-schools-pioneer-new-way-assess-students.

120 *"The Common Core, however dressed"*: Yong Zhao, "Common Sense Vs. Common Core: How to Minimize the Damages of the Common Core," Zhao Learning blog, June 17, 2012, http://zhaolearning.com/2012/06/17/common-sense-vs-common-core-how-to-minimize-the-damages-of-the-common-core/.

121 *We can begin, of course*: Lazarín, *Testing Overload in America's Schools*.

122 *Test scores are well known*: Sean F. Reardon, "No Rich Child Left Behind," *New York Times*, April 27, 2013, http://opinionator.blogs.nytimes.com/2013/04/27/no-rich-child-left-behind/.

122 *Dozens of high schools*: Jay Mathews, "A Rankings Boycott, of Sorts, Leads to an Invigorating Exchange," *Washington Post*, April 14, 2008, http://www.washingtonpost.com/wp-dyn/content/article/2008/04/13/AR2008041302372.html.

5. College Admissions: Break Free from The Frenzy

128 *For the class of 2018*: Nick Anderson, "College admission rates for Class of 2018: an imperfect but closely watched metric," *Washington Post*, April 3, 2014, http://www.washingtonpost.com/local/education/college-admission-rates-for-class-of-2018-an-imperfect-but-closely-watched-metric/2014/04/03/820ff578-b6af-11e3-8cc3-d4bf56577eb_story.html.

128 *Those odds may not*: Kevin Carey, "For Accomplished Students, Reaching a Good College Isn't as Hard as It Seems," *New York Times*, TheUpshot, November 29, 2014, http://www.nytimes.com/2014/11/30/upshot/for-accomplished-students-reaching-a-top-college-isnt-actually-that-hard.html.

129 *Dodds's charges are suffering*: Jeff Mitchell, "Harvard-or-Walmart Syndrome," essay published online, accessed June 19, 2015, http://jeffmitchellassociates.com/Jeff/harvardorwalmart3.pdf.

129 *The New York Times's Frank Bruni*: Frank Bruni, "How to Survive the College Admissions Madness," *New York Times*, March 13, 2015, http://www.nytimes.com/2015/03/15/opinion/sunday/frank-bruni-how-to-survive-the-college-admissions-madness.html.

130 *The craziest extreme*: Peter Waldman, "How to Get Into an Ivy League College—Guaranteed," *Bloomberg Businessweek*, September 4, 2014, http://www.bloomberg.com/news/articles/2014-09-04/how-to-get-into-an-ivy-league-college-guaranteed.

131 *As Deresiewicz tells it*: Deresiewicz, *Excellent Sheep*, 27–40.

131 *Between 1970 and 2010*: "Number Enrolled in College by Type of School and Enroll-

ment Status, 1970 to 2013," US Census Bureau, accessed June 5, 2015, http://www
.census.gov/hhes/school/data/cps/historical/FigureA-7_2013.pdf.

132   *In fact, over the past forty-five years*: Kevin Eagan et al., "The American Freshman: Na-
tional Norms Fall 2014," Cooperative Institutional Research Program at the Higher
Education Research Institute at UCLA, p. 44, http://www.heri.ucla.edu/monographs
/TheAmericanFreshman2014.pdf.

      Robert J. Panos, Alexander W. Astin, and John A. Creager, "National Norms for
Entering College Freshmen—Fall 1967," Office of Research, American Council
on Education, 34, http://www.heri.ucla.edu/monographs/TheAmericanFreshman
2014.pdf.

132   *The annual lineup purports*: "How U.S. News Calculated the 2015 Best Colleges Rankings," *U.S. News & World Report*, September 8, 2014, http://www.usnews.com/educa
tion/best-colleges/articles/2014/09/08/how-us-news-calculated-the-2015-best-col
leges-rankings.

132   Washington Monthly *deserves*: "2014 National Universities Rankings," *Washington
Monthly*, accessed June 19, 2015, http://www.washingtonmonthly.com/college_guide
/rankings-2014/national-universities-rank.php.

133   *Arizona State University psychologist*: Suniya Luthar et al., "'I can, therefore I must': Fragility in the upper-middle classes."

133   *Reed argued that*: "Reed and the Rankings Game," Reed College, last modified September 9, 2014, http://www.reed.edu/apply/college-rankings.html.

133   *The college paid a price*: Ibid.

133   *I was shocked to learn*: Daniel Golden, "Glass Floor: Colleges Reject Top Applicants,
Accepting Only the Students Likely to Enroll," *Wall Street Journal*, May 29, 2001,
http://www.wsj.com/articles/SB991083160294634500.

133   *A school's ranking*: "How U.S. News Calculated the 2015 Best Colleges Rankings."

133   *In part for these reasons*. Stephen Burd and Rachel Fishman, "Ten Ways Colleges Work
You Over," *Washington Monthly*, September/October 2014, http://www.washington
monthly.com/magazine/septemberoctober_2014/features/ten_ways_colleges_work
_you_ove051760.php?page=all. Lloyd Thacker, executive director of the Education
Conservancy, personal communication.

134   *The National Association for College Admission Counseling*: Melissa E. Clinedinst, Sarah
F. Hurley, and David A. Hawkins, "State of College Admission 2013," National Association for College Admission Counseling, 2014.

134   *College professors widely*: Deresiewicz, *Excellent Sheep*.
      Abigail Baird, personal communication. Alison Gopnik, personal communication.

136   Politico *reports that*: Stephanie Simon, "Advanced Placement classes failing students,"
Politico, August 21, 2013, http://www.politico.com/story/2013/08/education-ad
vanced-placement-classes-tests-95723.html.

136   *At the same time*: Janet Lorin and Lisa Wolfson, "Not-for-Profit College Board Getting Rich as Fees Hit Students," *Bloomberg Businessweek*, August 17, 2011, http://www
.bloomberg.com/news/articles/2011-08-18/not-for-profit-college-board-getting-rich
-as-fees-hit-students.

Rick Cohen, "Is the College Board a NINO (Nonprofit in Name Only)?" *Nonprofit Quarterly*, October 16, 2012, https://nonprofitquarterly.org/policysocial-context/21 184-is-the-college-board-a-nino-nonprofit-in-name-only.html.

136 *Yet in 2012*: Simon, "Advanced Placement classes failing students."

136 *The passing rates*: Ibid.

137 *A Harvard and University of Virginia survey*: Steve Bradt, "High school AP courses do not predict college success in science," *Harvard Gazette*, 2007, http://news.harvard.edu /gazette/2006/02.23/05-ap.html.

137 *And a study of more than*: Saul Gesier and Veronica Santelices, "The Role of Advanced Placement and Honors Classes in College Admissions," University of California, Berkeley, Center for Studies on Higher Education, Research and Occasional Paper Series, CSHE.4.04 (2004).

137 *Middlebury College math professor*: Priscilla Bremser, letter to the editor, *New York Times*, January 11, 2011, http://www.nytimes.com/2011/01/17/opinion/lweb17math.html.

137 *Besides, some private colleges*: Tamar Lewin, "Dartmouth Stops Credits for Excelling on A.P. Test," *New York Times*, January 17, 2013, http://www.nytimes.com/2013/01/18 /education/dartmouth-stops-credits-for-excelling-on-ap-test.html.

138 *The U.S. News & World Report "Best High Schools"*: Robert Morse, "How U.S. News Calculated the 2015 Best High Schools Rankings," *U.S. News & World Report*, May 11, 2015, http://www.usnews.com/education/best-high-schools/articles/how-us-news -calculated-the-rankings.

138 *And schools whose students*: Jay Mathews, "Jay Mathews's method of selecting America's Most Challenging High Schools," *Washington Post*, April 4, 2014, http://www.washing tonpost.com/local/education/abcs-of-americas-most-challenging-high-schools/2014 /04/02/bf19b1c2-b8f1-11e3-899e-bb708e3539dd_story.html.

142 *To restrain runaway competition*: Barry Schwartz, "Top Colleges Should Select Randomly From a Pool of 'Good Enough,'" *Chronicle of Higher Education*, February 25, 2005.

143 *Indeed, SAT scores parallel*: Josh Zumbrun, "SAT Scores and Income Inequality: How Wealthier Kids Rank Higher," *Wall Street Journal*, October 7, 2014, http://blogs.wsj .com/economics/2014/10/07/sat-scores-and-income-inequality-how-wealthier-kids -rank-higher/.

143 *Even the National Association*: National Association for College Admission Counseling, *Report of the Commission on the Use of Standardized Tests in Undergraduate Admission* (Arlington, VA: September 2008), http://www.nacacnet.org/research/Publications Resources/Marketplace/Documents/TestingComission_FinalReport.pdf.

144 *FairTest, a Boston-based organization*: "Colleges and Universities That Do Not Use SAT/ACT Scores for Admitting Substantial Numbers of Students Into Bachelor Degree Programs," FairTest, last modified summer 2015, http://fairtest.org/university /optional.

144 *A 2014 study backed by NACAC*: William C. Hiss and Valerie W. Franks, *Defining Promise: Optional Standardized Testing in American College and University Admissions* (National Association for College Admission Counseling, February 5, 2014), http://www.nacacnet .org/research/research-data/nacac-research/Documents/DefiningPromise.pdf.

145 *This "dimensional" application*: Scott Jaschik, " 'Dimensional' Admissions," *Insider Higher Ed*, September 25, 2014, https://www.insidehighered.com/news/2014/09/25/ben nington-introduces-new-option-applicants.

145 *Bard president Leon Botstein*: Ariel Kaminer, "Didn't Ace SAT? Just Design Microbe Transplant Research," *New York Times*, September 28, 2013, http://www.nytimes.com /2013/09/29/nyregion/didnt-ace-sat-just-design-microbe-transplant-research.html.

146 *It turns out that a college's admission rate*: "How U.S. News Calculated the 2015 Best Colleges Rankings."

147 *The 2013 Chegg Student Skill Index*: Chegg Inc., *Bridge That Gap*.

148 *Limit the number of times*: Wake Forest University, " 'Conscientious Objector' Opts Out of SAT," *Rethinking Admissions* blog, October 29, 2010, http://blog.rethinkingadmis sions.wfu.edu/2010/10/%E2%80%9Cconscientious-objector%E2%80%9D-opts-out -of-sat/.

150 *And individual educators*: Esther Wojcicki, "College Applications: Why Many Students Should Pass on Ivy League Schools," *Edutopia*, March 12, 2010, http://www.edutopia .org/college-admissions-school-choice.

6. Teaching and Learning: This Way Up

156 *"What was considered"*: National Education Association, *An Educator's Guide to the "4 Cs,"* http://www.nea.org/assets/docs/A-Guide-to-Four-Cs.pdf.

156 *A group of leaders*: "Framework for 21st Century Learning," Partnership for 21st Century Learning, accessed June 19, 2015, http://www.p21.org/about-us/p21-framework.

157 *Tony Wagner, an educator*: Tony Wagner, *The Global Achievement Gap: Why Even Our Best Schools Don't Teach the New Survival Skills Our Children Need—and What We Can Do About It* (New York: Basic Books, 2010).

157 *Yet when the*: American Management Association, *AMA 2012: Critical Skills Survey* (March 2013), http://playbook.amanet.org/wp-content/uploads/2013/03/2012 -Critical-Skills-Survey-pdf.pdf.

158 *One study published*: Robert C. Pianta et al., "Opportunities to Learn in America's Elementary Classrooms," *Science* 315, no. 5820 (March 30, 2007), 1795–96.

158 *Teachers of English*: Wagner, *The Global Achievement Gap*, 36.

159 *A 2014 study at the Universities of Washington*: Scott Freeman et al., "Active Learning Increases Student Performance in Science, Engineering, and Mathematics," *Proceedings of the National Academy of Sciences* 111, no. 23 (June 10, 2014), 8410–15.

163 *The outcome: 98 percent*: "Results," High Tech High, accessed June 5, 2015, http://www .hightechhigh.org/about/results.php.

       "Fast Facts: Graduation Rates," National Center for Education Statistics, accessed June 5, 2015, http://nces.ed.gov/fastfacts/display.asp?id=40.

164 *On the whole, though*: Brigid Barron and Linda Darling-Hammond, *Teaching for Meaningful Learning: A Review of Research on Inquiry-Based and Cooperative Learning*

(Edutopia, 2008), http://www.edutopia.org/pdfs/edutopia-teaching-for-meaningful -learning.pdf.

Neal Finkelstein et al., *Effects of Problem Based Economics on high school economics instruction* (Washington, DC: Institute of Education Sciences, US Department of Education, July 2010), http://ies.ed.gov/ncee/edlabs/regions/west/pdf/REL_20104012 .pdf.

Nate K. Hixson, Jason Ravitz, and Andy Whisman, *Extended Professional Development in Project-Based Learning: Impacts on 21st Century Skills Teaching and Student Achievement* (Charleston, WV: Office of Research, West Virginia Department of Education, September 2012), http://wvde.state.wv.us/research/reports2012/PBLEvalua tion_092012.pdf.

164   *Students learning this way*: Andrew Walker and Heather Leary, "A Problem Based Learning Meta Analysis: Differences Across Problem Types, Implementation Types, Disciplines, and Assessment Levels," *Interdisciplinary Journal of Problem-Based Learning* 3, no. 1 (2009).

Finkelstein et al., *Effects of Problem Based Economics*.

164   *And studies show that*: Walker and Leary, "A Problem Based Learning Meta Analysis."

164   *One study of five thousand*: Robert Geier et al., "Standardized test outcomes for students engaged in inquiry-based science curricula in the context of urban reform," *Journal of Research in Science Teaching* 45, no. 8 (August 29, 2008), 922–39.

164   *A US Department of Education*: Finkelstein et al., *Effects of Problem Based Economics*.

175   *And the state, like many others*: Taylor White, "Giving Credit Where Credit's Due: A 50-State Scan of Course Credit Policies," Carnegie Foundation for the Advancement of Teaching, August 5, 2013, http://www.carnegiefoundation.org/blog/giving-credit -where-credits-due-a-50-state-scan-of-course-credit-policies/.

175   *Trigg could choose to switch*: Shannon Burcham, personal communication.

178   *High Tech High also gets away*: School Report [High Tech High], 2012–13 Accountability Progress Reporting, California Department of Education, http://dq.cde.ca.gov /dataquest/Acnt2013/2013GrowthSch.aspx?allcds=37683383731247.

7. First, Be Well

183   *In a positive state of mind*: Carlos A. Estrada, Alice M. Isen, and Mark J. Young, "Positive Affect Facilitates Integration of Information and Decreases Anchoring in Reasoning among Physicians," *Organizational Behavior and Human Decision Processes* 72, no. 1 (1997), 117–35.

183   *Happy job candidates*: Jerry M. Burger and David F. Caldwell, "Personality, Social Activities, Job-Search Behavior and Interview Success: Distinguishing Between PANAS Trait Positive Affect and NEO Extraversion," *Motivation and Emotion* 24, no. 1 (2000), 51–62.

183   *Optimistic businesspeople*: MetLife case study, described in Shawn Achor, *The Happiness*

Advantage: The Seven Principles of Positive Psychology That Fuel Success and Performance at Work (New York: Crown Business, 2010).

183 *And students who were*: T. Bryan and J. Bryan, "Positive mood and math performance," *Journal of Learning Disabilities* 24, no. 8 (October 1991), 490–94.

183 *One study, published in*: Sonja Lyubomirsky, Laura King, and Ed Diener, "The Benefits of Frequent Positive Affect: Does Happiness Lead to Success?" *Psychological Bulletin* 131, no. 6 (November 2005), 803–55.

183 *International business leader*: Heffernan, Margaret, "Why it's time to forget the pecking order at work," TED Talk, Monterey, California, May 2015, http://www.ted.com/talks/margaret_heffernan_why_it_s_time_to_forget_the_pecking_order_at_work.

Juliet Blake and Kate Torgovnick May, "Career advice for millennials (and really, anyone) from Margaret Heffernan," TED Blog, July 3, 2015, http://blog.ted.com/career-advice-for-millennials-and-really-anyone-from-margaret-heffernan/.

184 *UNICEF, in a 2013 report*: Peter Adamson, *Child well-being in rich countries: A comparative overview* (Florence: UNICEF Office of Research, 2013).

184 *Researchers have found that, even in the most terrible circumstances*: Sara Truebridge and Bonnie Benard, "Reflections on Resilience," *Educational Leadership* 71, no. 1 (September 2013), 66–67.

184 *Children with the capacity*: Staci M. Zolkoski and Lyndal M. Bullock, "Resilience in children and youth: A review," *Children and Youth Services Review* 34 (2012), 2295–303.

Edward M. Hallowell, *The Childhood Roots of Adult Happiness: Five Steps to Help Kids Create and Sustain Lifelong Joy* (New York: Ballantine, 2002), 21.

185 *Ed Hallowell, psychiatrist*: Ibid., 33.

185 *Depression rates among first-year medical students*: Stuart J. Slavin, Debra L. Schindler, and John T. Chibnall, "Medical Student Mental Health 3.0: Improving Student Wellness Through Curricular Changes," *Academic Medicine* 89, no. 4 (April 2014), 573–77. Current data provided by Stuart Slavin via personal communication.

188 *This was an improvement*: National Association for College Admission Counseling, "Effective Counseling in Schools Increases College Access," *NACAC Research to Practice Brief* 1 (2006), 3.

188 *A high school in Naperville*: Mona Iskander, "A physical education in Naperville," PBS *Need to Know*, February 8, 2011, http://www.pbs.org/wnet/need-to-know/video/a-physical-education-in-naperville-ill/7134/.

189 *Research demonstrates that connections*: Hallowell, *The Childhood Roots of Adult Happiness*, 81–82.

Truebridge and Benard, "Reflections on Resilience."

Bonnie Benard, *Resiliency: What We Have Learned* (San Francisco: WestEd, 2004), 43.

189 *One study in New Zealand*: Craig A. Olsson, "A 32-Year Longitudinal Study of Child and Adolescent Pathways to Well-Being in Adulthood," *Journal of Happiness Studies* 14, no. 3 (July 25, 2012), 1069–83.

190 *"What resilience research"*: Benard, *Resiliency*, 66.

191 *A Palo Alto High School junior*: Carolyn Walworth, "Paly student tells of school

stress: 'Students are gasping for air,' " *The Almanac*, March 26, 2015, http://www
.almanacnews.com/news/2015/03/26/guest-opinion-on-school-stress-students-are
-gasping-for-air.

192   *He lost his first bid*: "Editorial: Catherine Crystal Foster and Ken Dauber for Palo Alto
      School Board," *Palo Alto Daily News*, November 1, 2014, http://www.mercurynews
      .com/peninsula/ci_26796880/catherine-crystal-foster-and-ken-dauber-palo-alto.

193   *In the 2012 survey*: Palo Alto Union High School District data compiled and published
      by We Can Do Better Palo Alto: https://docs.google.com/spreadsheets/d/1sYGu2
      -HNWsboTOOI3pCTrp61ara73SuOW0nxWZXEtkE/edit#gid=0.

195   *At the WINGS*: Grace Rubenstein, "The WINGS Story: An After-School Program
      Helps Students Beat the Odds," *Edutopia*, October 11, 2010, http://www.edutopia.org
      /stw-social-emotional-learning-after-school-wings-story.

196   *The earliest SEL programs*: "Social and Emotional Learning: A Short History," *Edutopia*,
      October 6, 2011, http://www.edutopia.org/social-emotional-learning-history.

196   *Now SEL is practiced*: Joseph A. Durlak et al., eds., *Handbook of Social and Emotional
      Learning: Research and Practice* (New York: Guilford, 2015), 3.

196   *Some entire city districts*: Lija Farnham et al., "Rethinking How Students Succeed," *Stan-
      ford Social Innovation Review*, February 17, 2015, http://www.ssireview.org/up_for_de
      bate/article/rethinking_how_students_succeed.

196   *A landmark 2011 study*: Joseph A. Durlak et al., "The Impact of Enhancing Students'
      Social and Emotional Learning: A Meta-Analysis of School-Based Universal Interven-
      tions," *Child Development* 82, no. 1 (January/February 2011), 474–501.

196   *Another study looking at*: Joseph A. Durlak and Roger P. Weissberg, *The Impact of After-
      School Programs That Promote Personal and Social Skills* (Chicago: Collaborative for
      Academic, Social, and Emotional Learning, 2007), http://www.lions-quest.org/pdfs
      /AfterSchoolProgramsStudy2007.pdf.

197   *Psychology "has been sidetracked"*: C. R. Snyder, Shane J. Lopez, and Jennifer Teramoto
      Pedrotti, *Positive Psychology: The Scientific and Practical Explorations of Human Strengths*
      (Los Angeles: Sage, 2010), 4.

197   *The ensuing research*: Martin Seligman et al., "Positive education: positive psychology
      and classroom interventions," *Oxford Review of Education* 35, no. 3 (June 2009), 293–
      311.

197   *They use stories*: "The Penn Resiliency Project," Positive Psychology Center, accessed
      June 19, 2015, http://www.ppc.sas.upenn.edu/prpsum.htm.

197   *The results so far*: Ibid.

197   *The skills for happiness*: University of Pennsylvania, "Positive Health," website of the Au-
      thentic Happiness program, accessed June 19, 2015, https://www.authentichappiness
      .sas.upenn.edu/learn/positivehealth.

199   *A UC Davis study*: Amy Smith et al., *Mindful Schools Program Evaluation* (UC Davis
      School of Education, June 2012), http://education.ucdavis.edu/sites/main/files/file
      -attachments/mindful_schools_final_report.081512.pdf.

199   *Studies of other mindfulness programs*: Kimberly A. Schonert-Reichl et al., "Enhanc-
      ing Cognitive and Social–Emotional Development Through a Simple-to-Administer

Mindfulness-Based School Program for Elementary School Children: A Randomized Controlled Trial," *Developmental Psychology* 51, no. 1 (2015), 52–66.

Sanford Nidich et al., "Academic Achievement and Transcendental Meditation: A Study with At-Risk Urban Middle School Students," *Education* 131, no. 3 (Spring 2011), 556–64.

199 *My favorite stat*: David L. Kirp, "Meditation transforms roughest San Francisco schools," *San Francisco Chronicle*, January 12, 2014, http://m.sfgate.com/opinion/openforum /article/Meditation-transforms-roughest-San-Francisco-5136942.php.

200 *In an interview*: "Segment: Sherry Turkle on Being Alone Together," Moyers & Company, October 18, 2013, http://billmoyers.com/segment/sherry-turkle-on-being-alone -together/.

202 *As to the confounding question*: "Media and Children," American Academy of Pediatrics, accessed June 19, 2015, https://www.aap.org/en-us/advocacy-and-policy/aap-health -initiatives/Pages/Media-and-Children.aspx.

202 *I take comfort*: "How much screen time is OK for my kid(s)?" Common Sense Media, accessed June 19, 2015, https://www.commonsensemedia.org/screen-time/how-much -screen-time-is-ok-for-my-kids.

204 *It also does not put the idea*: Adam Strassberg, "Guest Opinion: Keep Calm and Parent On," *Palo Alto Weekly*, March 16, 2015, http://www.paloaltoonline.com/news/2015 /03/16/guest-opinion-keep-calm-and-parent-on.

8. Action: How You Can Replace the Race to Nowhere

211 *Children should be going to bed*: "Sleep Duration Recommendations," National Sleep Foundation, accessed June 5, 2015, http://sleepfoundation.org/sites/default/files /STREPchanges_1.png.

215 *Parents have done this effectively*: Monty Neill, personal communication.

Epilogue

236 *The annual survey of entering college freshmen*: Cooperative Institutional Research Program, *The American Freshman*.

237 *Susan Engel, the Williams College psychologist*: Susan Engel, *The End of the Rainbow: How Educating for Happiness (Not Money) Would Transform Our Schools* (New York: New Press, 2015).

238 *Meanwhile, more than 550*: Lazarín, *Testing Overload in America's Schools*.

238 *The young and growing*: "The Student Bill of Rights," Student Voice, accessed June 19, 2015, http://www.sturights.org/.

239 *"You do have to say 'no'"*: Betty Friedan, *The Feminine Mystique* (New York: W.W. Norton & Co., 1963).

Selected Bibliography

T HE FOLLOWING RESOURCES were influential in shaping the thinking that went into this book and honing my ideas about the culture of
school and childhood. While far from exhaustive, this list includes a range
of materials that offer diverse insights and information that might be helpful for those delving deeper into the issues I've explored. To avoid duplica-
tion (and save paper), I've left out most of the citations that appear in the
notes, except a select few that I consider essential reading. However, there
are many valuable resources in the notes, as well.

In addition to the published works listed here, countless people and
school communities have helped to hone my perspective on childhood and
education over the last eight years. Together with my colleagues, I have observed practices firsthand in hundreds of schools, filmed at dozens of them,
and interviewed hundreds of experts, educators, and activists. The following organizations also supported some of the research in this book and are
valuable resources in their own right:

- The National Center for Fair and Open Testing, at fairtest.org

- The Buck Institute for Education, at bie.org

- *Edutopia,* a publication of the George Lucas Educational Foundation, at edutopia.org

- The Education Conservancy, at educationconservancy.org

- Colleges That Change Lives, at ctcl.org

- The Collaborative for Academic, Social, and Emotional Learning,
  at casel.org

New conversations, articles, blog posts, testimonials, TED Talks, and other inputs continue to mold my thinking every day. For up-to-date resources, visit the Race to Nowhere website at reellinkfilms.com.

Books

Baker, David P., and Gerald K. LeTendre. *National Differences, Global Similarities: World Culture and the Future of Schooling.* Redwood City, CA: Stanford University Press, 2005.

Benard, Bonnie. *Resiliency: What We Have Learned.* San Francisco: WestEd, 2004.

Bennett, Sara, and Nancy Kalish. *The Case Against Homework: How Homework Is Hurting Children and What Parents Can Do About It,* reprint edition. New York: Harmony, 2007.

Berger, Ron. *An Ethic of Excellence: Building a Culture of Craftsmanship with Students.* Portsmouth, NH: Heinemann, 2003.

Boaler, Jo. *Mathematical Mindsets: Unleashing Students' Potential through Creative Math, Inspiring Messages and Innovative Teaching.* Hoboken, NJ: Jossey-Bass, 2015.

———. *What's Math Got to Do with It?: How Teachers and Parents Can Transform Mathematics Learning and Inspire Success,* revised edition. New York: Penguin Books, 2015.

Bronson, Po, and Ashley Merryman. *NurtureShock: New Thinking About Children,* reprint edition. New York: Twelve, 2011.

Califano, Joseph A., Jr. *How to Raise a Drug-Free Kid: The Straight Dope for Parents,* revised edition. New York: Touchstone, 2014.

Carter, Christine. *Raising Happiness: 10 Simple Steps for More Joyful Kids and Happier Parents,* reprint edition. New York: Ballantine Books, 2011.

Damon, William. *The Path to Purpose: How Young People Find Their Calling in Life.* New York: Free Press, 2009.

Deresiewicz, William. *Excellent Sheep: The Miseducation of the American Elite and the Way to a Meaningful Life,* reprint edition. New York: Free Press, 2014.

Dweck, Carol. *Mindset: The New Psychology of Success,* reprint edition. New York: Ballantine Books, 2007.

Elkind, David. *The Hurried Child,* 25th anniversary edition. Boston: Da Capo Press, 2006.

Engel, Angela. *Seeds of Tomorrow: Solutions for Improving Our Children's Education.* Boulder, CO: Paradigm Publishers, 2010.

Engel, Susan. *The End of the Rainbow: How Educating for Happiness (Not Money) Would Transform Our Schools.* New York: New Press, 2015.

Frankenstein, Diane W. *Reading Together: Everything You Need to Know to Raise a Child Who Loves to Read.* New York: Perigee Books, 2009.

Frost, Maya. *The New Global Student: Skip the SAT, Save Thousands on Tuition, and Get a Truly International Education.* New York: Harmony, 2009.

Gardner, Howard. *Five Minds for the Future.* Boston: Harvard Business Review Press, 2009.

Green, Elizabeth. *Building a Better Teacher.* New York: W. W. Norton & Co., 2014.

Grolnick, Wendy S., and Kathy Seal. *Pressured Parents, Stressed-out Kids: Dealing with Competition While Raising a Successful Child.* Amherst, MA: Prometheus Books, 2008.

Guinier, Lani. *The Tyranny of the Meritocracy: Democratizing Higher Education in America.* Boston: Beacon Press, 2015.

Hagopian, Jesse, ed. *More Than a Score: The New Uprising Against High-Stakes Testing.* Chicago: Haymarket Books, 2014.

Hallowell, Edward M. *The Childhood Roots of Adult Happiness: Five Steps to Help Kids Create and Sustain Lifelong Joy.* New York: Ballantine Books, 2003.

Harris, Phillip, Bruce M. Smith, and Joan Harris. *The Myths of Standardized Tests: Why They Don't Tell You What You Think They Do.* Washington, DC: Rowman & Littlefield Publishers, 2011.

Hinshaw, Stephen, and Rachel Kranz. *The Triple Bind: Saving Our Teenage Girls from Today's Pressures.* New York: Ballantine Books, 2009.

Kohn, Alfie. *The Homework Myth: Why Our Kids Get Too Much of a Bad Thing,* reprint edition. Boston: Da Capo Press, 2007.

———. *The Myth of the Spoiled Child: Challenging the Conventional Wisdom About Children and Parenting.* Boston: Da Capo Lifelong Books, 2014.

———. *Punished by Rewards: The Trouble with Gold Stars, Incentive Plans, A's, Praise, and Other Bribes,* 2nd edition. New York: Mariner Books, 1999.

Koretz, Daniel. *Measuring Up: What Educational Testing Really Tells Us.* Cambridge, MA: Harvard University Press, 2009.

Kralovec, Etta, and James Buell. *The End of Homework: How Homework Disrupts Families, Overburdens Children, and Limits Learning.* Boston: Beacon Press, 2001.

Levine, Madeline. *The Price of Privilege: How Parental Pressure and Material Advantage Are Creating a Generation of Disconnected and Unhappy Kids,* reprint edition. New York: Harper Perennial, 2008.

Levitt, Steven D., and Stephen J. Dubner. *Freakonomics: A Rogue Economist Explores the Hidden Side of Everything.* New York: William Morrow Paperbacks, 2009.

Louv, Richard. *Last Child in the Woods: Saving Our Children from Nature-Deficit Disorder.* Chapel Hill, NC: Algonquin Books, 2008.

Medina, John. *Brain Rules: 12 Principles for Surviving and Thriving at Work, Home, and School,* 2nd edition. Edmonds, WA: Pear Press, 2014.

Mogel, Wendy. *The Blessing of a B Minus: Using Jewish Teachings to Raise Resilient Teenagers,* reprint edition. New York: Scribner, 2011.

Nakazawa, Donna Jackson. *The Last Best Cure: My Quest to Awaken the Healing Parts of My Brain and Get Back My Body, My Joy, and My Life.* New York: Hudson Street Press, 2013.

Payne, Kim John, and Lisa M. Ross. *Simplicity Parenting: Using the Extraordinary Power of Less to Raise Calmer, Happier, and More Secure Kids.* New York: Ballantine Books, 2010.

Pink, Daniel H. *Drive: The Surprising Truth About What Motivates Us.* New York: Riverhead Books, 2011.

———. *A Whole New Mind: Why Right-Brainers Will Rule the Future.* New York: Riverhead Books, 2006.

Pope, Loren. *Colleges That Change Lives: 40 Schools That Will Change the Way You Think About Colleges,* 4th revised edition. Revised by Hilary Masell Oswald. New York: Penguin Books, 2012.

Ravitch, Diane. *The Death and Life of the Great American School System: How Testing and Choice Are Undermining Education,* revised and expanded edition. New York: Basic Books, 2011.

——. *Reign of Error: The Hoax of the Privatization Movement and the Danger to America's Public Schools,* reprint edition. New York: Vintage, 2014.

Ripley, Amanda. *The Smartest Kids in the World: And How They Got That Way,* reprint edition. New York: Simon & Schuster, 2014.

Robinson, Ken. *Out of Our Minds: Learning to Be Creative,* 2nd edition. North Mankato, MN: Capstone, 2011.

Robinson, Ken, and Lou Aronica. *Creative Schools: The Grassroots Revolution That's Transforming Education.* New York: Viking, 2015.

——. *The Element: How Finding Your Passion Changes Everything,* reprint edition. New York: Penguin Books, 2009.

Rubin, Gretchen. *The Happiness Project: Or, Why I Spent a Year Trying to Sing in the Morning, Clean My Closets, Fight Right, Read Aristotle, and Generally Have More Fun,* reprint edition. New York: Harper Paperbacks, 2011.

Sahlberg, Pasi. *Finnish Lessons 2.0: What Can the World Learn from Educational Change in Finland?,* 2nd edition. New York: Teachers College Press, 2014.

Schulte, Brigid. *Overwhelmed: How to Work, Love, and Play When No One Has the Time,* reprint edition. New York: Picador, 2015.

Schwartz, Barry. *The Paradox of Choice: Why More Is Less.* New York: Harper Perennial, 2005.

Seligman, Martin E. P. *Authentic Happiness: Using the New Positive Psychology to Realize Your Potential for Lasting Fulfillment.* New York: Atria Books, 2004.

Selingo, Jeffrey J. *College (Un)bound: The Future of Higher Education and What It Means for Students,* reprint edition. Seattle: Amazon Publishing, 2015.

Senior, Jennifer. *All Joy and No Fun: The Paradox of Modern Parenthood,* reprint edition. New York: Ecco, 2015.

Siegel, Daniel J., and Tina Payne Bryson. *The Whole-Brain Child: 12 Revolutionary Strategies to Nurture Your Child's Developing Mind.* New York: Bantam, 2012.

Steinberg, Laurence. *Age of Opportunity: Lessons from the New Science of Adolescence.* New York: Eamon Dolan/Houghton Mifflin Harcourt, 2014.

Strauch, Barbara. *The Primal Teen: What the New Discoveries about the Teenage Brain Tell Us about Our Kids,* reprint edition. New York: Anchor, 2004.

Thacker, Lloyd, ed. *College Unranked: Ending the College Admissions Frenzy.* Cambridge, MA: Harvard University Press, 2005.

Thomas, Douglas, and John Seely Brown. *A New Culture of Learning: Cultivating the Imagination for a World of Constant Change.* Seattle: CreateSpace Independent Publishing Platform, 2011.

Tough, Paul. *How Children Succeed: Grit, Curiosity, and the Hidden Power of Character,* reprint edition. New York: Mariner Books, 2013.

Truebridge, Sara. *Resilience Begins with Beliefs: Building on Student Strengths for Success in School.* New York: Teachers College Press, 2013.

Turkle, Sherry. *Alone Together: Why We Expect More from Technology and Less from Each Other.* New York: Basic Books, 2012.

Twenge, Jean. *Generation Me: Why Today's Young Americans Are More Confident, Assertive, Entitled—and More Miserable Than Ever Before.* New York: Atria Books, 2007.

Wagner, Tony. *Creating Innovators: The Making of Young People Who Will Change the World,* reprint edition. New York: Scribner, 2015.

———. *The Global Achievement Gap: Why Even Our Best Schools Don't Teach the New Survival Skills Our Children Need—and What We Can Do About It,* revised and updated edition. New York: Basic Books, 2014.

Zhao, Yong. *Catching Up or Leading the Way: American Education in the Age of Globalization.* Alexandria, VA: Association for Supervision & Curriculum Development, 2009.

———. *World Class Learners: Educating Creative and Entrepreneurial Students.* Newbury Park, CA: Corwin, 2012.

Articles

Adolescent Sleep Working Group, Committee on Adolescence, and Council on School Health. "Policy Statement: School Start Times for Adolescents." *Pediatrics* 134, no. 3 (September 2014): 1697.

American Psychological Association. *Stress in America: Are Teens Adopting Adults' Stress Habits?* Washington, DC: February 11, 2014. https://www.apa.org/news/press/releases/stress/2013/stress-report.pdf.

Bacigalupe, Gonzalo. "Newton Suicides: Is High-Achiever School Culture Breaking Our Kids?" WBUR, February 17, 2014. http://commonhealth.wbur.org/2014/02/newton-suicide-stress.

———. "Teen Suicides in Privileged Suburb: We Have to Keep Talking." WBUR, February 21, 2014. http://commonhealth.wbur.org/2014/02/teen-suicide-suburb.

Barker, Jane E., Andrei D. Semenov, Laura Michaelson, Lindsay S. Provan, Hannah R. Snyder, and Yuko Munakata. "Less-structured time in children's daily lives predicts self-directed executive functioning." *Frontiers in Psychology* 5, no. 593 (June 17, 2014).

Benn, Melissa. "Education's culture of overwork is turning children and teachers into ghosts." *Guardian,* April 16, 2014. http://www.theguardian.com/commentisfree/2014/apr/16/culture-overwork-teachers-children-ghosts-schools.

Berliner, David. "Why giving standardized tests to young children is 'really dumb.'" *Washington Post,* July 19, 2011. http://www.washingtonpost.com/blogs/answer-sheet/post/why-giving-standardized-tests-to-young-children-is-really-dumb/2011/07/18/gIQAB7OnMI_blog.html.

Bhatia, Aatish. "Active Learning Leads to Higher Grades and Fewer Failing Students in Science, Math, and Engineering." *Wired,* May 12, 2014. http://www.wired.com/2014/05/empzeal-active-learning/.

Bronson, Po. "Snooze or Lose." *New York,* October 7, 2007. http://nymag.com/news/features/38951/.

Bronson, Po, and Ashley Merryman. "The Creativity Crisis." *Newsweek,* July 7, 2010. http://www.newsweek.com/creativity-crisis-74665.

Bruni, Frank. "Best, Brightest—and Saddest?" *New York Times*, April 11, 2015. http://www
.nytimes.com/2015/04/12/opinion/sunday/frank-bruni-best-brightest-and-saddest.html.

Bryant, Jeff. "Lani Guinier on our Ivy League meritocracy lie: 'You don't want only those
people who do well on the SAT.'" *Salon*, February 4, 2015. http://www.salon.com/
2015/02/04/lani_guinier_on_our_ivy_league_meritocracy_lie_you_dont_want_only
_those_people_who_do_well_on_the_sat/.

Burd, Stephen, and Rachel Fishman. "Ten Ways Colleges Work You Over." *Washington
Monthly*, September/October 2014. http://www.washingtonmonthly.com/magazine/
septemberoctober_2014/features/ten_ways_colleges_work_you_ove051760.php.

Canady, Robert Lynn, and Michael D. Rettig. "The Power of Innovative Scheduling." *Educational Leadership* 53, no. 3 (November 1995): 4–10.

Childress, Herb. "17 Reasons Why Football Is Better Than High School." *North Coast Journal
Weekly*, September 24, 1998. http://www.northcoastjournal.com/092498/cover0924.html.

Cooperative Institutional Research Program. *The American Freshman: National Norms Fall
2014*. Higher Education Research Institute at UCLA, February 2015. http://www.heri
.ucla.edu/briefs/TheAmericanFreshman2014-Brief.pdf.

Darling-Hammond, Linda. "Beyond the Bubble Test: Why We Need Performance Assessments." *Huffington Post*, July 15, 2014. http://www.huffingtonpost.com/linda-darlingham
mond/beyond-the-bubble-test-wh_b_5588990.html.

Davis, Joshua. "How a Radical New Teaching Method Could Unleash a Generation of Geniuses." *Wired*, October 15, 2013. http://www.wired.com/2013/10/free-thinkers/.

Divecha, Diana, and Robin Stern. "American Teens Are Stressed and Bored. It's Time to Talk
About Feelings." *Time*, April 10, 2015. http://time.com/3774596/american-teens-emotions/.

Dobbs, David. "Beautiful Brains." *National Geographic*, October 2011. http://ngm.national
geographic.com/2011/10/teenage-brains/dobbs-text.

Drew, Christopher. "Why Science Majors Change Their Minds (It's Just So Darn Hard)."
New York Times, November 4, 2011. http://www.nytimes.com/2011/11/06/education/
edlife/why-science-majors-change-their-mind-its-just-so-darn-hard.html.

Edwards, David. "American Schools Are Training Kids for a World That Doesn't Exist." *Wired*,
October 17, 2014. http://www.wired.com/2014/10/on-learning-by-doing/.

Emanuel, Gabrielle. "Among Dartmouth's Lathes and Saws, Lessons in Creativity." NPR,
December 1, 2014. http://www.npr.org/sections/ed/2014/12/01/353286773/among
-dartmoths-lathes-and-saws-lessons-in-creativity.

Enayati, Amanda. "Is homework making your child sick?" CNN, March 21, 2014. http://
www.cnn.com/2014/03/21/health/homework-stress/index.html.

Engel, Susan. "7 things every kid should master." *Boston Globe*, February 26, 2015. http://
www.bostonglobe.com/magazine/2015/02/26/things-every-kid-should-master/uM72L
Gr63zeaStOp9zGyrJ/story.html.

Entin, Esther. "All Work and No Play: Why Your Kids Are More Anxious, Depressed." *Atlantic*,
October 12, 2011. http://www.theatlantic.com/health/archive/2011/10/all-work-and
-no-play-why-your-kids-are-more-anxious-depressed/246422/.

———. "The Case for Recess." *Atlantic*, February 27, 2012. http://www.theatlantic.com/
health/archive/2012/02/the-case-for-recess/253549/.

Farnham, Lija, Gihani Fernando, Mike Perigo, Colleen Brosman, and Paul Tough. "Rethinking How Students Succeed." *Stanford Social Innovation Review,* February 17, 2015.

Fitzsimmons, William, Marlyn E. McGrath, and Charles Ducey. "Time Out or Burn Out for the Next Generation." Harvard College, 2000 (revised 2011). https://college.harvard.edu/admissions/preparing-college/should-i-take-time.

Flanagan, Caitlin. "The Ivy Delusion: The Real Reason the Good Mothers Are So Rattled by Amy Chua." *Atlantic,* April 2011. http://www.theatlantic.com/magazine/archive/2011/04/the-ivy-delusion/308397/.

Gladwell, Malcolm. "The Order of Things: What college rankings really tell us." *New Yorker,* February 14, 2011. http://www.newyorker.com/magazine/2011/02/14/the-order-of-things.

Gordon Commission on the Future of Assessment in Education. "Shifting Paradigms: Beyond the Abstract." *Assessment, Teaching, and Learning* 2, no. 2 (April 2012).

Gray, Peter. "The Decline of Play and the Rise of Psychopathology in Children and Adolescents." *American Journal of Play* 3, no. 4 (Spring 2011). http://www.journalofplay.org/sites/www.journalofplay.org/files/pdf-articles/3-4-article-gray-decline-of-play.pdf.

Greenfeld, Karl Taro. "My Daughter's Homework Is Killing Me." *Atlantic,* October 2013. http://www.theatlantic.com/magazine/archive/2013/10/my-daughters-homework-is-killing-me/309514/.

Hamilton, Jon. "Scientists Say Child's Play Helps Build a Better Brain." NPR, August 6, 2014. http://www.npr.org/sections/ed/2014/08/06/336361277/scientists-say-childs-play-helps-build-a-better-brain.

Hanscom, Angela. "Why so many kids can't sit still in school today." *Washington Post,* July 8, 2014. http://www.washingtonpost.com/blogs/answer-sheet/wp/2014/07/08/why-so-many-kids-cant-sit-still-in-school-today/.

Hawkins, Beth. "The Pursuit of Deeper Learning." *Atlantic,* December 2, 2014. http://www.theatlantic.com/education/archive/2014/12/the-pursuit-of-deeper-learning/383308.

Hoffman, Jan. "Anxious Students Strain College Mental Health Centers." *New York Times,* May 27, 2015. http://well.blogs.nytimes.com/2015/05/27/anxious-students-strain-college-mental-health-centers/.

———. "I Know What You Did Last Math Class." *New York Times,* May 4, 2008. http://www.nytimes.com/2008/05/04/fashion/04edline.html.

———. "To Keep Teenagers Alert, Schools Let Them Sleep In." *New York Times,* March 13, 2014. http://well.blogs.nytimes.com/2014/03/13/to-keep-teenagers-alert-schools-let-them-sleep-in/.

Hu, Winnie. "New Recruit in Homework Revolt: The Principal." *New York Times,* June 15, 2011. http://www.nytimes.com/2011/06/16/education/16homework.html.

IBM. "IBM 2010 Global CEO Study: Creativity Selected as Most Crucial Factor for Future Success." News release, May 18, 2010. http://www-03.ibm.com/press/us/en/pressrelease/31670.wss.

Jones, Todd, Mike Wagner, and Jill Riepenhoff. "Children may be vulnerable in $5 billion youth-sports industry." *Columbus Dispatch,* August 31, 2010. http://www.dispatch.com/content/stories/local/2010/08/27/day1-children-may-be-vulnerable-in-5-billion-youth-sports-industry.html.

Kamenetz, Anya. "Testing: How Much Is Too Much?" NPR, November 17, 2014. http://www.npr.org/sections/ed/2014/11/17/362339421/testing-how-much-is-too-much.

———. "Want your kids to opt out of standardized tests? The Constitution may be with you." Washington Post, January 9, 2015. http://www.washingtonpost.com/opinions/want-your-kids-to-opt-out-of-standardized-tests-the-constitution-may-be-with-you/2015/01/09/bea151b4–973a-11e4–8005–1924ede3e54a_story.html.

———. "What Schools Could Use Instead of Standardized Tests." NPR, January 6, 2015. http://www.npr.org/sections/ed/2015/01/06/371659141/what-schools-could-use-instead-of-standardized-tests.

Kohn, Alfie. "Why Self-Discipline Is Overrated: The (Troubling) Theory and Practice of Control from Within." Phi Delta Kappan, November 2008. http://www.alfiekohn.org/article/self-discipline-overrated/.

Kohn, David. "Let the Kids Learn Through Play." New York Times, May 16, 2015. http://www.nytimes.com/2015/05/17/opinion/sunday/let-the-kids-learn-through-play.html.

Kolker, Robert. "Cheating Upwards." New York, September 16, 2012. http://nymag.com/news/features/cheating-2012-9/.

Kreider, Tim. "The 'Busy' Trap." New York Times, June 30, 2012. http://opinionator.blogs.nytimes.com/2012/06/30/the-busy-trap/.

Lahey, Jessica. "Teach Kids to Daydream: Mental downtime makes people more creative and less anxious." Atlantic, October 16, 2013. http://www.theatlantic.com/education/archive/2013/10/teach-kids-to-daydream/280615/.

Lazarín, Melissa. Testing Overload in America's Schools. Washington, DC: Center for American Progress, October 2014. https://cdn.americanprogress.org/wp-content/uploads/2014/10/LazarinOvertestingReport.pdf.

Lifshitz, Jessica. "An Open Letter to My Students: I Am Sorry for What I Am About to Do to You." Huffington Post, March 5, 2015. http://www.huffingtonpost.com/jessica-lifshitz/an-open-letter-to-my-students-parcc_b_6808060.html.

Luthar, Suniya S., Samuel H. Barkin, and Elizabeth J. Crossman. "'I can, therefore I must': fragility in the upper-middle classes." Development and Psychopathology 25, no. 4, pt. 2 (November 2013): 1529–49.

Machado, Amanda. "Should Schools Teach Kids to Meditate?" Atlantic, January 27, 2014. http://www.theatlantic.com/education/archive/2014/01/should-schools-teach-kids-to-meditate/283229/.

McMillan, Rebecca L., Scott Barry Kaufman, and Jerome L. Singer. "Ode to positive constructive daydreaming." Frontiers in Psychology 4, no. 626 (September 23, 2013).

Merrow, John. "What Happens in Great Schools." Taking Note, November 7, 2014. http://takingnote.learningmatters.tv/?p=7311.

Miller, Claire Cain. "The 24/7 Work Culture's Toll on Families and Gender Equality." New York Times, May 28, 2015. http://www.nytimes.com/2015/05/31/upshot/the-24-7-work-cultures-toll-on-families-and-gender-equality.html.

Mitchell, Jeff. "Harvard-or-Walmart Syndrome." JeffMitchellAssociates.com. http://www.jeffmitchellassociates.com/Jeff/harvardorwalmart3.pdf.

National Association for College Admission Counseling (NACAC). Report of the Com-

mission on the Use of Standardized Tests in Undergraduate Admission. Arlington, VA: September 2008. http://www.nacacnet.org/research/PublicationsResources/Marketplace/Documents/TestingComission_FinalReport.pdf.

Noguchi, Sharon. "Teen health: Depression, anxiety and social phobias rising in kids, educators say." *San Jose Mercury News*, February 5, 2014. http://www.mercurynews.com/health/ci_25074044/teen-health-depression-anxiety-and-social-phobias-rising.

O'Brien, Keith. "Why have homework? Beneath a pillar of our education system lies a troubling uncertainty." *Boston Globe*, September 17, 2011. https://www.bostonglobe.com/ideas/2011/09/17/why-have-homework/oSYVu211Wz7TXa14cziH5I/story.html.

Organization for Economic Cooperation and Development (OECD). "Does homework perpetuate inequities in education?" *PISA in Focus*, December 2014.

Pappano, Laura. "Is Your First Grader College Ready?" *New York Times*, February 4, 2015. http://www.nytimes.com/2015/02/08/education/edlife/is-your-first-grader-college-ready.html.

Partanen, Anu. "What Americans Keep Ignoring About Finland's School Success." *Atlantic*, December 29, 2011. http://www.theatlantic.com/national/archive/2011/12/what-americans-keep-ignoring-about-finlands-school-success/250564/.

Pérez-Peña, Richard, and Daniel E. Slotnik. "Gaming the College Rankings." *New York Times*, January 31, 2012. http://www.nytimes.com/2012/02/01/education/gaming-the-college-rankings.html.

Ripley, Amanda. "Bored to Death: To learn just how bored kids are in school, look at Twitter." *New Republic*, December 16, 2013. http://www.newrepublic.com/article/115928/twitter-shows-epidemic-school-boredom.

Rivero, Lisa. "High School Years: College Prep or Life Prep?" *Psychology Today*, April 11, 2012. https://www.psychologytoday.com/blog/creative-synthesis/201204/high-school-years-college-prep-or-life-prep.

Rosen, Lawrence. "Buzzed: Energy Drinks + Stimulants = PEDs of Choice?" *Huffington Post*, January 30, 2013. http://www.huffingtonpost.com/lawrence-rosen-md/kids-energy-drinks_b_2581525.html.

Ryan, Richard M., and Edward L. Deci. "Intrinsic and Extrinsic Motivations: Classic Definitions and New Directions." *Contemporary Educational Psychology* 25, no. 1 (January 2000): 54–67.

Safi, Omid. "The Disease of Being Busy." *On Being*, November 6, 2014. http://onbeing.org/blog/the-disease-of-being-busy/7023.

Sahlberg, Pasi. "Finland's Educational Success is No Miracle." *Education Week*, January 2012. http://pasisahlberg.com/finlands-educational-success-is-no-miracle/.

———. "Teach for Finland? Why it won't happen." *Washington Post*, February 12, 2015. http://www.washingtonpost.com/blogs/answer-sheet/wp/2015/02/12/teach-for-finland-why-it-wont-happen/.

Schulte, Brigid. "In McLean, a crusade to get people to back off in the parenting arms race." *Washington Post*, March 23, 2014. http://www.washingtonpost.com/lifestyle/style/in-mclean-a-crusade-to-get-people-to-back-off-in-the-parenting-arms-race/2014/03/23/9259c6a2-a552-11e3-a5fa-55f0c77bf39c_story.html.

Schwartz, Barry. "Top Colleges Should Select Randomly from a Pool of 'Good Enough.'"

Chronicle of Higher Education, February 25, 2005. http://chronicle.com/article/Top-Col leges-Should-Select/14215/.

Schwartz, Katrina. "Does The Grit Narrative Blame Students For School's Shortcomings?" KQED *MindShift,* May 5, 2015. http://ww2.kqed.org/mindshift/2015/05/05/does-the -grit-narrative-blame-students-for-schools-shortcomings/.

———. "Harvard Wants to Know: How Does the Act of Making Shape Kids' Brains?" KQED *MindShift,* November 7, 2012. http://ww2.kqed.org/mindshift/2012/11/07/harvard -wants-to-know-how-does-making-shape-kids-brains/.

Schwartz, Tony. "Escalating Demands at Work Hurt Employees and Companies." *New York Times,* June 5, 2015. http://www.nytimes.com/2015/06/06/business/dealbook/excessive -demands-at-work-create-a-humanitarian-crisis.html.

Schwarz, Alan. "Risky Rise of the Good-Grade Pill." *New York Times,* June 9, 2012. http:// www.nytimes.com/2012/06/10/education/seeking-academic-edge-teenagers-abuse-stimu lants.html.

Shankar, Sri Sri Ravi. "Rethink. Redefine. Success." *Huffington Post,* March 5, 2012. http:// www.huffingtonpost.com/sri-sri-ravi-shankar/teen-suicide_b_1319009.html.

Shonkoff, Jack P., and Andrew S. Garner. "The Lifelong Effects of Early Childhood Adversity and Toxic Stress." *Pediatrics* 129, no. 1 (January 2012): 232–46.

Singh, Maanvi. "Why Emotional Learning May Be As Important As The ABCs." NPR, December 31, 2014. http://www.npr.org/sections/ed/2014/12/31/356187871/why-emo tional-literacy-may-be-as-important-as-learning-the-a-b-c-s.

Slaughter, Anne-Marie. "Rebellion of an Innovation Mom." CNN, June 5, 2011. http://global publicsquare.blogs.cnn.com/2011/06/05/rebellion-of-the-innovation-mom/.

Stipek, Deborah. "Relationships Matter." *Educational Leadership* 64, no. 1 (September 2006): 46–49.

Tierney, John. "Your Annual Reminder to Ignore the *U.S. News & World Report* College Rankings." *Atlantic,* September 10, 2013. http://www.theatlantic.com/education/archive/ 2013/09/your-annual-reminder-to-ignore-the-em-us-news-world-report-em-college -rankings/279103/.

Turker, Ron J. "All Played Out." *New York Times,* July 27, 2014. http://nyti.ms/X4hKxb.

Turner, Cory. "Kids and Screen Time: Cutting Through the Static." NPR, September 30, 2014. http://www.npr.org/sections/ed/2014/09/30/351521488/kids-and-screen-time -cutting-through-the-static.

Wagner, Tony. "Educating the Next Steve Jobs." *Wall Street Journal,* April 13, 2012. http:// www.wsj.com/articles/SB10001424052702304444604577337790086673050.

Walworth, Carolyn. "Paly student tells of school stress: 'Students are gasping for air.'" *Almanac,* March 26, 2015. http://www.almanacnews.com/news/2015/03/26/guest-opinion -on-school-stress-students-are-gasping-for-air.

Weissbourd, Rick, Stephanie Jones, Trisha Ross Anderson, Jennifer Kahn, and Mark Russell. *The Children We Mean to Raise: The Real Messages Adults Are Sending About Values.* Cambridge, MA: Making Caring Common Project, Harvard Graduate School of Education, Summer 2014. http://sites.gse.harvard.edu/sites/default/files/making-caring-common/ files/mcc_report_the_children_we_mean_to_raise_0.pdf.

Willingham, Daniel T. "How Knowledge Helps: It Speeds and Strengthens Reading Comprehension, Learning—and Thinking." *American Educator,* Spring 2006. http://www.aft.org/periodical/american-educator/spring-2006/how-knowledge-helps.

Wong, Alia. "In 2014, One Size Didn't Fit All." *Atlantic,* December 23, 2014. http://www.theatlantic.com/education/archive/2014/12/in-2014-one-size-didnt-fit-all/384001/.

Zinshteyn, Mikhail. "Should the U.S. Make Standardized Tests Harder?" *Atlantic,* November 24, 2014. http://www.theatlantic.com/education/archive/2014/11/should-the-us-make-standardized-tests-harder/383084/.

Lectures

Achor, Shawn. "The happy secret to better work." TEDxBloomington, May 2011. http://www.ted.com/talks/shawn_achor_the_happy_secret_to_better_work?language=en.

Brown, Brené. "The power of vulnerability." TEDxHouston, June 2010. https://www.ted.com/talks/brene_brown_on_vulnerability?language=en.

Heckman, James. "Cognitive Skills Are Not Enough." Address to policy and business leaders in Chicago, Illinois, December 16, 2010. http://heckmanequation.org/content/resource/cognitive-skills-are-not-enough.

Pausch, Randy. "Last Lecture: Really Achieving Your Childhood Dreams." Presented at Carnegie Mellon, September 18, 2007. https://www.youtube.com/watch?v=ji5_MqicxSo.

Robinson, Ken. "Do schools kill creativity?" TED Talk, February 2006. http://www.ted.com/talks/ken_robinson_says_schools_kill_creativity?language=en.

Rose, Todd. "The Myth of Average." TEDxSonomaCounty, June 2013. http://tedxtalks.ted.com/video/The-Myth-of-Average-Todd-Rose-a.

Index

academic extremism, 129

academic standards, 5, 10–12, 27, 35, 70, 86

Acalanes Union High School, 137

achievement measures, 76, 108–11, 123

Achor, Shawn, 183

Ackerman, David, 86, 92, 172–73

Acton-Boxborough, MA, 120

ACT scores, 133, 144–46

ACT tests, 27, 98, 101, 116, 148, 220

ADHD diagnoses, 27, 106, 124, 174

Advanced Placement program:
  AP exams, 12, 98, 101, 107–9, 136
  burnout from, 123, 127, 134, 137
  college applications and, 5–7, 10, 17, 114, 140
  college performance and, 137–38
  homework and, 88
  lack of sleep and, 20, 25
  minority students and, 136
  number of classes and, 18, 64, 140, 223–24
  school reputations and, 138

Adverse Childhood Experiences Study, 29

advocacy guidelines:
  AP program and, 213, 223–24
  collaborative efforts and, 229–33
  college admissions and, 148–52, 219–21
  curriculum standards and, 212
  for educators, 211–29
  family time and, 62–65
  for homework and testing, 210–15, 220, 233–34
  innovative teaching methods and, 216–19, 228
  Jacqueline and, 244
  opt-out movement and, 233
  for parents, 210–27
  performance pressure and, 12–14, 40–41

schedules and, 211–13, 217–18, 222, 227–28

school change and, 231–35

school rankings and, 216, 219

school schedules and, 56–60

social connections and, 227–28

sports and, 224

standardized testing and, 119–25

student surveys and, 214, 226

tutoring and, 211

affluence, 6, 32–34, 39, 154, 184, 238

Age of Opportunity (Steinberg), 8, 36

Alabama, 242

Allphin, Danielle, 82–83

Alone Together (Turkle), 200

alumni associations, 142

American Academy of Pediatrics, 24, 30, 55, 202, 226

American dream, 4, 244

American Gap Association, 220

American Management Association (AMA), 157

American Psychological Association, 19, 197

AmeriCorps, 242

Annual Review of Public Health, 31

anxiety:
  affluence and, 32–33
  of children, 236
  homework and, 68, 71–73
  of parents, 63
  performance pressure and, 8–11, 14–17
  sleep deprivation and, 55
  substance abuse and, 28
  teenagers and, 21–23
  testing and, 105, 122
  treatment for, 204

Appalachian State University, 21

Apple, 157

About the Authors

Vicki Abeles is an ex–Wall Street lawyer turned filmmaker, author, and education advocate. Her first feature documentary, *Race to Nowhere*, hit a nerve with its vivid portrayal of the pressure-cooker culture dominating America's schools. Her second film, *Beyond Measure*, about the groundbreaking leaders transforming schools for the better, premiered in 2015. She is also the founder of a nonprofit, grassroots organization that guides communities as they redefine student success and promote the health, learning, and wellness of the whole child. She lives in the San Francisco area with her family.

Grace Rubenstein is a multimedia journalist specializing in health, education, and immigration. Her stories—told variously in words, photos, audio, and video—have appeared in TheAtlantic.com and the *New York Times*. She is the multimedia editor at TED Books and a regular contributor at KQED public radio. Her five-year stint as a staff writer and producer at *Edutopia*, the publication of the George Lucas Educational Foundation, took her into innovative schools around the country. She is a fourth-generation San Franciscan.

Children's Grows Up

A Century of Caring

By Mary McGarey

HOSPITAL
Columbus, Ohio

Library of Congress Catalog No. 91-78242
ISBN 0-9631971-0-X
Copyright © 1992 Mary McGarey and
Children's Hospital, Inc., Columbus, Ohio

First Printing: February 1992

To All Children
and
Those Who Love Them

Introduction

When Children's Hospital was founded 100 years ago, the sole purpose of that courageous effort was to care for and treat every sick child who needed the hospital's help.

In 1992, that purpose hasn't changed, but Children's is in infinitely better position to fulfill it.

In the 10 decades of Children's existence, old childhood diseases have been conquered or tamed and new ones defined and attacked. The specialty of pediatrics has developed and matured, focused on the special problems and needs of children. Science has provided its practitioners with wonderfully precise and effective new tools and treatments, with masses of new knowledge, and with alluring signposts for the pediatric researcher tracking untamed killers and cripplers.

As it has grown to serve the fast-growing Columbus metropolitan area, Children's has embraced the benefits and responded to the challenges of meteoric change, particularly through the last five decades. It has extended its services into city neighborhoods and expanded them to counter the perils to childhood arising from late 20th century life. It has broadened its focus to a three-fold mission and become a premier regional center for pediatric treatment, education and research.

In its centennial year, Children's celebrates its past but looks to the future.

Its treatment expertise, increasingly challenged by more critically ill patients and more obscure problems, is in constant review in quest of new approaches and the improvement of established ones.

Its research programs, greatly bolstered in minds and materials and funding with the completion of the new research institute, are focused on a broad range of unanswered questions reflecting both long-established interests of Children's researchers and major national goals.

Its teaching programs, encompassing hundreds of students and health care deliverers, are constantly expanding and will be more efficiently and inclusively integrated with treatment and research when the new education building is completed in 1992.

A strong and vital 100-year-old Children's is prepared for the future. Its birthday, in a very special way, is cause for community celebration.

In 1892, as their written words attest, the founders of Children's launched their small hospital with little more than faith. That faith, in a Columbus community generous to the less fortunate and concerned for all children, was the bedrock on which Children's grew.

For a long way through its first 100 years, Children's was solely reliant on community efforts and generosity, particularly an incredible force of volunteers. Today, in the hospital's confident maturity, Children's and its extended community can celebrate a sound and thriving investment in our most precious resource—children.

Stuart W. Williams
Executive Director
Children's Hospital, Inc.

Ann I. Wolfe
President, Board of Trustees
Children's Hospital, Inc.

Grant Morrow III, M.D.
Medical Director
Children's Hospital, Inc.

Foreword

Children's IS a different kind of hospital. How it became one-of-a-kind in its Ohio region in pediatric treatment, teaching and research provides the exciting latter chapters of its 100-year history. How it was always different, in its availability and service to all sick children and its singular relationship with its community, forms the strong, rich chain linking the full century's achievements.

Walk through today's Children's, past a tiny newborn gaining strength to live helped by exotic monitors, a researcher tracking a defective gene in a state-of-the-art laboratory, a teenage mother being counseled for new responsibility, and see the scope of the hospital's 1992 uniqueness.

Traverse a crowded clinic area, through a skein of comfortably playing toddlers awaiting treatment, or drop in on a bedside birthday party, and see how a small hospital grown up has combatted the aloofness of size and specialization.

Read the names on new buildings and timeworn plaques or check the fund-raising events in almost any week's newspapers and see how a caring community has and does support the hospital for children it helped build.

Necessarily, and fortunately, this history relies as much on recollections as records. Many records are gone, but, even for the earliest days, someone or someone's comment was available to supply a word picture or family reminiscence to enliven dates and statistics.

In sum, several hundred doctors and nurses and staff members, trustees and administrators and volunteers, patients and patient families have helped compile this record.

I am grateful and indebted to them all. Their willingness to talk about Children's and their almost-uniformly positive approach are measures of the hospital's stature. I regret that we probably missed just as many other potential spokespersons, but a book twice the size we've compiled could not encompass all the large achievements and small triumphs of Children's 100 years.

It has been my special privilege in 40 years or so of writing about Children's to see the hissing respirators vanish with polio's conquest, to trace the battles and record the dwindling death rates for old foes like childhood cancer and new ones like Reye's Syndrome, to interview the same persons as perilously ill patients at Children's and as adults pursuing productive lives.

In this instance, it's a pleasure to conclude that the best and most exciting stories are yet to come.

Mary McGarey

Table of Contents

1892–1917
Faith and the Will to Survive

Like hundreds of the young patients it has served and cured, Children's Hospital has developed far beyond the greatest expectations of those who gave it birth.

They started a small local charity hospital to serve a dozen or so patients. Celebrating its 100th birthday, the precocious institution has become a complete children's medical center, competitive with any in the country and serving children far beyond the boundaries of Columbus and Franklin County.

The men and women who launched their little hospital with much more faith than funds could not have envisioned its potential from their turn-of-the-century vantage point. Nothing in their early efforts would indicate, however, that the larger vision would have deterred them. They had faith in a committed cadre of volunteers, which grew with the hospital, and in a community always responsive to appeals made in behalf of children.

Their faith held. The funds followed—never easily, often with great effort and ingenuity and individual sacrifice, through wars and epidemics and economic depression and the challenges of medical progress.

"The Lord seldom sends us a surplus, but He never lets this hospital want any necessary thing," Mrs. Truitt B. Sellers, a dominant figure in Children's history, declared in the mid-'30s.

The establishment of the hospital, like many of its later developments, benefited from good timing.

In the late decades of the 1800s, neither doctors nor hospitals were particularly well-armed to combat the ills of humanity, especially those of children.

There were no antibiotics, no vaccines, no instruments to seek out trouble deep within the body.

Contagious diseases, especially the more common ones, were accepted hazards of childhood. The kindly family doctor of legend relied on his own experience and limited training and a very small kitbag of medications to bring children through these and more serious illnesses. Sick children were usually treated at home, and wisely so, if the home was clean, warm and headed by capable parents. Children were hospitalized only if such care was lacking, if they were critically ill or if they could benefit from the limited surgical procedures available.

In fact, one Columbus medical historian said, family doctors tended to treat family members in a descending scale of priority, beginning with the father, the breadwinner; a survival-of-the-fittest notion was still surprisingly prevalent as it applied to delicate and sickly children.

In 1886, when the State Board of Health was organized, it gleaned from sketchy statistics on Ohio's health that "one-half of all deaths in our cities are children under 5 and one-third, children under one year . . ."

"The knowledge of the people regarding the laws of health is less perhaps than of any other subject so nearly concerning them," said the board's first annual report. "The erroneous beliefs and opinions of our ancestors are in many instances still entertained. People yet wear the bag of asafoetida to ward off contagious diseases."

The same report targeted major public health concerns in the state—stream pollution and drinking water contamination, poor sanitation, adulteration of foods, environmental hazards for children in school buildings. (It's an ironic footnote to progress that different problems, but under the same headings, are the concern of public health officials today.)

The new department detailed diphtheria outbreaks throughout the state, epidemics of typhoid fever in Bellaire and malarial fever in Columbiana County. It devoted extensive sections of the report to containment and home care of infectious disease cases.

However, in this same period, revolutionary change was beginning. The achievements of Pasteur, Lister, Morton and other 19th century pioneers were gaining attention and adherents in great medical centers of the world, effecting reforms and advances that would catapult the healing arts into the modern era.

In a parallel development, children's hospitals began to appear in the United States—Philadelphia's in 1855, others in the late 1800s in major urban centers, including Cincinnati's in 1873.

The Cincinnati venture sparked discussion in Columbus, undoubtedly heightened by the interest of Columbus women who had volunteered to sew garments and bedding for the Cincinnati institution.

It is a now-familiar story in Columbus annals that a group of girls and young women, members of the King's Daughters of St. Paul's Episcopal Church, met at the James Kilbourne home, 604 E. Town St., to discuss ways and means of securing a children's hospital for Columbus.

They planned and held a benefit fair, raised $125, and deposited that small sum in the Deshler Bank to gather interest while they gathered support.

One can imagine the gentle arm-twisting that went on between May of 1890, when the benefit was held, and Jan. 23, 1891, when a founding group of men and women met to plan a hospital. Years later, in a summary of the early years, Mrs. James Kilbourne spoke of "the enthusiasm of youth" among those very first fund-raisers for Children's.

A constitution and by-laws were drawn up, patterned largely after Cincinnati's, and the Articles of Incorporation were filed with the Ohio Secretary of State on Feb. 27, 1892. Two days later, at the Kilbourne home, the first 15 trustees were chosen and 15 women were appointed to a "Board of Lady Managers." A letter and a personal solicitation plan were devised to seek $5,000 from community donors, and a committee was appointed to look for a property or building site for the proposed hospital.

Nothing done at that meeting was more important than the naming of the women's board. It may have been the first instance in the building of Columbus institutions in which the talents of men and women were so equally and fully called upon.

Even though they were separately organized, they were certainly co-founders. The board of trustees, all male then and for more than 40 years thereafter, was charged with handling funds and investments, seeing to legal matters, and having the final word on all other matters pertaining to hospital and staff. It still is.

The women, for most of its first half-century, ran the hospital. To a large degree, they also sustained and promoted it. The latter, to a substantial extent, they still do.

Referred to in old minutes as both "lady managers" and "lady visitors," the 15-member women's board was enlarged within weeks to 25. Trustees increased its membership repeatedly through the early years as the women expanded their fund-raising and were entrusted by trustees with more and more responsibility for the hospital's operation and management.

The original trustees included Dr. C.F. Clark, an ear and eye specialist; Dr. Starling Loving, surgeon, medical educator and national medical leader; Dr. Thomas C. Hoover, surgeon; C.C. Waite, president of the C.H.V. and T. Railway; G.C. Hoover, a railroad contractor; W.F. Goodspeed, president of Buckeye Malleable Iron Co.; H.D. Lanman, manager of the Columbus Bolt Works; Edwin C. Kelton, lumber dealer; F.C. Eaton, treasurer of the Kilbourne-Jacobs Manufacturing Co.; John Siebert, vice president of the M.C. Lilley and Co. and president of the Ohio Savings Bank (later the Ohio National); G.W. Sinks, banker and business leader; A.B. Cohen, an executive of the Simon Lazarus & Sons retail firm; H.G. Dennison, attorney; and Col. Charles Parrott, president of the Paragon Oil Company.

Col. James Kilbourne, president of Kilbourne-Jacobs, member of a pioneer Franklin County family and a leading figure in city and state affairs, was the first president. G.W. Prentiss of the Clinton National Bank was treasurer, and Tod Galloway, attorney (and composer of the classic "Whiffenpoof Song") was secretary.

3

4

Wives of five trustees—Kilbourne, Kelton, Eaton, Clark and Good-speed—were named to the first women's board. Mrs. W.K. Rogers, wife of an attorney and mother of a physician, was the first president. Other original members included Mrs. E.B. Fullerton, Mrs. A.W. Thurman, Mrs. J.T. Holmes and Mrs. G.S. Parsons, wives of attorneys; Mrs. Frank Hickok, wife of a lumber dealer; Mrs. W.D. Brickell, wife of the "proprietor" of The Columbus Evening Dispatch; Mrs. P.W. Huntington, wife of a banker; Mrs. William Scarlett, wife of the Lilley Company's secretary-treasurer; and Mrs. A.N. Whiting, whose husband was associated with an oil company.

As a group, they were men and women whose paths crossed often in the commercial, social and philanthropic life of the city. Indeed, in a smaller Columbus one-tenth its present size, most of them were neighbors, their substantial homes in close proximity along E. Broad and E. Town Sts. and streets leading into them.

Nearly 100 years later, a current trustee observed that a perennial strength of Children's has been the consistent high quality of its trustee-ship—a standard begun with these original boards.

They planned for a growing city. Columbus population had passed 88,000 in 1890, and the Franklin County population exceeded 124,000.

The founders' intent was to rent or build a small charity hospital to give free service to children of poor families. A matron, nurse assistants and service personnel would comprise the entire paid staff. Doctors selected by the board of trustees would donate their services. The women's board and other volunteer groups would provide as many as possible of the furnishings and equipment, food and supplies, by direct donation or fund-raising projects.

Within a year, with more than $18,000 raised in donations, trustees began looking for a site. Several downtown rental projects were considered and rejected. Lengthy negotiations with the city for part of the Hare Orphans' Home site on Woodland Ave. were fruitless. The board voted to build, and land was purchased from James Nelson at Miller and Fair Aves., fronting on the "new" Franklin Park established by the city in 1884.

The site would assure small patients a pleasant outlook, fresh air and playground space, Col. Kilbourne told the board in his first annual report. He noted that the site was "away from the heart of the city" but "easy of access" on the Oak St. trolley line just a block away.

As president, and longtime board member, Col. Kilbourne was consistently chosen to chair the annual meetings through the early years. In his precise and formal language, at this first meeting, he defined the purpose of the hospital:

"With the general interest shown by the public, and the growing appreciation of the need of a hospital of this character, your trustees feel warranted in proceeding at once to the completion of the building, trusting to the generosity and liberality of our citizens to supply the necessary means.

"The hospital in its purposes is as broad as charity itself. It is strictly non-sectarian. It appeals to the members of all religious denominations, and to those who are members of none; to all who are interested in the class of unfortunates it seeks to help—sick, infirm and disabled children of every race, sect or condition, who through poverty or neglect need the shelter and the care such as only a hospital of this kind can give. From all such we ask liberal and prompt assistance that the hospital may be finished without delay and its good work be unhampered by debt."

Old records show the founders tried very hard, from their own reading, travels and inquiries and from a series of plans contributed by the architects, Yost and Packard, to plan a building suitable for small patients. That they weren't entirely successful was due to several factors:

• They built in the "institutional" style of the times, and the first hospital, while less castle-like than others erected in Columbus in the same period, was more imposing than it was homey or, indeed, functional.

• The shortcomings which were to grow so glaringly apparent within the first years of operation lay partly in changes and advances in medical care they couldn't have anticipated.

• Like many such projects then and now, the plans were tailored to available funds. The original building, according to the "long-range" plan, would eventually become largely an administration center when additional funds allowed for four wings to accommodate 100 patients and other hoped-for facilities.

However, these concerns lay ahead as a rejoicing city got its first glimpse of the new hospital on Dec. 30, 1893.

In its edition that morning, the Ohio State Journal reported that President Grover Cleveland and his party had returned from a duck-hunting trip, with no ducks; that a committee had been appointed to plan the inauguration of Ohio Gov. William McKinley; and that British Prime Minister William Gladstone was marking his 80th birthday.

Also, in two long columns headlined "A Noble Charity," the newspaper hailed the launching of Children's, termed the opening-day festivities "a brilliant social event," and described floor by floor the new hospital on the city's eastern edge.

A flight of stone steps led to the large entrance hall, which was flanked by an office and reception room on one side and the matron's room on the other. Beyond a broad staircase rising to upper floors from the hall, a dining room with service closets and butler's pantry lay on the left, an operating room to the right. The kitchen and food pantry, inexplicably, were on the third floor, together with storage rooms, rooms for the help and an obviously essential dumbwaiter.

The prevailing color scheme was blue and white, carried out in staff uniforms, chinaware, linens, bedding, etc.

A large porch across the entire front was to be added later, the article explained, as were an elevator and four "semi-detached wards," one on either side and two at the rear, which were to bring the bed capacity to nearly 100.

Available patient beds when the building opened were in one large second-floor ward; in the closed-in archways with which the projected wards would eventually connect; and in another large second-story room designated a "temporary" ward and intended eventually as the matron's bedroom.

Structurally, the building was adjudged up-to-the-minute in furnishings, heating, lighting, ventilation and "hot and cold soft water plumbing." Its architecture, said the Journal scribe, was "a free treatment of the French Gothic" with an exterior of mottled buff Roman brick, terra cotta roof, "local limestone" foundation and "Hocking Valley sandstone trim."

Times were bad, contributions slowed and a number of pledges were unfulfilled, while the community need for the hospital became more apparent—a demand-capacity dilemma which would confront Children's officials repeatedly in ensuing years. Even though they had trimmed the plans to match expected funds, the board had to secure a bank loan for $6,500 the only way they could—backed by the personal guarantee of board members.

Already, however, the enthusiasm and boundless ingenuity of volunteers—another constant in Children's history—were also being demonstrated.

The Young Ladies Sewing Society, a group of 25, had completely equipped the hospital with table and bed linens, and furnished clothing for the patients. A charity ball had provided funds for most of the furnishings; "Marriage Dramas" presented by the women's board at the Henrietta Theatre and benefit performances given by Sells Brothers Circus brought in more than $2,500.

Kilbourne, in his report, took special note of "a band of little girls" who had undertaken weekly visits to hospital patients and contributed $175 to support a bed for a year. This initial concern for brightening the days of hospitalized youngsters was also to become a hallmark of Children's. It was particularly important in this early period when parental visits were limited to once a week unless the child's condition was critical.

In its first year, the hospital's medical staff included a consulting physician, Dr. Loving; consulting surgeon, Dr. Hoover; and consulting oculist and aurist, Dr. Clark; two attending physicians; and a part-time house physician, Dr. Edgar M. Hatton.

Among the house physician's duties, as prescribed in the by-laws, were examining patients on admission, keeping records of their treatment and progress, making rounds with attending physicians, maintaining and keeping inventory of surgical instruments and apparatus, dispensing all medicines, seeing to the supply and proper handling of all drugs, and making postmortem examinations as required or requested.

The first matron was Miss Bertha Boswinkle, a registered nurse, graduate of the Episcopal Hospital of Philadelphia and experienced in caring for children. She was placed in charge of all household arrangements, the appointment and discharge of nurses and servants, supervision of nurses' activities not concerned with medical treatment, accommodation of visitors, emergency patient admissions, and general control over supplies and donations and domestic accounts. She was required to deputize an assistant to take charge during any absence from the hospital and to secure permission of the trustees or lady managers to be gone more than 24 hours.

(Four years later, this hard-pressed woman submitted her resignation but was persuaded to continue after a leave of absence—apparently her first vacation. A year later, after she did resign and a successor was named, the board voted to look into the question of paid vacations for staff members. It also took under advisement a proposal to "increase" the matron's salary to $50 a month, then referred it to the women's board to work out.)

Under original regulations, the hospital was open to patients between the ages of one and 16, no patient could stay longer than three months without a physician's request and board review, and no cases of infectious disease were to be accepted.

Through the first decades, the non-contagion rule proved almost impossible to enforce. One room had been designated a contagion room with one assigned nurse, should a case develop, but on several occasions so many cases of an interloping infection occurred that the hospital had to be closed to all other patients.

(In his history of Children's, Dr. Earl Baxter noted that, from 1908 to the late 1920s, children with smallpox, scarlet fever and diphtheria were cared for in a "pest house" on Greenlawn Ave., supervised by Dr. Elmer G. Horton, a Columbus physician expert in the care of infectious diseases, a former city health commissioner and, at a later time, assistant chief of staff at Children's.)

Children's first patient, Lucile Metzell, 6, was admitted on Feb. 3, 1894, with a diagnosis of hip-joint disease and a family history of tuberculosis. She was given familiar medicines of the day—cascara, cod liver oil, calomel and salicylic acid; was treated for the hip problem and taught to adapt to a brace; and was discharged Aug. 7.

In succeeding weeks, children came with other bone and joint ailments, eye and ear problems, respiratory infections, and one with polio. In less than a month, the original nine beds were filled and six more, all the hospital could accommodate, were added.

If the two projected front wards of 11 beds each could have been added, they "would be as quickly filled," Col. Kilbourne told the board at the first annual meeting after the opening, in March, 1895. At that meeting, both the matron and Dr. Dickson Moore, the new house physician, urged that the hospital be enlarged.

8

A report of expenditures through the shakedown period from April, 1892, to March of 1895 also gave some indication of the hospital's limited treatment ability, even allowing for 100 years' difference in pricing. The women's board, in that three-year period, spent $538 for all surgical supplies, $334 for drugs and $2,066 for salaries and wages.

While emphasizing the funding problems, Col. Kilbourne reported another instance of community response early in the previous year when the residual debt on the building stood at $7,701.98. Emerson McMillen, transit company executive, offered to contribute $400 if 20 such contributors could be found within 90 days. The money was raised "in less than one-fourth that time," Kilbourne said, and this windfall plus other public contributions enabled the hospital to end the fiscal year with a balance of $947.77.

Despite that, and the efforts of volunteers, trustees had to borrow $1,000 late that year and another $500 the next year. In 1897, the coffers swelled by another Sells Circus benefit, trustees authorized construction of the front porch—an expense minimized considerably by donations of 3,000 bricks from Lincoln Kilbourne, a ceiling from Kinnear & Gager, and $100 from Emerson McMillen.

In early 1899, the pressure to build increased. In April, 10 patients had to be refused admission for lack of space, and in May another 12 were turned away. The board voted to purchase and squeeze in six more cots and, with the treasurer reporting an operating balance of $382.81, began to talk of another expansion.

During that year, Columbus Elks staged a huge benefit fair with the enthusiastic help of many Children's volunteers, shared the proceeds, and turned over nearly $5,100 to the hospital. With that and the sale of some street railway stock, trustees paid off standing debts and, at the beginning of 1900, started plans for construction of an Elks' Pavilion "at a cost not to exceed $6,000."

By January, 1901, the additional 25 beds gained by expansion brought problems of greater expenses and occasional low occupancy. That month, the ending operating balance was $36. In September, the balance was 56 cents after the president covered an account overdrawn by $9.44 with his own $10 check.

It was a touch-and-go time for the hospital, despite occasional appeals for community support and the extraordinary efforts of the women's board and other volunteer groups in individual solicitation and special events. The women's board had assumed responsibility for the matron's salary and volunteered to contribute $150 a year beyond that to the trustees.

From the beginning, trustees had issued a voucher for $250, or occasionally slightly more, at the end of each month, to cover operational expenses incurred by the women's board. Late in 1902 Mrs. Kilbourne, as president of

James Kilbourne home on E. Town St.

View of 1894 hospital. Elks Pavilion, at left, and front porch were added later.

Play time on grounds of first hospital.

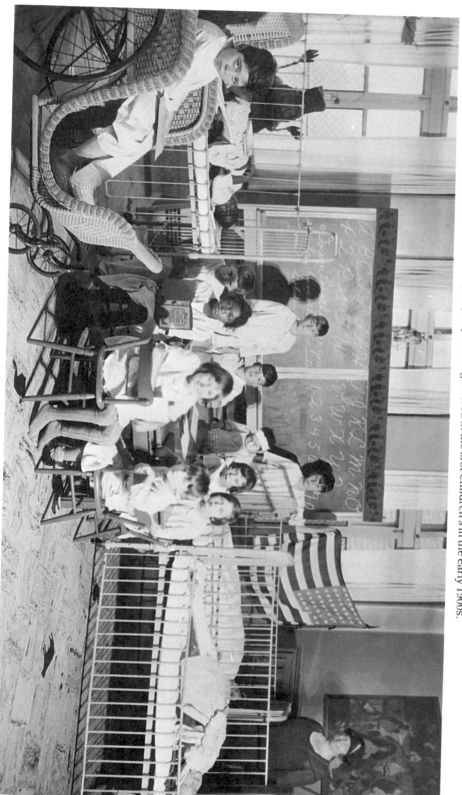

The spooky characters in the background suggest it must have been Halloween time when this group of patients gathered in the first Children's in the early 1900s.

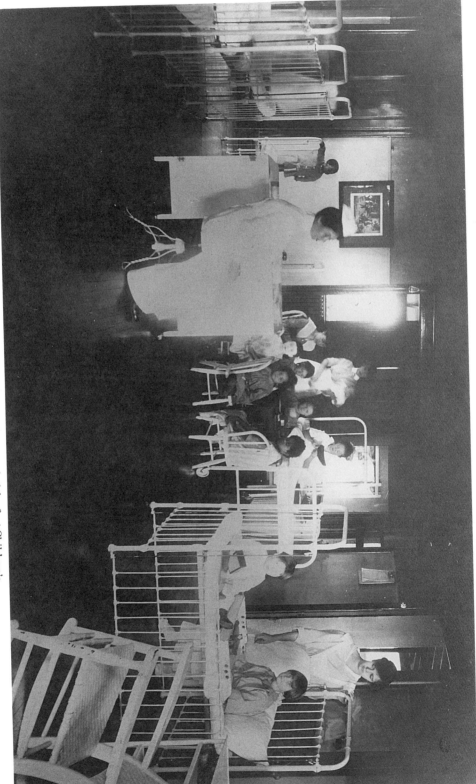

A tranquil turn-of-the-century moment in a ward of the first Children's.

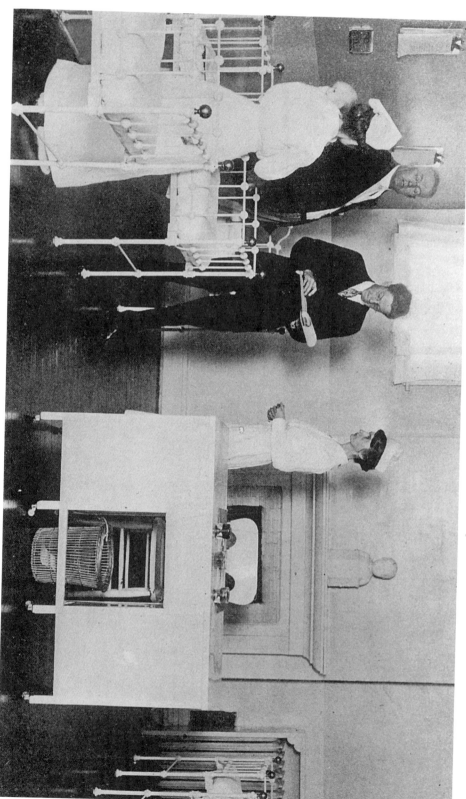

Dr. Dickson L. Moore, house physician in early 1900s, checks patient charts.

Elks' Pavilion, only major expansion of the first hospital, provided a fresh-air ward for patients in early 1900s.

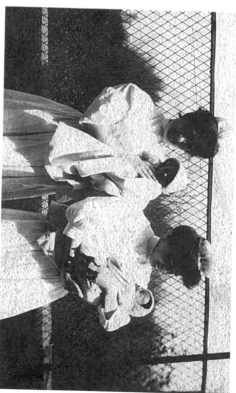

From former patient Isabelle Harper's album: Patients and nurses during her treatment in 1907.

Famed Dispatch cartoonist Billy Ireland recognized the dedication of James
Kilbourne to Children's in this early-1900 sketch showing his interests.

Trustee Fred Lazarus was also portrayed as a friend to Children's in this caricature by Ireland.

Ireland's sketch of F.O. Schoedinger suggests the longtime trustee and board president did occasionally get away from his business and philanthropic interests.

Miss Lily Dale Atkinson, superintendent of Children's, 1914-20.

the women's board, suggested to trustees that the $250 be given to the women directly "on a trial basis" out of which "all expenses formerly paid by the trustees, except insurance and repairs, should be met." Needless to say, trustees agreed.

From 1895 on, the women also conducted an annual Donation Day in November, a practice that was to continue through the '30s. On this fantastic day of combined socializing and accumulation, women volunteers received, sorted and stored huge quantities of jellies and potatoes, groceries and cash and other needed items donated by individuals and companies. It was the hospital's stockpile for the following year.

If handwritten secretary's notes, fully and formally entered in a crumbling ledger, can be termed poignant, the trustees' record for these early-1900 years is that. Louis F. Kiesewetter, a banker and son of a banker, was the faithful secretary-treasurer for more than a decade before he left Columbus to join a New York City bank. Month after month, it was his unpleasant task to report meager balances, bills deferred for payment, and frequent discussions of trustees on fund-raising possibilities.

In 1903, he also recorded two events significant to the hospital's future. The board was asked by the women's board and medical staff to consider the questions of a certification program for nurses and a change in policy to allow admission of paying patients.

It approved the program for nurses, thereby taking the first step toward the extensive education and training program in which the hospital would eventually become involved. It rejected the proposal for paying patients, one which would be repeatedly presented before the policy was finally changed decades later.

During these tough early years, the $100 annual memberships from a number of community contributors, the $200 annual membership paid by trustees, interest on small stock holdings the board had managed to accumulate and volunteer contributions of the women's groups and Columbus physicians kept the hospital afloat.

The value of the hospital property had already more than doubled, and several sizable bequests began to ease the financial picture somewhat. In June, 1905, the board approved a motion by Col. Kilbourne that all legacies "be placed in the form of endowments and that the income only be used for the hospital."

It was a renewed statement of faith that the men and women who founded Children's were in it for the long haul and that they looked to the future while relying on their own efforts to meet month-to-month obligations. At the same meeting, several months behind on their payments to the women's board, the board voted to borrow another $1,000 for running expenses.

It must have seemed like virtue rewarded, two months later, when the board learned that William W. Franklin, who died in January, 1905, had left the hospital $50,000 and residual stock holdings which, in interest alone, would greatly improve the hospital's annual income base.

(Since the Franklin bequest was the largest received by the hospital for decades, identifying him seemed important but proved difficult. Hospital records listed his address only as Madison County, where his will was probated. Although he was obviously a man of means, the only clue offered in a search of London, Ohio, historical, genealogical and newspaper sources was that he had, according to one old history, participated in a livestock sale in London.

(Finally, a surmise that his death might have been reported by Columbus newspapers led to a Jan. 22, 1905, obituary in the Dispatch. Franklin owned "one of the most valuable farms in Ohio" near London, the clipping reported, and was fatally stricken at age 71 in the lobby of the Hotel London—but he was a Columbus resident. He was president of the Columbus Forge & Iron Company and "director of many large corporations," the obituary noted. He was a native of Chillicothe, a bachelor, lived "near 4th and Broad Sts.," and had a sister, Mrs. Robert G. Dun, in Columbus and two sisters in Virginia.

(A subsequent search of Columbus directories and histories produced no further mention of Franklin, even his exact address. Obviously, he maintained a low public profile while amassing the fortune which, after bequests to his family, he shared equally between Children's and the Columbus Home for the Aged.)

At a 1906 meeting, with the financial picture brighter, trustees voted to decrease their annual dues from $200 to $100 and, in another year, to $25.

Meantime, while the founders struggled to keep it going, the little hospital was fulfilling its intended function for a succession of young patients. The facilities and organization were certainly less than ideal for physicians and staff. Outbreaks of scarlet fever or diphtheria or other infections and struggles with temperamental boilers and inadequate equipment must have been far more disruptive than a line in an old minute book shows. But all available evidence indicates children spent as pleasant a time there as a caring staff and dedicated volunteers could manage.

Before her death in 1988, Mrs. Isabelle Brunn Harper, a patient in Children's for 14 months in 1907 and '08, volunteered a five-year-old's recollection of that special time in her life.

"The hospital looked huge to me," she recalled, but she had pleasant memories of the spacious lawn, "bushes, trees and a big screened-in porch," of holiday fun especially at Christmas, and of the kindness of the staff.

Trustee minutes at this time reflect a greater feeling of affluence. More meeting time was devoted to the management of securities. The women's board got a $100 a month increase, to $550 a month, to run the hospital.

Already talking rebuilding or expansion that wouldn't materialize for another decade, the board acted on a committee's recommendation to purchase four Oak St. properties adjoining the hospital. (As frequently happened in transactions involving Children's, the real estate dealer, J.W. Davy, when the sale was finalized, donated his $105 commission to the women's board.)

Again, the perennial questions of paying patients and contagious cases emerged, and the board asked the medical staff for guidance. Trustees thought community physicians weren't using the hospital enough and proposed they might be permitted to admit patients, retaining complete control of patients' care during their stay.

On these terms, staff doctors rejected the plan, fearing it would create internal problems. They did respond favorably on the contagion question, proposing that a separate building be constructed for isolation of such patients. Later, after further study, they decided this plan also was not feasible.

In December, 1908, a name that was to loom large in Children's history appeared in trustees' minutes for the first time. Mrs. Truitt B. (Daisy) Sellers, a relative newcomer to Columbus, wrote as women's board secretary to ask an increase in the medical staff. The new members, increasing the staff to 11, were Dr. Andre Crotti, widely known throat surgeon, and Dr. O.H. Sellenings, one of the first physicians in Columbus with graduate training in pediatrics.

In 1910, Drs. Crotti and Sellenings, working with members of the women's board, planned and started a free dispensary, the forerunner of one of Children's most used and valued services—its extensive clinic program. At the same time, the hospital formed a significant relationship with the District Nursing Association which involved more training for staff nurses, follow-up of patients, and the kind of "outreach" effort so important for Children's today.

Gradually, the hospital's medical staff was building, bringing new expertise to the hospital service. Dr. E. Schilling, a pathologist, was appointed in 1911; Dr. Charles J. Shepard, a skin specialist, and Dr. Charles F. Bowen, an X-ray specialist, in 1912.

Trustees had been unsuccessful, however, in obtaining a recent graduate of the Ohio State University medical school as a resident physician. Physicians who came to the hospital to give service worked under difficulties. Those who needed special equipment had to bring it along. Laboratory equipment was almost nil, and any complex tests available were done in outside laboratories. Children who needed X-ray service were taken to downtown facilities, and surgical patients were carried up and down stairways from the first-floor operating room. (Dr. Leslie Bigelow liked to tell the story of how this latter practice was taxed to the upmost when a nurse of ample proportions had to have an emergency appendectomy.)

In 1912, the board had built and paid for an apartment building and another rental property adjoining the hospital. Eventual expansion was still the intent, apparently, but trustees turned down a recommendation of the women's board that the hospital add a maternity ward and contagion ward, responding that Children's was too recently self-sustaining to undertake immediate enlargement.

A year later, in July, 1914, the subject came up again after a possible purchaser for the hospital property had appeared. The board met with Dr. Sellenings, representing the medical staff, and Mrs. Sellers, now president of the women's board.

Mrs. Sellers stressed the urgent need for a contagion ward, a training school for nurses and better quarters for some staff personnel. A committee was charged with assessing the feasibility of using the existing hospital for administration (the original plan), the Elks' wing as a contagion unit and adding a new 60-bed hospital.

Days later, trustees, women's board, doctors and staff faced a crisis point, not financial this time, but one of policy and direction.

Board minutes for those years reveal little about internal operations. Women's board minutes, which would have been more concerned with such matters, have not survived. It does seem apparent from skimpy evidence that, while the physical property was showing signs of age, the organizational structure had also developed creaks and strains.

One can only speculate about why a succession of matrons signed on and departed within a relatively few years, why some physicians who joined the staff did not stay on or why some others whose community standing and expertise would logically have attracted them to Children's were not attracted.

The governing boards were obviously aware that their little hospital, three years short of its 25th birthday, needed a long hard look—that its vital components were at least out of synch if not out of communication. They invited Dr. John A. Hornsby of Chicago, secretary of the American Medical Association's hospital division and editor of "The Modern Hospital," to come to Columbus and take a critical look at Children's.

His verbal report, at the end of a day of touring and meetings, touched off debate even the laconic Mr. Kiesewetter in his minutes termed "lengthy and spirited"—about the hospital's role and image in the community, the quality of its service to children, its organizational structure and the advisability of building a new hospital. His written report a month later spelled out suggestions.

Hornsby was blunt. Taking note of a feeling among some trustees and women's board members that community agencies involved with children were less than cooperative in sending patients to the hospital, he said:

"I believe that if there were a conviction in the minds of the people of Columbus that your hospital was giving all it should give to the sick children committed to its care, the problem would be to take care of those who sought admission rather than to find more patients."

He recommended full reorganization of the medical staff into departments, a medical executive committee with access to the board on medical matters, and better "on-call" coverage of the hospital.

He recommended a laboratory with minimum adequate equipment costing about $400 and a pathologist on regular duty; X-ray facilities for another $500; scientific dietary service for the children, "a matter of method rather than money"; better admission service with an officer trained to examine incoming patients and specifically screen out those harboring contagious disease.

Finding the lack of an in-house medical officer "unthinkable," Hornsby proposed a young physician at the intern level who could care for the "constantly and quickly changing conditions of sick children" and also fulfill the expanded laboratory, X-ray and admission functions.

As for a new building, Hornsby thought the existing site ideal and suggested conversion of the old hospital to administration, nurses' and staff quarters, and construction of a new two-story 50-bed hospital expandable to four floors when necessary.

While reaction to the Hornsby report by those most concerned was immediate, action on its recommendations was to take far longer.

On the matter of paying patients, the women's board recommended one private room be established immediately at a rate of $15 a week for patients of staff physicians who would in turn render their own bill to parents. The doctors did not agree, but decided to support the proposal.

Trustees deferred action until they had a review of legally recorded stipulations in every will or memorial gift the hospital had received—more than two dozen—to be sure none had restricted the contribution to a strictly charitable institution. None had.

Trustees still hesitated. Although the hospital had for some time been accepting unspecified payment from parents willing and able to make it, it was to be another six years before hospital rules were changed to allow for paying patients.

The doctors wanted a facility for contagious cases, even an interim building, pending construction of a new hospital. The women stuck with the no-admittance rule, difficult as it was to enforce, and trustees agreed. They did find space for a better laboratory and authorized purchase of a microscope, incubator and other equipment for it.

Straightening out organizational problems and building a new hospital still called for attention.

Responding to the Hornsby report, the women's group insisted their board and trustees must be undisputed controllers of the hospital and the superintendent the final voice in enforcing rules and regulations.

Hornsby, in his report, had found Miss Lily Atkinson, recently appointed superintendent, both capable and knowledgeable, but echoes of friction with the medical staff sound through the board minutes.

At one point the usually diplomatic Mrs. Sellers, in a rush of plain-speaking, told the board of trustees that "there ought to be someone or ones (within the two boards) with the necessary authority to have it out with everybody who seems to be in disagreement." Early in 1915, trustees decreed a one-year trial for a new kind of controlling triumvirate, made up of the presidents of the trustees and women's boards and the dean of the medical staff. This failed, and reports of continuing friction were sent by trustees to the women's board to adjudicate as it could.

In retrospect, it is amazing that an organizational structure with such obvious built-in potential for misunderstanding and turf protection could have worked as well as it did for as long as it did.

Maybe the new hospital would solve that problem as well as many others. Children's was treating more patients year by year; use of the dispensary was increasing steadily; month after month, Mrs. Sellers and Miss Atkinson, by letter or in person, reminded trustees of the hospital's pressing needs.

Wary of contracting a large new debt, trustees were keeping a tight hold on the purse strings. In midsummer, when the women's board sought an increased allowance to defray expenses of establishing a nurses' training school, trustees allowed them an extra $20 a month.

However, they had begun negotiations with Miss Anna B. Conshaine for a fund-raising campaign the following year, and at their final 1915 meeting approved a contract with the fund-raiser for a campaign in March, 1916.

(It's an interesting footnote that at the same meeting Dr. George C. Schaeffer suggested Ohio State University and Children's had mutual interests in treating children and that OSU might be a proper site for the new hospital. The board appointed a committee to meet with President William Oxley Thompson and OSU trustees, but no result is recorded of an apparently fruitless discussion.)

The March campaign was disappointing. The goal was $300,000 to provide funds for a new building and an endowment to maintain it. Contributions totaled only half of that. The threat of war may have been a factor, but fund-raisers suspected the drive's failure hinged on public misconception about the hospital's legacy from the estate of Campbell M. Chittenden. The bequest, announced just prior to the fund drive, represented long-range benefit for Children's but not the immediate windfall many thought it to be.

(In fact, it took 48 years. Under terms of the tontine-type Chittenden will, drawn shortly before his death in 1916, six major beneficiaries shared income from the $2 million estate through their lifetimes before final disposition could be made. The legatees included names known in Columbus history—inventor Perry Okey, Hollywood actor Grant Mitchell and Harry F. West, attorney and public servant, the surviving beneficiary, who died in 1964. With his death, Children's became heir to six downtown properties valued at that time at more than $900,000.

(There were sad undertones to the 1916 Dispatch obituary of a dashing young citizen. Heir to the estates of his father, H.T. Chittenden, and grandfather, E.T. Mithoff, both hotel builders, Chittenden was a Yale law graduate, an art patron, traveled the world with his wife particularly in Egypt and Japan, and owned the first automobile in Columbus. But he died at 43 after a week's illness with peritonitis. His wife and principal legatee had been ill for a year and survived him only briefly, and the couple's only son had died at 12. During his last illness, the account said, a friend mentioned Children's building campaign, and Chittenden altered the provision he had made for his boyhood friends to make Children's residuary legatee.)

The year 1916 was a landmark for the hospital in other respects. Through the first quarter-century, the burden of volunteer effort and much fundraising had been shouldered by the 60-member Pleasure Guild and the women's board, now at 175 members. The latter group, established by trustees at the organizational meeting in February, 1892, with 15 members and referred to in early records as the board of lady visitors or lady managers, had accepted more and more of the day-to-day responsibility for hospital operation. In June, 1916, it became officially the Women's Board.

Meanwhile, a strong new auxiliary force was being mobilized—200 women originally, divided into small groups or "Twigs," each committed to supplying a specific need to the hospital. From 1916 on, the Twigs' contribution to Children's would become incalculable, both in supplies and services and in public relations.

The year also marked the founding of that remarkable little magazine, the Bambino, first issued in June, 1917, which became the voice of Children's for more than a quarter-century to its growing army of volunteers. With Mrs. Sellers, its founder, as business manager, and Mrs. Andrew B. Nelles as longtime editor, the Bambino was a well-edited, readable and highly informative monthly containing news of the hospital and volunteer activities, articles on child care and child welfare, selected stories and poems for children, and complete reports of hospital annual meetings. An invaluable line of communication, the Bambino was also a source of financial benefit for the hospital, realizing a profit each month from the very first issue on a publication initially sold at 50 cents for a year's subscription.

A most important step toward Children's future was the affiliation in 1916 with Ohio State University. It was tenuous at first, subject to termination by either party on seven days' notice, but the agreement had an immediate effect on the hospital's staff size and organization and marked the beginning of its eventual development into a treatment, training and research center.

Two other programs with long-range potential dating from 1916 were the establishment of a dental clinic and the employment of a trained social worker to visit homes and work with families of patients.

Contagion was a continuing problem. In 1917, the hospital was closed three times during outbreaks of scarlet fever, diphtheria and measles, and in 1918 the raging influenza epidemic closed the hospital to all but flu sufferers for two months.

Determined to build a new hospital but wavering between a new and old site, trustees were approached near the end of 1917 by W.K. Field, president of the Pittsburgh Coal Co. Field, whose wife was active on the Women's Board and who is mentioned year after year in old board minutes as donor of "a carload of coal" for hospital boilers, had a site to offer. He proposed that a new hospital be located on a city block at 17th and Stone Sts., southeast of downtown, fronting on Livingston Park, and offered to donate two lots which he owned within the site.

The entire area was part of the old Kelsey farm which at one time extended north to Town St., according to Dr. Samuel Robinson, whose wife is a member of the Field family. The lots, he said, represented the coal company executive's "entire inheritance" from his father.

Between the hospital site and Livingston Ave., land once used as a pioneer cemetery had been purchased by the city in 1839, according to old city records, and was converted to a park in 1885.

Trustees accepted Field's offer, purchased the remaining land, and began to plan the new hospital which, at a second site, would have room to grow and an adjoining park to offer open space and recreational area for patients.

At the 25th annual meeting in March, 1918, the managers of Children's, still including many of the founders, could look back on a quarter-century of struggle and achievement.

Compared to the brief statistics of its early years, Children's in 1917 had admitted 683 patients (124 medical, 135 surgical and 424 ophthalmological), logged 909 surgical procedures, served 5,387 dispensary patients and 89 in the new dental clinic.

Children's had come a long way, and the new hospital then shaping up in blueprints would again progress further than its planners could possibly envision.

1917–1942
Challenges of a New Neighborhood

The time a new or expanded hospital is most needed is not necessarily the best time to build one.

In 1918, while plans for the new hospital were being drawn, the community was caught up in World War I. Fifteen members of the medical staff had entered military service, hospital volunteers were involved in the work of wartime agencies, and the citizenry were preoccupied with the war's impact on their lives.

Special times called for special efforts, and Children's managers gleaned solid evidence of continued support. The Women's Board gave up its annual benefit entertainment and a committee headed by five men—J.L.V. Bonney, Mayor George J. Karb, F.O. Schoedinger, F.R. Huntington and Joseph Schonthal—sent out 500 letters, seeking $3,000 to replace the benefit's revenue. They received $3,142.

Donation Day produced more than a truckload of food and staples, 244 items of clothing and $600 in cash. The hospital handyman, from an $11 investment in seed, produced 21 bushels of potatoes, three crops of beans and similar lots of other vegetables from the hospital garden.

Unable to plan their annual Charity Ball in 1918 "without meetings and without men," busy members of the Pleasure Guild held the dance that wasn't. For their Camouflage Ball, they sent invitations on camouflage paper, sold tickets in the State House grounds beside a camouflaged cannon, and delivered boxed forget-me-nots to purchasers in lieu of staging the ball. "No one but the caterers seemed disappointed," Guild President Helen T. Miller reported, and the ball cleared more than $1,000.

The hospital staff was stretched to the limit, particularly during the two-month flu siege. Community physicians filled in for absent staff members. The new OSU affiliation brought the loan of a senior student as house officer and the assistance of OSU labs for testing procedures.

Progress on the new hospital was dishearteningly slow. The funds placed on interest after the disappointing fund-raising campaign of 1916 were not growing as fast as wartime costs, and it appeared another major fund drive would be necessary.

In other ways the hospital was moving ahead. The board finally voted to change hospital policy to allow for both full- and part-pay patients. In 1920, Miss Lily Atkinson retired as superintendent and Dr. Marion S. Reynolds, the first (and only) physician to hold the post, replaced her. Dr. Leslie Bigelow, who had become chief of the medical staff, reported a "cordial and sympathetic relationship" between staff physicians and the new superintendent.

New laboratory procedures and admission policies were paying off; due to required throat cultures for every child, the hospital remained free of the diphtheria epidemic which struck Columbus in 1921.

Under the new OSU affiliation, 61 medical students had added clinical observation at Children's to their training by 1921, and two interns from the senior medical class were assigned to the hospital. That year, the hospital admitted 1,136 patients, a sharp increase over 1920, and logged more than 6,000 dispensary visits and more than 1,000 home visits by the social worker.

In her annual report, Mrs. Sellers summarized in cogent terms where the hospital stood:

"The day is past when we can look upon the Children's Hospital as a simple charity. It is a vast plant whose economic value to this community cannot be measured by mere figures. For many years, it has been offering, free of charge to this city and county, the best medical and surgical skill for the safeguarding of the health of their children . . . this hospital plant belongs to the public of this community, and I believe now is the time to tell them of our difficulties."

In 1922, they did.

Trustees let the contract for a new hospital on June 21. On Sept. 15, with the governor, the mayor and other dignitaries looking on, they laid the cornerstone.

That same month, having demonstrated that the old formula—faith first, then funds—was still operative, they announced plans for a one-week campaign in October for $500,000 to pay for the new building.

F.R. Huntington was general chairman; Mrs. Sellers, chairman of women's activities; Simon Lazarus, publicity chairman. The estimate was that 1,000 volunteers were directly involved, and the goal was to reach as directly as possible every resident of the city and county. It must have been one of the most pervasive selling jobs Columbus had seen up to that time—perhaps even yet.

Pamphlets, posters, even tags on home milk deliveries were widely distributed. Sketches of the new hospital and photographs of the crowded old one appeared everywhere.

On the opening Sunday, all the churches hailed the campaign and a community concert was given in Ohio Stadium—the first public use of that proud new addition to the city. President Warren G. Harding endorsed the campaign in a letter to Huntington.

On Tuesday, 5,000 women dressed in white marched through the streets. On Thursday, Twigs demonstrated the variety of their work in a series of floats in a second parade, accompanied by young patients from the hospital and dispensary waving from automobiles.

On Friday, volunteers took over operation of the Deshler Hotel for a full day with proceeds going to Children's.

It was estimated more than 30,000 persons contributed, and the total in pledges was $517,911, surpassing the goal.

Amazingly, the old hospital continued to take more patients and to expand its services while the new one was being completed.

The big dedication day, June 16, 1924, finally arrived. Gov. Vic Donahey and Mayor James J. Thomas attended. The guest speaker was Dr. Joel E. Goldthwait of Boston, Mass., the ranking orthopedic surgeon in the United States, who pronounced the new Children's "the best in the country."

The Dispatch, in a long and laudatory editorial, said that, while other U.S. children's hospitals were larger and more costly, "we have good authority for saying that there is not one among them which can surpass it (Children's in Columbus) in the completeness and excellence of its equipment for its work."

In an excellent brief history, written for the June Bambino, Mrs. Thad Brown of the Women's Board traced the hospital's growth over its first 33 years.

The first three years, she said, it cared for 200 patients, and in 1923 alone with little space added, it cared for 1,276 patients and 6,563 dispensary cases.

With the $144,000 actually realized in the foreshortened 1916 campaign and the interest it had gathered, she said, trustees had purchased the new building site and land for an adjacent nurses' home, and had paid for architectural plans and equipment for the new hospital.

"Since the hospital has an endowed income of only $12,000 per year, and since it has been the aim of the hospital to avoid making annual appeals to the public for large sums of money . . . ," she wrote, "it depends entirely for maintenance on the financial aid given by the trustees, Women's Board, Twigs, Thrift Shop, Pleasure Guild, postage stamp machines, Bambino magazine, and other auxiliaries. The greatest help of all is the constant and unselfish service of the medical and surgical staff who do their work absolutely without remuneration."

She noted that Children's had been operating at the lowest cost of any like hospital in the U.S. and Canada, and that, although two pay beds had been provided by trustee action, they were available only when not needed for charity patients. (In his history, Dr. Baxter said that no real accommodation was made for paying patients until about 1930.)

The day after the dedication, Columbus got its first look at the new hospital it had helped build. An H-shaped structure with a basement and four upper

19

floors, the hospital was completed with 75 beds and was capable of immediate expansion to 150 and to twice that number with upper-floor additions to the rear section.

The exterior was red brick with terra cotta trim, the basic construction fireproof, the interior generally of hard plaster walls and terrazzo flooring.

The tendency to grandeur still prevailed in the main entrance and public rooms beyond it—a sweeping drive leading to a porte cochere and flight of stone steps; an entrance lobby of black and white rubberized tile with a blue tile fountain basin centered by a bathing-boy sculpture in white marble; paneled walls; and a wall plaque of a della Robbia bambino, the hospital's symbol.

Patient areas were decorated with the tastes of children in mind. Two solarium playrooms and an outdoor play area particularly were enlivened with animal pictures and finished with toys, books and child-sized furnishings.

To the hospital staff, accustomed to making do with the minimum of equipment and space, the more mundane niceties in heating, lighting, call signal systems, ventilation and refrigeration, and the advantageous placement of emergency rooms, surgical suites, dispensary, kitchens and dining areas, laboratory and X-ray facilities must have been a dream realized.

Meeting long-expressed needs were the isolation and observation ward, a premature nursery, rest and locker rooms for doctors, sleeping quarters for house and visiting interns, and an incipient medical reference library given by Twig 3 and made up largely of the personal libraries of Dr. Theodore Rankin of Columbus and Dr. Augustus Harper Buckmaster of New York City.

Pending the availability of funds for a much-needed home for nurses in training, quarters for 40 nurses were provided in eventual patient rooms on the third and fourth floors and the adjoining solariums. (A newspaper reporter, apparently unfamiliar with the architect's name for sunrooms, referred to these features of the new hospital as "cellariums.")

Interestingly, an area of the third floor was planned for a maternity department—a facility which was never developed for that use and which, to the present, some Children's officials believe is the one basic facility the hospital lacks. As recently as the late '70s, Children's and St. Ann's officials discussed a maternity facility, particularly for high-risk mothers, as a joint venture—an idea unrealized when St. Ann's closed its Bryden Rd. hospital and rebuilt in Westerville.

The medical staff had grown to 30 physicians plus an intern and two externs, with 14 other physicians serving the dispensary and clinics. Administrative personnel included Dr. Reynolds; her assistant, Miss Susan Anderson; a social worker; and Miss Vera Keyes, R.N., superintendent of the new nurses' training school.

The state-certified nurse-training program began with three nurses from Zanesville City Hospital, one graduate nurse from Virginia seeking pediatric experience, and two nursery maid students.

In January of 1925, Children's opened a school for patients with a teacher supplied by the Columbus Board of Education. For years thereafter, as the school program grew and developed, the reports of Mrs. Rhea McKee Taylor as school chairman for the Women's Board were an anticipated highlight of the annual meeting reports. Mrs. Taylor personalized her lively reports by describing individual patients and their needs and how the program was benefiting them.

21

Later, Mrs. Taylor's daughter-in-law, Lucile G. Taylor (Mrs. Livingston), continued this kind of reporting during her service as school chairman. She is a trustee emeritus, after serving both that body and the Women's Board, and Livingston Taylor was president of the board of trustees from 1959 to 1961.

By this early-1920s period, this "generational" kind of service to Children's had become established in a number of Columbus families—and the period probably produced the one holder of an unchallenged all-time record.

Franklin Oscar Schoedinger, a Columbus native and founder of his own sheet-metal manufacturing company, was the son-in-law of John Siebert, an original trustee and early board president. Schoedinger became a board member in the early 1900s, serving for years as chairman of the house committee, the one which worked most closely with the Women's Board in actual operation of the hospital. He served as board vice president and in 1920 began a term as president which continued until 1951.

He was a leader in Columbus civic and philanthropic affairs and past president of the Columbus Chamber of Commerce. Younger members of the Schoedinger family who worked at various times in the company recall a dignified, no-nonsense man who kept in touch with employees by personally distributing each person's salary envelope at his office desk. Asked how one man retained the presidency for such an unprecedented time, Clair E. Fultz, a fellow board member and later president, said, "I don't know. I guess he had such a commanding presence that we never thought about it."

Schoedinger, Mrs. Sellers and Dr. Bigelow were a remarkable triumvirate in this early-'20s period in their respective contributions and long service to the hospital. Alike in one respect, none of them ever presented an annual meeting report without injecting some personal observations on the state of the hospital, the community and the world in general.

Attempting to list Columbus families with whom service to Children's has become a tradition would be to risk omissions—but the list would be long.

Robert Lazarus, Jr., a current board member, recalling a family basement perennially used to house items for some hospital project, said, "It was something we grew up with. There were two or three organizations you always supported, and one of them was Children's."

His recollection could be shared by many, in a pattern of family involvement already well established when the hospital occupied its second, and permanent, home.

22

Adapting to the better fit and greater potential for service of its new environs, Children's could look ahead to ways to improve.

In his 1924 annual report, Dr. Bigelow mentioned the need for better record-keeping and follow-up of patients, and asked the cooperation of staff physicians.

Not only would this provide a gauge of the hospital's performance and the effectiveness of certain procedures and treatment methods, he reasoned, but it would also supply basic data for research. This new word "research" would soon and very rapidly become more important.

During 1925, the trustees raised the Women's Board annual allowance for operating the hospital to $20,000. It was more than six times their original allowance, but Board President Schoedinger noted it now represented only about a third of the total cost of one year's operation.

One good example of how this disparity was made up, through the years, was the Twig fund-raiser in October. Building on the success of their Deshler Day during the building fund drive, and with the help of a number of community organizations, they ran the "new Neil House" hotel for a day and raised more than $8,000.

Her death in November, 1925, when she was struck by a car on E. Broad St., ended the long service of Mrs. James B. Kilbourne, in whose home Children's began. A member of the executive committee from the hospital's founding until her death, she served for 18 years as Women's Board president.

In 1925 and '26, in her reports to trustees, Superintendent Reynolds noted trends in hospital service foreshadowing Children's future importance to a vast area beyond Franklin County. In 1925, she wrote that not only were physicians and surgeons of the city referring more cases to Children's but "also those of the county and state . . . referring cases for diagnosis as well as for treatment."

Many of these out-of-county patients were on the orthopedic service, supported by the Shrine organizations in a program overseen by Dr. W.D. Murphy. In the mid-'20s, the orthopedic service gained further impetus with the arrival of Dr. Harlan Wilson, who lobbied for the development of a state service to aid crippled children and to support their hospitalization. Dr. Baxter gave Dr. Wilson major credit for the expansion and improvement of the orthopedic service at Children's, which he headed until his death in 1952 during a medical staff Christmas dinner in the hospital.

In 1926, Dr. Reynolds told trustees, "We are beginning to realize that the value of the hospital to the community cannot be reckoned in terms of operations or cases treated. Rather the modern hospital must be measured in

Familiar names to Columbus, and to Children's, appear on this surviving fragment of a donor list for the 1924 building.

F.R. Huntington, secretary-treasurer of the board of trustees, was general chairman of successful 1922 campaign.

THE
NEW CHILDRENS' HOSPITAL
FUND

"A Half Million for Health and Happiness"

EXECUTIVE COMMITTEE
F. R. HUNTINGTON, CHAIRMAN
SIMON LAZARUS
F. O. SCHOEDINGER
MRS. T. B. SELLERS
J. J. STEVENSON

CAMPAIGN HEADQUARTERS, No. 47 NORTH FOURTH STREET
COLUMBUS

WOMEN'S ORGANIZATION
COMMITTEE
MRS. J. G. BATTELLE
MRS. FRANK C. MARTIN
MRS. HENRY C. TAYLOR
MRS. E. W. CAMPION
MRS. A. B. NELLES
MISS LUCILE ATCHERSON
MRS. THEODORE AUST

T
H
E

K
E
Y

I
S

I
N

Y
O
U
R

P
O
C
K
E
T

Appealing letterhead used in promotion for successful 1922 building campaign.

The Laying of the Cornerstone

===== for the =====

NEW CHILDREN'S HOSPITAL

"America,"—Led by Third Field Artillery Band

Opening Address—F. O. SCHOEDINGER,
President of Children's Hospital

Invocation—REV. THOMAS J. O'REILLY, St. Dominic's Church

"Rock of Ages,"—Led by Choir Boys of Trinity Episcopal Church

Address by GOVERNOR HARRY L. DAVIS

Placing of Mementoes in the Cornerstone
Introductions by MRS. T. B. SELLERS

Prayer by RABBI JACOB TARSHISH, B'Nai Israel Temple

Address—JAMES E. CAMPBELL, former Governor of Ohio

Address—LESLIE LAWSON BIGELOW, M.D.,
Dean of Staff, Children's Hospital

"All Things are Thine,"—Led by Choir Boys

Acceptance in behalf of Columbus—MAYOR JAMES THOMAS

The New Hospital—F. R. HUNTINGTON

Benediction—REV. S. S. PALMER,
Broad Street Presbyterian Church

"Star Spangled Banner,"—Third Field Artillery Band

Musical Program directed by KARL H. HOENIG,
Ohio State University

Friday, September 15, 1922.   Four O'clock

A governor, an ex-governor and the mayor were on the program for the cornerstone laying for the new hospital in 1922.

The hospital's cornerstone, laid in 1922, was rediscovered behind a dental clinic wall in 1992.

1924 hospital shortly after its completion.

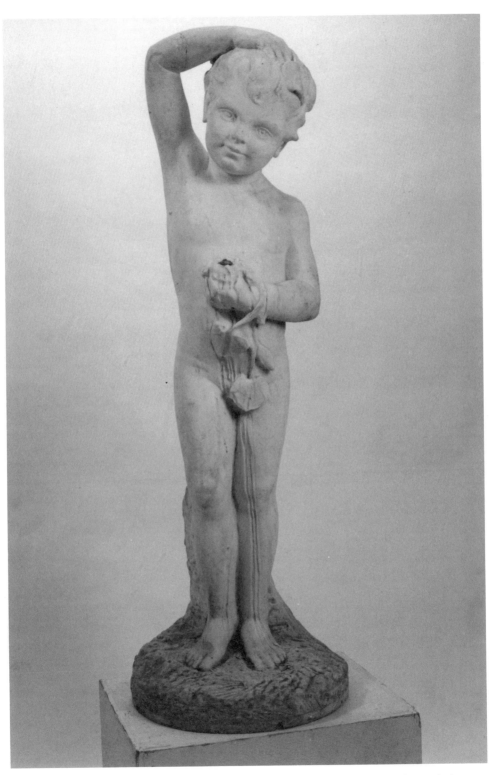

Bathing-boy statue by May Cook, Columbus sculptress, designed for lobby pool of 1924 hospital.

Feature of 1924 hospital—the solariums.

Livingston Park is framed in Children's front doorway in this 1931 view.

A 1942 operating room "perfectly equipped," according to a Bambino caption for this photo.

Dr. Marion S. Reynolds, superintendent of Children's, 1920-30.

A 1930 gathering of hospital stalwarts—Board President F.O. Schoedinger, left; Trustee Simon Lazarus and Dr. Leslie L. Bigelow, chief of staff, and Trustees Webb Vorys, left rear, and Erdis G. Robinson.

Student nurses in this 1938 class came from hospitals in six Ohio and two Kentucky cities.

Earth-movers became part of the Children's scene for decades after digging began in the late '30s for the Marks addition.

First major item in the constant expansion of the late century was the Amelia and Julius Marks addition, right, which provided more beds and needed facilities in the late '30s.

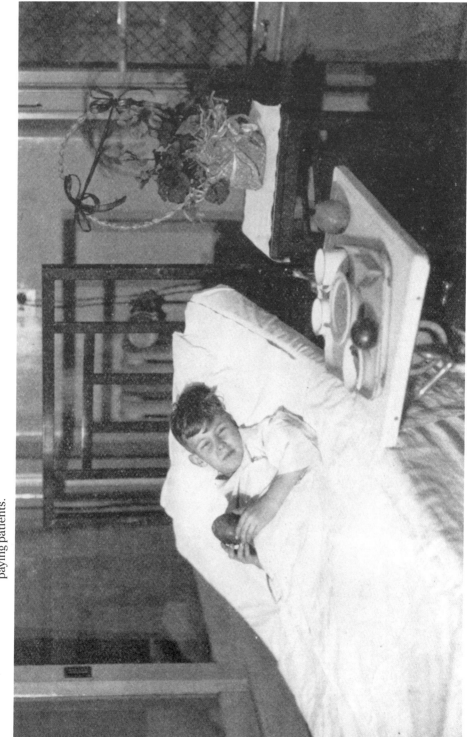

With the addition of 14 private rooms in the late '30s, Children's began to take more paying patients.

The dinner hour in a Children's ward in 1925.

Miss Eva Ellen Janson, last nurse superintendent of Children's, 1931-42.

terms of educational stimulus . . . and of the number of days of hospitalization it has prevented." The problem of steadily mounting costs and service
charges stemming from "enlarged community service," she said, must be
regarded as "our obligation as a community center."

During 1926, an intern affiliation was arranged with Ohio State University, giving medical students two months' training in pediatrics at Children's,
and the hospital was beginning to feel serious need of a resident physician.

In 1928, a heart clinic was established, and electrocardiograph equipment purchased for it. A convalescent camp for patients was opened in a
home on Big Walnut Creek equipped and maintained by Mr. and Mrs. Wilson
Carlile, and work was begun to prepare a fourth-floor area for a new nurse-
training program in affiliation with University Hospital.

Exhorting volunteers, as she usually did, to spread the gospel of
Children's services in addition to their fund-raising efforts, Mrs. Sellers noted
that the hospital's work was still "about 97 percent charity" and the services
of attending physicians at the same ratio. And in her report, Dr. Reynolds
commented:

"Inadequate incomes for the size of the family, incomes spent
unwisely . . . , mental incompetency, unemployment and dependency due to
death or desertion . . . all of these maladjustments are reasons for keeping
this hospital so filled with a high percent of charity and part-pay patients."

The next year, trustees and philanthropic citizens contributed more
than $18,000 to pay for the new nurses' quarters, and the Thrift Shop supplied
the money to furnish nine patient rooms.

The nurses' training school was opened with Miss Eva Ellen Janson, later
to become superintendent, in charge, and Dr. Paul Maxwell, product of Johns
Hopkins School of Medicine, signed on as house physician.

Aware that the hospital's very success was compounding its problems,
in the face of mounting costs, medical advances and the heavy charity load,
hospital officials were concerned about increasing income. The annual
operating cost, Dr. Bigelow warned, was edging toward $100,000.

During 1930, although it felt the effect of the countrywide depression in
many ways, Children's recorded a number of important "firsts" and forward
steps in its expanding mission.

Mrs. Sellers, while continuing her longtime service as Women's Board
president, was elected to the hospital board of trustees as its first woman
member.

In line with recommendations of the Hornsby report more than a decade
earlier, the medical staff was reorganized into departments, and each department chief made his separate report to trustees at the annual meeting.

The affiliation with Ohio State University was expanding, with medical
students working and observing in the hospital and clinic, home economics

students helping and observing in the nutrition clinic, and social science and psychology students involved with these hospital services.

A new mothers' clinic helped mothers plan for their children's dietary needs, budgeting and the family's general health.

The hospital began an eye clinic and a part-pay orthodontic clinic and reorganized its psychology, psychiatric and dermatology clinics.

Dr. Reynolds resigned and was replaced by Miss Janson. The Columbus Academy of Medicine attended a clinic presented by the hospital staff, and 65 members of the National Orthopaedic Society held a meeting at Children's to observe its work.

A bequest of $20,000 from the estate of Albert Riordan was the largest of several 1930 bequests—the largest indeed since the William Franklin bequest in 1905.

In 1927, with their shining new hospital just settling into expanded operation and service, Mrs. Sellers warned the hard-working volunteers they must remain "alert with noble discontent" and that a milestone reached was just that in the steadily growing demands on Children's. By the mid-'30s, with the original property at Miller and Fair Aves. just sold for $41,500 by trustees, it was apparent the new hospital was running close to capacity.

Through the worst years of the depression, Children's had kept all its beds open, retained its employees despite the necessary cuts in already-low wages, and intensified volunteer efforts to keep the hospital out of debt.

The annual operating costs were nearing the $100,000 mark. The nurses' training program was certifying nearly 100 students a year through its four-month course, some 200 medical students a year were rotating through the hospital, and the medical staff had reached more than 60.

The pressing needs were for a nurses' home which would release in-hospital space for a doubled number of patient beds and for attention to overcrowded dispensary and therapy facilities. The hospital was seeing an increasing number of infantile paralysis patients in need of such facilities and was aware an epidemic of the disease would seriously tax Children's capacity.

In late 1937, some of these problems were solved. Leo Marks and his sister, Mrs. Walter Franc, donated $150,000 from the foundation named for their parents to construct the Amelia and Julius Marks addition on the east side of the hospital. It would provide for extra beds, more dispensary space, a clinical demonstration area and a physiotherapy pool.

The gift was contingent upon the hospital's income being adequate to maintain and operate the addition. By March of 1938, a trustees' committee headed by Albert M. Miller had raised the $25,000 for the first year's operation.

The addition was dedicated Oct. 3, 1939. Dr. Bigelow, in his year-end report to trustees, assessed its importance to the hospital and staff in ways other than the needed increase in bed capacity. It also provided, he said:

24

• More extensive non-operative treatment of orthopedic cases, thanks to the swimming pool and a gymnasium.

• Extension of clinical and pathological laboratories and staff, which increased the number of tests performed by more than 10,000 in the first year.

This report was Dr. Bigelow's valedictory. After 25 years' service to Children's, he relinquished the post of chief of staff but stayed on as chief of surgery. On March 1, 1942, he became acting dean of the OSU College of Medicine; he was stricken by illness later that year and died in January, 1943.

Children's was approaching its 50th year. It was experiencing internal changes and facing greater ones which would far outstrip the solid accomplishments of the first half-century.

Again, as they had 25 years earlier, threats of impending war overshadowed the planning as new leadership moved into place.

In 1941, Mrs. Sellers declined to run for re-election, marking the close of a remarkable 26-year tenure as head of the Women's Board during which she had been prime mover, head cheerleader and continuing inspiration for the hospital and its volunteer army. She continued her membership on the Women's Board and board of trustees until her death a year later, on July 11, 1942.

Her contribution to Children's defies measurement. She was a leader in the building campaign which produced the new hospital. She founded the Twigs and helped build them to the vital financial and public relations bulwark they became. She founded the Bambino, which, for 25 years until the war stilled its voice in 1942, kept the volunteer legions informed not only about Children's but about developing issues and methods in child care—and which, with Mrs. Sellers as business manager, never failed to turn a profit to swell hospital coffers.

Mrs. Sellers was succeeded by Mrs. Philander S. Bradford, a longtime member of the Women's Board, who in turn would guide the women's auxiliaries through dramatic reorganization.

The shape of Children's future was drawn by Dr. Earl H. Baxter in his first report to the board as the new chief of staff in 1941.

A Children's staff member since 1924 and head of its medical department, Dr. Baxter was a practicing pediatrician, a longtime OSU faculty member and chairman of the medical college's division of pediatrics.

In 1941, when the division was given departmental status, he was named chairman. His joint appointment to this and the Children's post signified the meshing of the hospital's fortunes with the emergence of a new medical specialty recognizing children from birth through adolescence as a special class of patients.

In his history of the OSU College of Medicine, describing the beginnings of the pediatrics specialty, Dr. N. Paul Hudson wrote:

"More than one-fourth of all medical practice is concerned with children . . . The problems and diseases of this age group differ greatly from those of the adult. Children are not miniature adults, but individuals presenting different physiological and chemical reactions to infections and trauma, complicated by the problems of growth and development as influenced by genetics and environment.

"It is the firm belief and philosophy of the (OSU) Department of Pediatrics that the best medical care from birth through adolescence can be provided by those physicians who have been exposed to a thorough experience in the basic principles of pediatrics . . ."

A children's hospital, said Dr. Baxter in his first report to trustees, "deals with life at an age when all or most of the developmental years are ahead." While its primary duty, like any hospital's, is to "save lives, cure illness and correct defects," it must also, he said, be a training center "for the patient, the resident staff, attending staff, nursing personnel, both bedside and social service, as well as the medical profession and indeed the community at large."

Beyond this, he envisioned, it must be the recognized center for development and dissemination of "pediatric thought in the community" and must have the opportunity "to carry out certain investigative procedures and problems, commonly known as research . . ."

1942–1967
Growth and Specialization

$\mathbf{D}$r. Earl H. Baxter's farewell to Children's in 1963, after 23 years as chief of staff, was both retrospective and prophetic. "An institution without problems," he said, "is either stagnant or dead."

His administrative tenure, ranging from World War II to Sputnik, had involved every kind of problem arising from dizzying growth and change. Children's fourth quarter-century would mesh with charging medical advance at the same "fast forward" pace.

Many who were there firmly attest that the '40s and '50s were warm and wonderful years in a pioneering kind of way as exciting as it was frustrating. The hospital was old and limited, but the staff was young and eager, the first generation of specialists trained in treatment of children. Experimentation, cooperation and innovation became slogan terms.

Just as some structural bones of the old 1924 hospital still supported the shining new institution built around them through the '80s, the spirit of that mid-century surge—when Children's really began to grow up—became an integral part of what so many term simply "that special thing about Children's."

Quarter-century realignments were becoming a pattern. The hospital moved into the '40s with new leadership in key positions. Dr. Baxter, chairman of the new OSU pediatrics department, was named chief of the medical staff. Robert M. Porter, appointed by the Women's Board in 1942, became the first administrator with a background in hospital management. Mrs. Philander S. Bradford succeeded Mrs. Sellers as Women's Board president.

It was a major turning point, a deliberate relinquishing of control by the women who had nurtured and supported a small hospital now in need of direction and professional management.

Mrs. Bradford had made the appointment of a hospital-trained administrator a condition of her acceptance of the Women's Board presidency. Feeling that trustees had become too narrowly concerned with money matters, the Women's Board also saw the need of trustees' stronger voice in relationships with other community hospitals, questions of standards and policy, and pursuit of public funds then becoming available for hospitals.

While seeking and defining the limits of their respective roles, the new leaders faced two major challenges. A declining inpatient census was an immediate concern. Children's future role as an institution was a greater one. They recognized the hospital had to attract patients from a much broader segment of the community and had to improve its staff and facilities to encourage their coming.

Trustees supplied funds to add patient rooms, a new ambulance entrance, cafeteria and superintendent's office and for general redecorating and refurbishing. Recognizing that women's auxiliaries included hundreds of parents who were not using the hospital, Porter made a direct appeal to them to spread the word of Children's plans and improvements and to use its facilities for their own families. In just one year, with 20 new private rooms and 12 semi-private rooms made available, the hospital treated 365 more private cases.

Items on the hospital's standing agenda were all top priority and all interdependent:

• To modernize the administrative structure, clarify the administrator's role and lubricate creaky organizational machinery.

• To augment the medical staff with the best candidates available trained in pediatrics and its developing sub-specialties.

• To supply facilities and space for them and their patients and to look beyond that to certain building and expansion needs to be met after World War II.

• To take some definite positive action toward an established research program.

Beyond these considerable items, worrisome because still unsettled, were the uneasy relationship with OSU and the anomalous factors affecting medical staff positions.

Early in 1944, acting on a Women's Board proposal, trustees initiated a series of changes which eventually evolved in a board of managers made up of officers and selected members of the two boards. Porter became a member, then executive officer, of this board, speaking in its behalf to trustees.

In 1946, Mrs. Bradford resigned her Women's Board presidency after five years. Also a trustee, she accepted a new position created by that board as assistant secretary, to serve as ambassador-at-large and as their liaison with the auxiliaries, hospital management and the public.

Like other community hospitals, Children's had limped through the war years with medical and nursing staffs depleted by the military services. With the war's end, however, staff people began arriving who would help raise treatment and teaching standards to high levels and project Children's into the forefront among its national counterparts.

They had trained at premier medical centers, under the pioneers in pediatric medicine. They were pioneers themselves, and they found at Children's both the difficulties and challenges inherent in the trailblazer's role.

Dr. Warren E. Wheeler came in 1946, the first full-time professor of pediatrics at OSU and the first full-time medical staff associate at Children's. Revered as a remarkable teacher and insatiable investigator, Wheeler left a mark on Children's extending far beyond his years there after he left in 1963 to head the pediatrics department at the University of Kentucky.

Arriving four years later, and with similar impact, Dr. H. William Clatworthy had trained under the surgical giants, William Ladd, Robert Gross and Owen Wangensteen, and was the first pediatric surgeon not only in Columbus, but in Ohio.

A skilled surgeon, he was, like Wheeler, an excellent teacher, a strong advocate of research and insistent on the highest standards in care and treatment of patients. "With him," wrote Baxter, "came an entirely new concept in the surgical care of children. This included better nursing service, a better understanding of the physiology and pathology of children, and a closer relationship of the pediatric surgeon to the pediatrician."

Nationally recognized himself, Clatworthy built a nationally recognized department whose graduates now chair a significant number of pediatric surgery departments.

"It was kind of a clonical thing," said Dr. E. Thomas Boles, Jr., who joined the surgery staff in the early '50s and later became chairman. In the still-small world of pediatric medicine, the ones who came to Children's knew where other good people were—and it was quality Porter and Baxter were seeking.

Some came, contributed, then followed their careers elsewhere. Some came, left and were drawn back. Among other early arrivals of the post–World War II era whose names were linked with Children's progress through succeeding decades, Dr. William Newton in pathology and cancer research, Dr. Martin P. Sayers in neurosurgery, Dr. Morris Battles in ophthalmology, Dr. Thomas Shaffer in newborn pediatrics and adolescent medicine, Dr. E.V. Turner in administration and education, and Dr. W. Hugh Missildine in child psychiatry come immediately to mind.

"Word got around the country that Columbus was the place to be," recalled one alumnus of that period. Word also got around that doctors at Columbus Children's were doing new things to treat young patients, parents brought their children from farther and farther away, and Children's very success increased its problems.

The 25-year-old building was taxed beyond its limits. When an influx of polio patients added to the load in the epidemics of the mid-'40s and early '50s, the situation became critical. No one who visited the hospital in those hectic days will ever forget the hissing sound of the "iron lung" respirators, the pervading smell of "wet packs"—and beds of "overflow" patients ranged along corridors.

Nurses were moved to a Bexley mansion to free their living area for patient beds. Veteran nurses recall "all the little houses" around the hospital, former residences, into which offices and services were moved to gain more in-hospital space. One surgical secretary who logged nine office moves during her years at Children's remembered one such residential outpost when office operations filled the rooms and surgical files were stored in a shower stall.

All of the county's hospitals had building problems. The city was growing rapidly, the long war years had delayed expansion plans, and their aftermath brought an era of sharply mounting costs.

In 1944, a study of the county hospital system by Dr. Fred G. Carter, superintendent of Cleveland's St. Luke Hospital, recommended that general hospitals close their children's units and that Children's, possibly with a 50-bed expansion, become the center for treating young patients.

In 1945, the Columbus Hospital Federation was organized, having among its objectives the assessment of the area's health care needs and an orderly, equitable effort to meet them. Late that same year, Dean Charles A. Doan of the OSU College of Medicine suggested that Children's move to the campus area to become part of the OSU medical center complex. After long deliberation, trustees voted in 1946 to expand Children's on its existing site.

A year later, OSU's medical center expansion plans had to be pared to match available funding, a projected pediatrics facility was eliminated, and Dean Doan proposed that all pediatrics teaching and program development be transferred to and centered at Children's.

Moving the nurses to outside housing had given Children's some breathing room, making space for 75 more beds. A grant from the Timken Foundation helped fund construction of Timken Hall, the first free-standing addition to the hospital complex. The four-story red brick building on 17th St. at the Stone St. corner was opened in 1950 with residential quarters for 100 nurses.

In 1959, with hospital expansion creating the need for additional nurses, construction was begun on a three-story nurse education addition to Timken with residential accommodation for 88 more nurses. With its $100,000 gift to fund the addition, the Timken Foundation had given more than $350,000 to the total project.

Meanwhile, realizing hospital expansion was imperative, Children's trustees planned a building campaign. The United Hospitals Building Fund drive had also begun, and the participation of Children's, with its special appeal to donors, was sought.

Trustees, weighing community responsibility against certain delays and uncertain proceeds of a joint effort, agreed.

During those years, the county's general hospitals needed their bed space for adults and favored Children's serving young patients. To encourage Children's continued participation in a community building campaign, administrators of the county's hospitals reached a "gentleman's agreement" about Children's future role.

Mid-'50's view of hospital lobby shows information desk, a della Robbia bambino on the wall and the May Cook sculpture in the pool.

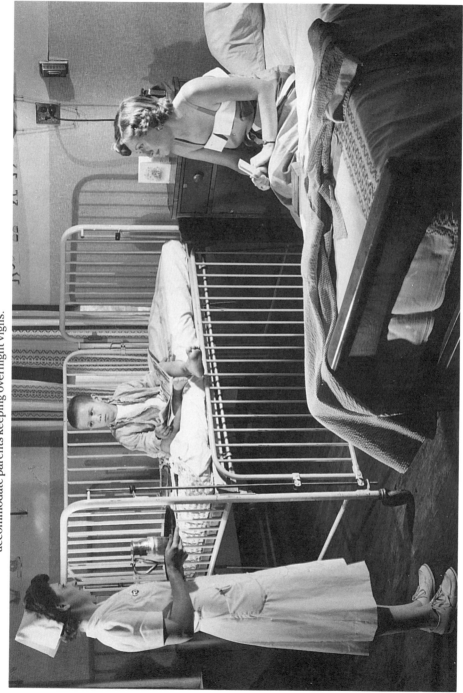

Mother and son in this 1950s photo benefited from Children's pacesetting efforts to accommodate parents keeping overnight vigils.

Houses surround hospital of the '50s.

An aerial view of the complex looking northeast, shortly after groundbreaking for the new south wing in 1958.

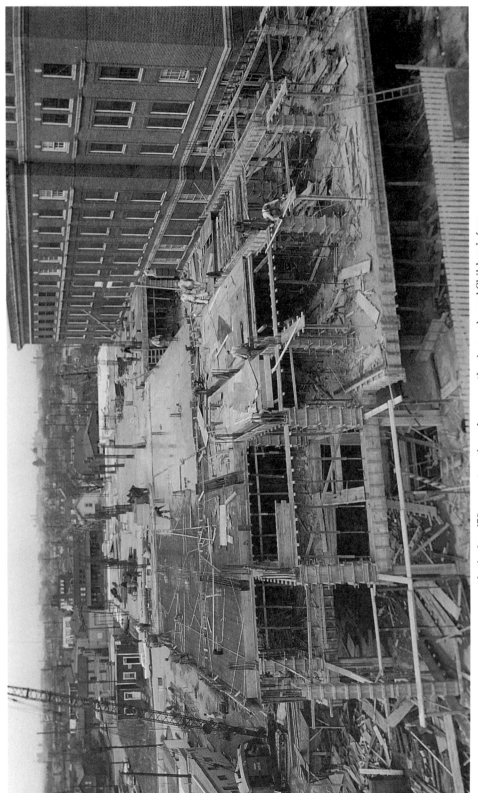

In the late '50s, construction of new south wing reshaped Children's face.

Dignitaries at 1960 dedication included, from left, Trustee E.A. Donnan; Leroy D. Gable, Timken president; Helen Bradford; Clair Fultz; Past President Albert M. Miller; Administrator Robert Porter, at rostrum; and President-elect Robert M. Rex.

Timken Hall addition, dedicated in 1960, gave nurses more dormitories and classrooms.

Drs. Wheeler and Baxter at a Children's staff dinner.

Board President Livingston L. Taylor, left, paid tribute to F.O. Schoedinger, 31-year board president, during 1960 south wing dedication.

Early 1960s view shows completed Timken additions, right, new south wing and first phase of Ross Hall, left.

At a mid-'60s hospital gathering: Drs. E.V. Turner, Bruce Graham, Henry Cramblett, Earl H. Baxter and former Administrator Robert Porter.

Delbert L. Pugh, longtime executive head of the Columbus Hospital Federation, recalled that agreement and the specificity of its wording. Children's was not designated as a "pediatrics center," which might be interpreted as a limitation referring only to difficult and long-term cases requiring specialized treatment, Pugh emphasized, but as "a general hospital for children," treating the full range of childhood diseases and difficulties.

Erosion of that agreement has become increasingly apparent in recent years of intense competition for hospital patients. Market-conscious hospitals are well aware of the appeal of children's faces in their brochures and advertising, and of the lucrative return in short-term, uncomplicated services offered children.

The turnaround is a threat to Children's, which must balance these "pluses" against the complex, long-term care it is often uniquely equipped to give and against an annual write-off for patients served but unable to pay— continuation of its century-old tradition.

Only the steady support of a community which appreciated Children's special character had brought it to this mid-century point and encouraged trustees to proceed with the most ambitious building program in the hospital's history.

A vital element in this community support was strengthened in 1949 with the organization of the Central Ohio Pediatric Society. Records of the society supplied by Dr. Edward W. McCall show that an initial purpose of the organization was to bring together physicians of the city and Central Ohio who were treating children, to acquaint them with the newly arrived specialists on the Children's staff and with the services the hospital was increasingly able to offer them and their patients.

Dr. Wheeler was first president of the Central Ohio chapter and Dr. McCall the secretary. A major topic for one of the society's early meetings, incidentally, was Dr. Oliver Hosterman's discourse on commercial infant formula at a time when most doctors were still advising whole cow's milk, a mixture of evaporated milk and Karo syrup, or dextromaltose for their small patients.

The hospital's relationship with area physicians has continued strong and mutually supportive, and Children's officials give it high priority in assessing the hospital's future. They recognize that any alienation between practicing pediatricians and the increasingly specialized hospital staff, an over-saturation of pediatricians in the area or the aggressive marketing of area hospitals are all factors which could affect Children's adversely.

By 1952, the Twigs had established their 100th unit and that year turned over to the hospital nearly $75,000 in proceeds from their annual bazaar, Thrift Shop, unit projects and other fund-raisers.

About this same time, responding to a request from the overworked hospital staff during a polio epidemic, Twig members were among the first to enlist in a new in-hospital volunteer service.

Kinder Key, formed from a former Charter Brace, an auxiliary unit of the Franklin County Society for Crippled Children, had signed on with long-established auxiliaries in 1954 to help support a new heart laboratory.

With the first half-million in hand from a building-fund drive, trustees began a program of additions and new construction that was to continue with little respite through the '80s.

In 1953, using an unexpected windfall, Children's gained new staff facilities in the James Merion addition. Merion was a former Columbus railroader and realtor and descendant of the Merion family, which owned much of southeastern Franklin County and for whom Marion Township (with spelling alteration) was named. At his death in Philadelphia in 1932, he left an estate of $121,168 in trust, providing that, when the fund reached $1 million, a charity hospital, "the James Edwin Merion Memorial Hospital," should be constructed on part of the old Merion land in Columbus.

Nearly 20 years later, realizing fulfillment of Merion's wish might take a century or so, the Huntington National Bank, as a trustee, asked Probate Court Judge C.P. McClelland for a ruling.

The Franklin County jurist turned to an ancient equity rule, the "Cy Pres doctrine," which provided that the instructions and intent of the testator in such cases be met as nearly as possible. Because of Children's proximity to the old Merion lands and of its strong charity commitment, McClelland selected the hospital in January, 1952, as the most eligible recipient. The bequest, after small deductions for trust settlements, totaled $150,000.

In 1953 also, a one-floor addition to the outpatient area was completed, and two years later, the two-story Daisy F. Sellers wing provided for 66 more beds, a gymnasium, hydrotherapy pool and other facilities planned particularly for rehabilitation of polio victims.

The fact that this much-needed addition became an anachronism in terms of its original purpose only makes those who treat children wish for more such anachronisms. After the Salk and Sabin discoveries, the Sellers building served a dwindling number of polio victims and was gradually converted to other purposes.

In the next two years, with remodeling of the north wing and addition of new emergency rooms, Children's updated and expanded basic facilities. In 1960, with its share of building campaign and bond issue funds and a $1,200,000 loan, Children's completed its new south wing, gaining a new exterior look and greatly increased treatment capability.

Within the red-brick rectangle fronting the old hospital were fourth- and fifth-floor patient rooms in a new alignment around center-island nursing stations and treatment rooms; a third-floor "rooming in" unit of single rooms with special provisions for parents; a new lobby and 180-seat auditorium; new administration and business offices, pharmacy and laboratories;

ground-floor accommodations for a complete outpatient department, and a second-floor surgical suite including nine operating rooms and a recovery room.

Children's had become the third largest children's treatment center in the country with 304-bed capacity and improved facilities to better accommodate the levels of treatment and care its staff had been developing during these busy years. Despite the overcrowding and disruption, the work going on inside was giving the same kind of impetus to Children's status as an institution.

Dr. Thomas S. Morse, who came from Boston Children's to join the surgical staff in 1960, recalled in his book, "A Gift of Courage," the climate he found in Columbus:

"When I finally saw the Columbus Children's Hospital, I knew at once that I wanted to work there. It had a striking vitality. The department heads were far younger than their counterparts in Boston. They were doing exciting things and were obviously happy in their surroundings. The new wing of the hospital was in the last phase of construction, and noise and bustle were everywhere."

Later, he observed how jurisdictional lines could be transcended in a pervasive spirit of "mutual respect and unselfish cooperation." The staff and physical plant were still small enough that "everybody knew what everybody else was doing," as another '60s alumnus put it, and each was willing to help— or learn from—another's experience.

Dr. Aaron Canowitz, retired anesthesiologist, remembered when Dr. Baxter, observing in surgery one day, suggested a better way of assessing a patient's blood loss which was immediately adopted. Dr. James Beesley, Lancaster pediatrician and the first full-time chief resident in the early '50s, recalled similar quick acceptance for a shortened IV needle he fashioned after nurses complained wriggly youngsters were pulling loose then-standard longer ones.

Preparing for the first open-heart surgery in the city in 1957 at Children's, Dr. Howard Sirak worked with hospital staff members and engineers to construct the necessary equipment.

In the hospital's cramped laboratories, new testing procedures were painstakingly worked out to give physicians the greatest amount of information from the small samples of blood and body fluids very young patients could safely yield.

Dr. Samuel Meites, who joined Children's staff as a biochemist in 1954, described in a 1959 interview how the laboratory staff labored to adapt or scale down procedures used with adults "to get tests to the level of one-half to one drop of blood—25 to 50 microliters for tests normally run on 1,000 microliters."

He demonstrated, with George Bates of the cardiopulmonary laboratory, another do-it-yourself adaptation they called "Dr. Wheeler's black box." With no available "micro" method of determining acidity of the blood, Wheeler modified a device he had seen in a catalog which reduced the blood volume needed from .5 centimeters to .005 centimeters.

With new diagnostic methods requiring day-after-day testing on patients with thread-size blood vessels and total blood volume ranging downward to less than a pint, the goal of just one drop of blood from a heel or finger puncture was of paramount importance.

Bates and Dr. Thomas K. Oliver, director of the respirator center, found a way to heat a child's fingers to draw arterial blood within needle range. Another modified "blood gas tension" test required .18 ccs. of blood instead of the 1.0-1.5 ccs. formerly needed.

In this pioneer work, Children's was serving not only its own patients and staff but other physicians and hospitals. Noting that any such equipment then commercially available was costly because of limited demand, Meites pointed out that the small-scale tests so vital to children could be used just as successfully for adults, were in many cases faster, and, because of much more precise standardization, were more accurate.

In scores of such ways, despite persistent problems of funds and space, Children's was riding the tide of progress and distancing itself from other hospitals in what it could do for young patients. Things were happening, some unplanned, that would establish the hospital's national credentials and shape its future.

Children's early participation in the long-standing, federally funded Children's Cancer Study Group, its selection as a regional reference center for blood typing, the nation's first birth defects study center and the world's first rhinovirus research laboratory were tangible proofs that the little hospital was coming of age.

These achievements, detailed in this history's chapter on research, resulted from investigative efforts carried on before much accommodation for research was possible.

In the late '50s, Children's applied for and received a $180,000 federal grant which, with a matching contribution from Ross Laboratories and other donations, provided funds for the much-needed two-story Ross Hall Research Building. It was opened in 1962 and completed with a two-story addition in 1965.

A 10-year summary of hospital activities presented at the annual trustees' meeting May 14, 1964, showed in dramatic terms what tremendous changes had occurred in the scope of Children's work and the kind of service it was giving.

Admissions had increased 105 percent, from 6,717 to 13,796, but the average length of stay had dropped from nine days to six, thanks to developments allowing for faster, more intensive treatment.

With expanded, improved laboratory and X-ray facilities, the hospital was doing many more and new kinds of testing. In increasing numbers, critically ill children from all over Ohio and adjoining states were being brought to Children's for specialized diagnosis and treatment, representing 50 percent of annual admissions by 1963. Twenty-six Ohio counties sent more than 50 patients each to Children's that year, and admissions came from all 88 Ohio counties and 17 other states.

Surgical operations had increased more than 100 percent. Clinic use was up 54 percent, emergency room visits up 106 percent, and the new Poison Control Center, established in 1957, had already shown a 109 percent increase in calls and contacts.

The 10-year report accurately predicted that future planning for Children's would be strongly affected by a steady population growth in its immediate area, an upward trend in ambulatory and outpatient care, and greater demand for treatment of critically ill patients with unusual problems.

The gleaming facade of the new hospital building now stretched across the former "front yard" of Children's, backed by the deeper red brick of the 1924 building. With its completion, Ross Hall and the Timken expansion, the hospital's 1954 assets had tripled in the decade—to $10.1 million.

Trustees were now focusing on a children's health center complex with the hospital at its heart. The city's slum clearance program was under way, removing older structures from neighboring blocks, and the new freeway provided direct traffic access to the hospital and reduced to minutes the travel time between Children's and OSU. The Franklin County Society for Crippled Children and the Children's Mental Health Center moved into the complex, and other allied buildings were projected.

In 1964, Children's Medical Center, Inc., was chartered, and in 1965, Children's Articles of Incorporation were amended to designate the hospital for tax purposes as a "scientific and educational institution" as well as a charitable one.

After the first surge of significant research, a Children's Hospital Investigative Laboratories Division (CHILD) had been formed in the mid-'50s to manage research programs. In 1964, this was superseded by the Children's Hospital Research Foundation with a board of directors more broadly representative of the hospital, College of Medicine and other OSU research areas.

In 1964, a major grant from the National Institutes of Health provided for establishment and maintenance of a six-bed Clinical Studies Center at Children's. Its purpose was to further the search for better diagnostic and treatment methods for unusual and puzzling childhood diseases.

Changes were also taking place in the hospital's administrative structure. Clifford A. Rostomily was hired in 1960 as associate administrator, and a controller, public relations officer, director of nursing and general services director were added by the mid-'60s.

And again, as it approached a 25-year milestone, the hospital had changes at the top.

Baxter's retirement in 1963 ended a 40-year association with Children's, 24 as chief of the medical staff. The following year, Porter resigned after 23 years as administrator.

Their contribution to the hospital, individually and jointly, was enormous, measured by their accomplishments and the testimony of scores of Children's associates, past and present.

In a quarter-century encompassing wars, epidemics, spiraling costs and incredible advances in medicine and technology, they oversaw Children's metamorphosis from small community hospital to nationally recognized regional treatment center.

The problems were not all space, staff, funds and facilities. In his candid memoirs, Baxter sketched the uneasy situation prevailing at the time of Porter's arrival. Miss Eva Ellen Janson, the last nurse superintendent and no favorite of the medical staff, had resigned suddenly in 1942, apparently on request of the Women's Board, and the chief of the nursing service was running the hospital. "My first contact with him (Porter)," Baxter wrote, "was when he came to my professional office and announced he was the new superintendent."

Not the best beginning, but in his history written after both men had retired, Baxter continued:

"It was a change to have a man at the head of the institution who had vision and tried to cooperate with the staff and anticipate what the staff might want. He also functioned well . . . as a liaison between the staff and the governing boards of the hospital. He put the hospital on a more firm financial basis . . . His cooperative efforts with the leaders of the staff aided the hospital to begin to assume its role of a greater institution. Much of the building program in the last 25 years (before 1965) occurred as a result, in part, of his persuasive efforts with the Board of Trustees."

While their respective positions were still being defined during much of their parallel tenure, Baxter and Porter shared the same dream for the kind of hospital they wanted Children's to be and the caliber of people they wanted to staff it. In a chaotic time, they worked cooperatively toward those goals.

In April of 1963, trustees gave equal status to the administrator and the chief of the medical staff, four months before Baxter's official retirement on July 1. Dr. Edward V. Turner served as acting chief until the arrival in January, 1964, of Baxter's successor, Dr. Bruce D. Graham.

A Wisconsin native, graduate of the University of Alabama, Graham trained in pediatrics at the University of Michigan and remained as a faculty member to attain a professorship in pediatrics in 1959. He came to Columbus from Vancouver, B.C., where he was chief of pediatrics at Children's Hospital, professor and chairman of pediatrics at the University of British Columbia, and pediatrician-in-chief at Vancouver General Hospital's Health Center for Children.

In January, 1965, with Porter's resignation, Rostomily, then director of administrative services, became acting administrator; he was appointed administrator in May. A North Dakota native, Rostomily was a hospital administration graduate of the University of Minnesota and came to Children's after five years at Cincinnati General Hospital and four as administrator of Lawrence County General Hospital in Ironton.

Shortly thereafter, to complete the dissolution of the triumvirate of the 1940s, Mrs. Bradford resigned her secretary's post on the board of trustees.

Nearing its 75th birthday, Children's launched two more important new programs while looking ahead to plans for the next quarter-century.

In 1966, the Columbus Invitational Pro-Am Golf Championship at Scioto Country Club was inaugurated, jointly sponsored by the hospital and Dispatch Charities.

Successful from the first, it would evolve into the Memorial Tournament at Muirfield, involve all the hospital auxiliaries and become an important new financial resource for Children's.

In 1966, the U.S. Children's Bureau began funding a cooperative venture of the hospital and other community agencies to provide health care to area children in a half-dozen neighborhood pediatric clinics—a program that would continue into the '90s.

Initially called the Children and Youth Project (C&Y), it is now known as Community Pediatric-Adolescent Services (CPAS) and provides quality health care from four inner city locations to a population that has been traditionally medically underserved.

Children's could look back on another period of amazing growth:

A patient increase projected for 1968 to 14,000 admissions, 35,000 treated in the emergency room and 90,000 as outpatients; a growth in grant-supported research from $50,000 in 1964 to over $1 million; a two-year staff increase from January '65 from 730 to 890; a 1968 operating budget of $8.3 million, up from $4.5 million in 1965.

Major items in a 10-year master plan for building being developed included expanded research facilities, a new hospital building with accommodation for all acute-care beds and expanded outpatient facilities, new parking lots, a sixth-floor addition to the south wing for an infectious diseases nursing unit (an early 1900s dream coming true) and further development of the health center complex.

To reach its centenary year in triumph, Children's had 25 years to go and much to do.

1967-1992
Confident Maturity, A Bright Future

One winter morning in late 1989, Stuart Williams, executive director, was reviewing early statistics on the first Children's Hospital. The original building's cost of $12,000; operating funds that often dwindled to a few ready dollars; the $500,000 campaign that built the first hospital on Livingston Park; an annual budget that did not top $100,000 until the '30s.

Shaking his head, he walked to the computer console in his office and did some rapid calculations.

"We now spend $2 million a week—$100 million a year. We spend $275,000 a day—more than $10,000 an hour."

Measured over little more than one lifetime on longevity charts, his assessment was one quick, startling way to illustrate what Children's had become.

Beyond Williams' office and the long corridor leading to other administrative suites ranged the enormous complex of patient rooms and treatment areas, laboratories and offices and classrooms, equipment and support facilities, clinics and outpatient services and public areas that comprise today's Children's.

At one end of the phalanx of buildings stretching across former residential blocks between the freeway and Livingston Ave. stands the new Wexner Institute for Pediatric Research, a major effort of the '80s. Beside Williams' desk were plans for the next one—a six-story, 130,000-square-foot education center extending the eastern limit of the main hospital complex to 18th St. This will better serve the vital and expanding third component of Children's treatment, research and education mission.

Like nearly everything that had happened at Children's, the need had been met and served before the facilities could be fully provided.

On the eve of the new century, Children's educational function had grown steadily to great lengths from the very early nurses' training and parent education efforts of the first hospital and the original Ohio State University affiliation of the early 1900s. Now, the program embraces hundreds of students, graduates and practicing professionals; patients and patient families;

staff, volunteers and community agencies and affiliations at the national and international level.

The broad impact of its educational effort, and its future potential, were major points made by Children's officials to a receptive legislature in seeking state support for the proposed education building.

Planned for completion in 1992, the anniversary year, the education and conference center will slide into place in the hospital complex as yet another major piece in a decades-long, catch-up construction effort.

The 100th year also provides stimulus for Children's continuing effort to build a major endowment fund to secure its present programs and support future needs.

The fund goal and the "Beyond Excellence" philosophy it embodies were directly or implicitly supported, in their comments on Children's history, by scores of physicians, department chairpersons, nurses and staff, community leaders and long-time volunteers. Committed to Children's importance and potential, they were in near-unanimity that the hospital's future depends less on major physical expansion, more on its ability to secure and maintain its three-fold mission to sick and injured children through periods of economic, social and scientific change.

In the final quarter of its first century, Children's made major advances toward that goal.

It was not all smooth sailing, and the early '70s were marked by high points and low ones as Children's struggled to launch the $20 million building program planned in the late '60s.

A beneficiary in the contested will of Gustav Hirsch, head of a communications corporation, Children's took its case to court and in 1971 received a settlement of more than $912,000.

In 1969, faced with the urgent need for new hospital facilities, trustees had voted to proceed with building, thereby making a conscious decision against any move to or near Ohio State. "I don't remember how the votes went," recalled a board member who participated, "but it was Webb Vorys and Bob (Robert, Sr.) Lazarus" who swung the decision that Children's should remain on its current site.

Later, denied certification for a $3.5 million bond sale it needed to fund the building, Children's received a "loan of last resort" from Battelle Memorial Institute through negotiations by then-Battelle President Sherwood Fawcett, who had recently joined the hospital board.

The final irony in that sequence, William R. Wise, Children's corporate director of finance, recalled, was that "construction business was nil right then, the bids were fantastic, and the Tower (the new building) only cost $10 million—less than we'd planned." Of the $10 million, $3.5 million was raised through a community campaign.

For whatever reasons, while the building program proceeded, those who were there recall a perceptible slowing of momentum in other areas.

The kidney transplant program, launched at Children's in the late '60s, became centered at Ohio State, as did for a shorter time thoracic surgery.

In 1973, Dr. Henry Cramblett, a key figure in Children's research program, moved to OSU to become dean of the College of Medicine and vice president for health services. Sharp cutbacks in federal funding for medical research nationwide affected liver transplant studies and other work in progress at Children's. Dr. Vincent Hamparian, now director of research services, recalls "a period when there was not much intellectual stimulation." Dr. Bruce Graham, then medical director, said it was a time when hard choices had to be made and priorities established, when facilities and trained teams had to be secured and assembled before Children's could go ahead with projects requiring such support.

Overall, however, the mid-'60s through the '80s comprised an era of great change and significant accomplishment:

Extensive construction, an intensification of the research effort, continuous advancement in treatment, effective work on financial accounting and cost control, incredible extension of services to encompass both medical progress and new societal needs, strengthened ties with Ohio State and adoption of a medical faculty salary plan with important effects on Children's, development of new funding sources and volunteer support, inevitable arrivals and departures of key personnel, expansion and particularization of the administrative structure—and a series of major changes in top positions.

In 1970, assessing hospital progress one department chairman termed "good but not great," trustees hired a new administrator. Declining to accept a subordinate position, Clifford Rostomily left following the appointment of John R. Jefferies as executive director. Jefferies had been administrator of a hospital in his native Salt Lake City, Utah, and of All Children's Hospital in St. Petersburg, Florida.

In January, 1977, he resigned as a result of what trustees termed "basic differences over philosophy and management." Williams was named to succeed him.

A Pittsburgh native and hospital administration graduate of the University of Chicago, Williams had been assistant director of the University of Michigan Hospital at Ann Arbor and administrative head of C.S. Mott Children's Hospital there. He came to Columbus as Children's administrative director in 1974.

Chief of staff from 1964 until 1970, Dr. Graham held the new position of medical director until late 1974. He continued as chief of pediatrics and as chairman of pediatrics at OSU until mid-1976, leaving both posts prior to his installation as president of the American Academy of Pediatrics in 1979. He continued as OSU professor of pediatrics and director of ambulatory services at Children's until his retirement in 1981.

During a lengthy search for a new medical director and pediatrics chairperson, Dr. Edward Turner, Dr. John P. Shultz and Dr. Juan Sotos fulfilled those administrative functions at Children's in acting capacities.

On September 1, 1978, Dr. Grant Morrow III became medical director and pediatrics chief at Children's, chairman of the OSU department and medical director of the Children's Hospital Research Foundation.

A native of Pittsburgh, graduate of Haverford College and the University of Pennsylvania School of Medicine, he had held faculty appointments at his alma mater and staff appointments at Philadelphia hospitals through the '60s. He came to Columbus from Tucson, where he was a professor of pediatrics in the University of Arizona School of Medicine and held staff positions with the University of Arizona and Tucson medical centers.

Morrow was a strong advocate of pediatric research, had already published extensively in his own particular areas of interest and came to Columbus with a firm commitment by Children's administrators in support of a strengthened research program. It was the major successful effort of the '80s.

In 1976, the community celebrated the crowning achievement of the Jefferies-Graham years—completion of the new six-story main hospital patient tower. Extended in two graceful curving arms west from the 1960 addition, the tower offered a welcoming contour to approaching visitors and an interior warmly and immediately recognizable as a children's facility.

Bright colors, curved and angled corridors, carpeting and lighting minimized an institutional feeling. Designed with parents in mind, there were admitting and service offices just off the main lobby; a center core of offices on each floor for physicians, social workers, nurse specialists and other counselors; and convertible window seats in patient rooms for parents keeping an overnight vigil.

Accessibility was a key goal also in locating patient rooms—surgical patients close to existing surgical facilities, infants near major diagnostic facilities.

Areas for the sickest children included the most up-to-date lifesaving and life-sustaining equipment. The neonatal intensive care unit designed to serve as many as 60 newborn infants had new overhead service modules. Each patient in other intensive care units was served by an individual system of normal and emergency power sources, oxygen and vacuum outlets.

In a long-established pattern, the building was occupied and used while the two top floors and part of the basement remained shelled in until finances permitted full completion. Its opening presaged a full decade of expansion, renovation and new construction through the '80s. The building sequence included:

• Renovation and remodeling of the Timken Building to house professional offices and clinics.

• Completion of the top two floors of the new hospital tower for patient units.

• Completion of a major surgical addition in late 1985 at the northwest corner of the hospital complex. The much-needed facility included a surgical suite of nine ultramodern operating rooms, 20-bed recovery room with three isolation rooms, 25-room outpatient surgery unit, expanded facilities for pathology laboratories, a new cafeteria and food processing areas, and space for receiving, processing and distributing hospital supplies.

• Construction of a parking garage and extension of surface lots to provide more than 1,000 off-street spaces in the immediate hospital area.

But with all of this, the major structural achievement of the '80s, in itself and in its importance to the hospital's future, was The Wexner Institute for Pediatric Research.

In 1984, after long consideration, hospital officials launched a capital campaign to raise a minimum of $7.5 million toward construction of a long-needed research facility. As so often before in Children's history, the community response was immediate and generous.

Mrs. Bella Wexner, Columbus businesswoman, gave $3,000,000, the first seven-figure "living gift" in Children's history. Nationwide Insurance gave $1,500,000 and, of 286 major donors, 23 exceeded $100,000, according to John Strick, executive director of the Children's Hospital Foundation. With total donations of $10.8 million and substantial support from the foundation, the $14.7 million building was completed debt free.

It was significant that the crowds attending the gala weekend of opening ceremonies in mid-November of 1987 included Dr. Albert Sabin, famed physician/scientist who had helped dedicate Ross Hall 22 years earlier.

It was significant that door after door in the gleaming, airy and state-of-the-researchers'-art building bore engraved nameplates honoring donors of the facilities—many of them family names first recorded on Children's turn-of-the-century donor lists.

It was most significant that a pre-opening tour, two months earlier, had included some 150 physicians and scientists attending the first institute-sponsored international symposium. Devoted to developmental gastroenterology, a subject in which Children's researchers have a long-standing and continuing interest, it was a demonstration of the hospital's position in the forefront of pediatric research and its vastly expanded capability to strengthen that position.

With 122,000 square feet of space on five floors and a lower level, the institute has room for 96 laboratories and support areas, great flexibility to meet changing demands and the most up-to-the-minute equipment to facilitate scientific effort and intercommunication.

At the core of the tiers of offices and laboratories is a spectacular atrium. Caught in the focus of a lofty skylight is an arresting, free-swinging mobile of healthy children—the ultimate beneficiaries of the institute's research achievements.

In 1980, Children's had opened a clinical laboratory made possible by a $207,000 gift from Wendy's founder R. David Thomas. With the opening of the Wexner Institute, space was freed up in Ross Hall, the former research building. In early 1989, a renovated Ross Hall was re-dedicated, housing such departments as Medical Records and Volunteer Services, as well as several clinical laboratories, although the R. David Thomas Clinical Laboratories are still very much in use.

In mid-1990, in a cooperative effort with the Childhood League, Children's opened a child care center for its employees in a shared new building at the northeast corner of Livingston Ave. and 18th St. The child care center is named in honor of Columbus philanthropist Betsey Kauffman Trumbull, from whose estate the hospital received a $1.92 million gift in 1983. With an entrance facing north toward the hospital, the center was designed to accommodate 48 infants and toddlers and up to 52 older preschool children. The move enabled the Childhood League Center to increase by 50 percent its educational services to developmentally disabled children.

In all of these new physical facilities, Children's was not only fulfilling the projected goals of two decades, but reflecting intense activity in honing its treatment skills and developing programs and services to meet new demands.

Indicative of almost-kaleidoscopic growth and change, a single paragraph from the 1980 annual report, from a joint summary by Williams, Morrow and Trustee President Arthur Vorys, detailed new patient care programs to be implemented just within 1981. It included:

"A pharmacology/toxicology program; chronic renal dialysis for children suffering from end-stage kidney disease (the only such unit specifically for children in Central Ohio); an expanded adolescent medicine service featuring a new program in sports medicine, special emphasis on early identification and referral for good prenatal care for 'high risk' teenage pregnancies, and continued efforts to treat and combat alcohol and other drug abuse; and an extensive behavioral science service which will provide for the expansion and better coordination and integration of existing programs dealing with the behavioral and developmental aspects of children."

To gain flexibility and strength for the task at hand and ahead, Children's reorganized at the top. In 1982, Children's Hospital, Inc., became the parent corporation to coordinate the activities of three subsidiary corporations: the Children's Hospital, the Children's Hospital Research Foundation and the Children's Hospital Foundation.

44

In the early '70s, with south wing completed, Children's looked to further expansion.

The new patient tower foreshadowed a new structural shape for Children's as construction proceeded through mid-'70s.

A major achievement of the '70's was the new patient tower, opened in 1976.

Symbolic of Children's progress over late decades of the century, a picture of the just-completed outpatient surgery wing also shows a crane in the background, where construction of the new research building was under way.

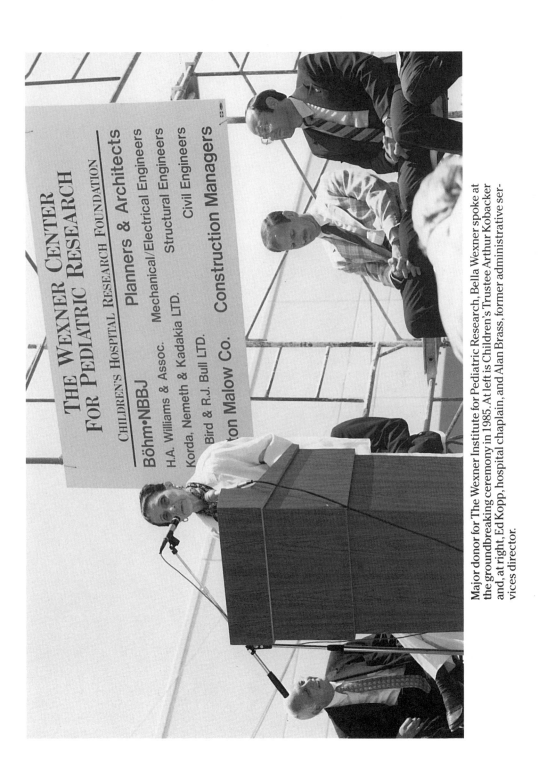

Major donor for The Wexner Institute for Pediatric Research, Bella Wexner spoke at the groundbreaking ceremony in 1985. At left is Children's Trustee Arthur Kobacker and, at right, Ed Kopp, hospital chaplain, and Alan Brass, former administrative services director.

The Wexner Institute for Pediatric Research

Stuart W. Williams

Dr. Grant Morrow III

The Ronald McDonald House, located on the Children's campus.

The Betsey Kauffman Trumbull Child Care Center opened in 1990 on the hospital's campus.

Children's and its community were growing up together in the 1990s, as this aerial view attests.

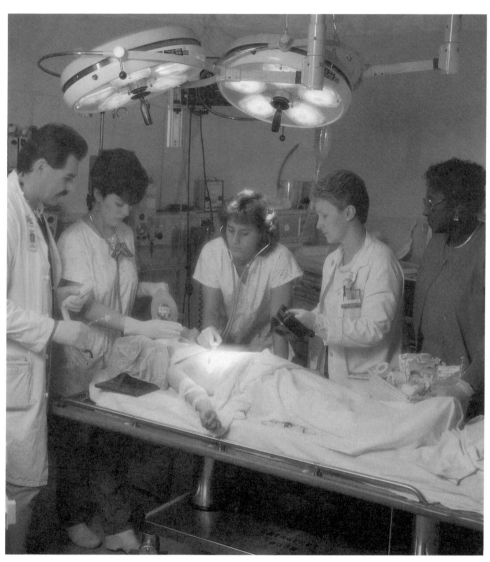

The hospital's trauma program was certified as Level I in 1991, the first pediatric program in the state to earn this distinction.

Two years later, Children's Hospital Guidance Centers (CHGC) became a fourth corporate subsidiary. The county's largest outpatient mental health system for children, adolescents and their families, then offering services at five community locations, CHGC evolved through much structural change from the Children's Mental Health Center which opened in 1950 under Dr. W. Hugh Missildine's direction in a small frame double next to the 1924 hospital.

Finalization in the early '80s of a medical practice plan for OSU faculty members within the Department of Pediatrics was a giant step, hospital leaders said, toward Children's future goals.

"We wouldn't be where we are without it," said Dr. Morrow. The three-track plan for medical staff salaries worked out with Ohio State enables the pediatrics department, and therefore Children's as well, to recruit and hire people interested in academic medicine at a scale competitive with other universities, Morrow said, if not with private practice. Competition for the best medical school graduates is increasing, he said, and the supply is smaller.

"Everything we can do for children can be done better," he declared, "and we have to have the people to do it. It's a matter of more research and its application to patient care."

The new plan, more space flexibility and undoubtedly changing treatment needs also prompted significant realignment of ambulatory services including the hospital clinics, Dr. Antoinette Eaton, corporate director of legislative affairs, said. "We looked at every clinic. A primary care clinic or one using a multi-disciplinary team stayed within the hospital (arthritis, birth defects, pediatric, teenage, allergy, etc.), while others moved across the street to the professional office building. It's a one-class system," she explained. "Patients are separated by category of need rather than ability to pay."

In the emergency department, the most significant change in a "very strong policy" implemented in 1981 was "a commitment to staffing by fully trained pediatricians, overall supervision. We still have a house staff but the medical direction is greatly enhanced," said Eaton, who served as the first woman president of the American Academy of Pediatrics in 1990-91.

With its tremendous emphasis on patient care, "the hospital's overall position is excellent," she said, "but our patients are sicker. There has been revolutionary change in the complexity of problems incoming patients present."

This has prompted such developments, Eaton noted, as the Level I trauma program in emergency services, neonatal intensive care, cardiology advances, and organ and bone marrow transplantation.

In the fall of 1991, Children's Hospital, Columbus, became the first children's hospital in Ohio to be certified by the American College of Surgeons as a pediatric Level I trauma center. This accreditation certifies that Children's is qualified and prepared to respond immediately with the highest quality care to the full spectrum of trauma patients it could receive.

Because of the sophisticated care it delivers, as well as the comprehensive array of child health care services it provides, Children's has become a major regional center serving a basic 37-county area throughout Central, Southern and Southeastern Ohio. Since the hospital has earned the respect and confidence of physicians and parents in this large region, virtually all pediatric care has been centralized at the Columbus facility. This, in turn, has enabled the hospital to provide extremely cost-effective care to the families it serves.

With this basic change in its in-hospital patient population, the tremendous upsurge in outpatient surgery and shortened hospital stays for more traditional ailments, Children's future treatment needs focus less on additional bed space, more on special teams and facilities and sophisticated new tools for both diagnosis and treatment.

As examples, a two-story addition to the emergency department, nearly doubling space and facilities for that much-used and fast-growing area, is scheduled for completion in 1993. By mid-1992 Children's will be doing magnetic resonance imaging (MRI) in a new one-story building on the hospital campus. MRI is an advanced method of producing very clear images of the human body without the use of X-rays. The procedure, which uses a large magnet, radio waves, an antenna and a computer, is capable of detecting diseases not detectable by other means—and at an earlier stage.

Despite its own rapid development and the changes and uncertainties in the health care delivery network generally, Children's made a major effort over two decades to achieve a new level of financial stability.

Until 1970, all contributions not specifically restricted were merged directly into hospital operations. With the creation of a development department and later the hospital's foundation, and a conscious commitment to a stronger research program, a portion of the annual contributions to Children's was diverted to building an endowment and supporting research—a foresighted action reminiscent of the action taken by Children's trustees in the early 1900s.

The hospital still received the major share of annual contributions to offset indigent care and other important but non–revenue producing programs such as the Poison Control Center and the child abuse program. With the change, the hospital's financial structure gained flexibility to function without so much reliance on annual contributions to make ends meet.

Children's does have "vulnerable" areas, Wise, the finance director, conceded, in programs subject to ups and downs in government funding; in the lack of a long-discussed maternity facility for high-risk mothers; in a shifting and competitive community health care picture that could affect the hospital's relationships with area pediatricians.

Marking its 100-year birthday with a new and vibrant face fashioned over a quarter-century, Children's has much to celebrate.

• The new education center, due for birthday-year completion, will serve not only students in training, but patients, staff, parents, volunteers and broad segments of the community.

47

• The research program, which has shifted into high gear with the Wexner Institute open and functioning, funding more than quadrupled over a decade to more than $5 million, one five-year plan successfully completed and another in place through 1993, a greatly expanded corps of investigators including important new sub-specialties, and a research agenda geared to Children's established strengths and to its own and national pediatric research goals.

• A treatment program in constant development and improvement, closely allied to research and training programs, and serving an increasing percentage of patients with critical illness and other serious problems.

• Expansion and increased use of outpatient services—surgery, clinics, emergency—and of the hospital's arms into the community—the guidance centers and comprehensive health care centers.

• Strengthened ties with OSU, not only in training students, but in cooperative programs in treatment and research.

• Increased stature for the hospital nationally and internationally and valuable interchange with foreign institutions in education, treatment and research. Doctors from foreign countries have come to Children's for training. An exchange of doctors, nurses and medical personnel was started with the Hadassah Medical Organization in Israel in 1988, and a similar program is being pursued with a children's hospital in Genoa, Italy. Major international conferences at the Wexner Institute have sharpened the research image. In 1989, Children's was one of only three U.S. pediatric centers selected to treat victims of an earthquake in Soviet Armenia.

• Children's current trustees, proudly vocal about recent accomplishments, but also well aware of chronic money problems through Children's early history, dwell on the 1991 hospital's smooth operation and financial stability.

• Children's volunteer fund-raising forces, grown as the hospital has in numbers, structure and activities, continue to be a hospital mainstay not only for the millions they produce but for the level of community commitment they represent.

Envisioning what lies ahead in the treatment of sick children, Dr. Morrow declared, "Our goal is to put ourselves out of business."

Reviewing progress made since his arrival in 1978, committed to a strengthened research program, Children's medical director commented, "Patient care helps a child at a time. Research helps a generation at a time.

To me, when we're talking 'vision', generating new knowledge is what it's all about."

He spoke of "areas where we've bridged treating children through research." He referred particularly to the proportionately greater number of pediatric patients today with genetic defects, a major focus of pediatric researchers, citing one recent case in which recognition of a treatable genetic defect obviated a child's need for a liver transplant. He decried a prevailing attitude which lays out funds for costly corrective procedures but withholds support for research which could produce preventive measures.

Basic in more than a decade of effort—completion of Wexner, intensive recruitment of personnel, coordination and expansion of research, the search for greater funding—has been, in Morrow's view, the creation of a questing, questioning atmosphere pervasive throughout Children's treatment, education and research activities.

"If you're not asking questions, you're giving anecdotal medicine," he said, "and that's not front-line health care."

It was not surprising that Morrow, who likes to point out that no research institution has a corner on medical breakthroughs, looked ahead for Children's in launching-pad terms.

"We got to an ignition point with the Wexner building," he said. "We fueled the venture with internationally prominent scientists. In our next phase, we're looking for more Ph.D. and M.D. scientists able to spend nearly 100 percent of their effort in research."

Beyond the hopes vested in its research in progress, "one of our goals," Morrow added, "is to train those people who will provide the next generation of researchers. You can't do that without recruiting a faculty from the best institutions who will come here, ask questions and inspire people to look for answers."

In the last year and a half, he noted, scientists from Johns Hopkins, Harvard, Yale, Princeton and from Cambridge, England, have joined the Children's staff.

How will Children's begin its second century? The executive director had some thoughts.

"We have set a strong foundation in the provision of patient care, then we strengthened the research arm, now the education arm," Williams said. "Now, as each element is improved, it in turn will enhance the other two."

He talked about research, not the hard sell it once was with hospital trustees.

"Some could look at research as a bottomless pit of expense," he said. "That is only because we have not yet solved all the problems that afflict children. Research at Children's is not an option; it is a necessity. There are only a handful of pediatric centers in the world that have accumulated the medical expertise, the facilities and the community support that we have in Columbus. We have an obligation to conduct research.

"The neat part," he added, "is that it enhances the care we deliver to the kids in our own backyard.

"As to what comes out next at Children's," Williams continued, "I think we will see an expansion on all fronts. Our inpatient programs will become more intensive as we learn how to care for children in short stays in the hospital, as children with more complex problems are referred to us from an ever-expanding region, and as we become more successful in curing children of problems that once were terminal.

"As external and internal pressures force a more economical model of health care delivery, we will treat an increasing number of children on an outpatient basis. We will perform more complex diagnostic tests and procedures as our knowledge and technology continue to improve.

"Our growth will also reflect the continued growth of the greater Columbus area."

What he was also seeing, Williams added, was "a health campus for children, from south of Livingston Ave. to the freeway," a concept first voiced at Children's with the slum clearance and land acquisition of the '50s and '60s.

"I counted once, more than 40 agencies in the county dealing with the problems of children. There is much that could be done to better coordinate our collective efforts."

He noted the presence of the Ronald McDonald House and Easter Seals Rehabilitation Center on the hospital campus and Childhood League's recent move to share quarters with Children's new child care facility in a building fronting on Livingston Park.

He envisioned a "cluster" of such facilities, in convenient proximity to Children's and each other, with possible associated housing and office space in a facing strip along Livingston Ave.

Williams advanced the health campus as an evolutionary possibility rather than a specific recommendation. The changing health care picture may point other ways. "There's a question about how much Children's should network with other hospitals. Will the health care system change sufficiently that we may be seeing a large community-wide system?"

He smiled as he added, "The U.S. health care system is very traditional— almost sacrosanct." But his own guideline for any long look into the future, he said, is "Let's keep an open mind."

He pointed out that Children's recently created a Department of Child Advocacy and Community Relations to expand its efforts toward keeping children healthy and working with the community to address the pressing problems children face today. "We do an outstanding job of making ill children well, but we see our role today and in the future as going beyond that," Williams said.

Children's Hospital received an outstanding national honor when it won the Gold Medal in the 1990 Health Care Forum Foundation/3M Organizational Innovators Awards competition for hospitals/medical centers of 300 beds or more. The award recognizes health care organizations which have applied fresh approaches to development or enhancement of their products and services, resulting in improved business performance and outstanding contributions to the community.

Within the lifetimes of people quoted in this history, Children's has undergone incredible change—from the first brave venture of 1892 to the triumphant achievement of 1924 to the giant regional institution of 1992.

In three distinctive ways, there has been no change. Children's continues to treat and care for EVERY CHILD who seeks its help. The men and women who work in and for Children's continue to do so with a special dedication engendered by the young patients they serve and the hospital itself. The community which helped build the first Children's continues its unflagging support.

That is because, in 1892 and 1992, the focus is on the most basic and appealing of human endeavors: to make sick children well.

Treatment
The Pediatric Focus Is on Lifetimes

The barest bones of information remaining from Children's early days are those relating to the two groups most essential to any hospital—the patients and the physicians.

Except for statistical summaries on hospital operation, old minutes and other records reveal little about the kind of treatment being given, who was receiving it and who was giving it. Even the few graduate studies done on the early history of Children's focus mainly on building, financial and organizational matters.

This is understandable. The hospital's survival was a major preoccupation of its managers in early decades. The aggregate of patients was very small compared with later years, the range of treatments was limited, and the primary concern of physicians who served the hospital was with their regular practices and patients.

After his retirement, conscious of this informational gap and at the urging of colleagues, Dr. Baxter compiled "Seventy-Five Years of Care" based on his 40-year experience at Children's, his own surmises about earlier years and the recollections gleaned from older physicians. Even with this background, he found very little specific material for the years before 1916, when Children's began plans to leave its first home across from Franklin Park.

Certainly, medical advances have altered the treatment and even the incidence of many of the problems presented by Children's first patients— contagious diseases, raging infections, deficiency diseases and bone-crippling tuberculosis. Certainly, at any given period in those early days, specialized service was geared to the expertise of the current staff.

Records do indicate that many of the physicians involved in the founding and early staffing of the hospital continued their active interest for varying periods. Among those most involved, and for the longest periods, were Drs. Dickson Moore, Elmer G. Horton and Leslie Bigelow.

Characterized by medical colleagues as "the society women's baby doctor," Dr. Moore was by their account a man of distinctive dress and tastes who took extra training to develop a highly successful pediatric practice and made his rounds in a chauffeur-driven car. Clearly, he also had an abiding interest in Children's, as one of the very early house physicians, as a longtime active member of the attending staff and, frequently, as its spokesman to the governing boards. But not perhaps his major interest . . .

"He kept a couple of dogs in his office," recalled one physician who remembered him. "When he died, he left all his money to the Humane Society—an outrageous thing to do."

Dr. Horton, product of the old Ohio Medical University, also combined an active interest in Children's with many other activities. He was an expert in infectious disease and directed a special community facility for infectious cases, served as Columbus city health commissioner, was an OSU medical faculty member and was chief of its pediatrics division from 1924 to '39. In a personal note in his history, Dr. Baxter recalls how Dr. Horton, overcoming his initial coolness toward a new chief of staff and pediatrics chairman, gave him "invaluable help" in his first years in the dual post.

Under Drs. Moore and Horton, Children's, small as it was, had two medical services from 1916 to 1930, Dr. Baxter records, with patients being assigned alternately to one or the other. The odd situation developed with the teaching affiliation between OSU and Children's and the appointment by OSU Dean E.F. McCampbell of a clinical staff made up of some 15 members of Children's medical staff. Why Dr. Moore wasn't named to this staff or why there were two staffs at all puzzled Dr. Baxter, but he surmised it was a case of two strong-minded individuals with different views on patient treatment.

A central figure in Children's internal operation through its second quarter-century, Dr. Bigelow joined the staff in the early 1900s, was chief of the medical staff from 1917 to 1940, then served briefly as acting dean of the OSU College of Medicine before his death in 1943.

For a detailed account of how the hospital's services developed, and the physicians involved in their growth, Baxter's unpublished history is an invaluable aid.

The first real staff organization apparently was into four services for both the hospital and outpatient areas—pediatric medicine, surgery, orthopedic surgery, and eye, ear, nose and throat diseases.

Orthopedic work (including fractures, then handled by general surgeons) accounted for a significant part of Children's caseload in very early days, and general surgery was the busiest service simply because it was the one kind of treatment children could not be given at home.

The only two turn-of-the-century patients who could be found to comment for this history were Isabelle Harper, who had hip surgery in 1907, and Gladys Scoles, who had a goiter operation in 1915. Mrs. Harper, a lifelong Columbus resident, died in 1988. Mrs. Scoles, a former Columbus resident, moved in 1974 to Albuquerque, N.M.

Besides Bigelow, a general surgeon, others active in the 1900-1920 period included Drs. Andre Crotti, Charles and Will Hamilton, J.F. Baldwin, and later Luke Zartman, Phillip J. Reel, J. Mitchell Dunn and H.E. Boucher.

New names in the '30s included Dr. Karl Klassen, whose interest was in cardiovascular surgery, and Dr. Harry LeFever, characterized by Baxter as a pioneer in neurosurgery, "a real scholar, excellent surgeon and rare individual." It was LeFever, the Hudson history records, who introduced air-contrast roentgenography of the brain to Columbus, who removed the first brain tumor at Children's in 1933 and the next year reported one of the first successful craniotomies for removal of a subdural hemorrhage in an infant.

World War II service depleted Children's surgical staff. Dr. Warren Harding (later superintendent of Grant Hospital) carried a heavy clinical load, Baxter noted, until he too entered the service, and general surgeons of the community (Drs. I.B. Harris, John W. Means, Verne Dodd and others) came to help.

After the war, Dr. Robert Zollinger, named chairman of surgery at Ohio State in 1947, became surgery chief at Children's as well to carry out a difficult and necessary changeover.

"We had 12 different men on the service," Zollinger recalled. "Children's was still doing a lot of hernias and appendectomies. The trend was to recognize pediatric surgery (another two years' training after general surgery), and Boston had the highest-class children's hospital in the country. We realized children's surgery was special and that we had to have it here."

Zollinger looked to Boston and his own alma mater, Harvard. Dr. H. William Clatworthy, who had trained there under the new leaders in pediatric surgery, came to Columbus in 1951 and soon thereafter became chairman of pediatric surgery.

General surgeons continued to work at Children's caring for their private patients and an occasional clinical case, Baxter noted, and the staff soon was augmented by others trained in the new specialty. Dr. Robert Izant, later chief of pediatric surgery at Western Reserve; Dr. E. Thomas Boles, recently retired department chairman; Dr. Thomas Morse and Dr. Blanca Smith Kent were among the first.

It was a hectic but exhilarating time, said Clatworthy, now retired. "We had three little rooms on the third floor, one orthopedic, one for ENT (ear, nose and throat), one for general surgery. Then we started doing lung surgery, heart surgery, Hirschsprung's disease, Wilms' tumor . . . We took a ladies' sewing room for a recovery room, established two little T & A rooms."

Despite "turndowns and shortages" and "reams of paper work," Clatworthy added, "we had great esprit de corps. Columbus Children's attracted the best residents because there was more excitement here."

In its rapid development, Children's surgical service was doing more things for small patients over a steadily broadening range of surgically correctable problems.

In 1961, Clatworthy and four fellow panelists, assessing progress in pediatric surgery before the American College of Surgeons, noted that 25 percent of surgery then being done, excluding tonsillectomies, was for children under 15; that the country had only 90 full-time pediatric surgeons; and that fewer than a dozen (including Columbus) of some 60 U.S. children's hospitals were adequately staffed and equipped as general hospitals for children.

They urged expansion of the specialty and prompt referral to specialized centers of problem cases, particularly newborns. They negated, from their own experience, the then-still-lingering notion that infants can't stand surgery. Clatworthy described studies done and measures taken at Children's (then and now) to counteract the emotional impact of hospitalization.

In a 1979 interview, returning to this favorite theme, he hailed the advent of outpatient surgery in the '60s. "We were really about the first institution in the country to begin to operate on little babies without keeping them overnight," he said, applauding a trend that not only reduces expense and emotional trauma but protects children from many possible infectious contacts.

His years in surgery, Clatworthy recalled, spanned life-saving victory over many childhood ailments, discouraging progress over others, and continuing gains in managing the major surgical problems among children—congenital anomalies, accidents and cancer. Many congenital anomalies have become "completely fixable," he said, and childhood cancer has yielded more to treatment than adult types. As for accidents, an increasingly violent society, he said, works against scientific advance in fighting childhood's worst killer.

The importance to patients of institutions like Children's, he said, is that the pediatric surgeon is part of a team of experts trained to deal with an array of physical and psychological problems.

The team approach—inter-departmental, multi-disciplinary and often involving many or all of the hospital's support systems—has become a hallmark of Children's, strengthened with each sub-specialty addition to the hospital roster.

In 1978, after weeks of testing and planning, two complete surgical teams worked with Dr. Boles on the successful separation of Siamese twins Mark and Matthew Myers. Dr. Morse, in his book, describes the months of study and testing involving not only surgical residents Marc Rowe and Arthur Pearson but Dr. J.P. Smith, urologist; Dr. Thomas Frye, radiologist; and Dr. Don Hosier, cardiologist, which preceded advances in treating kidney problems and the first kidney transplant in the '60s.

Hundreds of similar instances could be cited from hospital records.

Further development of its own transplant surgery program and an increasing emphasis on critical care surgery are on Children's agenda, Dr. Boles said, "both appropriate for a center like this," and both requiring "technical proficiency of large groups of people—the hiring, training and maintenance of whole teams."

Noting the continuing increase in outpatient surgery at one end of the spectrum, the foreseeable advent of fetal surgery and the research-level prospect of intestinal transplants at the other, the former surgery chairman and associate medical director said Children's need now is "to grow better rather than bigger."

Looking at Children's from a four-decade perspective, Boles said that, after establishing one of the finest pediatric training centers in the country and producing many advances in pediatric care, the hospital "went through a period of good but not great" but continued to be a leader in pediatric care and pediatric thought.

"An absolutely first-class community has supported it with very warm affection as well as respect, and we don't want to change that," he said. "Our situation is unique in the community. Children's comes close to having a monopoly on child care—there is no way a 150-bed hospital could have that. We have to have a certain irreducible volume of patients to have a specialized hospital work."

But also, in fulfilling its educational and research missions, he added, "we have to have people who have the time, interest and smarts to do more than take care of patients."

Children's officials always face the difficult decision, Boles said, in establishing priorities between equally expensive programs or tools which may be vital to a very few or beneficial to a much greater number.

An example of his final point might be the genito-urinary surgical program which was one of the first sub-specialties to be developed, according to Baxter, in the early days of the hospital. Dr. Milton Jones headed the division, succeeded by Dr. John Hoberg and later by Dr. John P. Smith, during whose tenure new ways to treat children's urinary problems became possible.

Transplantation/Dialysis

Children's was an early participant in kidney transplant and dialysis programs, Dr. Mark Mentser, chief of nephrology, said, but both languished after a time. Transplant work, still regarded as "expensive and experimental," moved to OSU with Dr. James Cerilli in the late '60s, Mentser said, and the departure of Dr. Carl Nelsen in 1972 for a time "basically ended the dialysis program."

Children's saw fewer patients of either type, Mentser said, until 1978 when he signed on at Children's to build a nephrology program.

The dialysis program, resumed in 1979, now includes a three-bed hemodialysis unit for patients who need regular access to the hospital machines, and a peritoneal dialysis program with equipment easier for small infants and usable at home to treat children while they sleep.

By the '80s, the transplant program was resumed and Children's now does five to seven kidney transplants a year, Mentser said, and has done seven or eight infants under a year old "who are doing well."

Medication is the first choice for children with renal failure, and only 2 percent need transplants, he said. When they do, he added, transplantation is "no longer experimental."

The most common urinary tract problem is infection, usually treatable and correctable, Mentser said, and another, blood or protein in the urine, may signal a kidney problem but is usually not serious.

"Technology has come a long way," Mentser said, "but it took interested people to make it happen. Now we're in the forefront of what can be done. It's an exciting place to be."

Subsequent to kidney transplantation, Children's began liver transplants and at the end of 1991 started a bone marrow transplantation program.

Neurosurgery

Neurosurgery at Children's, given initial impetus by Dr. LeFever, was further advanced through the mid-'40s by Dr. Peter Campbell, a pediatric neurosurgeon so active, the Baxter history records, that his surgical colleagues called him "Burr Hole Pete."

However, when Dr. Martin P. Sayers, a former intern, returned to Children's in 1951 after Navy service and a residency in Philadelphia, the life expectancy for children with congenital defects of the central nervous system, brain tumors or severe head injuries was uniformly bleak. Assessing the progress over the next decades—in new techniques, important new drugs and amazing new tools—the retired chairman of neurosurgery frequently resorted to the word "miracle."

"We had the third organized neurosurgery program in the country after Boston Children's and Philadelphia," he said. "We were on the forefront in children's neurosurgery. We had all the newest techniques but were not always first to get new equipment."

He ticked off advances and what they meant to patients:

• The first workable valve and subsequent improvements to treat hydrocephalus "which must have saved the lives of 200,000 people." Recalling he did 19 repeat operations for one hydrocephalic child long since grown to adulthood, he believes research will yet produce a more permanent treatment than valves and shunts.

• The postwar development of steroid drugs and antibiotics, "a boon to neurosurgeons"—"helped us combat forms of meningitis"—helped patients survive surgery for brain tumors, the second most common malignancy in children.

• X-ray developments and the "absolutely revolutionary" CT (computed tomography) scan. "The brain is like a switchboard, and up until then we could only tell what systems weren't working by dangerous, painful, time-consuming guesswork. CT took away all the guesswork, even educated guesswork."

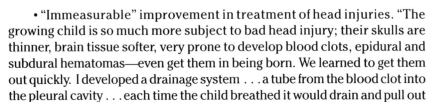

• "Immeasurable" improvement in treatment of head injuries. "The growing child is so much more subject to bad head injury; their skulls are thinner, brain tissue softer, very prone to develop blood clots, epidural and subdural hematomas—even get them in being born. We learned to get them out quickly. I developed a drainage system . . . a tube from the blood clot into the pleural cavity . . . each time the child breathed it would drain and pull out the liquid."

Sayers recalled a prevailing question, when he entered medicine, about saving children with serious defects—"kind of a feeling, the same way with preemies, that they had so many complications and problems working with them was bucking the tide."

Many more children are being salvaged, but he thinks questions remain. "Some parents can't have a normal child. With every new technique, we still lose a few patients. I've long been an advocate of amniocentesis and prenatal diagnosis. Genetic studies are really just beginning, but genetic guidance and advice are very important. We have much to do in educating the public and sorting out the morality of it."

Ophthalmology

Ophthalmology in the early days was a small service under general surgery limited mostly to the treatment of emergency injuries and refraction. Early staff members, the Baxter history records, included Drs. William Davis, Morgan Davies, Albert Frost and Harold Postle. In 1953, Dr. Morris Battles, the first physician in Ohio to devote his entire time to pediatric ophthalmology, became head of the service after four years' work in the eye clinic.

In the familiar pattern of those catch-up years, he recalled, the eye clinic was moved out of the hospital to a small house then to two other houses, while it doubled its patient load, expanded from three days to five each week and acquired its first OSU residents on rotation. Among Battles' early tasks was to plan for new clinic spaces and offices in the new south wing of the hospital.

His personal priority, a 15-year effort, was departmental status for ophthalmology which was granted in 1980. He recalls years of constant improvement in techniques and tools for the eye surgeon.

In treatment of cataracts, which children do have as a congenital problem or from trauma or German measles, first efforts were "reasonably unhappy," followed by a syringe aspiration method, then the great assistance of the microscope, then vitreous cutters, and now highly efficient instruments for "very delicate work" inside the eye, Battles said.

A major conclusion gleaned from his 40 years' experience, the retired chairman said, is that despite better tools and techniques, "there is no *minor* anesthesia, and there is no *minor* surgery."

58

Pursuing the retinopathy of prematurity problem which Battles first saw in the '50s as "retrolental fibroplasia," Children's has been involved in a long-term study by 23 centers to find out the effects of current treatment and the subsequent experience of children with the problem, said Dr. Gary Rogers, chief of ophthalmology.

"We will eventually be putting contact lenses in children," Rogers said. "Then refractive surgery, one of the next big frontiers, the technical aspects, a better understanding of how the brain and eye work together. The problem of the cross-eyed child is not really a muscle problem but something to do with the way the brain is wired up."

Ophthalmologists now "know when the critical times are from the vision development standpoint, when we can get in and do something for the child," Rogers said, and improved anesthesia, precise equipment allow them to "do things early and do them safely."

The pediatrician is the eye surgeon's first line of defense, he noted, in examining the eyes of a newborn. "During the '60s rubella epidemic, eyes were lost," he said, adding that, for some patients, the best time for surgery is from "days of age" to 10 weeks.

Recognition of eye problems is greatly improved, he said. Children's is "really doing everything" in treating eyes, he added, and is seeing fewer children for routine care, more on referral for specialized treatment, "probably half of them from outside Franklin County."

E.N.T.

Drs. John E. Brown, Sr., Hugh Beatty and Russell Means were major figures in ear, nose and throat treatment at Children's through the World War II years, the Baxter history records, and the service was the first casualty, repeatedly, to bed space requirements during the last polio epidemics. During the chairmanships of Dr. E.W. Harris and Dr. Trent Smith, Children's treatment reflected new approaches to ear, nose and throat problems and the service, Baxter noted, acquired its own 30-bed space in the hospital.

Dr. Herbert G. Birck, chief of otolaryngology since 1968, was the first U.S. graduate trained in the specialty.

Antibiotics, advanced microscopy and new synthetic materials brought improvements in ear, nose and throat treatment in the late '50s after decades of very little change, Birck said. "We were at the beginning."

Mastoid surgery and tracheotomies became less necessary and, when necessary, greatly refined. "Children have more airway distress than adults," he explained, and intubation, with plastic tubing rather than rubber, was the big change. With "fabulously small" instruments and great magnification, surgeons can do total reconstruction of the middle ear, he said, or correct an airway problem for a tiny infant.

The major problem now, he said, is fluid in the ear, when "the child just can't hear well. We started making a hole in the eardrum, using plastic tubing. At Children's now, we're doing 2,500 a year."

Several years ago, the outspoken Birck, in an interview, assailed an excessive number of tonsillectomies being performed and pronounced as highly suspect the occasional reported incident of several children in one family having the procedure at one time. This is happening less often, he said. Children's does about 1,500 tonsillectomies a year, he said, adding with a smile, "We do many more tubes than tonsils."

59

Like other department chairpersons, Birck thinks Children's is "better than it has ever been" and is entering an era of "general stabilization" with a possible increase in intensive care facilities.

Anesthesiology

Dr. Joseph Dunn was listed as the first anesthetist on Children's staff, in 1916 and '17, but the Baxter history assumes that anesthetics were probably administered often by general practitioners. Dr. W.D. Murphy, a general practitioner, was in charge of the service from 1922 until the late 1930s, assisted by Dr. Link Murphy and nurse anesthetists.

Dr. Aaron Canowitz came during the latter decade and, later, Dr. John Garvin, who became chief of the department. "Dr. Garvin and I didn't have pediatric training," Canowitz recalled, "and used to take turns visiting hospitals every vacation to learn."

Canowitz spans the full range of Children's growth about as well as anyone still associated with the hospital. He visited a cousin with tuberculosis of the bone in the old building across from Franklin Park and slipped into the "new" one as a schoolboy to stare at the ornate lobby. He was back in 1928 as an extern during a Christmas holiday week when two scheduled interns failed to show up and "the nurses practically hand-guided me," he said, through the necessary treatment routines.

"They were the good old days and the bad old days," he said of the pre–World War II Children's—a "family feeling," close doctor-patient and doctor-nurse relationships, but surgery procedures were imperfect—clumsy transfusion and wound cauterization methods, for instance, which sound primitive today, and there was a decided resistance to change in the Columbus medical community.

Like others, he hailed the advent of the Porter-Baxter era, the recruitment efforts, and the impact of Wheeler, Clatworthy and others not only within the hospital but in a quickened interest in pediatrics and its subspecialties among Columbus physicians.

Dr. Louise Warner has been a member of the anesthesiology team since the '50s. She got there in time to share the collective sigh of relief in 1958 when

Children's began using halothane as an inhalation agent, supplanting ether and cyclopropane, each with troublesome side effects and both explosive, necessitating special shoes and precautionary measures.

Halothane is now used in at least 90 percent of cases, but there are other new agents available for particular cases, she said, and there is a constant search for new and better ones both for inhalation and intravenous use.

Morphine is now used most often for post-operative and chronic pain: for the new post-operative patient-controlled analgesia method, for instance, which patients six and over can use up to a controlled safe level.

"There's a strange perception among some people that kids don't hurt as much as adults," she said. "We're pretty spoiled here, working with the best pediatric surgeons there are. We're focusing now on post-anesthetic complications, and we're pretty satisfied with what happens. We've been able to cut down on anesthesia and have arranged that no child has to have a shot, even for IV."

One of the busiest pediatric surgical centers in the country, Children's was among the first to do outpatient anesthesia in the late '50s, topped the 10,000 mark in inpatient and outpatient procedures in 1979, has now far exceeded that, and has "a very excellent safety record," Warner said.

Technology has greatly aided the anesthesiologist with the array of new monitoring and measuring equipment, she said, but hasn't lessened the responsibility. The anesthesiologist must rely on parents for a history of each child's medical problems, plan accordingly and react instantly if trouble develops.

Television hospital shows notwithstanding, "the absence of drama," Warner said, "is what we appreciate during surgery."

For more than a decade, Children's has been using an oral mixture for pre-operative patients which relieves anxiety, gives minimal sedation, has some anti-nausea effect and replaces the once-dreaded needle.

Even more child-specific is the anesthesia mask treated with a patient's-choice range of good smells like bubble gum or strawberry to override the anesthetic's odor.

Radiology

No vital service at Children's had smaller beginnings than radiology. When X-ray became available, well after Children's founding, patients were taken to the downtown office of Dr. Hugh Means. Later, when the new hospital was planned, Means designed the facility and headed it for a time, resigning, according to the Baxter history, when the administrator insisted the equipment be available to interns, residents and medical students.

From 1926 to 1945, under Dr. Huston Fulton's direction, a trained technician was on duty two or three times a week, with Fulton coming to the hospital when necessary to "read the films."

60

In 1946, Dr. William Howard, trained at Western Reserve, came to Children's to devote full-time to pediatric radiology and to become, said Baxter, nationally recognized in the specialty. Later, his assistants included Dr. Richard Klecker and Dr. Thomas Frye, now department chairman.

Even through a postwar decade or so, the service was small, the work volume low and limited to odd hours, recalled Frye, who joined the staff in 1960. "In those days, the worst things about X-ray were the open tanks for developer and fixatives . . . films that stuck together . . . damage to clothing. Somebody once asked Bill Howard what among all the developments in his 30 or 40 years in radiology was most important, and he said, 'Air conditioning.' "

He recalled early advances at Children's—the first image amplifier in Columbus, for which technicians needed red goggles; the first cardiac catheterization with Dr. Hosier; the developments and refinements which produced film within seconds and brought the innermost areas of the body within the radiologist's view and treatment scope; the CT scanner—"the most amazing thing I'd ever seen.

"We were the first in the city and among the first in the country to record all our examinations on videotape," he said.

Noting Children's continuing interest in "what radiation does to people," Frye said, "We do our best to keep radiation to the absolute minimum, to limit where the X-ray beam goes." Ultrasonic scanning, which penetrates without X-ray, is becoming a common procedure, he said, used particularly at Children's for kidney examination "as a successor to the old intravenous pyelogram with its needles and nausea."

Another basic change, "very expensive and very new," is the use of new contrast materials which have the same properties "but one-sixth the amount of reaction" of earlier materials. He also mentioned a "neat little machine," recently acquired, which is designed specifically to measure bone density in children.

From its small beginnings, the radiology department and its staff of more than 40 is nearing the 100,000 mark on the body-imaging procedures it conducts each year. Looking ahead, Frye anticipated great potential for the magnetic resonance imager (MRI) "which we're beginning to use for studies of circulation, metabolic work," and a resurgence in the field of nuclear medicine, established at Children's in the '60s, with current interests in monoclonal antibodies.

"We're positioned for the future," he said. "People are just beginning to realize not only the importance but the quality of Children's."

A prime beneficiary of dizzying technological advance, the radiology department offers some of the more arresting comparisons of how progress and specialization parallel hospital cost increases. In 1914, the Hornsby report told trustees they could establish and equip an X-ray facility for $500, which they did. In 1990, the estimated cost of just one wondrously versatile new tool, the MRI, was $3.3 million.

The Stubborn Killers

Dr. Frederick B. Ruymann was describing Children's notable success in the '80s with a new "8 in 1" chemotherapy treatment for brain tumors, the second most common—and traditionally lethal—type of childhood cancer. Detailing a heartening increase in the survival rate, he recalled one particular patient:

"We cured her tumor," he said, "but she died—of AIDS."

It was wry comment on a new dimension in children's medicine—the effect of the hazards and stresses of today's world on the enormous positive progress against disease and infection and physical defects. In this child's case, a gain against an age-old disease had been offset by earlier treatment with transfused blood tainted by a virus not defined until the '80s.

The Ohio Health Department supplied a graphic summary at the fatal level of how the perils of growing up have changed since Children's took a hand in the process a century ago. Gone from the latest (1988) top-five listing of the causes of death among Ohio children (and many vanished from longer listings) are scores of old bugbears conquered by immunization, antibiotics, better nutrition and prenatal care, new treatments, techniques and equipment.

The leading causes of death for infants under one year are changed but not surprising—a pared-down list headed by congenital anomalies, still-puzzling Sudden Infant Death Syndrome, respiratory distress, prematurity and complications of pregnancy. Then, the child's world extends beyond the nursery, and the picture changes.

Accidents are the leading cause of death for all age groups from one year into the 20s and early 30s in the Ohio count. Homicide enters the list at No. 5 for one- to four-year-olds, and for the 10-to-14 age group moves to No. 3, followed by suicide! Among Ohio teenagers 15 through 19, accidents, suicide and homicide rank 1, 2 and 4.

Only the stubbornest of childhood's traditional enemies—congenital anomalies for ages one through 10, cancer and heart disease from infancy on—retain a death grip on young lives comparable to the new, and preventable, interlopers of the late 20th century.

And this, of course, explains very clearly why Children's has grown so rapidly and in such focused directions through its first century and, most specifically, the last several decades. Its scope of concerns and programs, as a comprehensive child care center, expands with each new advance in its ability to improve children's lives and with each new challenge to that ability.

From mid-century on, Children's progress against cancer and heart defects and disease has been continuous and notable, in lives saved and lives improved.

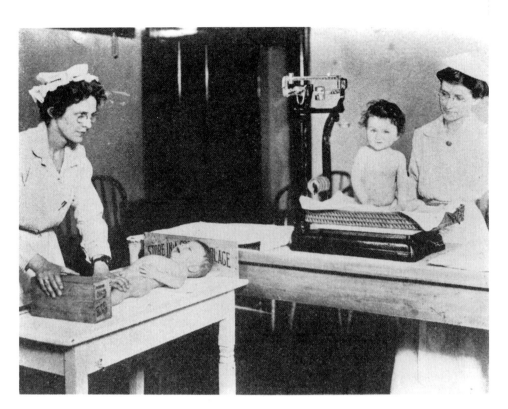

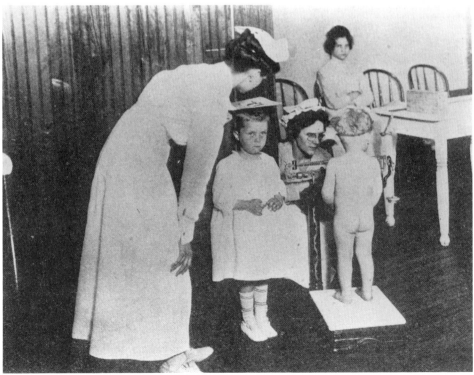

Weighing and measuring—1918 style.

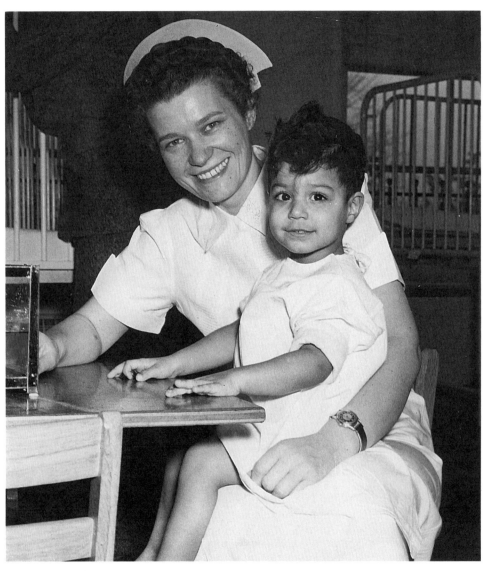

Venoie Olson Amey, trained in the Sister Kenny method of treating polio patients, was a key figure at Children's during the last epidemics of the '40s and '50s.

After polio's conquest, Sellers wing continued to serve its victims.

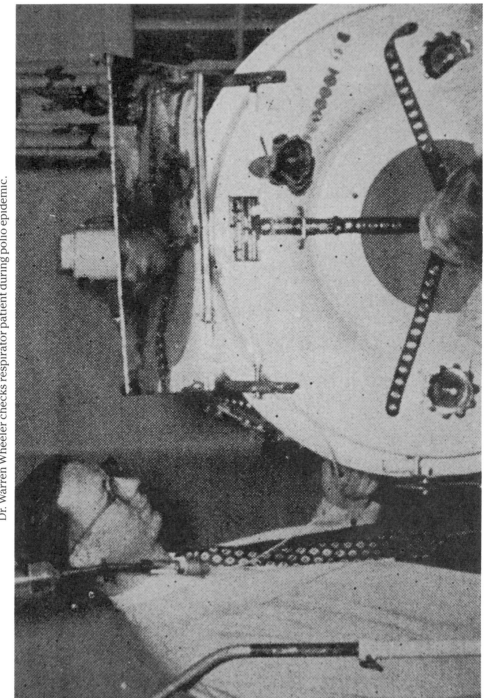

Dr. Warren Wheeler checks respirator patient during polio epidemic.

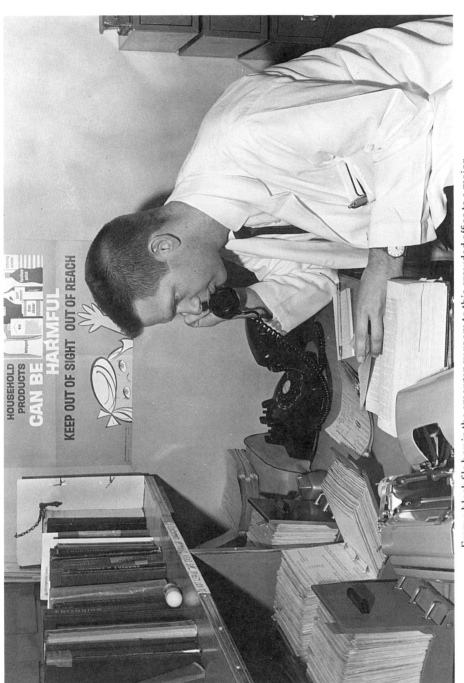

From a black file box in the emergency room to this crowded office to a major service, Children's Poison Control Center grew to meet growing demand.

Children's outreach to the community takes many forms—like this Poison Control Center display in an urban neighborhood in the 1960s.

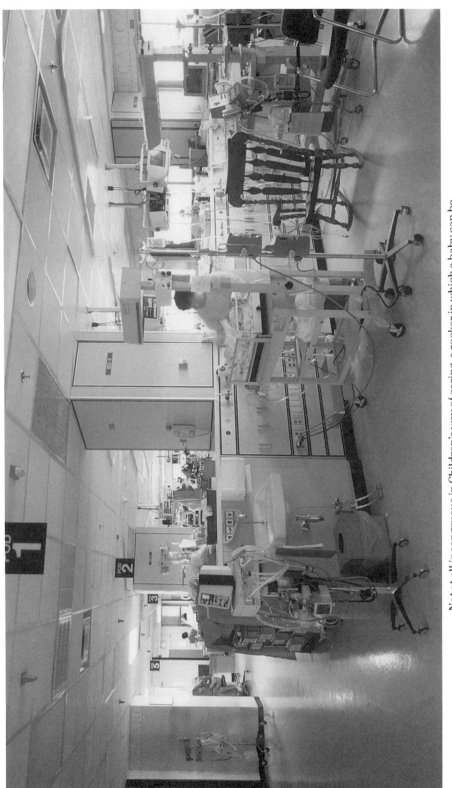

Not at all incongruous in Children's way of caring, a rocker in which a baby can be cuddled shares space with sophisticated monitoring and life-sustaining equipment in the Newborn Intensive Care Unit.

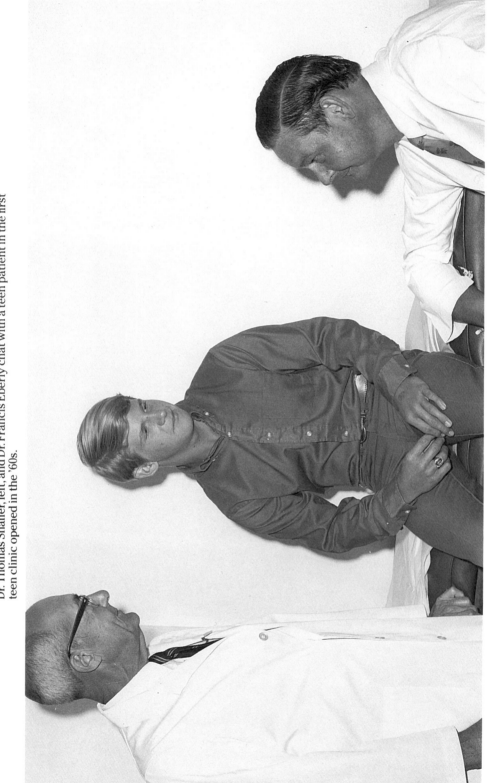

Dr. Thomas Shaffer, left, and Dr. Francis Eberly chat with a teen patient in the first teen clinic opened in the '60s.

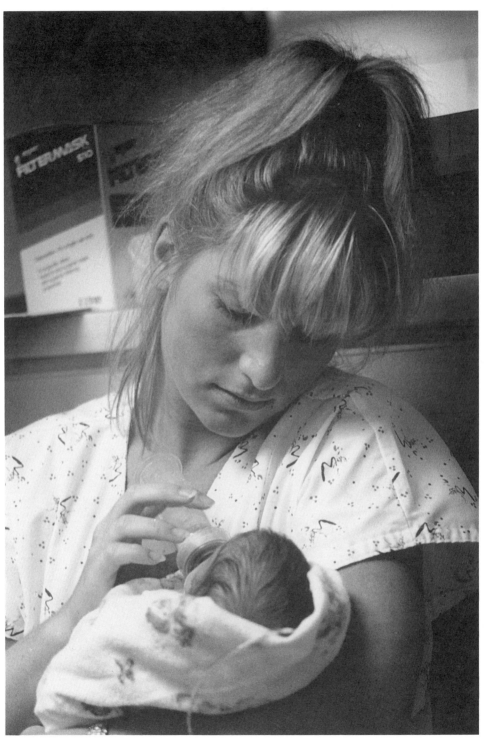

Stephanie Phillips, nursing assistant, feeds a tiny patient in the Newborn Developmental Unit, refurbished in 1990.

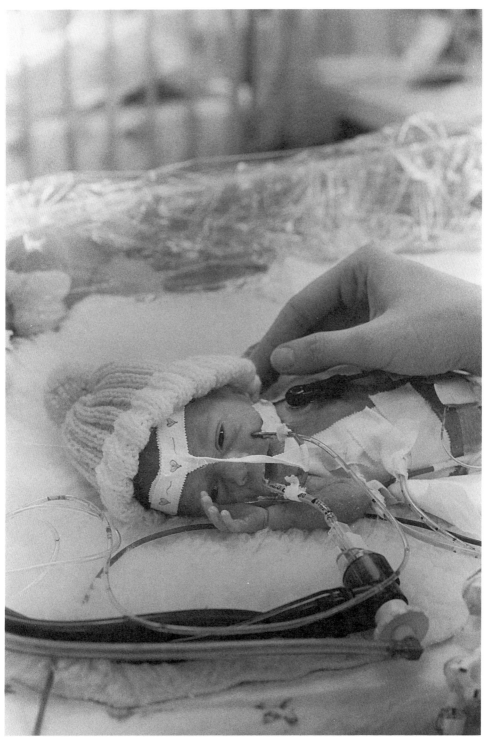

Assisted by marvelous devices and comforted by a soft nest and a loving hand, a tiny infant gains a firmer foothold on life in the Newborn Intensive Care Unit.

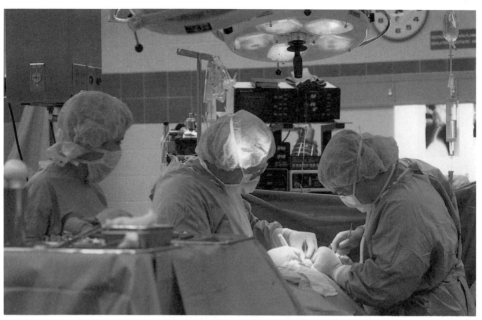

Children's in the '90s: Surgery

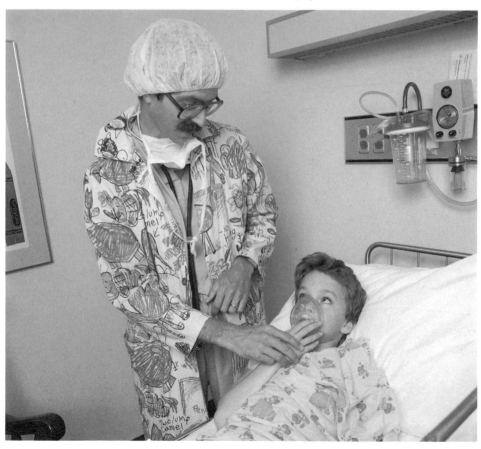

Children's in the '90s: Anesthesiology

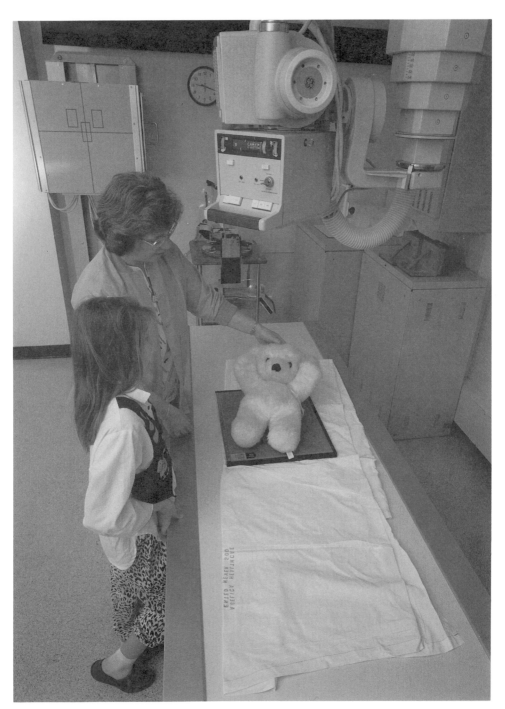

Children's in the '90s: Radiology

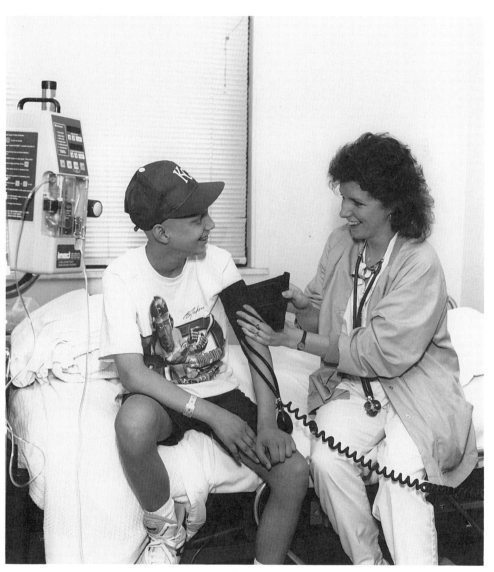

Children's in the '90s: Hematology/Oncology

Cardiology

Children's added the first cardiologists to its staff in the early '30s, but "when I was an extern in 1946," Dr. Don Hosier remembered, "there was little we could do for a child with a congenital heart defect." Hosier did his residency training at Johns Hopkins under the famed Dr. Helen Taussig, preeminent pioneer in pediatric cardiology, and returned in 1951 to direct the program at Children's.

"When I came in," he recalled, "we had an EKG machine in the basement, and they let me work in X-ray from 6 to 8 a.m. From then until now, the change has been fantastic, advancements in heart treatment perhaps more than any other."

His recollections are reflected in newspaper clippings detailing major advances in treatment of heart patients:

• Establishment of the Kinder Key Heart Laboratory in the mid-'50s.

• The city's first open-heart surgery at Children's in 1957. Trained in general surgery at OSU, Dr. Howard Sirak came to Children's to begin the program after two years' training at Columbia Presbyterian Hospital. "We developed the equipment here," Sirak said, recalling how a team including George Funakoshi, former chief perfusionist in the cardiovascular laboratory, assembled the device with its pump and rotating disk and trained to operate it.

Selection of a young patient was deliberate, he said, because the procedure was less complex and the patient's resiliency greater. "There was an enormous backlog of such cases," he recalled, "and after the first one, patients came from all over, even other states. Soon after the first experience at Children's, we set up a similar system at Ohio State."

Sirak, now retired, still receives phone calls "every now and then" from those early patients and enjoyed particular satisfaction when he learned that the very first patient, James Elliott, had helped relay the Olympic torch to the 1984 games in Los Angeles.

Later, Funakoshi said, he assembled a replica of that first open-heart apparatus for a permanent exhibit in Cleveland on the fight against heart disease.

• Stories through the next decades which recounted continuing advance in cardiac surgery—Dr. James W. Kilman, recently retired thoracic surgery chief, giving a blackboard demonstration of a new re-routing procedure of heart vessels or showing new materials like Teflon used to patch heart tissue.

• Opening in the late '70s of the new catheterization laboratory with its sophisticated equipment to assess heart function.

"Today, almost any congenital heart defect with which a child is born is correctable," Hosier said on the eve of his retirement in July, 1988. "Children get pacemakers as early as a month after birth, even younger," he added, and there are many more ways to help the child with long-range heart problems.

In the summer of 1988, surrounded by the best possible proof of Children's triumphs over heart problems, Hosier was a guest of honor at a Heart Party for several hundred of the hospital's heart patients and their families.

In 1990, with its cardiac patient total almost doubled in just a few years, Children's added personnel, services, equipment and space to accommodate them, including the first such unit in the hospital to serve jointly as a medical and surgical area. A multidisciplinary center for pediatric heart patients, it facilitates doctor-nurse collaboration, access of parents to education and support, the use of the most advanced monitoring equipment and diagnostic tools, and the care of each patient from diagnosis through surgery and/or other treatment and rehabilitation.

About seven children in 1,000 have heart problems, Dr. Hugh D. Allen, chief of cardiology, said, and most of them can be helped toward a normal or near-normal life.

He described some of the latest treatment devices—a new heart catheter to open narrowed valves and vessels, an umbrella device to "plug" an undesirable opening, and the exciting development of drug treatment of the unborn fetus and imminent fetal surgery.

Demonstrating some of the marvels technology has provided to aid the cardiologist, he anticipated further advances including, he is certain, "a three-dimensional heart projected into a room so you can walk through it to see how it is functioning."

Both Hosier and Allen stressed the importance of continuing collaboration between the clinician and researcher. Hosier mentioned the need to study the "familial" incidence of some heart problems, a way to permanently eliminate rheumatic fever, which showed a strange renewed vigor in the mid-'80s, and research needed on promising new drugs.

Besides the important fetal studies, investigations at Children's with important implications for heart patients, Allen said, include those on the importance of exercise, on how the heart relaxes and on childhood factors affecting adult heart disease.

Another concern in cardiology, Allen noted, is to follow up patients beyond 21, well into their adult years. The final step in effective research, he said, is to proceed beyond the basic work and its clinical application "to follow up what we have done and learn the consequences of it."

Childhood Cancer

Since the first real breakthroughs of the 1950s and '60s, Children's battle with childhood cancer has been steady and relentless, year by year.

They have been years of trial and error, of using available tools in new ways and combinations, of painstaking differentiation within cancer types and of modifying treatment to give each patient the greatest benefit at the least risk.

Children's has benefited from and contributed substantially to notable gains particularly through its long association with the Cancer Chemotherapy Study Group. Its increasing expertise in cancer treatment, closely allied with research advances, is a major thread in Children's post–World War II development.

Although the production of new cancer drugs has "sort of plateaued," as Dr. William Newton put it, experience, revised treatment protocols, information gleaned from research, and the precision and delicacy of new instruments have facilitated continued progress.

Newton's 40-year perspective spans the first notable gains over leukemia, most common and once-fatal childhood cancer, in the '60s and the achievements over brain tumor and rhabdomyosarcoma, a soft-tissue type, in the '80s.

At an international symposium in 1989 named in Newton's honor, Children's co-hosted an assembly of experts from nearly a dozen countries to discuss rhabdomyosarcoma. A long-term study begun in the '70s in which Children's laboratories had a major role resulted in a new treatment regimen and dramatically decreased mortality rate for this cancer type.

Looking to the future, Newton said, "Right now, we're stretching ourselves with tools, but new methodologies are enabling us to get inside the cells, gleaning new information. We now know most childhood tumors probably involve genetic defect. One of the things I'm doing right now is looking at the second tumor, if a child has a recurrence, to see how it is different. The overall incidence of childhood cancer hasn't changed. We're finding new ways to look for the 'why.' "

"We have the largest oncology practice in Ohio," said Dr. Frederick Ruymann, chief of oncology and hematology. Children's is seeing more than 100 newly diagnosed cancer cases a year, he said, and noted a five-year study showing half of the hospital's cancer patients come from Franklin County and another 25 percent from neighboring counties.

Much more progress has been made against childhood cancer than adult forms of the disease, he said, adding, "I think children have a more resilient immune system."

However, although childhood cancer accounts for only 2 percent of all cancer victims, advances against it and favorable results of current research and treatment efforts, he said, hold obvious promise for adult treatment. Despite this, he added, funding agencies like the American Cancer Society show an inexplicable reluctance to support work on childhood cancer.

Focusing on three current "areas of dramatic progress," Ruymann described how one achievement provides leads to another:

• The rhabdomyosarcoma study has led to treating other tumors of similar type and to a marker gene—"a molecular biology tool which can identify true 'rhabdos' from fellow travelers."

• Greatly improved survival for children with a type of brain tumor with a new "8 in 1" drug and radiation treatment which has led to a randomized study of children with brain tumors and an assault on the pediatric neurosurgeon's great remaining challenge, brain stem gliomas.

• The "sub-typing" of leukemia patients to specify the extent or even the need for cranial radiation treatment and a long-term follow-up study to assess latent effects of the treatment on patients. The follow-up studies extend to effects of childhood cancer and treatment on many facets of adult life, Ruymann said, and to the "fascinating" probability of a predictable pattern of cancer within families.

"We can look to a child's coming down with cancer as an index case to write a program for a whole family," he said. "We will be developing cancer control strategies for adults based on what we know about childhood cancer."

Trauma

Medical science has made great advances in keeping well children healthy and making sick ones well, but it hasn't much daunted the No. 1 child killer, accidents. Children's and major centers like it keep trying.

In fact, accidents as killers and maimers of children seem to feed on progress. Young victims of falls and fires and domestic mishaps were among Children's earliest patients, but the 20th century increased the perils of childhood sharply with motor vehicles, new poisons and toxic substances, and, most recently and tragically, the outbursts and weapons and addictions of a violent society.

The statistics are awesome and discouragingly constant. Nearly half of all deaths of children 14 and under are caused by accidents, more than all childhood diseases combined. In one recent year, 1986, nearly 8,000 U.S. children were killed in accidents and 50,000 were permanently disabled. Motor vehicles cause the most accidental deaths at all age levels, followed by fires and burns, drowning, choking and poisoning, and falls for those four and under; by drowning, fires and burns, firearms and falls for those five to 14.

For decades, Children's has combined its increasing proficiency in treating and salvaging accident victims with active support of accident prevention. Staff members have testified against dangerous toys and flammable materials and toxic substances available to children. The hospital has participated in community campaigns and conducted its own programs to educate parents and the public.

In the early '50s, Dr. Edward V. Turner worked with the Metropolitan Health Council on a public education program. A survey in March of 1951 showed that 500 Columbus children were hurt badly enough that month to require hospital attention, and the city's projected accident toll for the year, based on national estimates, was 25 children killed and 100 permanently crippled.

In the '70s, Dr. Thomas S. Morse devised and published a set of guidelines for initial care of the injured child and, later, with Children's ER head nurse Billie Lent, a list of equipment and supplies needed for emergency care of severely injured children.

In that same period, Morse was a leader among pediatric surgeons in support of the newly formed American Trauma Society, started by physicians seeking to raise the national consciousness about killer accidents the way other large organizations had done with killer diseases. The society, which Morse served as president during his final years at Children's, set as its first promotional priority the establishment and use of centralized trauma centers for critically injured children.

In more than 20 years during which it has functioned as the pediatric trauma center for Central Ohio, Children's has been moving toward that goal. It now has the full complement of facilities and trained personnel to qualify as a Level I trauma center, said Dr. Denis R. King, pediatric surgeon at Children's. In the fall of 1991 the hospital received notification it is certified as a Level I trauma center.

"We're really the first pediatric facility in the state to qualify. Eventually, others probably will," he said. Ideally, certain hospitals in a regional network will be certified at Level I, and all persons with a major life-threatening injury will be taken directly to such a center from an accident scene—adults to an adult center, children 14 and younger to a pediatric center.

There is good reason for the separation, King said. "Adults and children differ. Adults break and need to be fixed. They usually require more surgery. Children are more plastic, require more emergency resuscitation and monitoring. Injuries can be just as devastating (for both groups) but treatment and care differ."

As just one example, he noted that adult accident victims brought to a Level I trauma center will frequently require surgery for intra-abdominal bleeding. Children, while they need intensive care and observation, often simply stop bleeding, he said, and can be allowed to heal without invasive surgery.

Political and institutional resistance may well slow the implementation of a regional trauma network, King said, but "trauma is getting a lot more visible. It is THE BIGGEST public health problem."

Children's has joined forces with some 40 community groups in support of a five-year Safe Kids campaign launched nationally in 1988. Proving the need for public education, a survey of Franklin County parents in connection with that campaign showed, he added, that parents' greatest concerns for their children's safety do not square with the statistics.

Children's Hospital has made an enormous investment, he said, in facilities and personnel not only to treat accident victims but to treat those few who need it within the minutes that may mean life or death.

Emergency Department

At every juncture in its long effort to improve and expand, Children's has reshaped its emergency services and staff to serve patients better.

Emergency departments (ED) are the dramatic focal point of hospitals, certainly in the popular mind, but even in that context a children's ED is different—kind of a "microcosm" as one doctor termed it of the entire hospital population.

ED staffs have always been able to gauge their busy times by school hours, vacation times, doctors' office hours and, on occasion, an epidemic outbreak of a childhood ailment. Emergency patients have always ranged from the most critical to the complaint that is an "emergency"—but a very real one—to just one child and one set of parents.

Motor vehicles were once a separate, and small, listing on ED reports; now, they are a major cause of childhood injury. As late as the '50s, "wringer accidents" were a laundry-room peril. As they faded away, new cleaning agents and caustic chemicals emerged, one of the reasons for the ED's spawning of the special service that has become the Central Ohio Poison Center.

Through the years, as demand increased and facilities permitted, Children's learned to sort out incoming patients according to the extent and urgency of their need, expanded physician and staff coverage, added personnel specially trained in particular ED procedures and, most recently, the skilled trauma teams ready for action within the minutes that can mean life or death.

In 1990, Dr. Gary A. Smith, with extensive training in public health, pediatrics and preventive medicine, came to Children's as chief of the section of Emergency Medical Services and director of emergency medicine in the OSU Department of Pediatrics.

In recent years, approximately 50 percent of Children's inpatient admissions enter through the ED and overall patient visits have increased to more than 70,000 in 1991.

A two-story addition that will double the present ED space with more adequate facilities for patient treatment, teaching, and accommodations and support services for parents will be completed in 1993.

From Preemie to Pre-Adult

Among the sharpest contrasts between the Children's of 1892 and today's hospital is the greatly increased focus on the extremes of childhood—infancy and the teens.

The first hospital did not accept patients under one year, nor teenagers older than 15. Although that policy eventually changed, it was mid-century before modern medicine—and Children's—began to concentrate on the special and distinctly separate problems of the child just beginning life and the one about to enter adulthood.

Dr. Thomas Shaffer, who first came to Children's in 1946 and had a special interest in both age groups, remembers the old Hess incubators—"kind of like a double boiler with the baby placed in sort of a little boat"—and the arrival of the first modern isolette donated by a hospital friend.

He also remembers, a decade or so later, when Administrator Robert Porter, sensing teenage patients were uncomfortable among "little kids," established a separate ward, aptly named "Suite 1319," where they could convalesce more comfortably among their peers. In 1962, Shaffer started the first teen clinic at Children's with a grant and volunteer help from the Junior League and a "one morning, one afternoon" weekly schedule.

By 1964, two years after it opened, Children's first teen clinic, with its own staff and consulting specialist, was the largest of its kind in the Midwest. From the 1,368 teenagers who came during 1963, Children's staff began to get a picture of the age group's special needs and problems.

The late Dr. Francis Eberly, then clinic director, in a Dispatch interview that year detailed "real pain" and distress suffered by young patients from individual concerns and external stresses that were a "tip of the iceberg" preview of those the next quarter-century would produce.

Some of those looming problems were anticipated in the spring of '65 when Children's co-hosted a three-day symposium involving many of the country's ranking experts in the new field of adolescent medicine. While agreeing that troubled adolescents warranted special attention, the experts also worried about how a kind of separateness and greater visibility might compound their difficulties.

Through the next decades, while its adolescent patients shared in the benefits of progressing medical care and treatment, Children's expanded its programs and services to encompass old adolescent woes and emerging ones—notably, drug and alcohol abuse and a new "prematurity" problem, teenage pregnancy and parenthood.

Responding to the latter problem, the hospital's section of Adolescent Health, as it is known today, developed a Teen/Tot program, the only one of its kind in Central Ohio. It provides medical care for babies and serves the needs of their teenage mothers for parenting education. A separate but complementary program called Parent Enrichment is an effort to prevent child abuse among teenage parents.

Infants were prime beneficiaries of major treatment advances and early research efforts at Children's throughout the '40s and '50s, detailed elsewhere in this history. Since then, almost year by year, Children's has increased its ability to sustain life through the hazards of prematurity and through the early detection, treatment and often correction of inborn problems.

By 1990, while its research teams focused on myriad unsolved problems, Children's treatment expertise, facilities and parent support for its smallest patients were a distinctive feature of the hospital. When the expanded, intensive care and developmental units for newborns were opened in midsummer of '90, Dr. James Menke, chief of neonatology, said only three or four hospitals in the country were staffed and equipped to match Children's program.

Newborns in trouble, only a few hours or a few days old and as small as 1¼ pounds, are referred to Children's from all over Central and Southeastern Ohio and sometimes neighboring states. Many, several hundred a year, are rushed to the hospital in a custom-made mobile intensive care unit by a highly skilled Children's transport team trained and fully equipped to give continuous care and meet emergencies en route.

Quiet, softly lit, staffed by attentive and skilled personnel, the newborn units are equipped with an array of supportive, monitoring, measuring and "remembering" devices, all designed to sustain and strengthen each tiny infant's will to live.

"Each" is a key word, Menke emphasized. Care and treatment are shaped by vigilant staff and machines to the individual needs of each infant. This focus continues in the newborn developmental unit in which parents, given special accommodations to be near their infants, learn to interact with their children and to give the care that will be necessary at home.

Latest additions to the electronic marvels serving the newborn units include a high-frequency ventilator to regulate an infant's breathing over a wide range and the long-awaited Extra Corporeal Membrane Oxygenator (ECMO) which takes over heart and lung functions for babies at high risk.

Depending on their individual problem, infants may be in the intensive care units from two days to eight or nine months, Menke said, and the average length of stay is about 20 days.

Child Health Problems Still Exist

With all of its acquired expertise and state-of-the-art facilities, Children's is acutely aware of other imperatives affecting all its patients and most particularly the very youngest: education at all levels of care-giving; public advocacy of programs concerned with child care; research, which alone can fill still-yawning gaps in medical knowledge.

Dr. Antoinette Eaton, corporate director of governmental affairs, pinpointed some of the problems as the newly installed president of the American Academy of Pediatrics in 1990.

She cited the "deplorable" figures that rank the United States 22nd in infant mortality rates (9.7 deaths per 1,000 live births) behind No. 1 Japan's

5.5; the 22 percent of children and adolescents (the largest segment of the population) living in poverty; the 35 percent lag in the immunization of the country's pre-school children; the lack of good, affordable child care for working mothers; the financial and non-financial barriers to health care access.

She noted the favorable position of Central Ohio and, indeed, the state, in the placement of children's hospitals and the accessibility of all levels of care. She hailed the advances, within a few decades, in neonatal intensive care, in genetic engineering, in helping children with chronic disability and chronic illness. She saw unmet needs as the responsibility of health care professionals, parents and every citizen.

Looking at what's done and what's to do from a different perspective, Dr. Juan Sotos, chief of endocrinology and metabolism, measured significant advances against a formidable array of unknowns—recently devised testing of newborns, for instance, for four known and manageable deficiencies from a list of hundreds of still-unharnessed genetic problems.

"We don't have enough knowledge yet," he said. "Mental retardation, epileptic seizures we can treat but often don't know why. Diabetes. We don't know where it comes from, how to prevent it, how to treat it without daily injections."

Research, "interminable research," he said, is the only route to new knowledge, the prime source of medical advance. He said the most fascinating areas of research currently are genetics and immunology, studies of the individual human cell and the internal "microchip" which contains "the millions and millions of messages that make you you." In such basic and narrowly focused research, he said, "one bit of new knowledge feeds into another, and any new knowledge is going to help."

The Enigma SIDS

Significant progress against Sudden Infant Death Syndrome (SIDS), the puzzler persistently lodged among the top killers of babies under one year, is almost nil, Dr. Charles Reiner, Children's pathologist, said.

Mentioned in the Old Testament and "clearly recognized by pediatric pathologists as early as the '30s," SIDS claims as its victims apparently healthy babies under a year old, "peaking about two to four months," Reiner said. It is unpredictable, so far unpreventable and accounts for an estimated two deaths per 1,000 live births in the nation's infant mortality rate.

Thus far, nationwide efforts against SIDS in which Children's has participated have produced largely tangential results—support groups to combat the psychological effect of SIDS on parents and families; conferences to share new information; and encouragement of what Reiner termed "an investigative type of autopsy" which can at least establish a SIDS diagnosis, occasionally pinpoint another latent cause of death and possibly produce a durable clue.

"We have what we call a 'cause a month club,' " Reiner said, referring to many promising leads later proved invalid. "We do have some research money," Reiner said, which he hopes will implement studies at Children's based on new SIDS data that warrants investigation.

Finally, at a point where societal problems *have* invaded the nursery, Children's infant care extended in the '80s to babies born with AIDS or affected by parental drug abuse.

Clinics
Neighborhood Doctor and Regional Specialist

Children's hadn't been established very long, back in the 1890s, before the first parents and children began dropping in, seeking medicine and advice. That was the origin of two important functions—a "family doctor" role in its urban neighborhood that Children's has continued to fill and a network of clinics grown to a comprehensive array of ambulatory services.

In 1910, with an established dispensary and programs in child nutrition and family health, trustees authorized Dr. O.S. Sellenings of the house medical staff, Dr. Andre Crotti of the surgical staff and Miss Martha Deshler of the Women's Board to plan a clinic program.

For a long time, the use and growth of outpatient services depended to a considerable extent on space, facilities and the time community physicians could devote to them. As late as the early '50s, Dr. Morris Battles recalled, his arrival at Children's had allowed for extension of the ophthalmology clinic from two to three days a week and Dr. Morgan Davies, then chief of the service, "frequently came out to the hospital and did retinoscopies during his lunch hour."

Nevertheless, from the very early years, the clinics developed steadily and met increasing demand. In March, 1920, urging their expansion, Women's Board President Daisy Sellers told trustees:

"A well-managed dispensary service ought to develop new lines of public interest because it is concrete, because it deals with large numbers, because it relieves suffering in very obvious ways, and because it is a preventive and can be put before the people who give, not only because their hearts are touched but because their heads approve."

Marvin Ware, familiar with Children's clinics from two perspectives, said similar things in a different way. Growing up in a neighborhood where most children didn't go to a doctor but "to Children's," he remembered, "I wanted to go to the hospital so bad." Eventually, he made it to the clinics, "mostly for dental work" and for childhood ailments.

Back in Columbus in 1957, after a career in military service, he went to work in Children's clinics, retiring 16 years later as assistant to the clinic director.

"I got a little cynical in the Army, used to say I didn't like kids," he confessed. "But working in the clinic—it becomes more than just a job.

"You see so many kids in distress," he explained, recalling a little girl suffering from drug abuse, another who had lost her hair to chemotherapy—"She came and worked for me awhile and just loved it."

He remembered the patience of waiting families, particularly in an earlier time "when we booked everyone in at 8 a.m.," and the policy, unchanged from his boyhood and earlier, of "never looking at whether they could pay or not."

Children's clinics have changed in important ways since he left in 1972, said Dr. Philip C. Ambuel, now retired, who devoted much time and study to clinic development during his 19 years at Children's.

"Even at the time I came, in '53, clinics were primarily for low-income patients," he said. "For a large part, they still are, but there's been a shift, a good shift," to a much broader service base. The other, "bigger" change, he said, is that clinics have in a way "come in from the cold" in the hospital hierarchy in staffing and service range, thanks to changing treatment patterns and research interests.

Describing a program that, by 1991, included 35 clinics serving nearly 100,000 outpatients a year, Catherine Lancaster, R.N., M.S., director of ambulatory services, pointed to a crowded weekly schedule with dozens of different listings all day long, Monday through Friday, plus primary dental care every weekday after 5.

"We divide the services into 'clusters' for organizational purposes," she said, the clusters including primary care, acute care, chronic care, hematology and dental services.

She elaborated. Primary care clinics meet basic health needs of children—diagnostic evaluations, physical assessments, immunization, nutrition; a range of services for adolescents; health care for infants of teenage mothers.

Acute care covers "very acute, short-term needs"—allergy and asthma; dermatology; ear, nose and throat problems; eye problems; orthopedic problems; surgical and urologic problems.

Chronic care clinics serve children with cerebral palsy, arthritis, physical and developmental handicaps, learning disabilities and neuromuscular physical handicaps. In the chronic cluster also is "family development," focused particularly on counseling, prevention and treatment in child abuse cases.

The hematology/oncology clinic serves children with cancer, hemophilia, sickle cell anemia and other hematologic disease, and those with immunodeficiency problems including AIDS.

The dental clinic, "one of our big growers," she said, along with primary care and ear, nose and throat clinics, provides services to patients through age 21 and attracts patients from a wide area.

Two small clients at the dispensary entrance in 1920.

A 1922 crowd of parents and children in the old hospital's dispensary.

Comfortable accommodations and decor shorten waiting time for patients and parents in Children's busy clinic areas.

During all the construction of the '50s and '60s, hospital services were temporary occupants of area houses. The one at left accommodated the child development clinic and pediatric surgery offices and the one at right, the eye clinic.

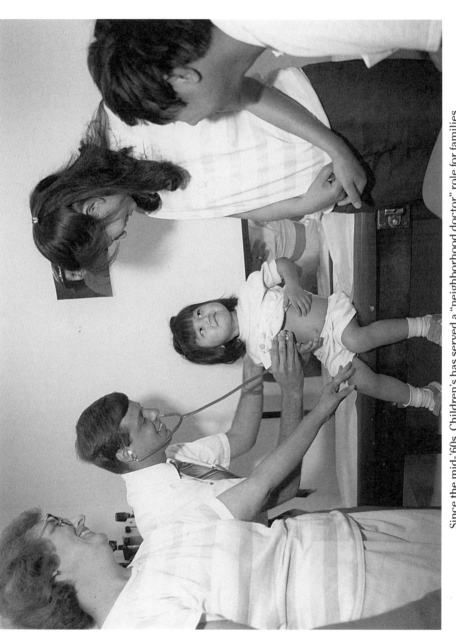

Since the mid-'60s, Children's has served a "neighborhood doctor" role for families like this little girl and her parents in four neighborhood clinics, now called Community Pediatric-Adolescent Services (CPAS).

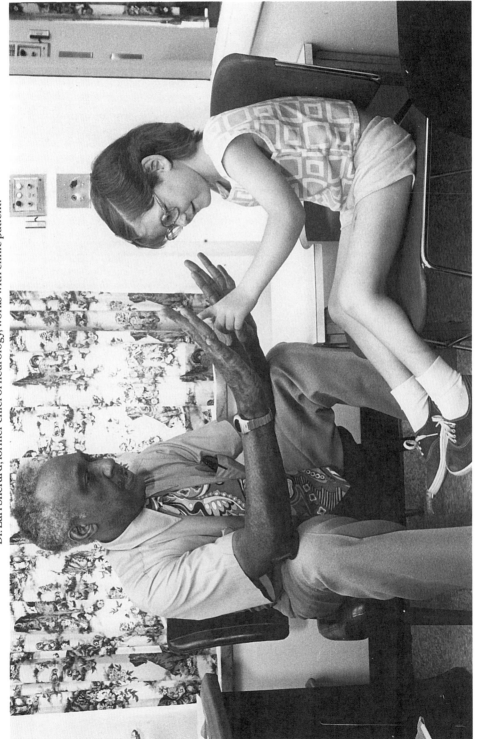

Dr. Earl Sherard, former chief of neurology, works with clinic patient.

The Ambulatory Services entrance at Children's Hospital in 1990.

Many people aren't aware, Lancaster said, that a child with any one or several other problems may have dental problems also and need treatment under special facilities a dentist's office doesn't have. "We do a lot of dental procedures in surgery," she said, and have trained personnel "steps away" from the dental clinic in case of emergencies.

The dental clinic is among several special enough to attract referrals beyond the hospital's normal service area, she said. Others include physical medicine's seating program, which was created to provide adaptive seating devices or wheelchairs for any patients who need them, and the myelomeningocele clinic that provides multidisciplinary care to patients born with spina bifida.

Probably closest to the old "neighborhood doctor" image in the hospital's clinic structure are the four inner-city community clinics, started as the federally funded Children and Youth project in 1966. Their programs broadened and deepened over more than three decades. They provide comprehensive health care services for families in their respective areas of the city under their new name, Community Pediatric-Adolescent Services (CPAS).

Each of the in-hospital clinics is served by an array of staff specialists who can best help with a particular problem—for the cerebral palsied child, for instance, experts in physiatrics, developmental pediatrics, orthopedics, family dynamics and community service; for the child with learning disability, a pediatrician, psychologist, pediatric nurse associate, educator and medical social worker.

In all of the clinics, "one thing we are absolutely committed to," Lancaster said, "is one level of care for all patients."

Noting a 21 percent increase in clinic patients in one year and anticipating further growth, she added, "Children can't get some of the services we offer anywhere else in Ohio."

Sketching idly on the back of a pamphlet, she illustrated Children's "continuity of care" approach to its clinic patients—not a straight-line progression but a circle encompassing home, hospital and ambulatory clinics and perhaps repeated many times during a child's growing-up years.

Research
The ONLY Road to New Knowledge

Challenges to the researcher in pediatric medicine have never been more exciting. Children's Hospital has never been so well-positioned to meet them.

It has a state-of-the-art research facility, a growing corps of able investigators, dramatically improved financial resources, and an established research agenda projected past its centennial year toward the 21st century.

Through its doors each day, seeking its specialized treatment, come the children from Central Ohio, the state and region, and beyond, presenting myriad problems. Every year, with new knowledge and technology, Children's makes further gains in saving and improving young lives. Every such gain brings into sharper, more tantalizing focus the unconquered diseases and unanswered problems.

Logically, from a teaching-treating-investigating milieu like Children's the elusive answers should most readily be tracked.

Research was a latecomer to Children's. Occasional references were made to better record-keeping and systematized data collection in early years, but it was 50 years before limitations in personnel and facilities could be overcome to allow for any real research development. It was still so new an idea in 1941 that Dr. Baxter felt the need to define it in his first annual report as chief of staff.

With a new administration and an expanding postwar staff, all supportive of research, results came quickly through the '40s and '50s. Within little more than a decade, the first real investigative efforts were having positive effects on patient care and in recognition for the hospital.

As laboratory space was minimal and staff time limited by multiple duties, early studies focused logically on problems presented by patients being treated. In his history of the OSU College of Medicine, Dr. N. Paul Hudson describes some early work and its significance.

Responding to problems arising from the then-new practice of transfusing babies with erythroblastosis, Dr. Wheeler started an Rh reference laboratory in which new testing and typing methods for blood and its components were developed. Children's not only became a center for treatment of so-called "Rh babies" but was selected in 1958 by the American Association of Blood Banks as one of its 12 regional blood-typing reference centers.

In the spiraling nature of research, this work led to an interest in cross-matching blood for open-heart surgery and in new ways of detecting other antibodies in the blood.

78

After a siege of infectious diarrhea at Children's, Dr. Wheeler and Dr. Bertha Wainerman published a study describing the efficacy of a new drug in treating the disease and detailing principles for controlling such infection. During a series of staphylococcal infection outbreaks in area hospital nurseries, Drs. Shaffer, Robert Sylvester and others did a series of studies, one using specimens from 19 institutions, on the nature and effective control of the staph strain involved.

The Hudson summary of what Children's investigators were doing in this early period included studies by Dr. Don Hosier in cardiac treatment; in identification and management of neurophysiatric disabilities by Dr. Hilda Knobloch and the child development clinic staff; in thyroid disease and renal disorders by Dr. Robert Blizzard and others. Dr. Philip Ambuel and outpatient staff personnel worked on a range of problems including the cause and treatment of enuresis (bedwetting), treatment of Vitamin D–resistant rickets, and the use of sulfonamides in throat and ear infections.

Another major study grew from a problem brought to Children's by M. & R. Dietetics Laboratory (later Ross Laboratories). Babies receiving an infant formula produced by the laboratory, particularly those receiving no supplemental nutrition, were developing a form of anemia. A research team headed by Dr. Leonard Lubhy was able to pinpoint the deficiency in processing which solved the problem.

When polio victims flocked to Children's in the last big epidemics of the mid-'40s and '50s, the hospital became a regional treatment center for both child and adult patients. Faced with their acute and long-term problems, the staff honed its treatment skills and focused research efforts on respiratory paralysis and permanent tracheotomies.

After a regional respirator center was established at Children's by the National Foundation for Infantile Paralysis, including a well-equipped pulmonary laboratory, Dr. Thomas K. Oliver and others expanded those studies to problems of pulmonary function in the newborn and congenital fibrocystic disease.

On Jan. 4, 1960, Basil O'Connor, president of the National Foundation, came to Children's to dedicate the first March of Dimes–sponsored Birth Defects Study Center in the country. Before the development of new surgical techniques through the '50s at Children's and other hospitals, few children born with congenital malformations had lived beyond infancy. At the center, a team of specialists headed by Dr. William O. Robertson would be concentrating on early diagnosis, evaluation, treatment, rehabilitation and long-term care of children with birth defects of the central nervous system.

The leukemia saga at Children's, through fortuitous twists, led to one of the hospital's longest-standing and most important research involvements—as a core member of the National Cancer Institute's Cancer Chemotherapy Study Group.

Converted to pediatrics during his internship at Children's and signed up to become chief resident, Dr. Robert Sylvester had been invited to work in the Harvard pathology laboratory of Dr. Sidney Farber, who was testing folic acid antagonists as a possible treatment for childhood leukemia.

"At one of Bob Porter's famous staff parties at Nightingale Cottage," Sylvester remembered, he suggested to Porter and Dr. Wheeler that they "farm me out" for the Farber project. They had no money available, but Porter mentioned the opportunity to Mrs. Elizabeth Bigelow, widow of the former chief of staff. She provided a fund for such use and "should be recognized," Sylvester said, "for that kind of commitment."

When the first paper on the Farber study was published in the New England Journal of Medicine, Sylvester was listed as a co-author. Farber's subsequent presentation of his data in 1948 to the Massachusetts Academy of Medicine is now a medical landmark—the beginning of cancer chemotherapy.

Opting to return to his post at Children's, Sylvester began treating leukemia patients and "the word got around pretty well," he said, bringing parents and leukemic children in greater numbers and from greater distances.

Eventually, Sylvester revived his long-delayed wish to enter private practice, and Dr. William Newton entered the picture. He had joined the Children's staff in 1951 as chief of pathology and director of laboratories, charged with developing that much-deprived facility.

"The day I arrived," he said, "Dr. Sylvester came in with a stack of charts, and I inherited about 20 leukemia patients. There was no hematology clinic—because I was primarily responsible for the laboratory this became an add-on—so in a couple of years we just built a wall around a desk."

Through the '50s, the treatment of children with leukemia—then and now the most common childhood cancer—was mostly a delaying action. For a number of years, Newton and the staff planned an early Christmas party for leukemic patients unlikely to survive until the holiday itself.

The Farber discovery sparked the development of other anti-cancer drugs, and in the mid-'50s Children's became an early member of the federally sponsored Cancer Chemotherapy Study Group (CCSG), sharing its data with other major centers on treatment of leukemia and, later, solid tumors as well.

Though Children's did not seek the credit, Newton suspects that some important advancements occurred as early at the Columbus hospital as anywhere.

"Dr. Wheeler said one day, 'Why not treat leukemia like an infection, with more than one drug at a time?' " Newton recalled. It was tried at Children's, and it worked. The NCI took the idea, using four drugs and adult patients, and reported the work, Newton said, "but it was still the single greatest thing that happened in curing leukemia in children."

By the early '60s, the dramatic reversal in childhood leukemia had begun, and the cure rate began to climb from near zero to the present 60 percent.

In the mid-'50s, "Dr. Clatworthy was the dominant figure in the area in surgical treatment of tumors," Newton continued, and the Children's researchers joined forces in attacking other types of cancer, using combinations of drugs, surgery and radiation to eradicate cancer and forestall its recurrence.

Among major advances since then to which work at Children's contributed were the conquest of Wilms' tumor (kidney), once nearly always fatal and now almost 100 percent curable; the first use of drugs in treating brain tumors (neuroblastoma); an extensive CCSG study of rhabdomyosarcoma centered in Children's laboratories; and changes in national treatment protocols for these and other cancer types.

Under Clatworthy's leadership, surgical data were also being compiled and reported on such diverse problems as aortic coarctation, esophageal atresia, intestinal atresia and obstruction, infantile inguinal hernias and hemangiomatous tumors (birthmarks).

Launched at an exciting and exacting level, research at Children's has continued to grow, subject to inevitable peaks and valleys due to funding problems, staff departures, institutional priorities and other factors.

In many ways, the effort has broadened, to encompass not only medical problems but the many other influences—social, emotional, economic, environmental, etc.—which affect children from infancy through adolescence. In another way it has narrowed—to single cells and single cell components which by their behavior, presence or absence can determine the course and quality of a child's life.

In 1960, a Dispatch story on Children's search for answers to childhood ailments detailed a broad range of work in progress—studies relating to then-new open heart surgery, thyroid function and cretinism, care and treatment of burn patients, hydrocephalus and other congenital anomalies. The outpatient department had completed a study of 100 patients to find out why some children do not grow well and, in a study of similar scope, the surgery department was achieving dramatic reduction in the mortality rate in cases of perforation in appendicitis.

Space was still a problem, and these and other studies were being done, one researcher commented, by investigators working "elbow to elbow and back to back." A 1959 article in the hospital house organ, Pediascript, featured the laboratories as department of the month, describing their multiple functions in support of patient care, education, physicians' and their own staff research. The article noted only incidentally that the small staff of 40 or so, full- and part-time, worked in laboratories "scattered from a penthouse on the roof to neighboring houses."

In the mid-'50s, the hospital's first formal research organization, CHILD (Children's Hospital Investigative Laboratories Division), had been established to give stature, impetus and accountability to a research program and to seek funding resources. An initial goal of CHILD was a research building.

In 1958, in response to the hospital's request, NIH awarded $180,000 to Children's toward a research building. A matching contribution by Ross Laboratories and other substantial donations supplied the funding. Erected on a site west of the newly expanded hospital building, Ross Hall was opened in 1962 as a two-story building, one floor for clinical research, one for pathology, and a ground floor for animal work. It was filled upon completion, and plans were soon under way for an addition.

Pediascript articles in July, 1959, and January, 1960, indicate the kind of work going on and the recognition it was receiving. In July, papers by eight staff members—Drs. John P. Garvin, J.P. Smith, Clatworthy, Boles, Wheeler, Robert Blizzard, Martin P. Sayers, and Howard Sirak—were presented at the International Congress of Pediatrics in Montreal; Clatworthy presented a paper on primary liver tumors, co-authored with Drs. Newton and Boles, before the British Association of Pediatric Surgeons in Liverpool; and the American Academy of Pediatrics scheduled a spring post-graduate course at Children's on problems of the newborn.

The early '60s brought more recognition in terms of research investment.

In 1963, NIH made a $750,000 grant for a Clinical Studies Center, a six-bed unit in a remodeled area of the Sellers wing with government funding for facilities, personnel and patients selected for treatment because of a puzzling medical problem. Dr. Juan Sotos, former chief resident, returned from his post in endocrinology at Massachusetts General Hospital to be center director.

A 1963 Pediascript update noted work in progress or planned on a range of problems from rheumatic disease in childhood to inborn errors of metabolism. With open-heart surgery an established procedure, the surgical staff looked toward organ transplants with weekly conferences and facilitating studies.

Through most of the '60s, Dr. Blanca Kent, then chairman of surgical research, worked on and published a number of studies including a technique of liver hemostasis pioneered at Children's and other work on the characteristics of the liver looking to new treatment methods and, eventually, liver transplants.

In 1989, when a Chicago surgical team reported success of a partial liver transplantation from a mother to her daughter, Dr. Charles B. Reiner, a Children's associate, reminded Columbus in a letter to the Dispatch of Dr. Kent's contribution to that advance.

82

Ending its first year in 1963 and already recording 250 to 300 visits a month, the new teen service was devoted to a special stage of growing-up just being recognized for the distinct problems it presented to medical practitioners and researchers.

Two additional floors of Ross Hall were under construction, with one major occupant on hand before adequate space was available. One of the most encumbered new arrivals in Children's history, Dr. Henry G. Cramblett, nationally known researcher in virology and microbiology at Bowman Gray School of Medicine, Wake Forest, N.C., came in the summer of 1964 to direct basic and clinical research in infectious disease. With him, packed in dry ice for the plane transfer to Columbus, came some 10,000 specimens related to his ongoing, NIH-sponsored research.

That summer the hospital also established the Children's Hospital Research Foundation (CHRF), a separate corporation designed to seek, direct and coordinate research activities. With an initial board representative of the hospital, university and community, it had a stated purpose to "foster and conduct basic and applied research in the physical, biological and medical sciences and other branches of learning." Three years later, total funds expended on grant-supported research at Children's passed the $1 million mark.

In early 1965, the National Institute of Allergy and Infectious Diseases announced establishment at Children's of the world's first rhinovirus reference center under the direction of Dr. Vincent Hamparian. It was to be kind of an international clearinghouse of data and material about a numerous and newly recognized group of viruses associated with the common cold and other respiratory diseases. The next year, a classification system developed by a team led by Hamparian and Dr. Robert Conant, which established 55 rhinovirus prototypes, was ratified by the International Congress of Microbiology at a Moscow meeting.

The rhinovirus center took over a renovated second-floor area when the Ross Hall addition was opened and dedicated in the fall of '65, and the fourth floor was occupied by laboratories and isolation-type areas particularly designed for viral research by Cramblett and other staff members. Dr. Albert H. Sabin, famed developer of oral polio vaccine, addressed the opening-day crowd of community leaders on the value of research.

The mid-'60s period brought others to Children's with research goals.

The U.S. Children's Bureau announced its first-ever national nutrition survey among preschool children, a five-year study to be launched at

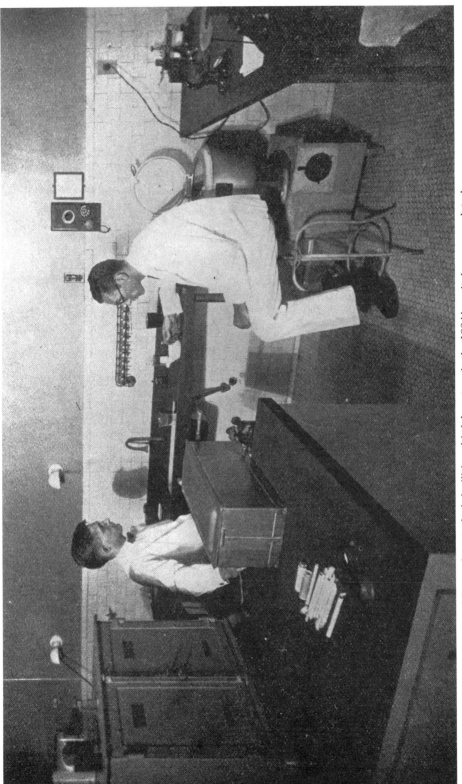

A far cry from today's facilities, this laboratory in the 1924 hospital accommodated Children's first real research efforts.

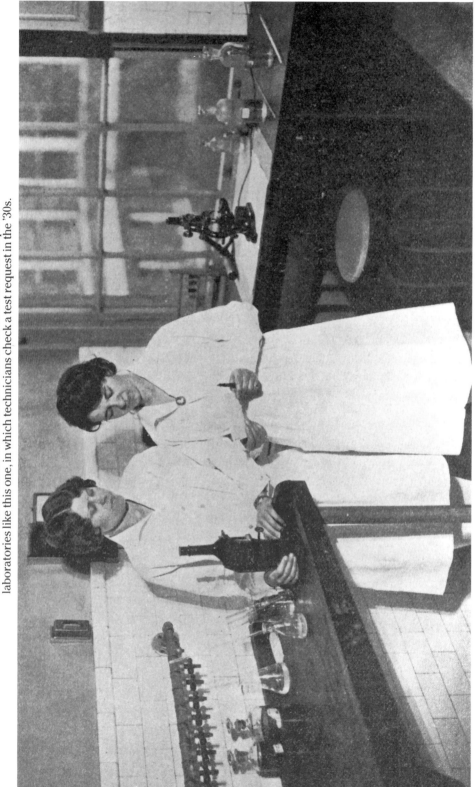

Advances in treatment and research taxed the staff and facilities of hospital laboratories like this one, in which technicians check a test request in the '30s.

Ross Hall, first stage, 1962.

Ross Hall, completed, 1965.

Greeted by Richard Sensenbrenner, son of the late Columbus mayor, Dr. Albert Sabin, conqueror of polio, came to help dedicate the Ross Research Building in 1965. In the reception group, from left, are Trustee George Kauffman, Administrator Clifford Rostomily, Dr. Bruce Graham, Dr. Henry Cramblett and Trustee David Cox.

Dr. S. Addanki with firefly "lanterns" for his space-age research.

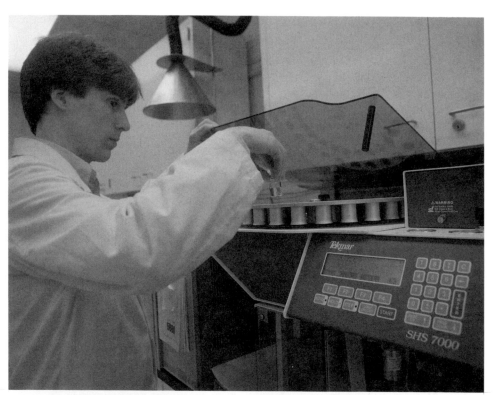

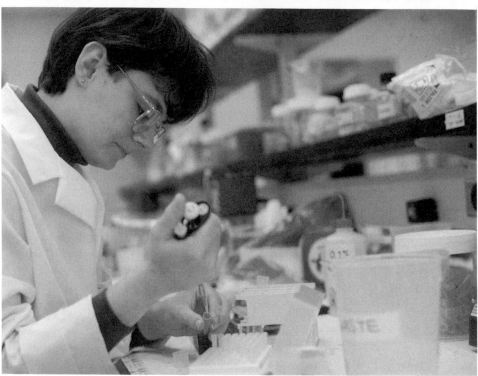

The spacious, well-equipped laboratories in The Wexner Institute provide the optimal setting for productive pediatric research.

Atrium of Wexner Institute.

Children's under the direction of Drs. George Owen and Carl Nelsen, chiefs of the hospital's nutrition and renal divisions, respectively.

The National Cystic Fibrosis Research Foundation signed on to support the work of Dr. Gordon Young in a clinical center at Children's focused on that puzzling hereditary disease. The State Health Department funded a rubella research and diagnostic laboratory.

Children's found a common interest with the burgeoning U.S. space program in one "far out" 1965 project for which Columbus-area Boy Scouts and other children collected and contributed several thousand fireflies. Both Children's and NASA scientists at Greenbelt, Md., were interested in secretions in the firefly lantern which light up in the presence of a chemical compound, adenosine triphosphate (ATP), found in living cells. NASA was interested in the extract to detect and signal living matter in space and help map the "terrestrial biosphere" around the earth. Dr. Somasundaram Addanki, working on childhood metabolic disease at Children's, found the firefly extract a faster, more sensitive means of measuring ATP content of tissue.

Now more than 20 years into significant research activity, Children's leadership saw much still to be done in broadening and strengthening the program and making it as impervious as possible to the vagaries of funding.

These needs were underscored in the early '70s when a major change in research funding by the National Institutes of Health not only reduced available grant money but greatly diminished federal support for the academic faculty, research facilities and equipment.

In the mid-'70s, studies under way embraced longstanding interests in birth defects, cancer, nutrition, genetics testing and evaluation of new drugs and vaccines, and environmental concerns such as lead poisoning control.

In 1974, climaxing a concentrated, all-out attack against a ferocious interloper of the '60s, Reye's Syndrome, Children's hosted an international conference for an exchange of research findings and treatment information. Thanks in large part to effective therapy developed at Children's, the mortality rate of 90 percent claimed by the swift killer in a peak period in the '70s had declined by the '90s below 20 percent.

In the late '70s, Dr. Earl Sherard, chief of neurology, supported efforts of a Columbus optometrist, Dr. Bernard Abrams, to secure for his daughter a drug used in Europe but not approved in the United States for a type of epilepsy. Sherard obtained supplies of the drug, sodium valproate, as a licensed investigator and treated patients from many states before the drug's eventual approval for commercial use. His published report in 1979 on 100 cases treated at Children's not only corroborated the drug's efficacy but, as the first U.S. study of a "pure pediatric population" of under-21 patients, provided useful additional data.

In the '80s, Children's took long strides toward a well-balanced, well-funded, comprehensive and competitive pediatric research program.

In October, 1983, CHRF approved the first five-year plan of a long-range planning committee. Its major goals were to foster basic research, attract physician scientists to expand both clinical and basic medical research teams, gain national recognition for CHRF, increase external funding and expand research support systems.

In 1989, with a second set of goals through 1993, the planning committee chaired by Dr. William Zipf could report almost full achievement of the first five-year effort.

Basic to the achievement, the committee pointed out, were the establishment of an academic practice plan to provide the financial base for faculty expansion and the completion of The Wexner Institute for Pediatric Research to attract and house the expanded research force.

The staff additions, a dramatic increase in both research proposals and research funding, two major international conferences held at Children's and the increasing use of the Institute for work and study by national and international scientists all attested to Children's growing stature among research centers, the committee noted.

In setting goals through 1993, the committee looked at national pediatric research priorities and, division by division, at research proposed and in progress at Children's. Each area was analyzed on the basis of its current strengths and potential and its interaction with other research areas, and areas were categorized as to needed development.

Other committee recommendations included establishment of a research endowment of $45 million consistent with those of other pediatric research institutions, development of a fellowship program, continued emphasis on research relating to nutrition and energy metabolism, and continued development of molecular biology and molecular genetics areas.

From 1981 until mid-1990, research at Children's had increased from 50 projects valued at $1.6 million to more than 150 with a total value of about $4.2 million.

Of particular importance, Dr. Hugh Harroff, CHRF administrative director, pointed out, was the substantial base of NIH-funded investigations in progress at Children's which qualified it to seek major, multi-million-dollar grants from the federal funding agency.

The vital importance of research to Children's total mission was explained in particularly lucid fashion during the annual "Science Day" program in 1988 by Dr. Grant Morrow, CHRF medical director.

"Parents and the community need to realize," he said, "that if you have a research environment and a group of professionals who are questioning how to do things better, then it makes for a more exciting and creative environment.

"It makes a big, big difference; by fostering such an environment, we are able to attract some of the best and brightest—people who want not just to provide state-of-the-art care, but who seek still better methods of care. We can attract the house staff, who are the residents in training, and the up-to-date, well-trained faculty to come here. And that whole process makes us double and triple check everything we're doing, as well as asking how we can do it better."

He added that research projects, which must be self-supporting, also bring dollars and their positive effect on the economy to the Columbus community.

Later, commenting that "we need to develop certain areas of excellence," the medical director noted that programs in cancer immunology, gastroenterology and nutrition are "doing well" and that other areas of major interest include virology, heart disease, trauma injury, and "the area of excitement for the '90s," molecular biology.

Also noting that "big programs like these take big dollars," he said CHRF trustees and grants personnel are aware of the vulnerability of a program that is 60 percent government-funded and are looking to for-profit corporations and the regional area Children's serves to build a broader base of support for research.

In the early '90s, research under way at Children's focused on some intriguing problems:

• Studies in infant nutrition and food assimilation with possible relevance to the world food shortage and to adult afflictions such as heart disease and osteoporosis.

• A search for communication pathways between the brain and immune system and for a way to detect and replace aberrant genes associated with deficiency diseases and some forms of cancer.

• Studies related to dietary programs for patients with such diseases as cystic fibrosis, chronic dysentery, colitis and cancer; on teenage obesity; and on the effect of various dietary regimens on teenage physical and mental performance.

• A search for the proper stratagems for successful intestinal transplants.

In the summer of 1990, Dr. Long-Sheng Chang from Princeton University and Dr. Chack-Yung Yu from England's Cambridge University, both molecular biologists, joined the CHRF staff, adding that important expertise to the research team.

Ticking off the gains in facilities, funding and staff that are bringing the Children's investigative force to fighting strength, Morrow spoke of several disease problems—cystic fibrosis, Down's Syndrome—so tantalizingly close to solution. "No one," he said, "has exclusivity on a breakthrough."

The Reye's Syndrome Story

When Children's celebrated the 25th anniversary of the Children's Hospital Research Foundation in 1989, the program focused on the hospital's long, triumphant battle with Reye's Syndrome, a fast-acting killer disease. It was an apt choice, demonstrative of Children's special capabilities and resources.

When CHRF was founded in 1964, the disease had just emerged in medical literature, described by an Australian pathologist and others—an onset of severe flu-like symptoms followed rapidly by organ degeneration, brain swelling and, all too often, death.

As Reye's took its toll over the next several years, a fearsome scourge in winter months as polio had once been in summer, its U.S. attack focused on the Great Lakes area of Ohio, Michigan, Wisconsin and neighboring states. Children's was seeing more and more cases with discouragingly few means to help them.

Researchers, clinicians and parents of Reye's victims joined forces in a retaliatory attack that became centered at Children's.

In an effort Dr. Dennis Pollack, OSU microbiologist, described in 1974 as "one of the most intensive study groups in the country on this disease," Children's had five teams working "steadily, constantly since 1968," he said, on the pathology, diagnosis, etiology, management and therapy aspects of Reye's.

Pollack made his published comment in announcing the first international symposium on Reye's, sponsored in Columbus by CHRF in October, 1974.

At the anniversary celebration, Dr. Juhling McClung, associate medical director, described the intensive effort as he found it when he came to Children's in the '70s—"a siege, or 'war-room' mentality" that was focused and pervasive against "a raging illness where the battle was won or lost within 36 hours."

McClung described the wide-ranging, never-definitive search for a cause—studies of aspirin, a major suspect, and forays by the Ohio Health Department's Dr. Thomas Halpin into homes to check tablet counts in aspirin bottles; a long look at agricultural chemicals; suspicious triggering toxins across the world including "a fungus that grows on peanuts."

Parents enlisted in the fight after two Bryan, Ohio, couples whose daughters had been Reye's patients at Children's determined to help raise research support. By 1977, the National Reye's Syndrome Foundation had more than a dozen working chapters in Ohio and neighboring states. In 1977 also, the family and friends of 13-year-old Tommy Fisher of Worthington met most of the cost, as a memorial to Tommy, for sophisticated monitoring equipment designed at Children's to track vital signs of Reye's victims.

In sum, Children's major role in the Reye's fight, McClung said, included establishment of the foundation, the assembling of the scientific community for a focused thrust and the development of innovative therapy.

He noted the special input of Dr. Earl Sherard, former chief of neurology, who "used to lie awake at night thinking about ways to understand the bio-chemical findings"; Dr. Carolyn Romshe, first to present a Reye's test that didn't require liver biopsy; Dr. Milo Hilty, who with Sherard formulated the drug using glycerol, a natural nutrient produced by the body, to treat the disease.

A special guest at the silver-anniversary party was Dawn Howard of Summit Station, Ohio, who, 12 years earlier, was the first child treated at Children's with glycerol therapy. An attractive, healthy 18-year-old, she listened with her fiance as her mother described the sequence of terror and joy as the therapy brought her daughter back from a once-irreversible coma.

Education
Training for Today and Tomorrow

T hroughout its first 100 years, Children's has shared its growing expertise in the care and treatment of children with students, health professionals and the community.

The hospital's involvement with education dates from the very early days when the first nurse supervisors trained newcomers to the staff, set up classes in child care for nurses in the community, and began to offer instruction to parents bringing children to the dispensary. Today's complex, many-faceted and far-reaching educational programs grew from those beginnings.

Most important in the development of Children's educational mission, and indeed to the stature and growth of both participants, is the affiliation with the Ohio State University College of Medicine which started in a cautious, tentative way in 1916.

Through most of the next two decades, OSU medical students, and students in allied fields, came to Children's for some part of their training, although the program was far short of ideal. Pediatrics training through those years consisted largely of lectures, Dr. Baxter noted in his history, and students saw patients in two small and widely separated units at Children's and at OSU's Starling Loving Hospital.

House coverage for Children's by staff physicians or physicians in training was a persistent problem, Baxter added, and was intermittent at best. He found sketchy records of a 1918 OSU graduate who was an extern at the first Children's in 1918, several more interns through the '20s, and a pediatrics resident in 1931.

Residencies approved by both OSU and the hospital were not possible, he added, until the university's pediatrics division was given departmental status in 1941.

It was only after that, and with Baxter now holding joint titles as chief of Children's medical staff and chairman of the new OSU department, that the full program of pediatrics teaching was centered at Children's.

Meanwhile, a years-long debate (which some still argue) continued on whether Children's should become a part of OSU (physically and/or organizationally) or retain its geographical and organizational separateness as a community hospital with a strong teaching affiliation with the university.

Nearly everyone now agrees that the hospital trustees' decision in 1969 to proceed with construction of the new hospital building finally determined Children's future on the latter course.

However, these years of interim decisions and rejected overtures paralleled a steady expansion and enrichment of the affiliation itself.

Significantly, during the time trustees were determining the hospital's future course, Dr. Richard L. Meiling, dean of the College of Medicine, became a member of the hospital board, the first in that position to do so. (Dr. Starling Loving, a member of the original Children's board and a nationally known medical educator, came close. He was still a Children's trustee when he resigned as dean of the faculty of the old Starling Medical College just before its 1907 merger with the Ohio Medical University to form Starling-Ohio Medical College. Seven years later, Starling-Ohio merged with the OSU College of Medicine.)

While education is the strong core of the Children's-OSU affiliation, now grown in size and scope to include hundreds of students in medical and related career fields, the affiliation also involves collaboration and cooperation between the two institutions in the other major missions common to both, patient care and research. In 1988, the hospital's research foundation and the university signed a formal research agreement.

Amazingly, as officials of both institutions attest, the basic affiliation is still loosely constituted, built much more on good faith than formal documentation—perhaps the only such pact, Dr. Manuel Tzagournis thinks, involving institutions of such size.

"It's good for us, and good for Children's," said Tzagournis, dean of the medical college and OSU vice president for health services. "Children's is a large pediatric hospital—the fourth in the country in the number of medical students. We need it."

In the area health care system, Children's and OSU are mutually "set apart," he noted, "in the way we operate, the way we're organized, with more than patient care as our primary mission."

Like Children's officials, Tzagournis termed the establishment of the OSU medical practice plan in July, 1979, an important step for both institutions in guaranteeing more equitable remuneration for physicians devoting their time to academic medicine and research.

He also noted that the OSU College of Medicine was a co-applicant for state funding for Children's new education center and that funds granted by the legislature will be administered through OSU.

A member of Children's board of trustees, Tzagournis, like many of his Central Ohio medical colleagues, did his two months' rotation in pediatrics at Children's as an OSU medical student, returned for three months' elective training in surgery, and takes more than official interest in its welfare.

Students from 13 schools of nursing listen to lecturer Marilyn Webster in a Timken classroom in the '60s.

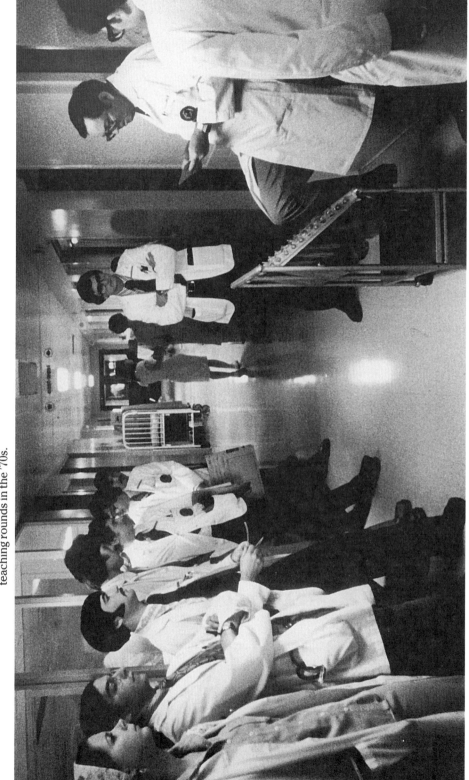

Dr. Henry Cramblett lectures in hallway of new infectious diseases unit during teaching rounds in the '70s.

The education of medical students and residents is a major focus of teaching hospitals such as Children's.

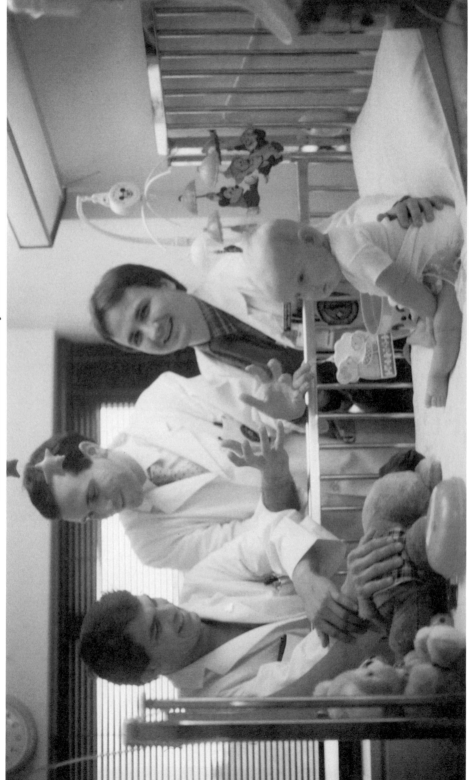

Children's residents make their daily rounds.

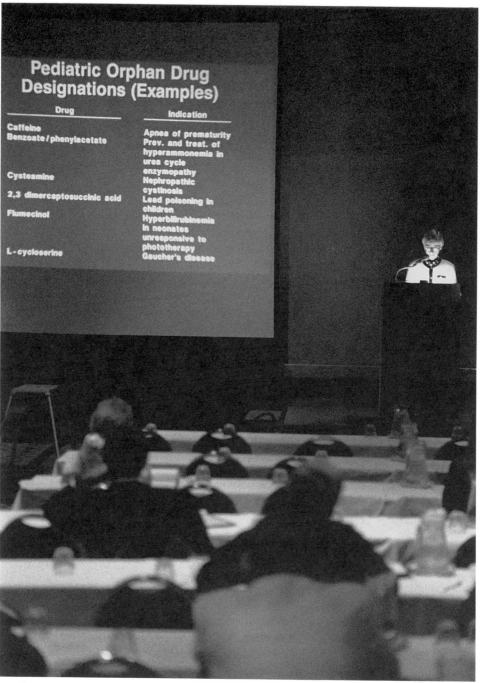

Drug therapy for children was the topic of the Third International Wexner Symposium in 1990.

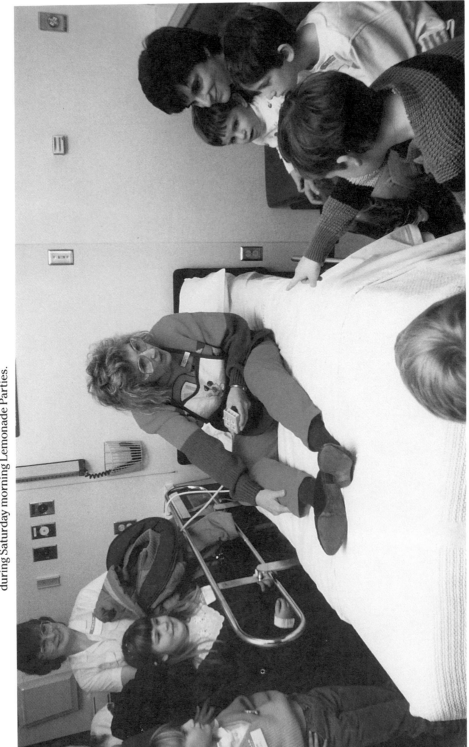

Patients scheduled for hospital admission, with their families, learn about Children's during Saturday morning Lemonade Parties.

An architectural rendering of the hospital's new Education Building.

He believes the Columbus training program is producing "about the right number" of pediatric physicians, perhaps with somewhat fewer in cities and more in less-populated areas. He thinks Children's merits the community's support as "the appropriate place" for treating children.

He also thinks the OSU-Children's affiliation, with its "good faith" basis, is working fine and that "there is nothing I can envision that would affect it."

Other medical colleges have difficulties with pediatric training, he said, adding with a smile, "I feel fortunate as dean that I have no problem trying to connect a pediatrics program and a hospital."

In the "apartness" Tzagournis found in the three-fold mission Children's and OSU share, Dr. Grant Morrow, Children's medical director, also noted an advantage.

"There are a couple of things about an institution that distinguish 'good' from 'excellent,' " he said. "One is that the academic mantle allows us to get that small margin of excellence in recruiting people."

Children's educational program has grown incredibly through the years, not as an extra or separate function, but one steadily focused on the needs of the children seeking the hospital's help. They are the ultimate beneficiaries of every lecture and seminar, every training course for staff or parents or community workers, every support group meeting and international symposium.

In 1991, education was more than a $6 million item in Children's budget. Dr. Karen Heiser, director of education, detailed where the funds go.

• Student affiliation. In addition to 65 full-time pediatric residents, Children's provides pediatric training each year to more than 200 residents and 240 medical students from all over Ohio, more than 700 nurses from 13 Ohio colleges of nursing, and another 250 students in psychology, occupational and physical therapy, pharmacy, radiology, biomedical engineering, social work and hospital administration. Hospital space is provided for nearly 100 OSU faculty members and support staff.

• Professional outreach. In 1989, 15,000 participants came for conferences including international research symposia, specialty programs in new clinical procedures, social and behavioral concerns of children, and professional continuing education.

• Community education involved 13,000 children, adolescents and adults in conferences, community appearances by hospital spokespersons, health fairs, hospital tours and Explorer Groups (twice-a-month programs for high school students considering health careers); 33 support groups for families of patients with special problems; tours and special events for Children's Adopt-a-School projects at Colerain and Livingston schools.

• Staff development includes some 350 in-service and continuing education programs for the hospital's 2,800 employees and 500 in-hospital volunteers—from orientation and annual updates to advanced skill and management development. Children's gives 125 scholarship awards, gives tuition assistance to 250 staff members and offers career assessment and counseling services.

• Inpatient and family education involved some 8,000 children and parents during 1990—preadmission programs, inpatient Child Life activities, school instruction and closed circuit TV for children, special classes (prematurity, renal dialysis, etc.), written materials and home-going instructions for parents.

Although Children's is one of the few pediatric centers with a centralized education department, Heiser said, its programs are carried on in facilities inadequate in both space and design. Although some recent hospital-sponsored gatherings of specialists have necessarily been held outside the hospital complex, it is amazing how much has been ventured beyond comfortable accommodation.

"The new building will enable us to do so much more," Heiser said. Education forges a special link between the hospital and its patients and the community, she said, "and gives us ways to repay the community." She mentioned specifically training classes for paramedic squads and for "about 2,500 child-care workers just in 1990."

While the new building will have the latest in instructional and informational technology, it will also fill long-unmet basic needs for faculty offices and study and locker space for students.

Heiser detailed some of its features:

A conference center with an auditorium and meeting rooms "for internal and external use"; an extensive library, maintained jointly with OSU, and with a special section for parents and patients; a computer instruction center and a skills laboratory with special equipment to teach medical and nursing students; an audio-visual studio and publications office, both of which the hospital can use in producing its own educational materials.

Special equipment will allow for satellite teleconferences with medical and hospital groups—"maybe one speaker talking to thousands," Heiser said—and even for an "uplink hook so we could transmit for an international conference."

Children's did a survey among physicians, Heiser said, asking them how much time they spent on patient education, and they responded, "60 percent."

That is an indication of the increasing emphasis on education in providing good health care, she said, and underscores Children's intent to accommodate and expand its educational programs.

In their application for state funding for the education building, Children's officials pointed out that, through its history, the hospital has fulfilled its educational commitment without financial support from the state, Ohio State University or other affiliated colleges.

They also said that the hospital will continue that commitment and, when the new center is completed, will meet its operating costs from hospital funds.

Even before the first symbolic earth-turning for the new center in July, 1990, discussions were in progress on how the hospital's strengthened educational arm can now be used even more broadly and effectively in behalf of children.

Nursing
A Tradition of Caring

Nurses who care for small children meet special needs of their patients, but nurses throughout the history of Children's have gone beyond that. Through most of its first 50 years, the nursing staff was the resident constant for the levels of care and treatment the hospital sought to give.

Until Robert Porter's appointment as administrator in 1942, all but one of the matrons and superintendents had been graduate nurses. Their nursing staffs, gradually increasing in professionalism, carried out the instructions of doctors who came and went, performed myriad duties today allotted to an echelon of staff workers, were the first line of defense in inevitable emergencies, and served as surrogate comforters and cuddlers to small patients who saw their parents only on one-hour weekly visits.

Although a study of Children's as early as 1914 stressed the urgent need for a physician on regular duty in the hospital, attempts of the governing boards to fulfill this need from graduate rosters of the OSU medical school remained an on-again, off-again kind of effort through several decades.

Nowhere in Children's first 100 years is there more dramatic contrast than between those first "assistant nurses" who signed on with Miss Bertha O. Boswinkle in 1893 and skilled, highly trained professionals on the hospital's nursing roster today.

Significantly, the original by-laws of the hospital prescribe that "assistant nurses must be able to read and write" and be "subject to the direction of visiting physicians, the house physician and the matron."

Significantly also, the by-laws made provisions for "nurses in training." Records reveal that from the very beginning the nursing staffs sought to improve their own performance and share their experience with incoming staff members and other nurses in the community.

Through the years, the training program evolved with advances in treatment. As early as 1903, Children's had a certification program for nurses trained at the hospital. In the '30s it established the first training course for student and graduate nurses from hospitals in Ohio and neighboring states. In 1943, after the arrival of Elgie M. Wallinger as director of nursing, she worked with Porter and Baxter to establish the Department of Nursing Education which at that time included 75 students from nine affiliating schools.

By 1960, the hospital's program was serving approximately 100 students from 11 affiliated schools each academic quarter whose time was divided between classroom instruction and care of patients. More and more the four-year college degree course was replacing the three-year training program, hospitals were closing their schools of nursing, and the students' role in the hospital's patient care service diminished.

By 1971, most of the three-year programs had been phased out, Children's closed its affiliate program, and students from the OSU School of Nursing under instruction of OSU faculty members came to Children's for that phase of their training.

Veteran nurses at Children's regret the change, insofar as it reduces students' early contact with patients, but recognize the vastly greater knowledge and expertise today's graduate nurse must have.

Combining more years of service to Children's than the hospital is old, a group of longtime nurses shared their memories and filled in sparse records of people and events from their distinctive points of view.

Like Jacqueline Kruman, former director of nursing, Grace Ellis, Kathyrn Cottrell and Phyllis Fristoe ranged from the patient's bedside to an administrative desk during their nursing years.

During her years in the emergency department, Evalee Leeper was the first port of call for news reporters in the era before television and hospital public relations departments. Venoie Olson Amey, trained in the Sister Kenny method of caring for polio patients, was an equally valuable source of information and explanation after she came to Children's in 1948 to supervise the hospital's jam-packed polio unit.

The scrapbook collection of Mrs. Leeper, who died in 1988, reaches back furthest to those 1890 counterparts who formed Children's first nursing staff. The original by-laws provided for a 9 p.m. to 7 a.m. shift for night nurses, apparently leaving to day nurses the other 14 hours. Later, and for a long time, nurses worked one of two 12-hour shifts with two half-days off a week. No record of their salary exists, but it was somewhere below the original less-than-$50 a month the matron received and, like hers, included meals and lodging.

Most of all, today's nurses empathize with those early predecessors about the limitations and frustrations they must have felt in trying to help small patients—the frequent notation on early records of a child sent home "improved" with a disease or deformity modern medicine can cure.

Within the lifetime and/or professional career of many of Children's nurses came the great breakthroughs that conquered so many infections and diseases, made so many more corrective procedures possible, and decreased children's hospital stays to shorter and much pleasanter periods.

Among crisis times they remember, World War II and the polio years loom large. With wartime shortages and depleted staffs, nurses and supervisors worked long hours and took on extra duties which could range from instructing a student while assisting a surgeon to, on occasion, scrubbing the floors.

The polio onslaughts were distinguished not only by overcrowding, Mrs. Amey said, but by the initially tentative approach to both pain relief and rehabilitative therapy for polio sufferers.

The work of Salk and Sabin conquered polio while better ways to treat its effects were still being sought. (The best hope of cancer researchers is for a similar breakthrough—a way to prevent or cure that complex and dreaded disease even before it is fully understood.)

Since Children's became the recognized center for polio treatment in the area, an influx of adult patients brought extra stresses and strains to a hospital tailored to small patients. Mrs. Amey recalled a mother's delivery of a baby with an oxygen bubble over her head and the man who continued to run his insurance business from an iron lung.

As for the crowding?

"At one time, in old Room 200, which was comfortable for six patients, we would have 16," she said. "We would have to pull each bed into the hall to give that patient care."

Meanwhile, Mrs. Leeper saw another facet of the epidemics—an always busy emergency area, which had just three examining rooms and a surgical room, occasionally overrun by anxious parents and children.

"If one child in a family got polio, or one child in a school, parents would panic. They'd bring in the rest of the kids, sometimes we'd get a school bus load, and we'd do spinal taps on each one—the only way we had to confirm diagnosis."

The emergency room also got the first frantic calls when a child had swallowed something caustic or poisonous. The proliferation of new chemical products after World War II increased these calls, Mrs. Leeper said, and "we had a little black box with a card file on ingredients, antidotes, who to call." From that black box and its increasing inadequacy grew the Central Ohio Poison Center, one of Children's most valued services.

Nurses who watched Children's grow and change are proud of the initiative it showed in improving and extending care of children, and in the role nurses played in those changes.

"During the war years, nurses were evaluated on their ability to improvise," Miss Kruman remembered. Nurses were the first hospital staff units to write out procedures, she said, and became early students of emerging new concepts about child growth and development.

With the gradual decline of "the old idea of keeping mothers away from sick babies," Miss Ellis recalled, came installation of the first folding cots for mothers in patient rooms and Children's national preeminence since then in accommodating parents of sick youngsters.

They remembered the "big step" to intravenous equipment and the early requirement that a nurse sit by the patient's bedside until the fluid flow was completed.

Noting that care of the acutely ill patient is one of the great demands on nurses today, they recalled the beginnings of an intensive care unit at Children's, spearheaded by Dr. Clatworthy.

"First we had to find a room, finally found one for three or four patients, then we had to have a staff," Miss Kruman said. "Then, we got a regular ICU unit'for six or eight. Now, we have great equipment, but the nurse still has to make decisions at the bedside or in monitoring the patient."

With all the options today's nursing graduates have, will hospitals like Children's continue to attract enough of the good ones?

The women who have spent their professional lives there hope and believe so. But it's not for everyone.

"Pediatric nurses and doctors have to have great compassion or they couldn't do it," said Miss Cottrell. "They have to interact with patients, and they have to have a sense of humor. Children can be trying—then so naive, and so pathetic. They get sick so fast, and get well so fast."

Agreeing, Miss Kruman remembered, "When we did the first heart surgeries, they'd be sitting up reading comic books the next day.

"I've always felt something different about a children's hospital," she added, "in the way we treat, not just technically but psychologically. In many ways, pediatric hospitals have taken the lead in improved patient care."

One such pioneering concept, which she inaugurated in 1963, was the continuity of care program with Mrs. Leeper as first coordinator and Dr. Clatworthy as physician advisor.

Focused on the patient who would require short-term or long-term care at home, the program involved working with parents, medical and nursing staffs, other hospital departments and public health agencies to facilitate and support the hospital-to-home transition. Further development of the concept throughout the years has included the popular and useful Helping Hand program of educational material for parents, initiated by the Children's nursing division and utilized throughout the country.

Although her death in 1988 precluded her direct contribution to a history of Children's, Miss Wallinger, nursing director from 1943 through 1960, played a major role in it and in the positive changes her fellow nurses recalled.

Small, trim, brisk and a complete professional, she was a standard-setter, they said, both in nursing education and in the care given sick children. The author of a widely used nursing textbook, Miss Wallinger worked with other Children's administrators to improve those standards during her busy years at Children's.

Nurses' sitting room in the "new" 1924 building.

Elgie M. Wallinger, Nursing Director, 1943-61.

Children's nurse meets the friend of a friend.

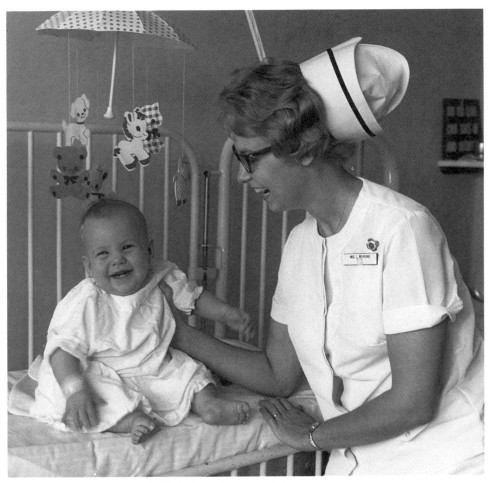

Children's nurse L. Wehrling and a happy baby share a precious moment.

Evalee Leeper, R.N., first contact for news media in Children's emergency room in the '50s.

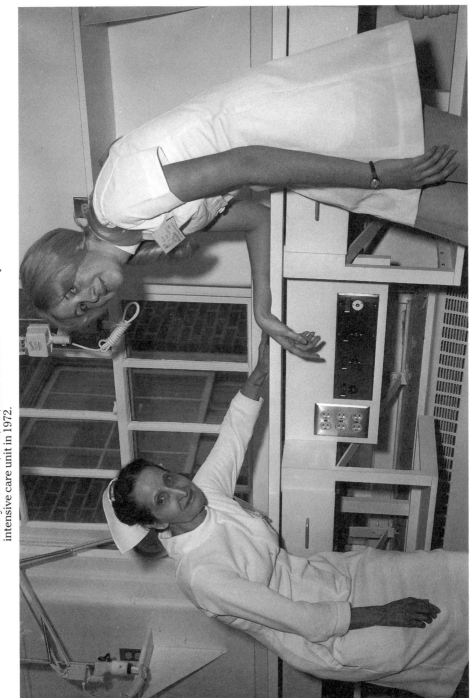

Kathryn Cottrell, R.N., left, and Pat Kabbes in the newly-remodeled infant intensive care unit in 1972.

She spent her nursing career in Ohio but was "very devoutly southern," as Miss Fristoe put it, and returned to her native Tennessee after retiring.

An excellent paper from Children's nursing files, unfortunately neither titled nor dated, gives a fascinating picture of the responsibilities of the pediatric nurse, probably in the late '60s or early '70s.

"Today's pediatric nurse . . . must be at once a biochemist and a hydraulics engineer; an electrician and a technician in humidity conditioning and air handling; a plumber, a mechanic, and a physicist; a statistician and an accountant; a social worker, a sentinel and a mother.

"She must have a deep technical understanding of everything she does and *everything the physician does.* With children, minute variations in progress and reactions are important, and she must know what to look for and what to report, whether the actual procedure is her own responsibility or the doctor's."

Details may change, but the basic premise is the same as two decades ago or in the old, old Children's. Nurses are still the largest single professional force within the hospital, and they are still the first line of defense for sick children when problems develop.

In recent years, in the face of widening career opportunities for nurses, a general shortage of hospital nurses and the concerns of nurses about professional status and advancement, Children's has looked for solutions.

A major step for nurses, patients and patient families was the implementation of the primary nurse plan in which one nurse has particular responsibility for and contact with each patient throughout the child's hospital stay.

In October, 1988, Children's began to phase in a new clinical advancement program designed to encourage and reward nurses who want to continue direct care of patients with increased salary and responsibility.

Work on the advancement program had begun in 1987, when Children's formed a Nursing Recruitment and Retention Task Force for a long-range attack on the nursing problem. In 1989, that effort was rewarded by a $50,000 planning grant from the Pew Charitable Trusts of Philadelphia in collaboration with the Robert Wood Johnson Foundation. With or without hoped-for further funding, Children's would develop and carry out a five-year plan for restructuring patient-care delivery. The ultimate goal is the best possible patient care; the study involves not only nursing but its interaction with ancillary and support services, and how they all might benefit from changes.

This five-year Patient Care Planning program started in 1990 with 23 interdisciplinary teams of employees, representing every patient unit. Individually, teams discussed the type of patient care they would like to see in their areas by 1995 and created "vision statements" listing their goals.

One year later, in a series of "revisioning retreats," they reviewed program strengths and accomplishments, refined their original "vision statements" and defined specific goals for the next years, always within the context of the five-year planning process for better patient care.

"Each individual has the ability to improve patient care every day," said Sharon Stout-Shaffer, R.N., project coordinator, who presided over most of the retreats. "But program goals, as developed by staff on units, provide an opportunity for all staff to work as a team to improve care for our patients and families."

Recruitment and retention of excellent nurses will be essential to the hospital's growth and development as the institution expands current programs and adds new ones.

A good example of an innovative program is Children's Homecare Services (CHS). Established Dec. 4, 1990, CHS provides an alternative for children who need specialized medical treatment but do not require hospital care.

"CHS is a hospital-based but community-oriented program," said CHS Director Sam Chapman, R.N., who was instrumental in founding the program. With the expertise of pediatric clinical personnel and with equipment designed and sized for children, she added, "I believe we can offer a better, more family-focused program than any now available. Kids recover better at home, and I see our agency becoming an important advocate for that kind of care."

The program offers such in-home services as transfusions, total parenteral nutrition, enteral nutrition (tube feedings), IV antibiotics, chemotherapy, hemophilia therapy, pain management, fluid replacement therapy, blood drawing, and physical, occupational and respiratory therapy.

For the nurses involved, CHS is another extension of the major satisfaction of pediatric nursing—working with children and families, and helping sick children get better.

Tamar Gilson was a student nurse at Children's in the Elgie Wallinger era, returned as a staff nurse in the '60s, and was a nursing administrator and director of nursing through the '70s and '80s. Currently corporate director of community and education services, she envisioned the role of today's pediatric nurse as an exemplar within her own profession and an increasingly important force in the hospital and the community.

"I see the nurses in pediatric hospitals setting the example," she said. "More nurses will be doctorally prepared, involved in scholarly pursuits for their own growth and with minds directed to better methods of delivering service and to research for new ideas in care, treatment and systems."

In the increasing influence of computerization and technology on the delivery of nursing service, the nurse is still "the coordinating mainstay," Gilson pointed out. At a time "when hospitals are being decentralized to living rooms," families will rely on nurses in new ways. Nurses will also be "partnered in new settings," she predicted, to assist school systems "just overwhelmed with the health and social problems of children."

Nurses are becoming "far more attuned to community leadership," she said, and will become increasingly involved with public and political affairs.

Finally, she spoke of staff involvement in the hospital's overseas affiliations. "Here we are, in a magnet center, reaching out in a global sense to teach health care—in Israel, Italy, now Romania. That is a very special opportunity, very exciting for our hospital, very meaningful to Columbus."

Staff
A Commitment to Quality

Originally, they were fewer than a half-dozen, handling the simple cooking, cleaning, building and grounds maintenance work required for a larger-than-average family home. Today, they number more than 2,800, performing the myriad services that keep a huge, sophisticated specialty hospital running smoothly.

Implicit in every expansion move, treatment advance, research effort, new program or any other development recorded in this 100-year history are the individual contributions of hundreds of personnel.

Sharing their memories, observations and feelings, a group of men and women with more than two centuries' worth of collective service to Children's talked of good times and bad times.

They included Mary Lou Herron, former assistant director of nursing and night supervisor; Wayne Potts, programming manager in data processing; Dan Kozelek, former internal auditor in administration; Albert Goss of personnel and environmental services; Arletta McGill, unit clerk specialist; Roswell "Whitey" Thomas, formerly of engineering; and LaVerne King, former acting director and long-time assistant director of clinical social work.

Children's has been spared major disaster, but, with patients dependent on life-sustaining equipment and controlled temperatures, every weather-related emergency or major service disruption calls for extraordinary response.

"We almost lost the heating during the 1978 blizzard," Thomas remembered. "I had just got to the hospital and started down the ramp when a six-inch steam pipe burst. Everybody with a four-wheel vehicle was recruited. Everybody stayed and worked. I remember (Executive Director) Stu Williams folding diapers and helping to cook breakfast one morning."

There was the time the hospital lost all electricity, they recalled, when "all the disciplines pulled together for 27 hours" to carry on with makeshift measures. "We kept sending over to Kroger's for extension cords" to keep vital support systems in operation.

There was the 1979 flood, when one January working day for most marooned employees was extended to three days and nights.

Sometimes, even eventual blessings come disguised in confusion and disruption, the staff veterans remembered: computerization, new communications systems, the many moves dictated by expansion.

Relocation has become a decades-long way of life as the hospital encompasses new space. "Just yesterday," said Goss, "we moved all the time cards from one end of the building to another."

As in most institutions, the initial impact of the computer age in the mid-'60s was anything but time saving, they agreed. However, the gradual transition to new information and communication systems, starting with accounting procedures, extends now to every part of the hospital, stilling the clacking typewriters in offices and saving countless hours and steps.

Push-button communication has, for some personnel, limited their direct contact with patients, they said, but has in no way decreased their awareness of the children they serve.

That, said King, is a hallmark of the hospital. "It's an infectious thing. You are always aware, in what you do, of who you are doing it for."

Agreeing, Thomas added some personal motivation. "My son had three major surgeries here, the last one at 13. He's 22 now, and six feet two."

Even today, he said, there are special things the hospital needs and cannot buy. He recalled building two cradles and constructing an operating table to meet a particular need. "You're not a doctor," he said, "but you do what you can."

In the summer of 1990, Children's initiated a new recognition program for employees who exemplify by acts or services the meaning and values of the hospital—a monthly "From the Heart" award to persons nominated by parents, patients, visitors or their peers.

Early recipients included:

• Albert Goss, one of the employee spokespersons for this chapter, who devoted more than a year's time in appointments, interviews and paper work to help a fellow employee obtain a prosthetic device.

• Sally Jo Zuspan, former trauma coordinator, who was on duty when a one-year-old child died from auto accident injuries soon after arrival in the emergency room. Knowing the critically injured mother was in intensive care at another hospital, she took the child to the mother for a last farewell.

• Ernestine Roe, medical lab technician in hematology/oncology, who keeps the toy box filled for small patients, sees that patients and families receive Christmas remembrances and on one occasion used vacation time to accompany a patient who could not otherwise have gone to receive a bone marrow transplant in Seattle.

• Cheryl Rodgers, administrative secretary, CHRF, whose charitable activities include spearheading an effort to provide food for volunteers on telethon day and spending hours compiling a cookbook to raise funds for Operation Feed.

Woody Hayes was a surprise guest at a special after-midnight party for Mary Lou Herron, R.N., given by her night-shift cohorts.

Children's looked besieged by the snows of the 1978 blizzard, but the staff coped with the emergency as it has with many through 100 years.

Children's Hospital staff members celebrating major service anniversaries and earning other honors are saluted at an annual recognition dinner.

Rosalyn Bandman

• Sandra Sass, who led an "adopt-a-family" Christmas project in the personnel department, found out needs and provided specifics for the nine-member family on sizes, wished-for toys, etc., and delivered a van-full of wrapped gifts shortly before Christmas.

From the well-remembered nurse who befriended a lonely little girl in 1907 to these heartwarming stories in recent employee publications, Children's annals are full of instances in which staff care and concern for small patients far exceeded job descriptions.

The caring attitude of the Children's staff, McGill wanted to be first to attest, extends not only to patients, but to each other. She grew up in the shadow of the hospital, volunteered at 12 to distribute water to patients, and signed on as an employee—on a paper towel supplied by a nurse—during a hospital visit in 1956 with one of her five sons.

Honored as November, 1988, Employee of the Month for her own dedication, she described how doctors and fellow staffers took personal interest in her advancement and how nurses adapted their commuting schedules to give her transportation during the seven years she held two jobs to pay for her home.

The high point of staff camaraderie for Herron, an avid Buckeye fan, was when her night-shift cohorts planned a wee-small-hours party for her with a section of then-new Ohio Stadium Astroturf, secured from Woody Hayes, as a featured gift. The real surprise, which rendered her uncharacteristically speechless, she said, was when Woody, intrigued by the plans, showed up at 2 a.m. to join the party.

Not all night visitors were as welcome, she remembered, when the security force, now well-staffed and well-equipped, consisted of one man armed with a gun that had no firing pin.

"I used to encounter some weird characters in the elevators," Herron said, "but I could usually stare them down. I think it was the cap," she added, referring to that symbol of authority most nurses no longer wear.

Most welcome, she said, were the frequent after-hours visits by Stu Williams, "one of the most people-oriented persons I've ever known."

The executive director may show up anytime, "even three o'clock in the morning," she said. "First, he'll ask about the patients. Then he'll say, 'And how are all the people doing?' That's us."

Others noted that Janet Porter, administrative director, has taken to such nocturnal visits, and that another recent drop-in caller, one time at 5 a.m., has been Arthur J. Kobacker, immediate past president of the board of trustees.

"Children's is employee-oriented," said Goss. "The retirees' club, for instance. You'd be amazed at the response we have for every event scheduled for them. They all know that when they leave they're not going to be forgotten."

Collectively, this articulate group of veterans gave the strong impression that the people who work at Children's, and make Children's work, share a distinctive pride.

"When you meet someone, and you say you work at Children's, they look at you differently," said Kozelek.

"Nothing in the world takes the place of caring people," declared Herron, "and there are none greater than the people who work here."

"You know you work for a place where no child is ever turned away," said King. "And that is a beautiful thought."

Social Work

With many families coming to Children's comprehensive health care centers, said Dr. Antoinette Eaton, corporate director of governmental affairs, "their social service needs can outweigh their medical needs."

"I feel good about where we are now," said the late Rosalyn Bandman, longtime director of the Department of Clinical Social Work. "We've grown from giving meal tickets and providing transportation to looking at the total needs of a family."

The evolution of social service illustrated by their comments began very early in Children's history with the realization that total care for the sick child in the hospital extends to and involves the family back home.

The early hospital did what it could, with its own small staff and the help of community agencies. In 1916, Children's acquired its first trained social worker and began to build a staff. In 1950, with the arrival of Bandman, the Department of Clinical Social Work was established.

In an interview shortly before her retirement in 1989, and her death the following year, she assessed the changing, and unchanging, nature of family problems from a 39-year perspective.

"In the broadest sense, the same problems were all here when Children's started," she said. "Types of problems change. Family mobility is greater. We have more violence today, drugs and alcohol, teenage pregnancy. Thirty years ago, we didn't identify child abuse as such."

The impact on a child and a family of critical and chronic illness, disability and handicaps and scores of other problems can't be measured nor solved with dollars, she said, and the role of the social worker has grown from "financial evaluator" to a team specialist dealing with those problems.

She spoke particularly of the child abuse program, in which she became a recognized leader and for which she secured a $250,000 Federal Demonstration Grant, the first in Ohio, in 1975.

"In 1971, we reported 71 cases of child abuse," Bandman said. "In 1987, we assessed more than 1,100 and reported 800. But—we know more, people are more alert to the issue, kids (even preschoolers) are better educated, and our ability to evaluate kids is becoming more efficient."

With the best efforts, however, she conceded, sexual abuse cases were still on the increase and physical abuse cases seen at Children's had dropped in number but were more serious.

On the positive side, she ticked off "a lot done in prevention" through the '80s in education and special programs for parents and for staffs of child-protection agencies in dealing with children with a range of special problems.

Gratified with the changed role of the social worker during her years at Children's, she envisioned even greater opportunity. The expert on psycho-social relationships, she said, should be "as normal a part of treatment as the doctor and the nurse" and the social service department "more a total part of teaching and research."

Plainly, she helped this happen at Children's. Recalling the small hospital she joined in 1950, and the subsequent development in complexity and sophistication, she declared:

"We have to change with society, and this place has never stopped challenging. There are institutions that stagnate. Children's isn't one of them."

In her memory, the Rosalyn Bandman Scholarship for Social Work was established by her family, friends and co-workers.

Guidance Centers
Coping with Childhood Stresses

T he domestic disruptions and societal turbulence affecting normal, healthy children in the 1990s have dictated the comprehensive services offered by Children's Hospital Guidance Centers (CHGC).

The 40-year development of a vital program progressed from a one-man clinic in a small house near the hospital to a corporate subsidiary of Children's Hospital operating from four facilities conveniently located for the families they serve.

The CHGC growth story is a singular example of community cooperation and support, through a succession of changes in location, supervision and funding.

Dr. W. Hugh Missildine, trained at the University of Iowa and Johns Hopkins, came in 1949 to establish a child guidance clinic through joint efforts of the hospital, OSU and the Junior League. The first mental health center opened the next year under his direction in half of a hospital-owned frame double near Children's.

The first staff and service expansion, to the other half of the house, came two years later, with the help of the state and United Community Council.

In 1962, with community, Junior League and federal support, the first unit in the present CHGC network was opened at 721 Raymond St. near the hospital. In 1969, the center became a contract agency of the Franklin County Mental Health and Retardation Board, with funding from the state, county and United Way.

By the mid-1970s, the center's share from a new county tax levy and a grant from the National Institute of Mental Health allowed for significant expansion. A downtown youth service branch and a mobile mental health team had also been established.

In 1978, the mental health network became one of the first in the nation to be accredited by the Joint Commission on Accreditation of Hospitals. In April, 1985, a year after Children's Mental Health Centers became a subsidiary of Children's Hospital, Inc., the present name was adopted.

The hospital's concentration on CHGC's development "reflects the beginning of society's understanding of the needs of families," said John T. Clark, Jr., former CHGC administrative director and executive director since July, 1991. "We are seeking, in a comprehensive way, to respond to the emotional, spiritual and behavioral needs of kids and families."

The single focus of the centers' specialized, many-faceted effort, said Clark's predecessor, James K. Jackson, Children's corporate director of campus and facility development, is "guiding children and families through stressful times."

The largest outpatient mental health facility for children in the community, the centers recently have been treating more than 3,000 children and adolescents a year, Jackson said.

Relocated, some several times, to best serve their immediate neighborhoods, the centers now include:

East Central, the first unit, 1015 E. Broad St.; East, 6421 E. Main St., Reynoldsburg; North, 595 Copeland Mill Rd., Westerville; and Northwest, 3242 W. Henderson Rd.

Patients come on referral from physicians, social service agencies, schools, parents—and sometimes on their own. They present the tangential but very real ills of late 20th century childhood—from physical and mental abuse to school problems and delinquency, from family disruption to their own physical illness or a family member's; from suicidal tendencies to eating disorders; from an alcoholic parent to a like problem of their own.

The general age range of patients is from six through 18, Jackson said, presenting the same range of problems except for drug and alcohol abuse, which is a particular and alarming pitfall of the middle school and high school years.

Serving them is a staff of professionals—child psychiatrists, clinical psychologists, clinical social workers and educators—with programs and approaches ranging from emergency treatment and problem assessment to scheduled treatment courses and continuing care. Parents and other family members are involved when indicated, notably in divorce services.

Noting that "during 1990 we saw more than 3,200 children, fewer than half from two-parent families," Clark said dealing with children of divorce is becoming a real area of specialization. Working with children and parents, he said, "we begin with custody mediation, help them examine the alternatives and develop detailed long-term plans."

Research which earlier showed effects of a bad marriage on children is now disclosing that bad divorces can have their own injurious effects, he noted.

Despite the severity of the drug and alcohol problem, Clark believes that, too, is giving ground to better approaches and expanded programs. "The

Dr. W. Hugh Missildine

CHGC East Central Branch

CHGC Northwest Branch

CHGC North Branch

CHGC East Branch

overall drug education and prevention program is becoming increasingly effective," he said. "We are changing attitudes about drug abuse, catching children younger, giving them positive alternatives."

In helping children with problems literally as old as Solomon and as new as the latest street drugs, CHGC is always seeking more ways—and means— to give that help.

More than a half-million dollars in grants and new program funding received by CHGC in the early '90s will make possible intensification and expansion of programs in teenage drug abuse, child abuse and emotionally disturbed children.

Volunteers and the Community
The Lifeblood of Children's Hospital

T he relationship between Children's Hospital and its community is a major factor, perhaps THE major factor, in any history of the hospital's growth.

From the very beginning, the investment of men, women and children in terms of money, materials, time and effort has been critical to the hospital's survival—and impossible to quantify or measure.

Neither is it possible to separate donors from volunteers. So many, from the first, would rank in both columns. Beyond that, how do you separate donated time from donated dollars—or from bills for materials or professional services simply never presented?

If such a detailed account could be written, it would be a lively one. The slogan "No gift too small" has been a constant in Children's history, and many such gifts are painstakingly recorded in early minutes. The variety of their donations and innovative fund-raising makes records of the women's auxiliaries fascinating reading.

Among all of the written reports and oral recollections, certain items in this vast panorama of giving stay in the mind. For instance:

• Each year after the death of her husband, a Children's trustee, in 1917, Mrs. Fred Lazarus gave a party on his birthday for the children at the hospital.

• During his board service in the early days, Col. N.B. Abbott received a used surrey as a donation to Children's. The month he sold it, for $85, the hospital's operating budget balance had dipped to $19.

• The three cents contributed by a small bedfast patient during the second building campaign was a larger sharing of resources, percentagewise, than leaders on the donors' list—and was duly recorded.

• The famous Camouflage Ball given by the Pleasure Guild during World War I was a success that grew out of necessity. Counting on novelty to replace entertainment, they carried the camouflage theme through their promotion and ticket-selling and made their usual tidy sum on a ball that never happened.

• An entry in the January, 1912, minutes is typical of many. "The secretary reported that Mr. F.O. Schoedinger (house committee chairman) had repairs made at the hospital to the amount of $51.88 and had made a donation of same. The hearty thanks of the trustees were extended." Board members through the years made many such personal gestures, recorded and unrecorded. Many recent board presidents, for instance, mentioned particularly the valued, perennial legal services given by longtime trustee Webb Vorys— for which none could recall any billing.

• Crisis time came for the Twigs in November, 1951, when labor problems closed the Neil House hotel to them just six days before their mammoth annual bazaar was to be held there. In that short time, they re-tailored an entire year's planning to fit old Memorial Hall, got the word out to members on switched assignments and booth locations, did their final setting up after the wrestling matches vacated the hall on bazaar eve—and turned over a net profit of more than $11,000 to the hospital.

Assessing Children's past and future, those who have headed the board of trustees through most of the second half-century have been unanimous in stressing the vital role filled by the women's auxiliaries.

In a typical comment, Sherwood Fawcett, former president of Battelle Memorial Institute, conceded the assurance which a much greater endowment base would give the hospital, then added immediately:

"The greatest endowment Children's has had through the years is all those wonderful women."

Just one set of figures, gleaned from the 25th anniversary report of the Women's Auxiliaries Council in 1987, shows the contributions of the auxiliaries for just that 1961-86 period, which totalled nearly $13 million.

With their annual bazaar, Thrift Shop and unit activities, the Twigs led the list with more than $8 million raised for the hospital. Kinder Key's total was $541,779; Pleasure Guild's, $475,000; Women's Board, $250,000; and, from council events, $1,602,646 from the Memorial Tournament and other golf events; $217,000 from a '76 Walk-A-Long; $1,658,688 from the Festival of Trees; and $63,606 from six years' redemption of Heinz baby food labels.

Those kinds of efforts, in infinite variety and like result, extend back to the hospital's beginnings.

Early trustees' minutes do not clearly sort out how the original volunteer groups evolved into the present, potent fund-raising organizations.

For instance, the March, 1894, minutes state specifically that the Young Ladies Sewing Society, organized with the establishment of the hospital, completely equipped the original hospital with table and bed linens, garments for patients, etc., and also originated the Charity Ball and raised $559.60 on the first one.

The same report credits the Children's Hospital Helpers, "a band of little girls," with raising $175 to support a bed for a year and with undertaking weekly visits to the hospital to take fruit, flowers and other gifts to patients.

Subsequent mention of these two groups is only as "reports received" in annual meeting minutes over the next several years. It seems likely that one or both groups formed the nucleus of young people organized by Mrs. Erskine B. Fullerton, an original women's board member and niece of President Rutherford B. Hayes, to make and sell items for a Pleasure Fund for Children's patients.

First extant reports of that group were made by Mrs. Frank Hickok, another women's board member and secretary of the Pleasure Fund. She succeeded to the presidency after Mrs. Fullerton's death and organized it into the Pleasure Guild. The Guild made its first report to trustees in 1909 and at some point took over the Charity Ball as a private event with an invited guest list. In 1912, the ball was expanded into a community-wide social event and the date set permanently on Thanksgiving Eve. For years, the ball's proceeds were a significant item in hospital income.

While the ball was its major fund-raiser, the Guild, true to its original purpose, continued to brighten the days of hospital patients in many ways and to take on a wide variety of volunteer chores—transporting patients to and from clinics, helping in the clinics and making surgical dressings.

In the '20s, the ball was replaced by annual Touchdown shows, then by horse shows, annual hospital maintenance fund drives and, in the early '50s, sponsorship of exhibition baseball games. Since 1958, the Guild has annually presented a children's play. That year, it was "Hansel and Gretel," staged in the Little Theater of the art museum. The locale changed with expanding audiences—to Battelle Auditorium and, in the last several years, the Palace Theatre.

A year-long effort, the production includes selecting the play and director, auditioning a cast, making all costumes and sets, and fashioning hand-crafted items related to the production for sale at the performances. From its 1991 production, "Charlotte's Web," the Guild realized $82,000 for the hospital.

In its service functions, the Guild supplies stock and personnel for the library cart of books and magazines trundled through the hospital each weekday; staffs the Tuesday evening "welcome walks" for children scheduled for outpatient surgery and their parents; helps with Saturday "lemonade parties" for children scheduled for hospital admission and their parents, and assigns members to help with major hospital fund-raisers like the Memorial Tournament, Festival of Trees and the Children's Miracle Network Telethon.

True to its original plan, the Guild meets in the homes of members, membership is limited (originally to 60, now 80) and vacancies are filled by invitation.

By far the largest of Children's auxiliaries, the Twigs, started by Mrs. Truitt B. Sellers in 1916, now number more than 220 groups with a membership of 4,600.

As Children's has developed into a regional center, its volunteer support has crossed county lines also. Granville's Twig 1 was the first in a state network established in the early '70s, and some 10 Twigs are now functioning in Licking, Fairfield, Pickaway and Fayette counties.

Forty-two women in 15 Twigs made up the auxiliary for its first official meeting April 4, 1916. Within a year, the numbers grew to 26 Twigs and 200 members who, in 1917, contributed 1,336 new articles—towels, curtains, stockings, sheets, 50 dozen eggs, linen for one bed for a year—and $1,411.40 in cash to the hospital. Each new Twig formed focused on a particular need of the hospital, from graham crackers to thermometers, from light bulbs to ether.

Besides their individual projects, Twigs have always been on call for special needs of the hospital. In the early days, one or several Twigs would respond to supply a new piece of equipment or replace an old one. In World War I days, they helped can the vegetables produced in the hospital garden.

During the polio epidemic of the '50s, they helped feed the children at mealtimes to relieve the hard-pressed nurses—thereby beginning a new cadre of in-hospital volunteers.

The annual pre-Thanksgiving Donation Day began with the hospital, but the Twigs took over and ran that one-day spectacular from 1925 until it was discontinued in the early '40s. In her history of the Twigs' first 50 years, Mrs. William H. Kersker, Jr., asks:

"Can you imagine the work done by the Twig members assigned to the storeroom to sort the provisions, when over 4,000 glasses of jelly were donated in one day?"

One answer to that might be—only in comparison with the thousands of hours Twig members and their children must have spent counting little scraps of paper during later years when they redeemed thousands of dollars for the hospital from used Ohio sales tax stamps.

Ever alert for a money-making opportunity, Twig members have also, for certain periods, collected tinfoil and toothpaste tubes and harvested a share from gumball machines placed in strategic locations. As Mrs. Kersker noted about such slow-building money-makers, "It only took a hundred pennies to make a dollar."

Major milestones in the fund-raising efforts of the Twigs were the establishment of the Thrift Shop in 1920 and the annual Christmas Bazaar, spawned by the Thrift Shop, two years later. Both projects have been distinguished by frequent location changes prompted by downtown development and their own success, and both have contributed substantially to Children's.

Traditionally, the Thrift Shop offered for sale both first-quality used clothing and new, donated merchandise. After a half-dozen moves, its last quarters at 260 S. 4th St. allowed space for a lucrative section of used furniture.

Managed and staffed by volunteers, the shop reaped profits ranging from $5,800 its first year to $72,612.63 for its first 11 years to $74,000 in 1965 alone.

In 1991, after seven productive decades, the Thrift Shop closed due to the changing residential patterns of the city, staffing difficulties and other factors associated with urban progress. Meanwhile, a new venture attracting a similar clientele of browsers, the Twig Attic, was in its fourth year as a kind of flea market held on a single day in mid-spring.

The Twig Bazaar began as a special Christmas-season feature in the Thrift Shop with Twigs contributing money for toys and holiday novelties as well as handmade clothing and household items. More Twigs became involved, producing and contributing more and more items. A pre-sale was added for women of the hospital, held first in downtown hotels or storerooms and for three years in the hospital. In 1946, the bazaar went public with a three-day, two-night sale in Memorial Hall and made a profit of $8,000.

It grew steadily in scope and side attractions, becoming the pre-Thanksgiving event at which hundreds of Columbus and Central Ohio women began their Christmas shopping.

During 13 years at the Neil House, it featured afternoon card parties and evening dances, both eventually eliminated in deference to merchandising space. Its size, its customer service area (now extending to neighboring states) and its profits have continued to rise through moves to Veterans Memorial and, at present, to the Multi-Purpose Building at the Ohio State Fairgrounds.

Grown from one table to more than 500 and now "departmentalized" into foods, home decorating items, collectibles and a wide range of gift items, the bazaar netted $340,000 in 1990. Even its five-year-old preview party has outgrown its first location and was moved in 1988 to the Aladdin Shrine Temple, where customers paid an admission price to shop for the latest feature items and bid at special auctions in a relatively uncrowded milieu.

As individual units, in groups or in all-Twig projects, the auxiliary, through the years, has sponsored and worked on every imaginable kind of fund-raising effort—dances and ballet performances, concerts and book reviews, carnivals and style shows, theater performances and movies, flower and garden and puppet shows, baseball games and dance recitals. They have operated hotels for a day, staffed downtown department stores and, at least once, made a quarter a person listening to manufacturers tout their products on in-plant tours.

The Twigs were 75 years old in 1991, the year before the hospital turned 100. In all that time, just two major changes have occurred in their organization.

In 1942, with elimination of Donation Day, obligations assumed by individual Twigs to supply specific items for the hospital were also abolished.

Instead, Twigs were asked to clear their treasuries twice a year of project proceeds and make donations to the hospital to be used for whatever purpose they were needed.

In 1935, black women of the community who wanted to work for Children's formed the first King Branch, named in memory of Wilbur King, a prominent attorney and civic leader believed to have been the first black contributor to the hospital. Patterned after the Twigs in organization and projects, the King Branches grew to five units and approximately 100 members before they became part of the Twig organization.

In 1954, another Children's auxiliary, Kinder Key, was formed from Charter Brace, an auxiliary unit of the Franklin County Society for Crippled Children. Created specifically to provide support for the then-new heart laboratory at the hospital, Kinder Key has fulfilled that commitment with its caroling program each Christmas season as well as working with other hospital auxiliaries on fund-raisers.

In 1970, Children's gained both financially and in volunteer expertise when Nightingale Cottage, opened in 1931, ceased operations as a convalescent center for young victims of tuberculosis and, later, of polio. Several units of the cottage's active Wings joined the Twig organization, and the remainder of the cottage's endowment fund was given to the hospital. Although not a part of the hospital's auxiliary structure, some Wings groups still exist today and support Children's pulmonary program.

In 1961, the Women's Auxiliaries Council was formed as the advisory and governing body for the four hospital auxiliaries—another move toward modernizing and increasing the intercommunication and effectiveness of the organization.

The communication factor is highly important. From the beginning, Children's leadership has appreciated and sought the help of women volunteers not only in fund-raising but in spreading the good word about the hospital and its services.

So it was that, in 1916, the Twigs and the Bambino, that informative little monthly magazine, came into existence almost together. So it was that, with the Bambino's demise at the beginning of World War II, the Twigs general chairman took over with an extensive newsletter covering not only Twig projects but news of the hospital. And so it is that the hospital's public relations and marketing programs, as they have evolved, put a high priority on informing not only the staff but the people all along the community support network about what Children's is doing and planning.

Contributors of that increasingly valuable item, time, are the men, women and teenagers who make up the volunteer group most familiar to Children's small patients.

They work in the hospital days, nights, weekends—whatever best fits their personal schedules, and every hour they give, supervisors note, frees staff members for other duties.

118

Volunteers store the proceeds from an early Donation Day.

After all the sorting, counting and storing of Donation Day, volunteers gathered for tea.

In 1952, Twig president Betty Shepherd presided at the celebration hailing formation of the 100th Twig.

Board stalwarts Robert Lazarus, left, and Webb I. Vorys admire plaque dedicated to Vorys and his long service to Children's in 1969.

Children's can always use volunteers, as this donated billboard proclaims.

Twig Bazaar draws throngs of Christmas shoppers.

Memorial Tournament founder and host Jack Nicklaus signs autographs during the 1980 event.

Festival of Trees has become pre-Christmas tradition.

Children, hospital officials, phone bank volunteers and WBNS-10 TV share the successful conclusion of 1991 Children's Miracle Network Telethon.

All that is available in old records certainly indicates that women volunteers worked in the hospital at various tasks from the very beginning. Impetus for the present program seems to have come with the polio epidemic of the '50s and the need for extra hands to help feed children who couldn't feed themselves. Mrs. Frank Shepherd, Twig chairman at that time, remembers that 98 Twig members answered that call.

Virginia Denman, longtime director of Children's volunteer services, recalled her initial uncertainty about how much an in-hospital volunteer group would want to be involved with patients directly. She found that many were willing to take on any task they could do, so a training program was devised and a nurse consultant obtained.

"Children's has special needs," she said. "There are a lot of things a child in a hospital can't do that an adult can—and that nurses and aides don't have the time to do." One of her favorite stories occurred when a nurse asked a volunteer, who was cuddling a child in a rocker, to run an errand, and the child protested, "Please don't take my lap away."

Jo Taylor, Denman's successor through the '80s, described the selection of in-hospital volunteers on the basis of an application, an interview and a testimonial of physical and mental fitness from their physician, and training including a two-session orientation and a day's on-the-job experience under a supervisor.

Volunteers who work directly with patients are in two groups, she said—those who assist nurses with bathing and feeding children, running errands, reading to or playing with patients, and those in the Child Life program of play therapy who work with and under the supervision of staff therapists.

Those who choose to work with sick children have many motivations, she said—the "empty nest syndrome, gratitude for treatment given a child they love, the need to be needed, just a desire to serve." Children's, she added, "is never over-supplied. It always needs volunteers."

The need is there, and more are volunteering, said Liz Nusken, director since January of '89. "We're coming out of the 'me' generation. People are more stirred to act. We've seen an increase of about 150, up to now about 400 depending somewhat on the time of year." The age range is 14 to 80, and the in-hospital force, once mostly women and girls, is now about 25 percent male.

"We have a group of retired RNs from Lancaster, husband-wife, mother-son and mother-daughter teams. Some people come with a specific agenda—'I'm studying radiology' or 'I want to be a pediatrician'—and we have 'specials'—a teenager interested in genetics, for instance, who works in the genetics office. We have young professionals in the 25-40 age group, many coming straight from work to the hospital. We have a good number of college students, and we have some Children's Hospital employees."

In the summer months, she said, about 20 percent of the volunteers are high school students in the 14-to-18 age group.

Much of the program's success lies in matching volunteers with a task, she said. "Some who work with people all day want quieter work, but 80 percent of our volunteers come in some contact with patients."

Volunteers use the hospital library and other ways to improve their skills, and the new education center, she said, will be a significant benefit. "Our need for volunteers will become greater," she said. "For the 'crack' babies, for instance, the many more infants we're seeing because of parental substance abuse. And there's a growing volunteer role in home support."

In-hospital volunteering is "very personal, individual," and attracts a special kind of person. "I get to work," said Nusken, "with the neatest people in town."

In the organizational complexity Children's has attained, fund-raising volunteer activities are part of a structure of giving within the Children's Hospital Foundation.

Norman Myers, senior associate director of the foundation, joined Children's in 1970 with the organization of the development department, the predecessor of the Children's Hospital Foundation. He explained some of the fund-raising efforts that benefit the hospital.

The women's auxiliaries and development board together generate approximately $1.5 million for the hospital each year, he said. The development board, new in the '70s, was organized by the late business leader John Fergus, who thought such a group, composed of young men and women of the business community, could support the hospital as auxiliaries do.

The board's membership has grown from an original 20 to 25 to about 125 and includes a Ross County unit, Myers said. Their contributions to the hospital, from the Woody Hayes Sports Spectacular, an Annual Giving Campaign and other events, was more than $400,000 in 1990.

"FFA-FHA" stands for Future Farmers of America and Future Homemakers of America. These groups have raised an average of $55,000 a year for Children's through statewide fund-raising efforts, Myers said. In its first three years, the Bobby Rahal Columbus Charities Pro-Am has generated $250,000 for Children's Hospital.

The Children's Miracle Network Telethon, aired by WBNS-10TV, has become an important fund source. In 1991, this annual event generated a record $1,462,193 for Children's, bringing its nine-year total to nearly $9 million.

During 1990, the Children's Hospital Foundation received donations totalling $5,062,027, Myers said, noting that the funds are spread to meet many needs.

A sizable amount helps support research. Another allotment goes to valued hospital programs which produce no revenue—Child Life, the Poison

Control Center, summer camp programs for children with special problems (cancer, cystic fibrosis, etc.) and the child abuse program.

Another substantial portion is placed in trust for an emergency situation or sudden unexpected drain on hospital resources. "There have been times this hospital couldn't make ends meet," Myers pointed out, and its endowment funds are limited.

121

John H. Strick II, executive director of the Children's Hospital Foundation, said, "Given the needs that exist and the opportunities Children's could pursue, we're not at all comfortable with our endowment fund balance. However, by the year 2000 we hope to establish a major endowment fund that will generate significant investment income on an annual basis.

"This won't be a finite campaign with a cut-off point, but we need to set a different tone of need," Strick said. "There are so many things we could do that are worthy of support. What we have to sell is an investment in the future."

Donors identify easily with sick children under treatment, Strick explained, but perceive less clearly the hospital's major needs in education and research—the programs that extend to preventing disease and to keeping children well. "Most of our annual gifts are $100 or less," he said, "and to a great degree spontaneous, not investment-type decisions."

Of the hospital's $11 million endowment fund at the end of 1989, he said, $8,473,148 was earmarked for patient care, the guidance centers, etc., and $2,769,687 specifically for research.

Only in recent years have individual gifts and bequests to Children's topped the $1 million mark. Among these are the deferred gift trust funds established by Dedger and Rose Jones, valued in the late '80s at $6.5 to $7 million; the $4.371 million endowment gift of Elizabeth and Harold Derrer; Bella Wexner's $3 million gift for construction of the research institute; the $2 million endowment for research from Robert E. Jones; the $1.925 million construction and equipment needs gift from Betsey Kauffman Trumbull; $1.4 million from John C. Fergus; and $1.2 million from Hester Funk Dysart. Organizational million dollar–plus donors include the Aladdin Crippled Children's Hospital Association, Battelle Memorial Institute, Nationwide Insurance Company and The Kobacker Company.

"People who are philanthropic have their favorite causes," Strick said, "and people who make investments are planners who expect big term returns. Philanthropic investors want to truly make a difference, to help ensure Children's Hospital's future ability to care for and improve the quality of life for all children."

To attract substantial support from those interested in investing in Children's and children, the foundation has defined a number of major needs and devised an array of giving plans to mesh with individual charitable desire and financial plans.

From the very early days, when two Sells Circus performances kept a fledgling hospital afloat and the Elks underwrote the first addition, Children's has received material and financial support from community organizations and special groups literally too numerous to mention.

Some have consistently supported a particular program—the Shrine and crippled children; the Lions' Club and Auxiliaries and vision; the Firefighters and burns treatment, and the Ruth Lyons Christmas Fund for patients being among the most long-standing. The Junior League has helped launch a number of new programs or facilities. At holiday times, most particularly Christmas, Children's is the perennial recipient of special gifts and treats from many organizations and individuals.

Forged over 100 years of mutual service and support, Children's links with a caring community continue strong.

Women's Board

The most regrettable loss from the early annals of Children's are the records of the Women's Board. If any of them ever surface, from an attic or an heirloom trunk or a forgotten file cabinet, they will give color and form to the tapestry of Children's early days.

Because the women did it. They were the originators of the idea, at least co-founders and drafters of the hospital's first policies and goals, certainly the major overseers for its day-to-day operation for nearly 50 years.

The doctors, of course, were the essential element, and Children's could not have existed without their service, given freely for so many years. The trustees were equally important—influential, experienced community leaders who husbanded the little hospital's meager resources and set the policies that assured its growth and development.

But it was the Women's Board, its own growing membership and the auxiliaries it established who handled the nitty-gritty details and special problems peculiar to Children's early operation. Aside from their own extensive fund-raising activities, they hired the paid staff and guaranteed some salaries; shouldered a major share of the furnishing, equipping and maintaining of the hospital; saw to the entertainment and education of the patients; helped begin and staff such all-important developments as the dispensaries and clinics; served as the vital liaison between employees and supervisors and medical staff and trustees; and took on all the special chores involved in building campaigns and other fund drives.

Always, they asked trustees' approval of their decisions and activities. Occasionally, they lobbied strongly for a policy change or piece of equipment they thought essential. Often, after presenting a particularly thorny problem, they would get it back for solution—a major flare-up between physicians and a matron, for instance, or the complaints of neighbors about crying infants on the old hospital's open-air porch.

Two entries from old records stick in the mind as illustrative of the spirit and will of the women volunteers. In the 1919 annual report, the mending committee chairman reported apologetically "only 5,002 garments mended" during the previous year. In 1925, announcing trustees' authorization "to pay the Ladies' Board $20,000 per annum for maintenance of the hospital," President Schoedinger added that the amount was "less than one-third of what it requires to operate this institution." It was understood volunteer effort would produce the rest.

It is never easy for the builders of an institution to relinquish its control to other hands, and it couldn't have been easy for the Women's Board to realize, by the end of the '30s, that their little hospital had grown beyond them. Recognizing it could and should continue to grow, they knew it needed professional management, its own medical staff and a strengthened financial and administrative structure. In 1942, with the hiring of Robert Porter, they turned over the managerial reins to a professional after an incredible 50-year achievement.

Of course, they continued to work for Children's. For a time, Women's Board members continued their Bambino Shop on E. Broad St. and, for much longer, staffed the hospital gift shop. In 1961, the board joined with other volunteer units in formation of the Women's Auxiliaries Council. Its membership largely composed of women who had given extensive volunteer service, the board continued its support of Children's through one annual event and individual contributions, staffing the hospital information desk and participating in annual all-auxiliary projects.

In 1990, the Women's Board launched a new fund-raiser of its own, the Junior Golf Tournament at the new Shamrock Golf Club. The July event was a success, raising $3,700 for the hospital, and the 1991 tournament raised about $6,000.

Board Presidents
Prudence, Vision and Leadership

Arriving at Children's for a board meeting, Clair E. Fultz, trustee emeritus, board president from 1967 to '69 and former chairman of the Huntington National Bank, parked his car several blocks away and walked to the hospital.

"I wanted to look at license plates," he explained. "All those people from so many different places, all coming to Children's."

Just back from a business trip and due to leave on another, Arthur J. Kobacker, board president for 1987-90 and chairman of The Kobacker Company, dictated a final letter, put his calls on hold, and launched into a detailed description of recent research at Children's like a man with all the time in the world.

Molly Caren Fisher, former Women's Board and Women's Auxiliaries Council president and a trustee emeritus, took her place on the phone bank for the ninth straight year during the 1991 Children's Miracle Network Telethon.

Ann I. Wolfe, elected for the 1990-93 term as the board's first woman president, talked of new hospital funding sources, the importance of new nursing programs and of her own children's experience as hospital patients.

Collectively, and in company with many others, they represent the long-term commitment and proprietary interest Children's has enjoyed through the years from community leaders.

Of the 20 men who served as board president from the hospital's founding through the '80s, nine survived to contribute personal recollections.

During his tenure in the early '60s, "we were very loosely organized . . . met pretty much as a family," Robert M. Rex, former president and general manager of Columbus Bolt & Forging Co., remembered shortly before his death. Board procedure was more limited to final approvals, he surmised, and the tendency lingered in those lower-budget years to depend on women volunteers. "It was the most fascinating thing. We'd say, 'Gee, we can't afford this,' and they'd come up with the money."

Recalling "no time we ever thought we weren't going to make it," Rex declared today's Children's is "a very aggressive operation, in better shape than ever," but "people in Columbus still don't realize what a great institution it is."

Fultz, whose 22-year tenure from 1949 through his '67-'69 presidency spanned the final two years of F.O. Schoedinger's longtime leadership, recalled the 1920-51 president as "a very large man, very persuasive manner, one of the builders of the hospital." He remembered the first purchase of small lots and residences around the hospital; the "very wise" decision to keep Children's a community hospital; the Timken pledge toward a nurses' home—"one of the first matching gifts I ever heard of."

"Well-satisfied" with Children's development as "one of the most worthwhile organizations in our community, philanthropic or otherwise," he anticipated the hospital's increasing role "in the health and welfare of our Central Ohio residents."

David Cox's first involvement with hospital affairs in the early '60s was in connection with Children's first real research facility. U.S. Rep. Clarence J. Brown, whose granddaughter had been a leukemia patient at Children's, had sponsored legislation through which a hospital could get federal matching funds, Cox recalled.

"Dr. Baxter called me (about a possible grant), and I got my company, Dick and Melvin Ross, to match it," said the former president of Ross Laboratories. Recruited to the board by Fultz, whom he followed as president in 1969, Cox also recalled the valuable assistance of OSU's Dr. Alfred Garrett in establishment of Children's research foundation; the debated decision to contest the Hirsch will ("That money really saved us from a very difficult time in the early '70s"); a proposal by OSU Dean Richard L. Meiling, "who basically didn't believe in specialty hospitals," that Children's relocate as a "semi-autonomous institution" on a site near Battelle and OSU; and "the overwhelming consensus that we did not want to be taken over by OSU."

Cox elaborated on the hospital's troubled financial situation as he found it—"something like 49 different accounts, no overall compatibility, a legacy of hand-to-mouth funding"—and the disappointing return from Children's participation in the United Hospital Campaign.

"Here we were, running the biggest outpatient program in the country, and they used to give us $50,000—then wanted to cut it. Trustees decided Children's had to raise money on its own."

Watching Children's affairs from a Florida retirement, Cox sees a gravitation toward larger and larger hospital systems but thinks that "children will remain a distinct medical responsibility from the rest of society" for decades. He believes "Children's is on firmer ground than it's ever been (although it still doesn't have prenatal care for women, and should have it)" and that it is "living with certain immunities and endowed with tremendous emotional appeal.

"My one regret," Cox concluded on his 20-year board service, "is that I was a liberal when the environment was conservative."

His comments, and those of his successor, Sherwood Fawcett, reflect changing board attitudes during these years, particularly toward financial procedures and the importance of research.

In his memoirs, Dr. Baxter describes his frustrations a decade or so earlier in urging more aggressive pursuit of research funding and facilities. He also credits Meiling, who became OSU dean in 1960, with "reorganizing the College of Medicine on a thoroughly business basis."

Fawcett, and his successors in the Children's board presidency, date much of Children's improved financial organization from the arrival of William R. Wise, currently corporate director of financial services, in 1964.

His own major achievement, said the former Battelle Memorial Institute president, was securing that all-important "last resort" loan in the early '70s for Children's new patient tower. From then on, through his presidency and to date, it's been "onward and upward," Fawcett declared. "The annual budget has gone from about $12 million when I was president to more than $100 million, and Children's has become a world-class operation."

Taking a tempered approach to larger endowments and future growth, he added, "You live by your wits. I hope we'll always worry a little." He thinks Children's should "do what it has to do, be of a size to serve its population" but be somewhat focused in its services and "always try to be really good in certain areas."

Robert (Tad) Jeffrey, a descendant of the Kilbournes in one of many family lines represented on the Children's board, served the eventful '75-'78 presidential term. He had the happy task of presiding over the opening of the new hospital in 1976 and the more difficult one of top administrative change.

Arthur I. Vorys also followed a family tradition to the Children's board. A bronze tablet in the hospital recognizes the four-decade board service of his father, Webb Vorys, and an even longer period as Children's volunteer legal counsel.

Children's great advantage over any other hospital, Vorys said, is its "cadre of volunteers, most important the women's auxiliaries, not only as money-raisers but for public relations."

He conceded trustees have been "very, very conservative, very reluctant to commit funds until the most recent renovation. If they hadn't been, we'd probably be out of business," he added, noting that trustees have been very conscious of the commitment never to turn a child away, of Children's role as "the nursing center for many indigent children, and as a family doctor for thousands."

In its present leadership, Morrow and Williams, Children's has "one super management team," Vorys declared. "One thing that is very appropriate," he added, is the use of Children's by those who serve it. "My kids were patients; my brother and sisters were. Children's will continue to fare well as long as it is serving a 'critical mass' of children."

Frank Wobst, president of the Huntington National Bank and board president in 1981-84, hailed the success of two unusual relationships the hospital enjoys—the co-leadership of Williams and Morrow and the longstanding affiliation with the OSU College of Medicine.

"It's one of the best-managed institutions in town," Wobst declared, "and—somewhat unique for a hospital—the medical administration and business administration complement each other."

He referred particularly to the downturn years of the '80s when Williams told him he thought hospital costs could be held to a very slight increase and Wobst, the banker, said in effect, "If you can do that, why have any?" In that troubled period, Wobst said proudly, "Our zero price increase showed a very positive intent . . . resolve on the part of the board, administration and medical staff to run an efficient operation."

The OSU affiliation is "built on good will—not even a document exists," he said, but is "a very positive working relationship I hope will continue. The university is by far the stronger partner materially, but Children's is a wonderful asset to the university."

Hailing "tremendous progress" in research activity, exemplified by the Wexner Institute, Wobst declared Children's "works best as long as it is acknowledged by the medical community as the children's treatment facility." The loss of any part of its program to other hospitals would be "a community problem" and "a major concern," Wobst said. "The care of children is something special . . . special nursing, special doctors, special facilities. Healing is more than medical care."

The president of Nationwide Insurance and a father whose four children were all Children's patients, John Fisher also hailed "the fulfillment of our research goal. Children's has always been credited with excellent patient care, then excelled in teaching. Now, we're reaching the full flower of our third major mission."

Board president in 1984-87, he sees many pluses for the Children's of the '90s—"a great job in space planning, increased professionalism in the medical governance system, in all candor good working capital, good insurance protection" and a "harmonious" updating of its internal structures and affiliations such as with OSU.

Fisher thinks the expanding research program will inevitably be accompanied by more highly specialized procedures but does not foresee a time Children's will "want to afford everything" or "be all things to all people."

He thinks Children's has thus far withstood, perhaps better than expected, any harmful effects of new insurance patterns, marketing competition and hospital "feeder" centers, changes in medical practice, even a fluctuating birth rate. "It's my impression that Children's has become such a

Robert Rex

Clair Fultz

David Cox

Sherwood Fawcett

Robert Jeffrey

Arthur Vorys

Frank Wobst

John Fisher

Arthur Kobacker

Ann I. Wolfe

recognized viable resource," he said, "that parents expect to see their children treated there."

He does not think this obviates "constant concern" about these and other factors—the effects of substance abuse on children, for instance, or the need to keep health care affordable—that will affect Children's future.

"When you send your kid to Children's, you're not only getting the best possible care for him or her," Arthur Kobacker declared, "but making it more likely your grandchild will get that kind of care."

Children's is "one of the largest and best pediatric hospitals," reasoned the 1987-90 board president. "We have more than 270,000 patient visits each year. Because of that, we may see even very rare maladies several times in a year. Our doctors are familiar with them and know what to do. They can also build enough of a data base for research."

Noting that essential items of this set of circumstances would not be present in an adult hospital, he summed up, "In the absence of large pediatric hospitals, we would never improve" in children's care and treatment.

Excited about "tremendously dramatic" instances of treatment and research advance he has seen at Children's, Kobacker anticipated new programs—home care and bone marrow transplants, for instance—and declared, "Children's should remain at the forefront in every new area that comes along."

And that, he added, includes not only the best treatment for children but comfort and convenience for them and their families, in ways ranging from greatly expanded parking facilities to waiting-room amenities and quicker test results. "We want to treat them just as we would want to treat them in a fine salon or a fine store."

As she tells it, Ann Wolfe's long volunteer service to Children's has been paralleled, as it is with many, by her own family's experience with the hospital and its resources. From her "first encounter" as a Pleasure Guild member, she took on a succession of volunteer tasks leading to board memberships, presidency of the Children's Hospital Foundation and, in 1990, presidency of the board of trustees.

Meanwhile, as their three daughters grew up, she and her husband, John F. Wolfe, turned to Children's for short-term and emergency room visits and the sudden frightening illness of one child. That resulted in an emergency admission, a stay in the Clinical Studies Center, surgery, and, 14 years later, a healthy young woman launched on a business career.

Mentioning friends who have had similar experience with seriously ill children, Mrs. Wolfe declared:

"Children's is just a special place—nurses and doctors who spend their whole lives dealing with children, the amount of unpaid care the hospital gives."

When the sick child is your own, she added, all the reasons to support Children's are accentuated. "You just know you have to do something."

She spoke of particular interests—the new child care center, promising research projects under way, the hoped-for major grant for nursing research. On the eve of its 100th anniversary, the new board president declared, "Children's is at the moment in better shape than any institution in the city."

The varying perspectives and informed concern of these latter-day board presidents is typical of the kind of trusteeship Children's has enjoyed through the years. In the very early days, the boards were smaller and both membership and leadership changed more slowly.

From 1892 until 1915, Col. Kilbourne and John Siebert alternated in the presidency except for five years. Col. N.B. Abbott, an engineer historically recorded as the man who imported the city's first Trinidad asphalt to pave parts of High and State Sts., was president from 1899 to 1903. In 1904, Rutherford H. Platt, prominent legal scholar and jurist, took the office in March and resigned in September, and his replacement, Frederick W. Schumacher, philanthropist, gold miner and art patron, resigned in December. Both continued to serve on the board.

Longtime member Fred Lazarus, Sr., president of the F. & R. Lazarus & Co., was president from 1915 until his death in 1917, and Foster Copeland, president of the City National Bank, from then until 1920. Following the 30-year tenure of F.O. Schoedinger, Albert M. Miller, president of the Central Ohio Paper Co., headed the board from 1951 to 1959; Livingston L. Taylor, attorney, from 1959 to 1961; and George W. Kauffman, president of the Kauffman-Lattimer Co., succeeded Robert Rex in 1962 and served until 1967.

The service records of these board leaders could be matched by many other individuals and many husband-wife teams whose dedication to Children's spans years of active involvement and a continuing interest.

Typical of many others, the Leigh Koebels shared their respective reminiscences in a living room brightened by pictured generations of younger Koebels the summer before Mr. Koebel's death.

She was Pleasure Guild chairman when the Marks family funded a hospital addition and recalled Guild dances at old Memorial Hall. She was president of the Twigs in the late '30s—"We made $16,000 my first year and $17,000 the second"—and on the Women's Board "when Hattie (Mrs. Robert) Lazarus started the Bambino Shop" and when, at an SOS from the hospital, "we'd begin calling businessmen and just never get turned down."

Recruited to the board of trustees by Livingston Taylor, Koebel was longtime treasurer of the board. He recalled the "almost tearful" valedictory of F.O. Schoedinger and estimated his own service at about 25 years. "I resigned when I was 75," said the veteran ex-trustee, who was still active in his real estate business, "and that was nearly 20 years ago."

Dr. Baxter used to joke that pediatricians appeared younger than their medical peers, because of constant contact with children. The benefit would seem to extend to Children's volunteers.

Presidents, Board of Trustees

1892-98, Col. James Kilbourne
1898, John Siebert
1899-1903, Col. N.B. Abbott
1903, Col. James Kilbourne
1904, R.H. Platt, resigned
1904, F.W. Schumacher, resigned
1904-05, Col. James Kilbourne
1906-09, John Siebert
1910, Col. James Kilbourne
1911-14, John Siebert
1915-17, Fred Lazarus
1917-20, Foster Copeland
1920-51, F.O. Schoedinger
1951-59, Albert M. Miller
1959-61, Livingston Taylor
1961-62, Robert Rex
1962-67, George Kauffman
1967-69, Clair Fultz
1969-72, David Cox
1972-75, Sherwood Fawcett
1975-78, Robert Jeffrey
1978-81, Arthur Vorys
1981-84, Frank Wobst
1984-87, John Fisher
1987-90, Arthur Kobacker
1990-   , Ann I. Wolfe

Vignettes
Portraits from Children's Family Album

The Kilbournes

When Col. and Mrs. James Kilbourne helped found Children's Hospital, they signed on for a lifetime. He was a board president for 10 years, perennial chairman of the annual hospital meetings for two decades and a trustee until his death in 1919. Her service spanned the opening of both hospitals—continuous membership on the Women's Board until her death in 1925 and 18 years as its president.

Member of a pioneer Franklin County family, Col. Kilbourne founded the Kilbourne-Jacobs Manufacturing Co., which shipped its principal product, wheelbarrows, all over the world. A man of broad interests and attainments, he served leadership roles in charitable, military and veterans' groups; the Columbus Public Library and the Columbus Board of Trade; Democratic politics including a candidacy for the Ohio governorship; college alumni groups and historical, archaeological and horticultural societies. He was also, Children's records show, one of the very few early trustees who rarely missed a meeting.

The Kilbourne home at 604 E. Town St. was the site of the first planning for Children's and of many board meetings and benefits thereafter. A granddaughter's recollections provide some warm glimpses of the Kilbourne home, no longer standing, and of her grandparents.

Anna Kilbourne Smith, who died in 1988, remembered the colonel as "a darling, very erect but very grandfatherly." He was a "passionate fisherman," she recalled, and "a great scholar. He spent a year at Heidelberg University and spoke German fluently."

Impressive but more daunting to a small granddaughter was Anna Bancroft Kilbourne, daughter of Gen. George Bohan Wright of Granville, whose social, charitable and cultural interests paralleled her husband's.

"Grandma Annie," said Mrs. Smith, "was very slim, elegant, haughty," and in her later years made her social rounds in an electric Pierce-Arrow "driven by a chauffeur who was also a butler and lived in an apartment over the garage."

The house, typical of its day, had a large, cherry-paneled center hallway, a parlor to the left, library to the right, huge kitchen to the rear, seven bedrooms and two baths upstairs.

The parlor was "very stiff but nice," Mrs. Smith remembered, but the library, bay-windowed and lined to the ceiling with books, was her grandparents' favorite room.

"That's where they spent their evenings," Mrs. Smith said, "with Grandmother reading to Grandfather and knitting at the same time."

It was also the site, on many other evenings, for the first plans and dreams that produced a hospital.

In 1919, following Col. Kilbourne's death, Foster Copeland, then board president, assessed the Kilbournes' joint contribution in his annual report. "It is hard to see how this hospital could have come into existence," he said, "if it had not been for these two."

Mrs. William King Rogers

Mrs. William King Rogers, first president of the Women's Board, was a dedicated worker for Children's from its founding until her death in 1924. The former Mary Lord Andrews was the granddaughter of a pioneer fur trader who settled in Steubenville as an agent for John Jacob Astor, and the daughter of Dr. John Andrews, a practicing physician who became head of the Steubenville branch of the State Bank and, later, president of that bank in Columbus.

Mrs. Rogers' husband, William King Rogers, was a law partner of Rutherford B. Hayes until Hayes' election as Ohio governor and later served as President Hayes' private secretary. Her son, Dr. William King Rogers, educated at Georgetown University during the family's Washington years, received his medical degree from the University of New York, studied in European eye and ear clinics, and served for many years as eye, ear and throat surgeon at Children's and other Columbus hospitals. Until her death, Mrs. Rogers was president of the Lincoln Twig (Twig 6), so called because its members were all residents of the old Hotel Lincoln on E. Broad St. at Jefferson Ave.

Isabelle Brunn Harper

Isabelle Brunn Harper's recollections of a turn-of-the-century Children's Hospital were of a warm, caring staff, huge rooms and stairways, and a broad green lawn.

Her description of a 14-month stay at Children's in 1907 and '08 may be the earliest available from a patient's point of view. Mrs. Harper, who died at 86 in 1989, was admitted to the old Children's at age four with a hip problem.

She remembered being "in a ward with a lot of other little kids," and being carried to the first-floor surgery. "I had a big cast for months," she said. "When they'd change it, they would lay me on a table and saw the old one off. Then I'd have to lie there until the new one dried."

Two of her memories illustrate the old hospital's constant battle with contagion and its careful husbanding of supplies. Mrs. Harper had both measles and mumps while a patient. Her mother told her, she said, that, on one of her rare visits home, she was given a slice of bread topped with butter and jelly and informed her family, "At the hospital, we get butter or jelly—never both."

Her parents also told her, she said, that her surgeon went to Chicago, before her operation, to learn details of a similar case involving "a daughter of the Armours." The surgery was successful.

Mrs. Harper recalled walking down the broad center stairway, one hand on the banister and the other held by a nurse, when her father came to take her home for good. She enjoyed normal activity through her life, she said, until arthritis forced her back into a wheelchair in her 80s.

The daughter of a Columbus electrical contractor and the widow of Willard Harper, a chemist at the Dublin Rd. water treatment plant, Mrs. Harper was a statistician for the State Welfare Department before her marriage.

Hospitalized at a time when parental visits were limited to one hour a week, she surmised her long sojourn earned her a little special attention from the staff.

"I was the only one who got a doll for Christmas," she remembered, and recalled her delight when nurses would occasionally allow her to hold one of the infant patients and when a favorite nurse, Miss Margaret Nicklaus, took her on a weekend trip to visit a new baby.

"They had stacks of red sweaters," probably the work of hospital volunteers, "and we all had one," she said. "I used to dream of having a child of my own to dress in a red sweater—but I never did."

Daisy Sellers

Daisy Sellers' final report to Children's Hospital trustees in March of 1940 was upbeat, philosophical and uncharacteristically brief.

She thanked everyone—physicians and staff, auxiliary units and their chairmen, Columbus citizens and the local press—as she always had during her 26 years as Women's Board president. But she didn't exhort either volunteers or citizens to greater effort, as she usually did, nor did she list, as was her custom, the unmet needs Children's always faced.

A torch was being passed. At year's end, Mrs. Sellers declined to be considered for the board presidency again. In mid-1942, she died. For a key to a rare personality, one is drawn back to a paragraph rather gratuitously inserted into her final report: "The longer I live the more deeply I am convinced that which makes the difference between one man and another is energy, invisible determination."

Gleaning from her own achievements and recorded comment and the memories of those who knew her, Daisy Sellers had both qualities in vast measure, devoted in large part to Children's Hospital.

Born in Louisville, Ky., Mrs. Sellers was schooled in philanthropic concepts and the way to activate them by her father, Gen. John Finnell, a lawyer and statesman, and her mother, a founder of the Kentucky Children's Home. She moved to Columbus in 1902 with her husband, Truitt B. Sellers, an insurance executive, and became active in community organizations, most particularly the new charity hospital.

She was a leader in the building campaigns of 1916 and 1922. In one of her first acts as Women's Board president, she founded the Twigs. She started the Bambino, Children's first magazine, and served as its business manager. She became the first woman member of the board of trustees.

Obviously, she spent countless hours—in the hospital, in talking problems and needs with the staff, in keeping up with the progress of medicine and what other hospitals were doing, in pursuing and assessing all kinds of fund-raising ideas, in seeing in every experience and chance encounter some possible benefit for Children's.

One story has it that the rather ornate design of the "new" 1924 hospital (which many liked and many didn't) markedly resembled a chateau Mrs. Sellers had seen on a trip to Europe.

Those who remember her recall her energy most vividly—a small, brisk woman, kind, tactful, but always moving. "A little dynamo," said one. "The doingest woman I ever knew," said another.

Even through the requisite-statistics of her annual reports to trustees, glimpses of the Sellers personality can be gleaned. In 1919, thanking the board for the hospital's first automobile, a Dodge, and for an operating fund increase from $10,000 to $12,000, she added:

"Someone has truthfully said that nothing is more effective in raising standards than a spirit of helpfulness, concerted action and cash."

A fellow board member, Molly Caren Fisher, in a casual exchange one day, may have plumbed a deeper incentive for Daisy Sellers' singular contribution. Asked if she had attended a graduation ceremony the previous night, the childless Mrs. Sellers responded in effect: "No, I can't bear such ceremonies. I look at all those young faces and think, 'One of them might be mine.' "

It would have been characteristic of the Daisy Sellers revealed by her achievements to convert a personal disappointment into life-giving benefits for the children of Central Ohio.

Dr. Leslie L. Bigelow

The man who headed Children's medical staff during its "growing-up" years is remembered by family and friends as a person of charm, wit, broad interests and strong philosophical bent. They are traits he must have needed often in speaking for his medical colleagues during difficult times, and they are traits apparent in his lively annual reports to hospital trustees. His valedictory report as chief of staff at the 1940 annual meeting had typical elements.

He had a little story: Bigelow, a general surgeon, Harvard trained, and his Children's associates handled a broad range of cases. Unknown to him, his fellow surgeons had vied for the distinction of being the first to use the new operating room on the 1924 opening day of the "new" hospital. When the man who had won the honor arrived for his 7 a.m. case, he met Dr. Bigelow emerging from surgery—after taking and completing a rush appendectomy at 5:45 a.m.

He looked to a future Children's: During his tenure as chief he had urged staff doctors to summarize and analyze their work each year to provide a data base for improving patient care and "to promote the scientific spirit." Anticipating growth and change in the 1940 hospital as both inevitable and desirable, he cited a favorite example of human complacency. The great French surgeon, Ambroise Pare, he said, prefaced his 16th century surgery textbook with the bit of folly: "It may be doubted if . . . future generations will ever be able to add anything that is new or of fundamental importance to what is here set down."

Finally, in summarizing the credo guiding his own long service, he defined succinctly that "special something" about Children's. "What we are trying to do here, all of us who work for the Children's Hospital," he said, "quite simply is to be kind and generous to little children who are in need of help; and that, in a world where there is so much unkindness and so little generosity, is a very important thing."

Dr. Earl H. Baxter

Dr. Baxter liked to point out that he and Children's shared an 1892 birthdate, "both conceived by and born to devoted women." Later on, through more than 40 years, the lives of the physician and the hospital ran closely parallel, bringing him, in 1963, to honorable retirement but the hospital only, as he put it then, to "the midst of its adolescence."

Many, that retirement day and since, have termed Baxter, teacher, administrator and pediatrician for hundreds of Columbus-area children, as a major force in the fledgling hospital's growth and development.

It was during his two decades as chief of staff and chairman of pediatrics at OSU that Children's attained established identity as a pediatric treatment, research and education center.

"It has achieved almost full physical size and growth," he said in his valedictory, "and now must develop a maturity of function . . . From now on, highly technical and trained personnel are necessary for its successful future."

Tall, white-haired, with twinkling eyes and a ready wit, Baxter was an effective speaker and, to the benefit of future Children's generations, a prolific writer. His comments on past events and personalities are often the only ones in existence.

Interestingly, although so much of his time was focused on the hospital and its problems, the Baxter legacy of papers, speeches and published interviews deals almost as much with the profession of pediatrics and its importance in the lives of children.

Noting that pediatricians, in the '60s, had already progressed from "baby feeder" to scientific guardian of a child's growing years, he envisioned a growing role for pediatricians as educators. Anticipating and helping with problems of young parents. Monitoring the school progress of their patients.

Beyond that, he thought teacher training programs should offer expanded study of child growth and development, taught by pediatricians, and that it would be a fine idea if "every school or series of schools" had a full-time pediatrician on staff to oversee school environment, teach health courses and be the schools' liaison with family physicians.

Like others of his generation, Baxter was a latecomer to his chosen specialty. Reared on a Mt. Vernon, Ohio, farm, he received his medical degree from Ohio State in 1918 and worked first in "war pathology" at the University of Michigan on the problems of sick and wounded servicemen. Back at OSU as an instructor in clinical diagnosis and microscopy, he was drawn to pediatrics by his own interest in children and a developing scientific and social focus on their special problems.

Children's and pediatrics were both in their growing years when he became chief of staff of the hospital in late 1939 and, two years later, professor and chairman of OSU's new Department of Pediatrics. Like the good athletic coach, his careful recruitment of a staff trained in the new specialties was a major factor in Children's development.

Two Baxter maxims form a recurring refrain in his written legacy and undoubtedly in the memory of students he taught and parents and patients he counseled. They are:

• That "child power" is the country's greatest natural resource, deserving of every effort expended to realize it fully.

• That a child is born with all the mental potential he or she will ever have and can fulfill it only with the proper environment and good health care.

Robert M. Porter

Robert M. Porter was one of the young men in a hurry in post–World War II Columbus—cherubic and ruddy-faced; busy but accessible; usually with a new plan to discuss or a blueprint to display; always projecting the sense of a call waiting or another appointment pending.

Those with a long perspective of Children's history place him on the short list of those most responsible for the hospital's rapid development in mid-century. Twenty years into his post as Children's first trained administrator, he revealed in a 1962 interview that he took it on as more of a challenge than a mission, as a career twist he hadn't planned.

He graduated from Wooster College, planning to be a doctor. Student jobs at Western Reserve University diverted him first toward pharmacy, then hospital administration. Later as pharmacist and pharmacy instructor at Western Reserve, he set up a hospital pharmacy course and wrote a set of minimum standards in hospital pharmacy for the American College of Surgeons. He moved into administration at Cleveland's Lakeside Hospital, then as assistant administrator at Akron City Hospital.

The Columbus position, he recalled, offered a challenge to change things he didn't like about most children's hospitals in the '40s—exclusionary policies toward parents, limited services, inadequate financing, and insufficient tie-in with education or research programs.

In his first talk with Dr. Baxter in Columbus, Porter recalled, he found "we were in accord a children's hospital ought to be a general hospital for an age group, with all facilities for all children."

They were also in accord on the importance of education and research and on seeking the best medical staff possible and using not just their expertise but their counsel. "An administrator can't do a job at all without the help of the medical staff . . . to agree and disagree," he said in his 20-year retrospection, "and sometimes a good disagreement is better than acquiescence."

While he was almost constantly involved with funding and planning for staff and building expansion, Porter is remembered by staff veterans for other innovations.

A strong believer in public relations, he mobilized volunteers to spread the word about Children's, initiated publications to introduce parents and children to hospital facilities and procedures, supported access and accommodation for parents of sick children and took an active role in community projects involving children.

In the 1962 interview, Porter anticipated the hospital's future as a center for treatment, education and research and the keystone of a complex for related organizations serving children and families.

Porter is remembered for fostering the "family feeling" at Children's, for his enthusiasm for staff parties and his interest in staff members' problems. A former secretary recalled his compassion for small patients.

For some time, before he moved his family to a Licking County farm, the administrator lived in a frame house directly across from the hospital. Asked by the secretary one day if he had become used to children's crying at night, Porter replied:

"No, never. And I often get up, come over and walk through the corridors, just to be sure everything is all right."

Helen Shields Bradford

Helen Shields Bradford's singular contribution to Children's development was as the trustees' effective liaison agent during the crucial early-'40s period among physicians, staff, administration and the community.

The widow of Philander S. Bradford, a Columbus attorney, and a long-time volunteer as a member of Twig 2 and the Women's Board, Mrs. Bradford succeeded Daisy Sellers as Women's Board president in 1941. The next year, in her first presidential report to trustees, she said, "Although we are unusually well prepared to care for private patients, we have never realized the possibilities of service or of financial revenue from this source."

Despite the disruptions of wartime, she worked with Dr. Baxter and Robert Porter on the internal improvements and community approaches that implemented Children's evolution from small charity hospital to regional pediatric treatment center.

A volunteer who became an expert, Mrs. Bradford served five years as Women's Board president and hospital trustee but continued to serve trustees through the early '60s in the liaison role. Strongly supportive and articulate about the work of hospital auxiliaries, she helped effect change in the Children's volunteer structure and later served as chairman of the Women's Auxiliary councils of the Ohio Hospital Association and American Hospital Association.

Mrs. Bradford died in 1971 at the age of 81. It is a fitting tribute that the Employee of the Year Award given to recognize dedication and outstanding performance by hospital staff members is named in her honor.

Dr. Warren E. Wheeler

He might be called the Edward R. Murrow of Children's Hospital, a standard-setter by whom those who worked with him and came after him measured each other and themselves.

Dr. Warren E. Wheeler looked neither formidable nor imposing—slight, bespectacled, unassuming, identifiable by the gray lab coat he favored over the traditional white. A product of Mt. Union College and Harvard Medical School, he came to Columbus and Children's in 1946 as the first full-time faculty member in OSU's Department of Pediatrics.

It was largely through Wheeler's efforts, Dr. Earl H. Baxter has written, "that the residency training program increased to its highest efficiency, and that adequate full time supervision of patient care, development of laboratory facilities, and an incipient research program were started."

Those are major contributions, but men and women who worked with Wheeler speak first of his frontal assault on unanswered questions, his ability to spot the small factor in a patient's history or condition that made a large difference, his encouragement to young researchers, his excellence as a teacher.

"He had an enormous broad, deep intellectual curiosity," said Dr. Robert Sylvester, retired Granville pediatrician, former chief resident and staff member. "Everybody (in the medical world) knew Children's Hospital as Warren Wheeler's training ground."

Col. James Kilbourne

Anna Wright Kilbourne, hostess for Children's first organizational meetings.

Mary Lord Andrews Rogers, first president of Women's Board.

Isabelle Harper, Children's patient in 1907.

Daisy Sellers, Women's Board president for 26 years.

Dr. Leslie L. Bigelow, chief of medical staff, 1915-40.

Dr. Earl H. Baxter

Robert M. Porter

Helen Shields Bradford

Dr. Warren E. Wheeler

Dr. H. William Clatworthy

Terry Metcalf

Janice Williams Merrow

James Elliott, first open-heart surgery patient.

Tommy Burr

Ilse Kershner, longtime in-hospital volunteer, with Virginia Denman, retired director of volunteers.

The Myers twins, Matt, left, and Mark, in 1991.

Mark and Matthew Myers, surgically separated twins, leave Children's with their parents after a checkup.

Jennifer Nath

Sean Elliott

Sylvester remembered how physicians usually jealous of their leisure hours would flock to "Warren's Saturday morning syphilis clinics." The disease can involve every organic system of the body, he explained. "It was a rich learning experience, just to share the breadth and depth of his knowledge."

Dr. Wheeler's extensive contribution to early research work at Children's is detailed in that section of this history.

He left Children's in 1963 to become chairman of pediatrics in the new University of Kentucky College of Medicine, presiding over its growth for the next decade. He continued his interest in infectious disease and continued his contributions to medical publications.

He was the president of the American Pediatric Society in 1971-72, returning to Columbus during that period to give the Earl H. Baxter lecture at Children's. He retired from the chairmanship of the Kentucky department in 1974 but continued a schedule as lecturer and consultant until his death in October, 1976.

Dr. H. William Clatworthy, Jr.

In a community largely unaware it was happening, Dr. Clatworthy built at Children's and Ohio State through the '50s and '60s one of the earliest and most respected pediatric surgery training programs in the country.

A Denver native, graduate of Stanford University and Harvard Medical School, Clatworthy served with the Army Medical Corps in Europe during World War II, was chief surgical resident at Boston Children's in the mid-'40s, and came to Columbus from a general surgical residency at the University of Minnesota. Chief of surgery at Children's and head of pediatric surgery at OSU from 1952 to 1972, he was honored nationally and internationally for his contributions as practicing surgeon, educator and researcher before his retirement in 1986.

In 1985, in a presidential address to the American Pediatric Surgical Association, Dr. Judson Randolph, surgeon-in-chief of the Children's Hospital, Washington, D.C., paid tribute to the "pioneers" of pediatric surgery—the founder, Dr. William E. Ladd of Boston; the first practitioners, Dr. Herbert E. Coe of Seattle and Dr. Oswald S. Wyatt of Minneapolis; and the "teachers," the seven men who developed pediatric surgery training, including Robert Gross of Boston, C. Everett Koop of Philadelphia and Clatworthy of Columbus.

Clatworthy, said Randolph, "has contributed richly to our body of scientific knowledge" but even more to "sweeping new concepts" in pediatric surgery. A five-year study by a committee organized and chaired by Clatworthy in the mid-'60s, he said, reviewed and upgraded educational standards for all U.S. and Canadian training programs and was "the bedrock" on which the new specialty founded its approach for recognition to the American Board of Surgery.

The Columbus training program, preceded only by those in Boston, Chicago and Philadelphia, is Clatworthy's "greatest monument," Randolph said, "and has provided many of our current leaders in pediatric surgery." The achievement, in the midst of the problems of growth and development besetting the mid-century Children's, is even more noteworthy.

142

Clatworthy students, in comments gleaned by Randolph, saw their surgical mentor as "concerned, compassionate, a perfectionist, a motivator, explosive but fair, forgiving, trusting, and above all a superb teacher."

Medical colleagues recall his surgical prowess, his talent for innovation, his cooperative support of research efforts and his insistence on the highest standards in patient care and treatment. Veteran nurses remember gratefully Clatworthy's continuing efforts to reduce the stresses and fears of hospitalization for small patients and their families.

Dr. Clatworthy himself has described the experience of a first-generation pediatric surgeon as a ride on an express elevator that never stopped—"a great, soaring, thrilling ride."

Accepting the William E. Ladd Award from the American Academy of Pediatrics in 1979, he declared, "I sometimes feel sorry for anyone who is not a pediatric surgeon," in the specialty "where surgical success is not rewarded by a few salvaged years . . . but by whole lifetimes."

Terry Metcalf

Terry Metcalf may have been one of the very few one-of-a-kind patients in Children's history, past or future.

Victim of a disease which medical science has virtually eradicated, she fought a special battle against polio during her six months' stay at Children's and scored a rare triumph over disability for 40 years thereafter.

Twenty-five and an active sportswoman, Mrs. Metcalf had a two-year-old son and was five months pregnant when polio struck her during a weekend vacation at Lake Erie. Recognizing the telltale signs, her physician rushed her back to Columbus and the polio unit at Children's.

Confined to a respirator, only able to sustain her breathing for five minutes without its help, she worked hard with doctors to extend that time before her baby's birth. "A minute meant a lot, even 30 seconds," she recalled in a 1988 interview. Even so, it was "quite a tricky procedure," she said, when daughter Judy arrived on schedule "on Election Day, 1949." It was the first such birth reported in the country.

"With paralytic polio, you don't lose feeling, like with a spinal injury," she said in describing the painful birth procedure. "You know it when you bump your toe."

She remembered the long slow fight at Children's against crippling polio—the hot wet packs that felt "so wonderful," the twice-daily sessions with therapists "who would go over every muscle in your body, and there are a LOT of muscles, and grade them for any change."

Freed from the respirator, Mrs. Metcalf spent Christmas with her family, then went to Warm Springs, Ga., "to learn to do as much as I could" using the wheelchair to which she would be permanently confined.

143

With polio, "after two or three months you know what you have to deal with," she said, and she shaped her life accordingly. She and her husband, former Probate Judge Richard Metcalf, became active participants in community events. She proudly managed her home and family without help, and welcomed visits with her children and four grandchildren.

Mrs. Metcalf was a past officer and 45-year member of Children's Twig 80, was president of the sustaining board of Creative Living and was 1980 March of Dimes Showcase chairman.

Recounting these details, she confided she was detecting a gradual weakening and loss of function which fellow polio victims had told her sooner or later to expect. Within months, she died of heart failure in November, 1989.

The memorable quote from that final interview, because it was so patently true, was Terry Metcalf's happy assertion, "I've had a very normal life."

Janice Williams

Janice Williams was Children's first television star. On May 25, 1951, she was featured in a page-one Dispatch story and a WBNS-TV special telecast that night to help promote the United Hospitals Building Fund campaign.

She had been in Children's three years and would be there another year, recovering from terrible burns from flaming kerosene that had warped and scarred 85 percent of her body. Appearing with her in a six-column newspaper photo and on the telecast were representatives of the scores of doctors, nurses, technicians and other hospital personnel involved with her treatment—and of the Ohio Penitentiary inmates who had donated skin grafts to help her.

Referred to Children's after initial life-saving treatment at Hocking Valley Hospital in Logan, Janice was a classic illustration of the kind of long-term, complex case Children's so often receives.

Lying on a Stryker frame, swathed in sheets except for her pretty smiling face, which the flames had spared, Janice was calmer than most of her hospital associates under the TV lights. At the close of the program, she charmed a Central Ohio audience with her unaccompanied version of "Abadaba Honeymoon," one of the "hillbilly" numbers she often sang to hospital roommates.

After another year at Children's and at Nightingale Cottage, a convalescent facility, and after 200 or so surgical procedures, Janice went home to Haydenville in a body cast to resume her life.

She regained her ability to walk, and to roller skate and dance. She finished high school, trained as a linotypist, and worked for newspapers in Logan and Marietta, married Harold Merrow and had two daughters.

Today, in her early '50s and living in a retirement community in North Carolina, Janice is the same bubbly, upbeat person who once smiled at a photographer through tears as her ravaged body was lowered into a soapy, healing whirlpool bath.

"I've had a blessed life," she declared, although it hasn't been all that easy.

Her marriage ended unhappily. She has been back in the hospital repeatedly, for serious surgery, although she quickly pointed out, "My burn tissue (so carefully grafted and nurtured over long months) has never broken down." She gradually had to give up full-time work.

But Janice treasures the laminated clippings that dubbed her "a walking miracle"—and believes she is. Getting acquainted with her neighbors, settled within driving distance of her two daughters, the burn victim savors the life doctors feared for when they first saw her. "I'm thinking of writing a book," Janice said, "called 'Thank God for another day.' "

James Elliott

James Elliott doesn't remember much about the 1957 surgery which gave him a small niche in Children's history as the first open-heart surgery patient at the hospital—and in Columbus. He was only eight.

He does remember being "all hooked up" for the procedure but not specifically the machine designed and assembled by Dr. Howard Sirak and a hospital team which kept him alive while Sirak repaired the septal defect in his heart.

He also remembers a long stay in Children's and his later frustration as a sports-minded teenager in an era when former heart patients weren't encouraged toward exercise and strenuous sports. "My only outlet was playing the drums because that was regarded, mistakenly," he said with a laugh, "as a sedentary activity."

A Central High School graduate and former Ohio State University student, Elliott moved to California in 1976. Today, 43 and the father of three, he works for the city of Long Beach, plays the drums with musical groups and at the Baptist church he attends, and spends a lot of time counseling young people about the dangers of substance abuse and the importance of exercise and sensible diet.

He also likes to tell them about the high point of his life to date—the day in 1984 he ran a kilometer through Corona del Mar, California, relaying the Olympic torch toward the summer games in Los Angeles.

Running, competitively and for the sheer joy of it, has become his avocation—kind of a personal celebration for the former "boy with a hole in his heart" which modern medicine, in good time for him, learned how to fix.

144

Tommy Burr

Tommy Burr may be the best known and is certainly the most deliberately publicized patient in Children's history. His ties with the Columbus community are very special.

For a month and a half in 1966, as 10-year-old Tommy fought through a dangerous siege in Children's, his progress was closely monitored and reported by the Columbus media, churches had special prayers for him—and more than 1,000 donors gave blood to keep him alive.

In his book, "A Gift of Courage," recalling young patients who had given particular meaning to his surgical years, Dr. Thomas S. Morse concluded with Tommy's case as the most rewarding.

Tommy had a double problem. He had a tumor on the adrenal gland, a rare type but surgically correctable, but he also had hemophilia, lacking in his blood enough of the factor which causes normal clotting.

He was fortunate on other counts. Children's recognized his immediate problem and what to do about it. A California scientist, just two years earlier, had devised a way to glean the vital "Factor VIII" from blood plasma. The media campaign was started to collect the 200 pints it was estimated Tommy would need. The Red Cross assigned technicians to the factor precipitation process and screened prospective donors for the 12 percent who had Tommy's blood type and were otherwise eligible.

The community effort continued as repeated surgery was necessary to stem a persistent blood leakage. By the time he was ready to go home, some 45 days later, he had received 960 pints of blood, nearly five times the original estimated need.

Hospitalizations and injections and the exaggerated effect of bumps and scratches haven't deterred him from shaping as normal a life as possible—active sports, college, work as an electronics technician, a woodworking hobby.

Married in 1984, he took his new wife to Massachusetts to meet Dr. Morse, now retired, with whom he has kept in touch. As a teenager, he had made the tough decision to have a vasectomy, and he still, like many others long dependent on the blood of others, has a lingering fear of AIDS.

Generally, Tommy treats himself with the vital clotting factor he needs, but he has been hospitalized, most recently in 1988, for short-term bleeding episodes and for arthritis surgery on joints weakened by his disease.

However, like so many former Children's patients who have come to terms with special problems and learned to savor life, Tommy's outlook is upbeat. He is active in the Central Ohio support group for hemophiliacs and sums up his Children's experience and the Columbus community in one word: "Fantastic!"

"I was lucky that medical science had found the factor before I needed it," he said of the crucial '66 surgery, "and that I was in a place that knew about it. When I left Children's for the last time as a patient, it was like leaving home."

Ilse Kershner

Ilse Kershner is a special person among special people—the volunteer legions who work for Children's Hospital and its patients.

An immigrant from Germany just before World War II, Ilse learned English, became a U.S. citizen, moved to Columbus, and became a one-woman task force to help the hurting and the troubled.

No stranger to tragedy, she knew how to help. She lost more than 40 relatives to the Nazi gas chambers. Two of her three children did not survive childhood. She nursed her first husband through an ultimately fatal seven-year illness. When she turned to helping others, she looked for those in greatest need of a hand to hold and an ear that listened.

She became the only woman volunteer one day a week in the "no visitors" area of the Columbus State Institute. She counseled the hopeless and desperate visitors and callers at the Mental Health Center's Suicide Prevention Bureau. When she was named the Citizen-Journal's Community Volunteer of the Year in 1970, her volunteer hours at Children's alone totaled in the thousands.

In her years at Children's, she has shown special concern for the parents of seriously or fatally ill children, sensing that their great need sometimes is to voice their fears. For a long time, Ilse's destination each week has been the hematology area—long enough that she remembers when "none of them got well."

She arrives with a supply of small candies and small toys for children bored by waiting, speaks to those who know her (as many regulars do), helps the staff any way she can, and is most importantly "just there," to listen.

Ilse's son, Dr. Robert Levy, is a practicing oncologist in Modesto, Calif. Her husband, Barney Kershner, is a proud supporter of her volunteer activities. Ilse herself reduces her countless hours of giving to a simple statement: "If I can make just one soul a day happy, it's worth it."

Mark and Matthew Myers

One 1989 sixth-grade class in Bucyrus was a little special, with four sets of identical twins.

Even in such select company, Mark and Matthew Myers had an extra distinction, as the first set of Siamese twins to be surgically separated at Children's Hospital, or in Ohio.

Other than that vital bit of history, Mr. and Mrs. Frank Myers report, their sons are normal, healthy, happy boys.

One of the few surgical procedures at Children's for which a full-scale "dress rehearsal" was done, the operation was performed three months after the twins' birth Dec. 9, 1977, in Marion General Hospital. It took seven hours and two complete surgical teams.

Born joined from chest to abdomen, the twins had separate organs and body systems except that they shared a liver, diaphragm, pericardium and breastbone. In the delicate, carefully plotted surgery, this common tissue and bone were separated and the open wounds sheathed by the twins' own skin and surgical sheeting.

The twins recovered well and have grown and developed with little deference to the dramatic surgery they shared as infants. They have participated in Little League baseball and football, play trombones in the school band and are already challenging their dad's five-feet-ten height.

147

Each has his own friends and interests, their parents report, but the Myers boys' "twin-ness" does show up in their reliance on each other. "When they play with their friends, they'll choose opposite sides," their father said, "but when they were put on opposing football teams, they didn't like that much."

Jennifer Nath

After spending her first two years in Children's, Jennifer Nath has enjoyed a happy, active childhood normal in all ways but one. She still gets her food supply through tubes.

Jennifer was born in 1978 with a relatively rare and once-untreatable problem. Surgery shortly after her birth revealed she had far too little usable intestine to enable her to digest and absorb food normally. She was among the first patients at Children's to be placed on a special feeding system largely dependent on an intravenous "lifeline."

Jennifer learned to walk, talk and meet the media during her long stay in the surgical intensive care unit. Meanwhile, her parents, Rudolph and Katy Nath of Newark, became the first "graduates" of a lengthy training program at Children's on how to continue her feeding regimen at home.

Since she went home in late 1980, Jennifer has thrived on her special diet with few complications, receiving her food supply in a 10-hour period overnight through one tube directly into her stomach and another into her blood stream.

In a 1991 interview with the Dispatch, Jennifer talked about friends who know about her problem and make little of it and of an active pre-teen schedule that has included ballet, tap and jazz dance lessons, playing softball and basketball at Fulton Middle School in Heath.

Jennifer's mother gratefully reports that her daughter has not let her problem affect either her activities or her self-image. She's been elected a cheerleader for 1991-92 and, when they talk career choices, Jennifer thinks she'd like to be a model.

Meanwhile, in one of the major research areas at Children's, investigators continue to seek better ways to help children with a whole range of difficulties in handling and assimilating food.

Sean Elliott

Fate dealt Sean Elliott a difficult assignment—coping with a rare form of a rare disease. It also, at Children's, gave him essential help—doctors who recognized his problem and a research program that made possible the procurement and careful administration of a new drug to combat it.

148

Within a week after his birth in 1979 as an apparently healthy infant, Sean's mother, Michele Elliott of Springfield, recalled, he began to develop the recurrent difficulties—eating problems, infections, allergies—which necessitated hospitalizations, surgery, varied diagnoses and treatments.

In 1980, recognizing Sean's wiry, stiff hair as a clue, doctors at Children's pinpointed his problem as Menke's Kinky Hair Disease, a genetic defect affecting the body's ability to utilize small but essential amounts of copper. Fewer than 200 cases of the devastating, usually fatal disease have been reported worldwide since an Australian physician first identified it in the '60s, and Sean is only one of three reported patients with an atypical, partial form of Menke's.

Speculating that the low case totals may represent non-recognition as well as rarity, Dr. Grant Morrow cited Children's experience with Menke's as an illustration of its special strengths.

The questing approach of a teaching environment led to the diagnosis of Sean's case. The "total research program" made possible the series of consents, authorizations and careful planning preceding Sean's treatment with an investigational drug called copper L-histidine.

So far, Sean's mother reported in early 1991, the drug is working. Sean, at 12, is more energetic, healthier, addicted to baseball and his favorite Cincinnati Reds, and has "mainstreamed" into most of his sixth-grade classes, she said. The "weird hair," an outward manifestation of the kinked-up vascular systems of Menke's patients, has taken on more normal color and texture.

Mrs. Elliott, a former legal secretary, completed training to become a nurse after Sean's problems started and has become active in a support group of Menke's families. Their interest is not only in sharing the burden of a devastating disease, she said, but in encouraging research that may help future Menke's victims.